EYESHIELD 21

Vol. 30: This Is Football

STORY BY **RIICHIRO INAGAKI**   ART BY **YUSUKE MURATA**

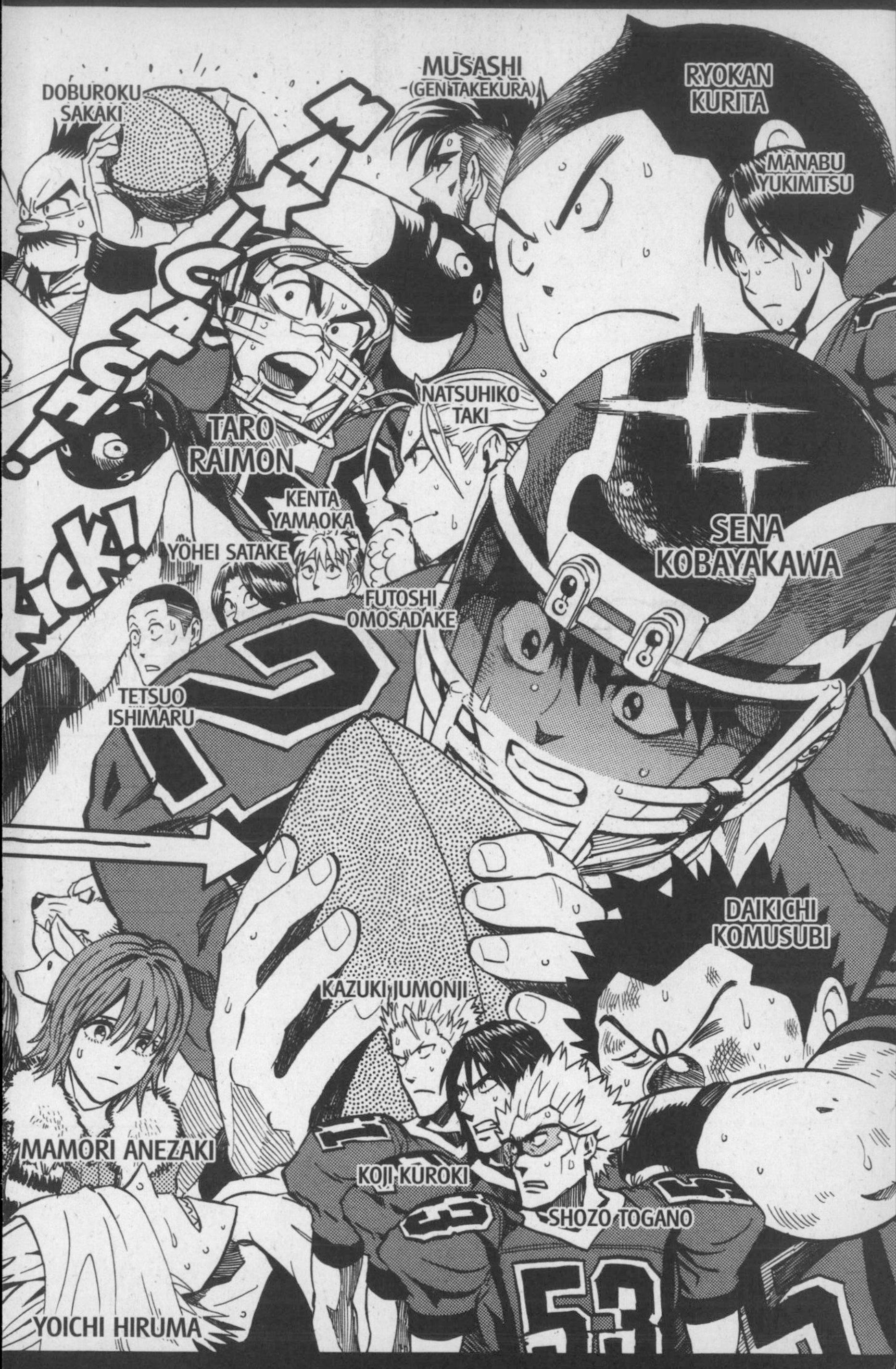
RYOKAN KURITA
MUSASHI (GEN TAKEKURA)
DOBUROKU SAKAKI
MANABU YUKIMITSU
NATSUHIKO TAKI
TARO RAIMON
SENA KOBAYAKAWA
KENTA YAMAOKA
YOHEI SATAKE
FUTOSHI OMOSADAKE
TETSUO ISHIMARU
DAIKICHI KOMUSUBI
KAZUKI JUMONJI
MAMORI ANEZAKI
KOJI KUROKI
SHOZO TOGANO
YOICHI HIRUMA

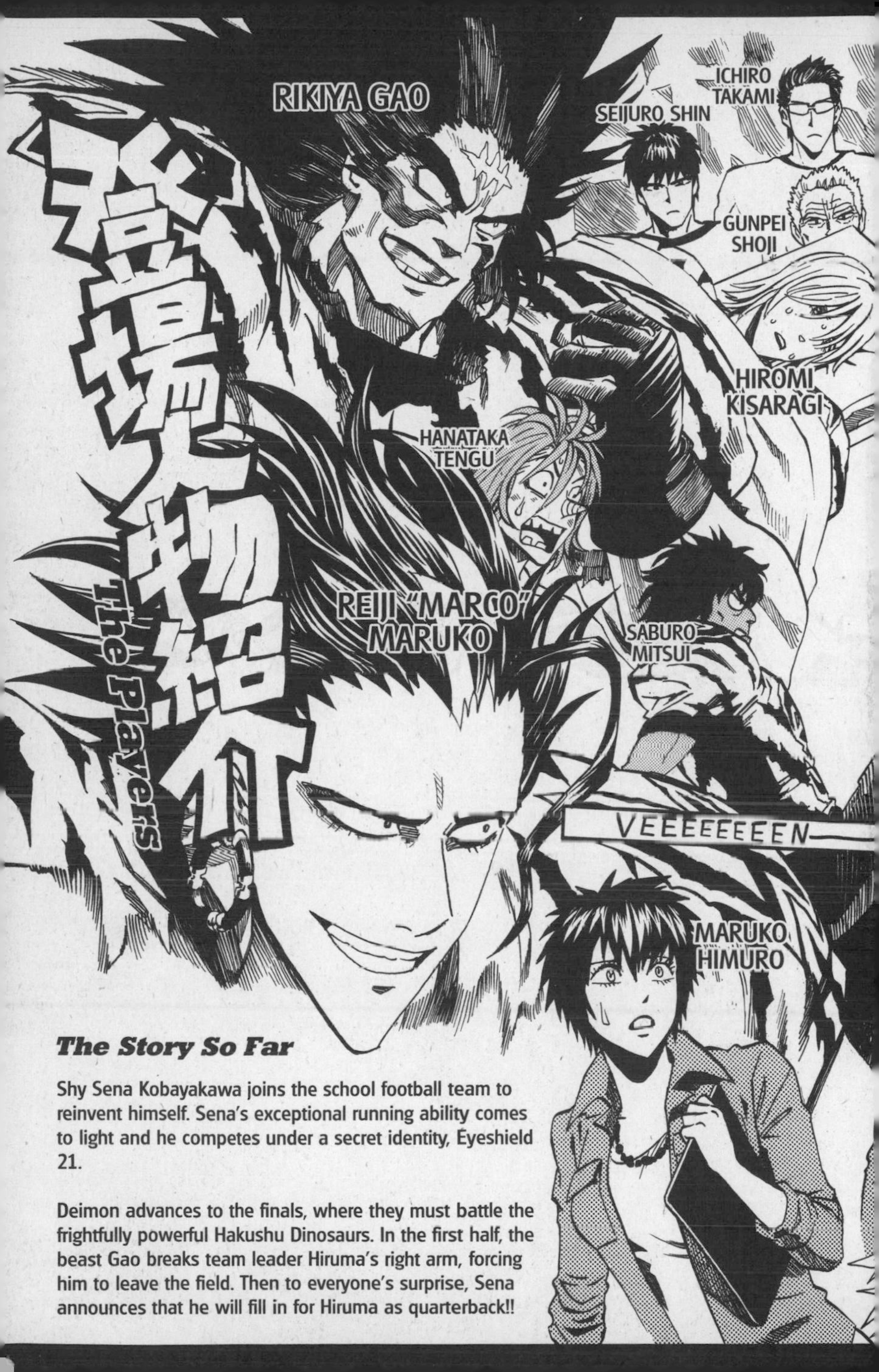
ICHIRO TAKAMI
SEIJURO SHIN
GUNPEI SHOJI
RIKIYA GAO
HIROMI KISARAGI
HANATAKA TENGU
SABURO MITSUI
REIJI "MARCO" MARUKO
VEEEEEEEEEN
MARUKO HIMURO
登場人物紹介
The Players

The Story So Far

Shy Sena Kobayakawa joins the school football team to reinvent himself. Sena's exceptional running ability comes to light and he competes under a secret identity, Eyeshield 21.

Deimon advances to the finals, where they must battle the frightfully powerful Hakushu Dinosaurs. In the first half, the beast Gao breaks team leader Hiruma's right arm, forcing him to leave the field. Then to everyone's surprise, Sena announces that he will fill in for Hiruma as quarterback!!

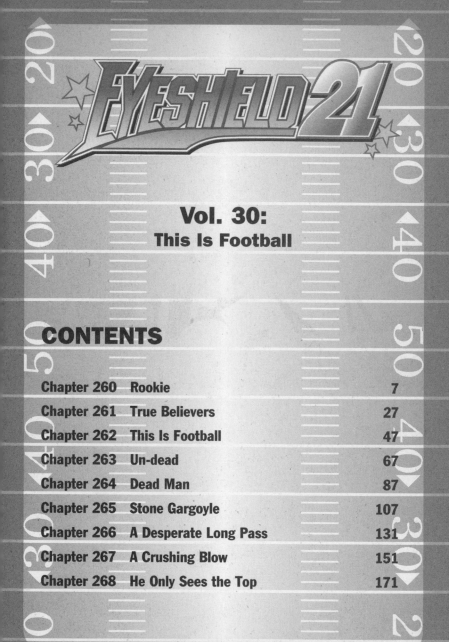

EYESHIELD 21

Vol. 30:
This Is Football

CONTENTS

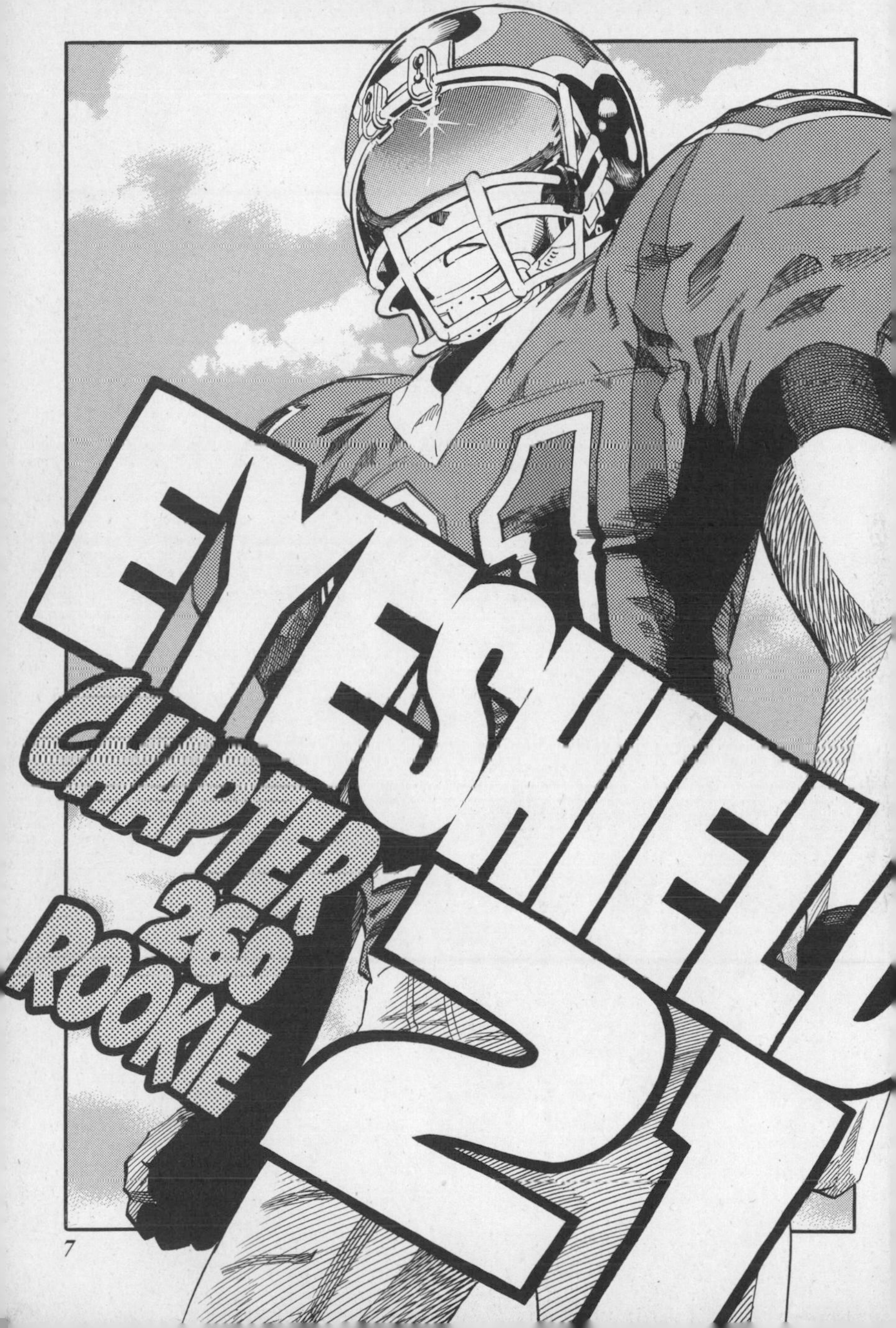
EYESHIELD 21
CHAPTER 260
ROOKIE

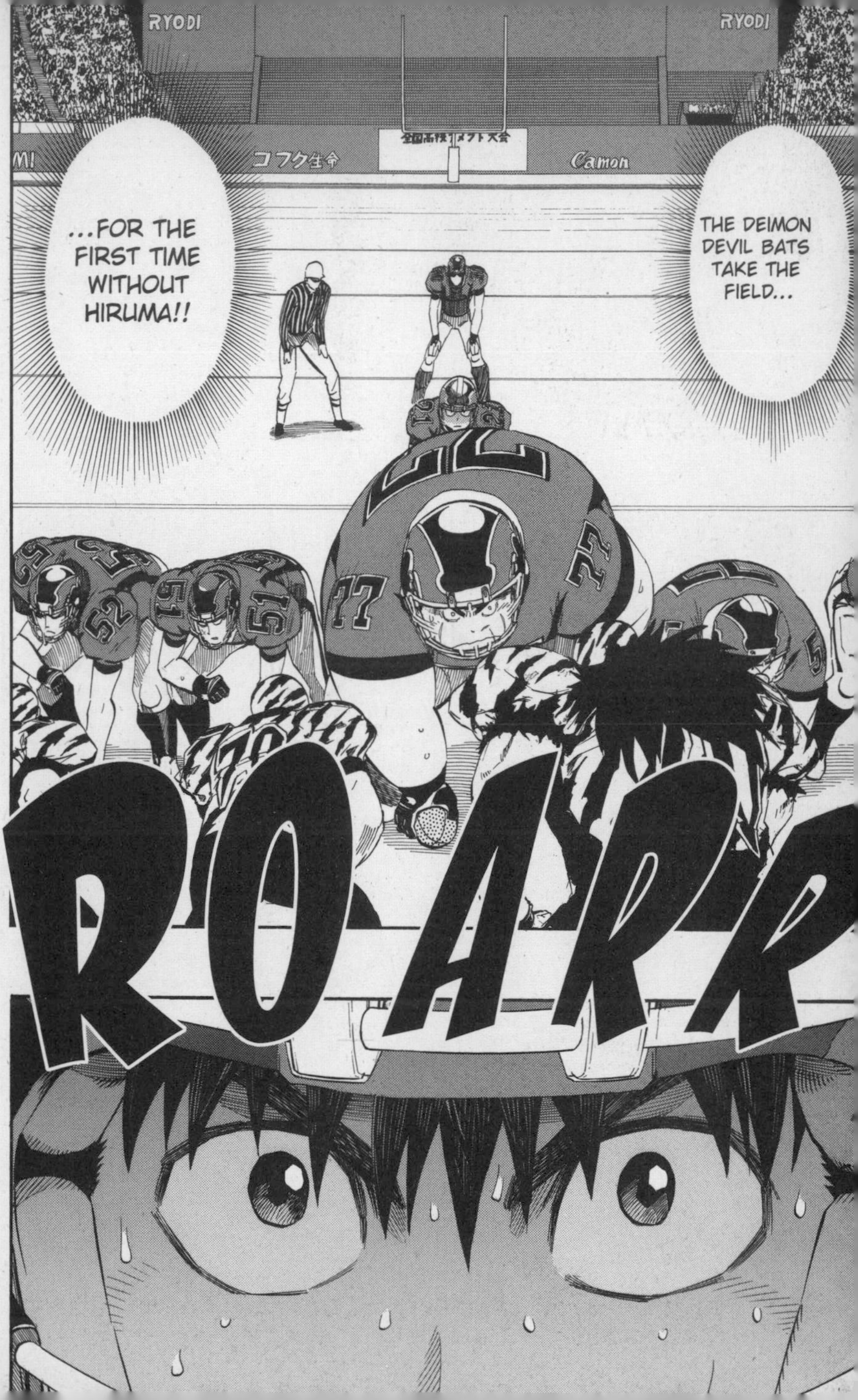
RYODI
RYODI
Camon
コフク生命
THE DEIMON DEVIL BATS TAKE THE FIELD...
...FOR THE FIRST TIME WITHOUT HIRUMA!!
ROARR

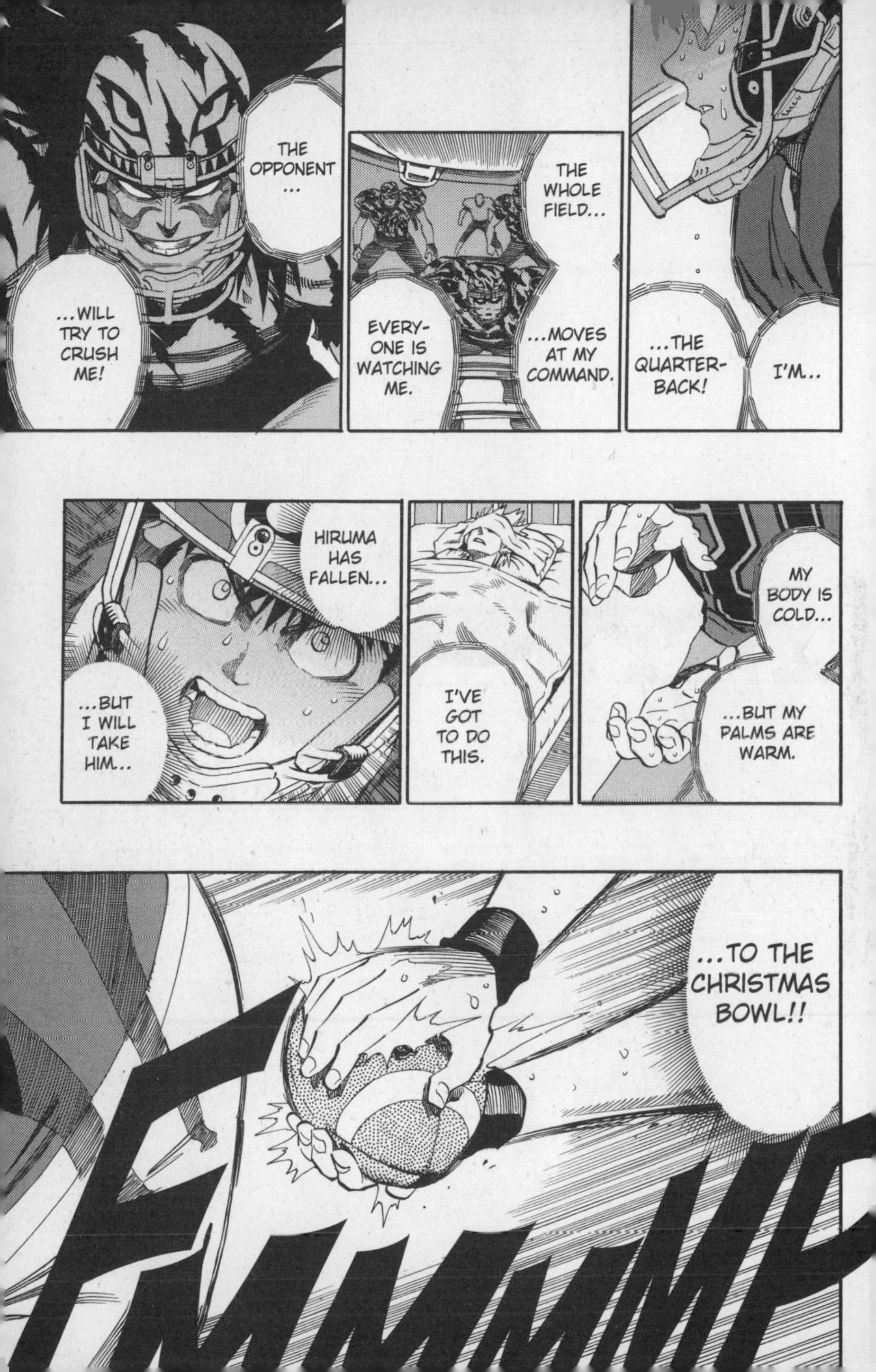
I'M...
...THE QUARTER-BACK!
THE WHOLE FIELD...
...MOVES AT MY COMMAND.
EVERY-ONE IS WATCHING ME.
THE OPPONENT...
...WILL TRY TO CRUSH ME!
MY BODY IS COLD...
...BUT MY PALMS ARE WARM.
I'VE GOT TO DO THIS.
HIRUMA HAS FALLEN...
...BUT I WILL TAKE HIM...
...TO THE CHRISTMAS BOWL!!

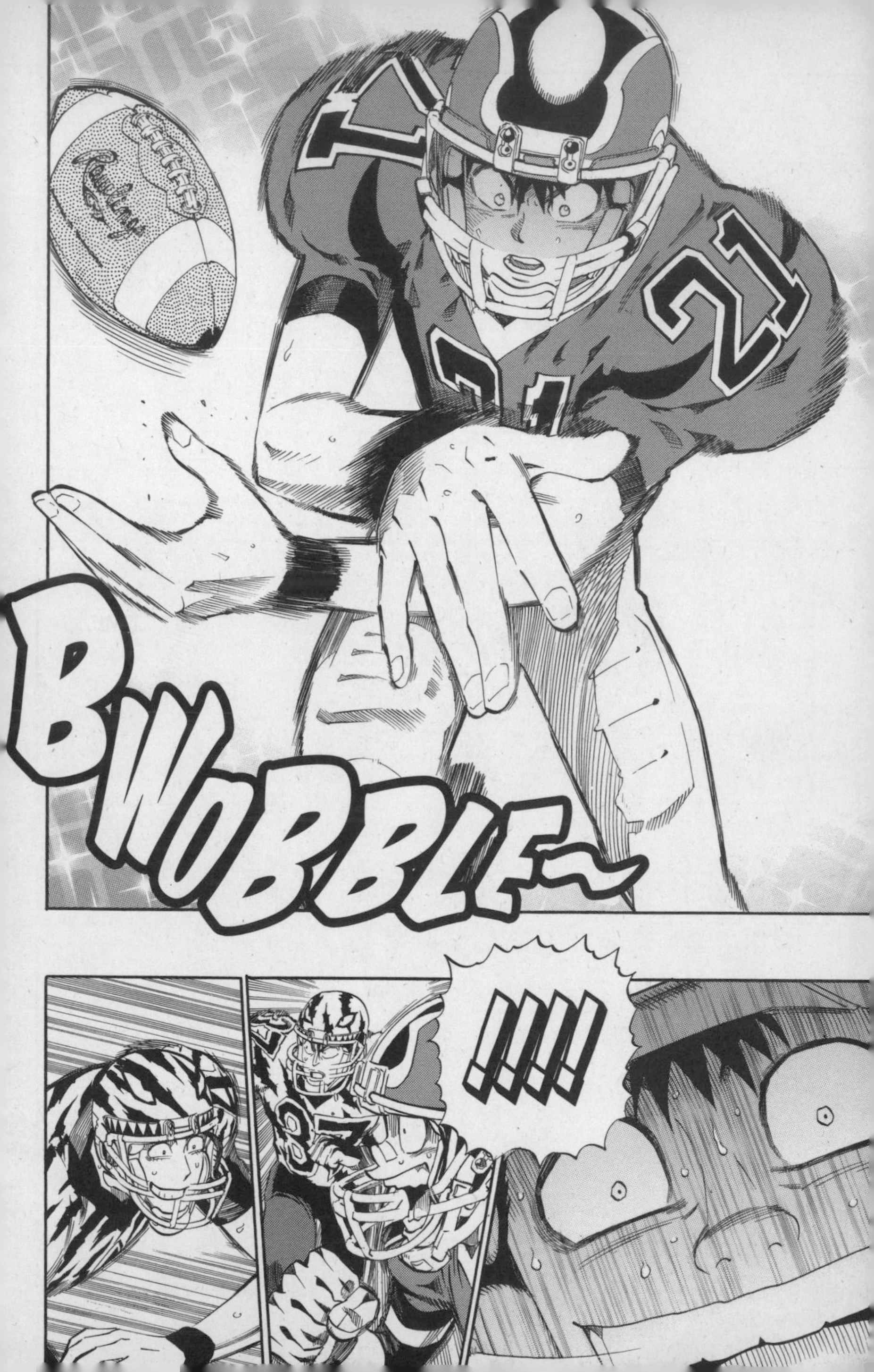
BWOBBLE~
!!!!

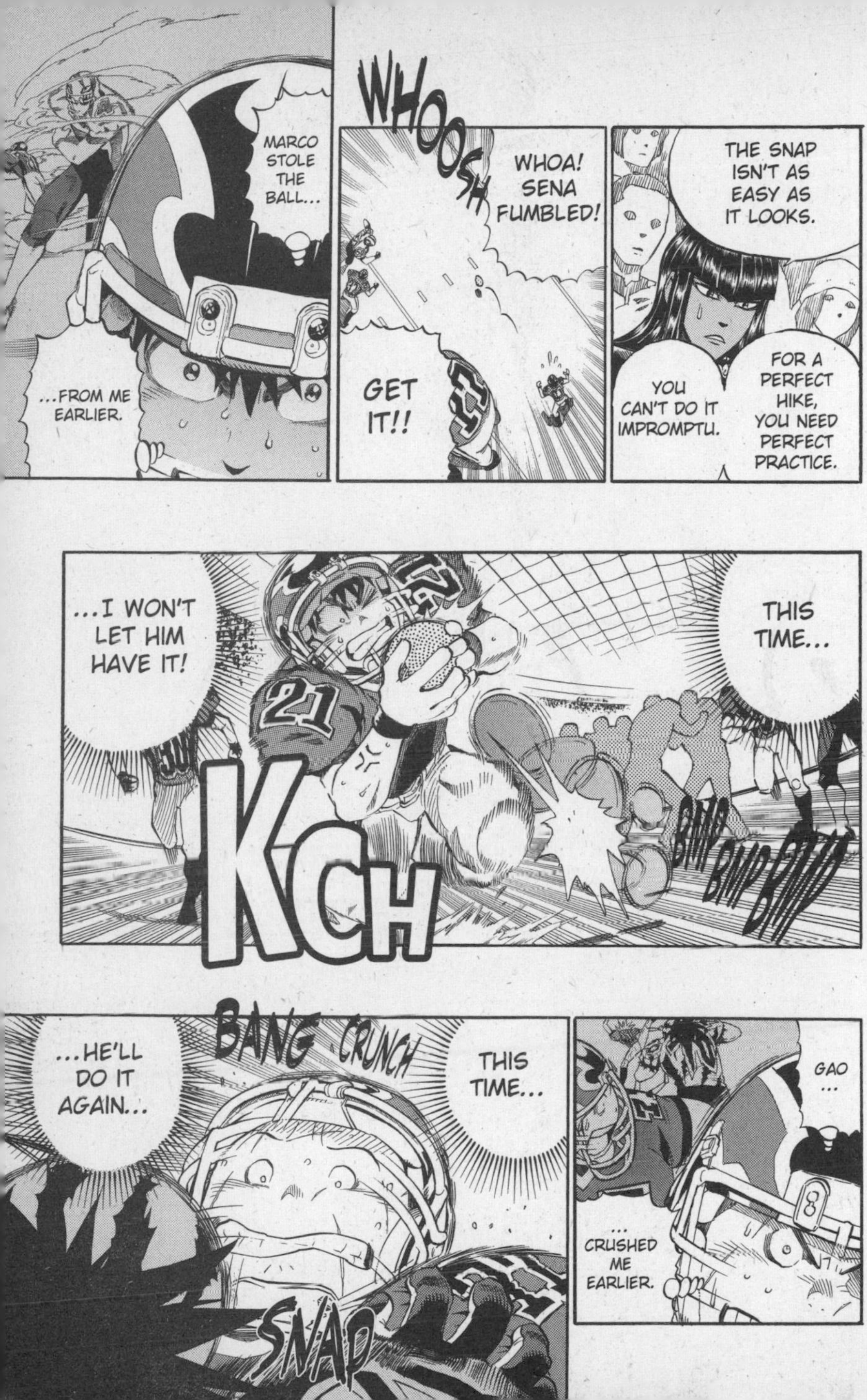
THE SNAP ISN'T AS EASY AS IT LOOKS.
FOR A PERFECT HIKE, YOU NEED PERFECT PRACTICE.
YOU CAN'T DO IT IMPROMPTU.
WHOOSH
WHOA! SENA FUMBLED!
GET IT!!
MARCO STOLE THE BALL...
...FROM ME EARLIER.
THIS TIME...
...I WON'T LET HIM HAVE IT!
KCH
BMP BMP BMP BMP
GAO...
...CRUSHED ME EARLIER.
BANG CRUNCH
THIS TIME...
...HE'LL DO IT AGAIN...
SNAP

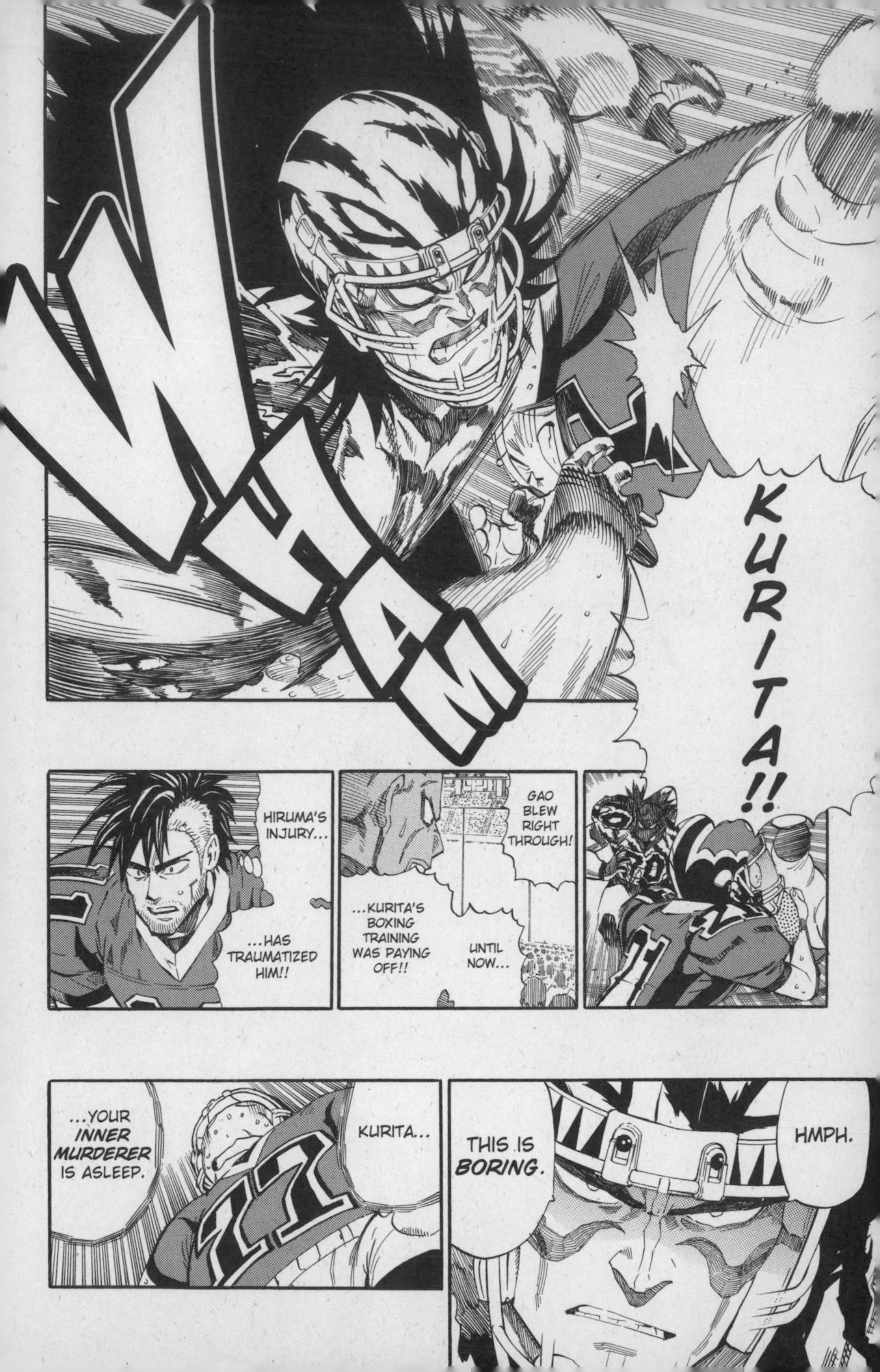
WHAM
KURITA!!
GAO BLEW RIGHT THROUGH!
UNTIL NOW...
...KURITA'S BOXING TRAINING WAS PAYING OFF!!
HIRUMA'S INJURY...
...HAS TRAUMATIZED HIM!!
HMPH.
THIS IS *BORING*.
KURITA...
...YOUR *INNER MURDERER* IS ASLEEP.

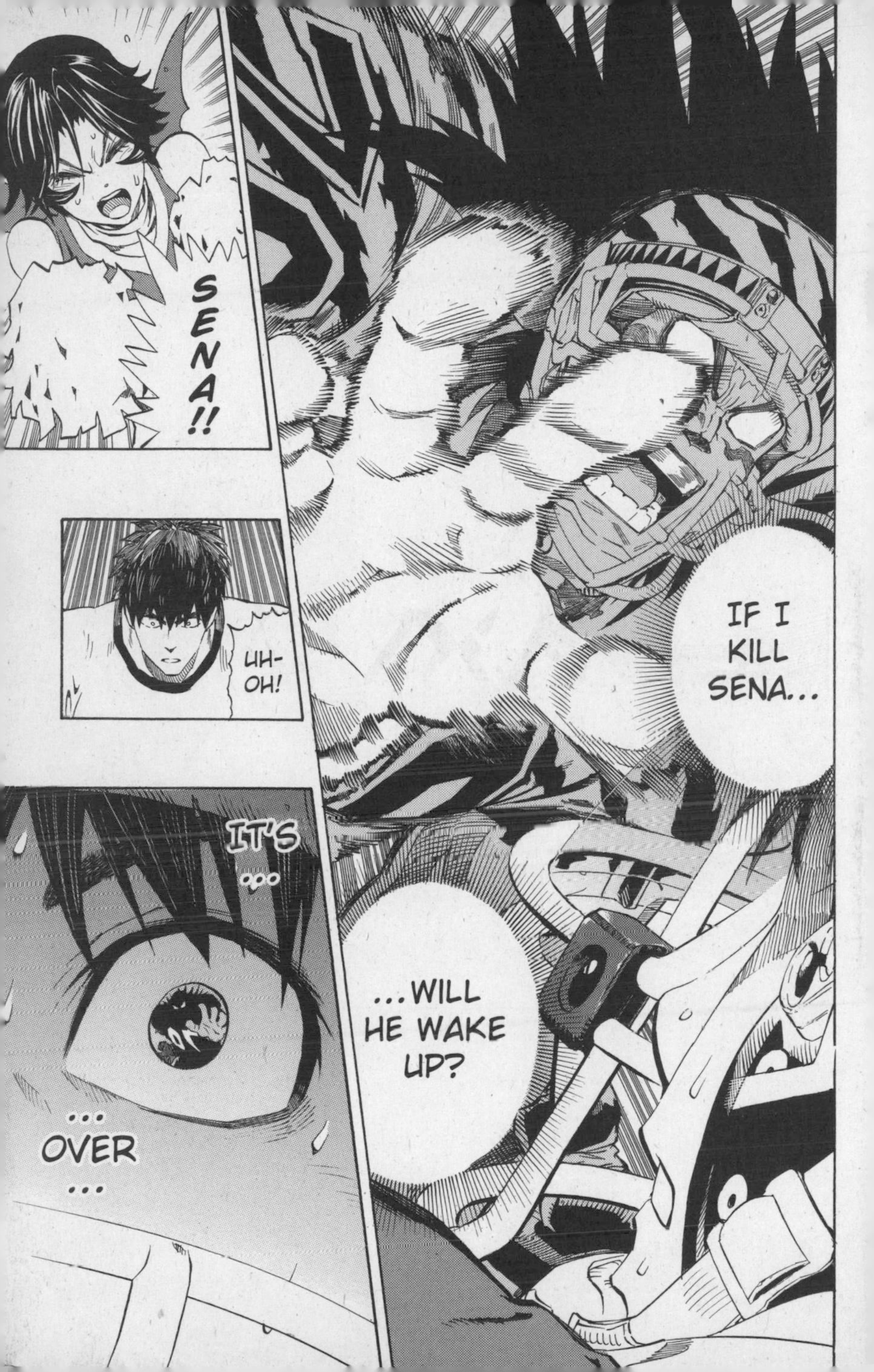
IF I KILL SENA...
...WILL HE WAKE UP?
SENA!!
UH-OH!
IT'S...
...OVER...

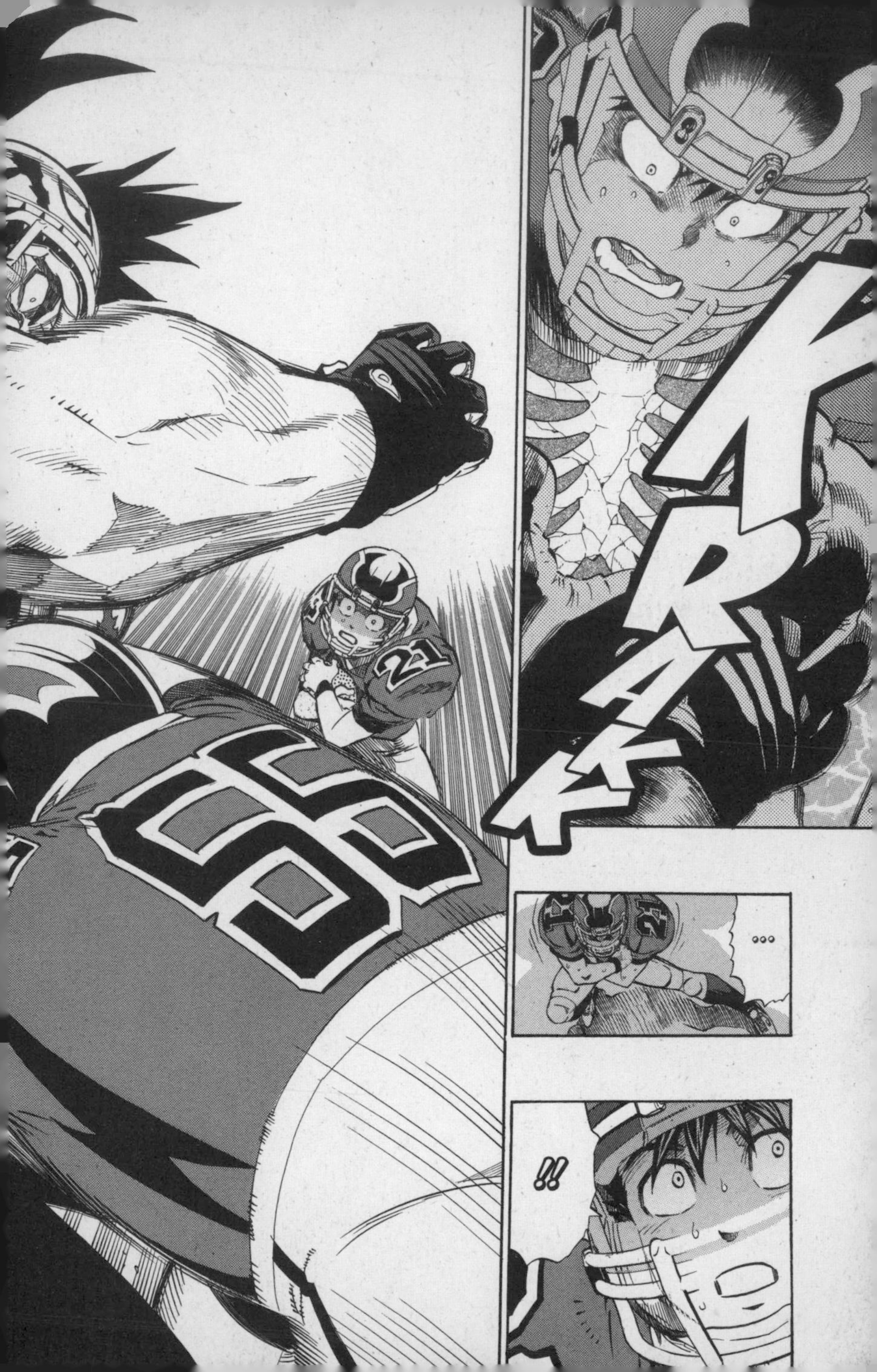
KRAKK
...
!!

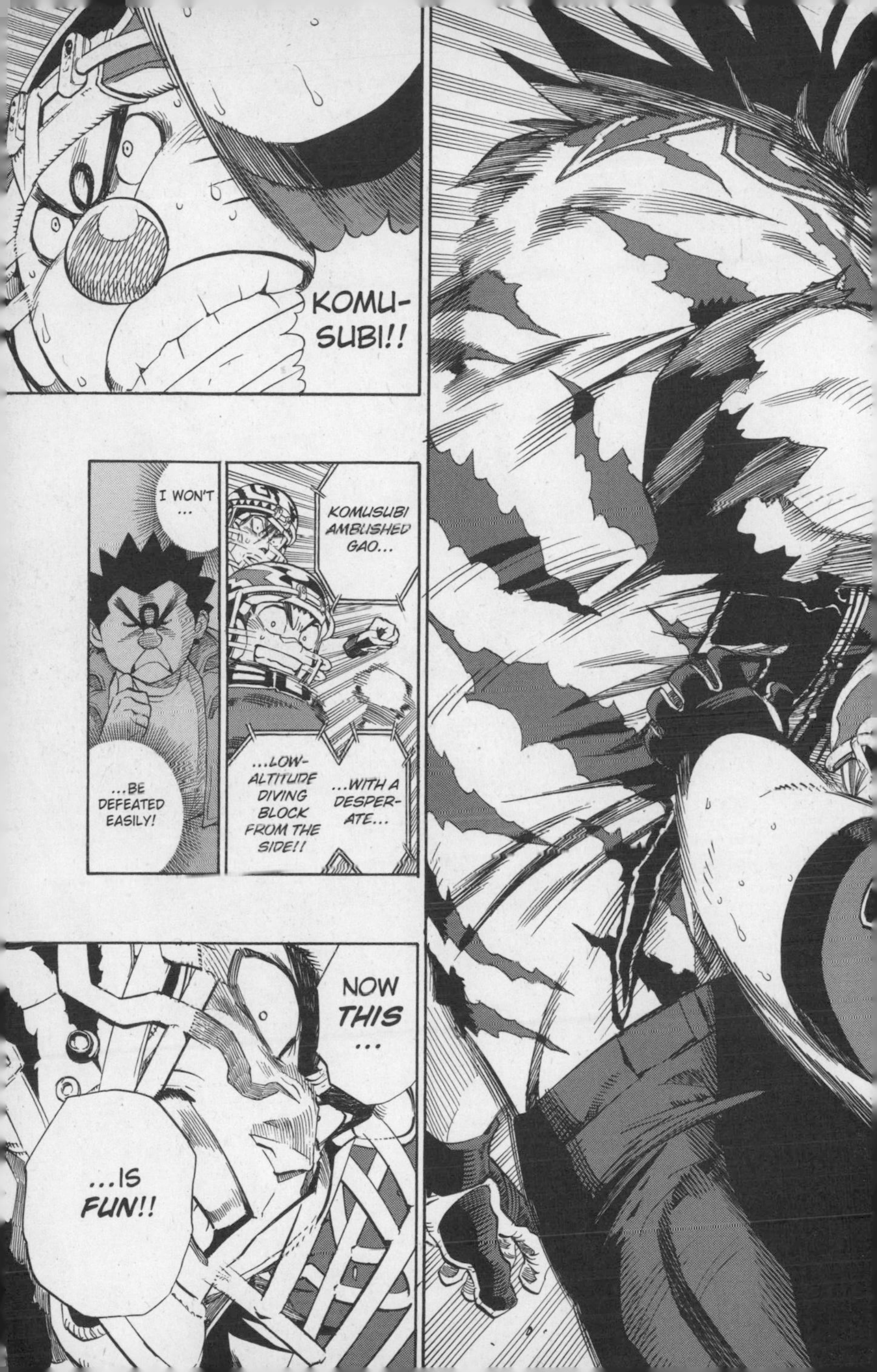
KOMU-SUBI!!
KOMUSUBI AMBUSHED GAO...
...WITH A DESPERATE...
...LOW-ALTITUDE DIVING BLOCK FROM THE SIDE!!
I WON'T ...
...BE DEFEATED EASILY!
NOW THIS ...
...IS FUN!!

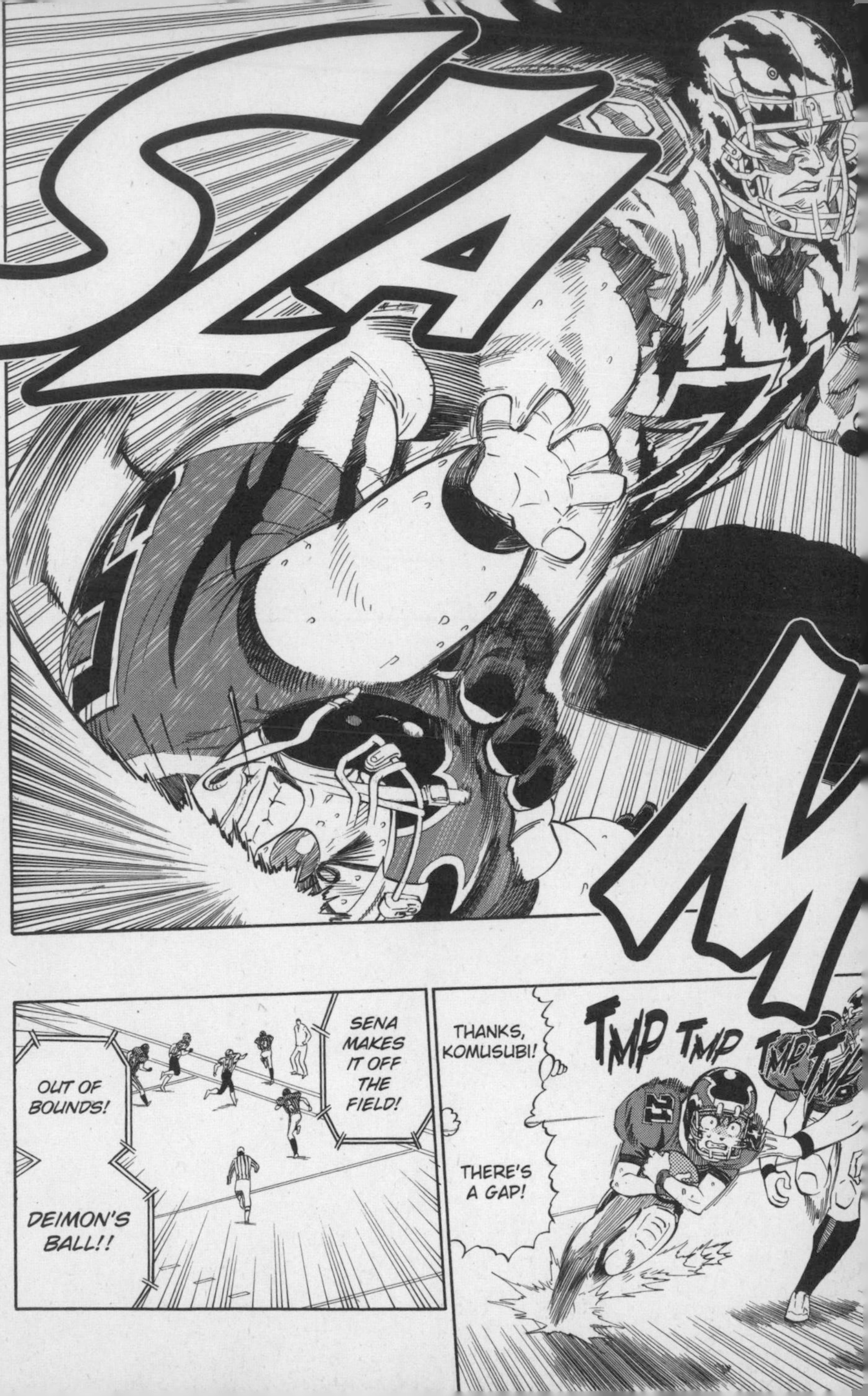
SLAM
TMP TMP TMP TMP
THANKS, KOMUSUBI!
THERE'S A GAP!
SENA MAKES IT OFF THE FIELD!
OUT OF BOUNDS!
DEIMON'S BALL!!

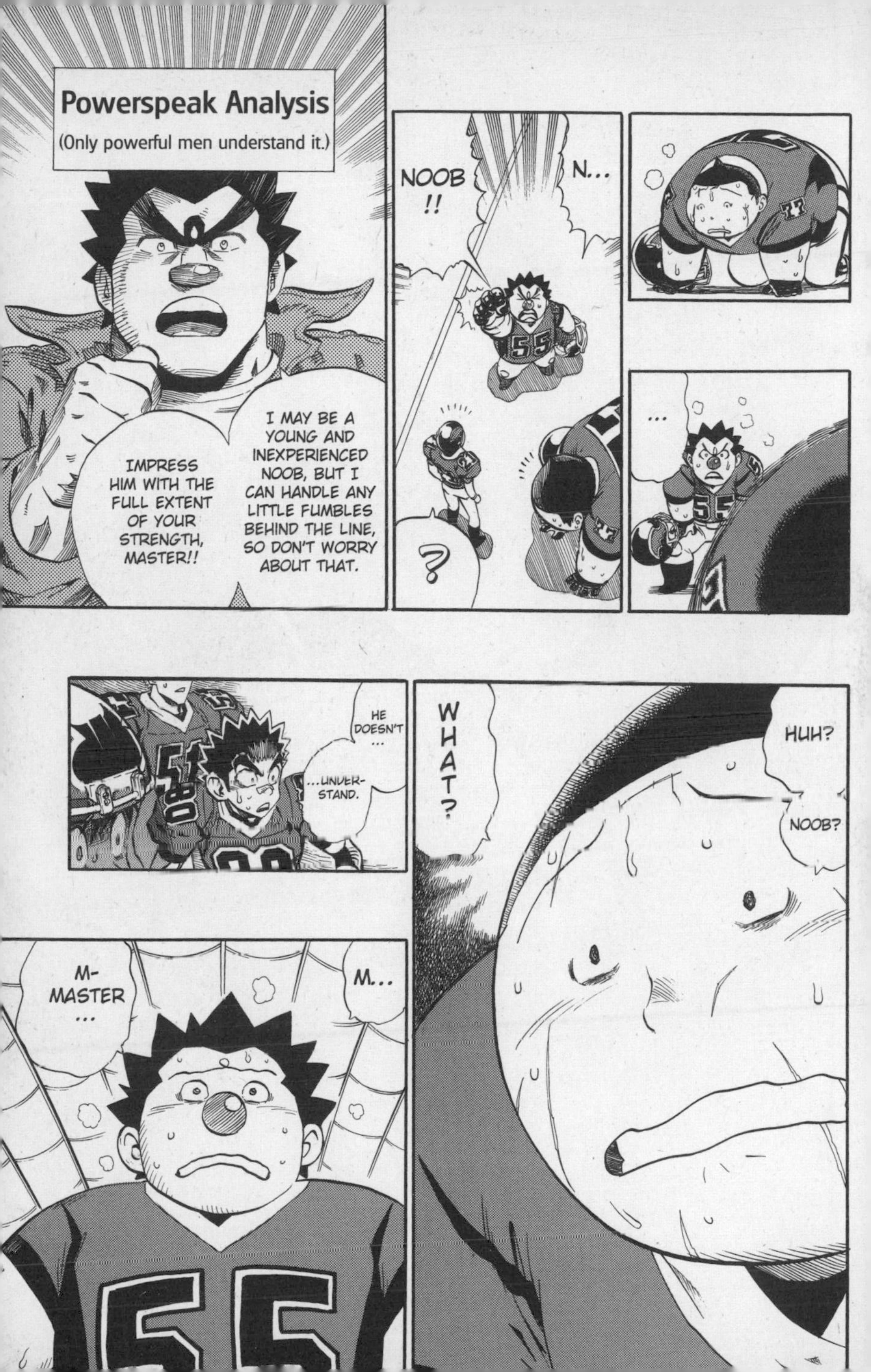
...
N...
NOOB!!
?
Powerspeak Analysis
(Only powerful men understand it.)
I MAY BE A YOUNG AND INEXPERIENCED NOOB, BUT I CAN HANDLE ANY LITTLE FUMBLES BEHIND THE LINE, SO DON'T WORRY ABOUT THAT.
IMPRESS HIM WITH THE FULL EXTENT OF YOUR STRENGTH, MASTER!!
HUH?
NOOB?
WHAT?
HE DOESN'T...
...UNDERSTAND.
M...
M-MASTER...

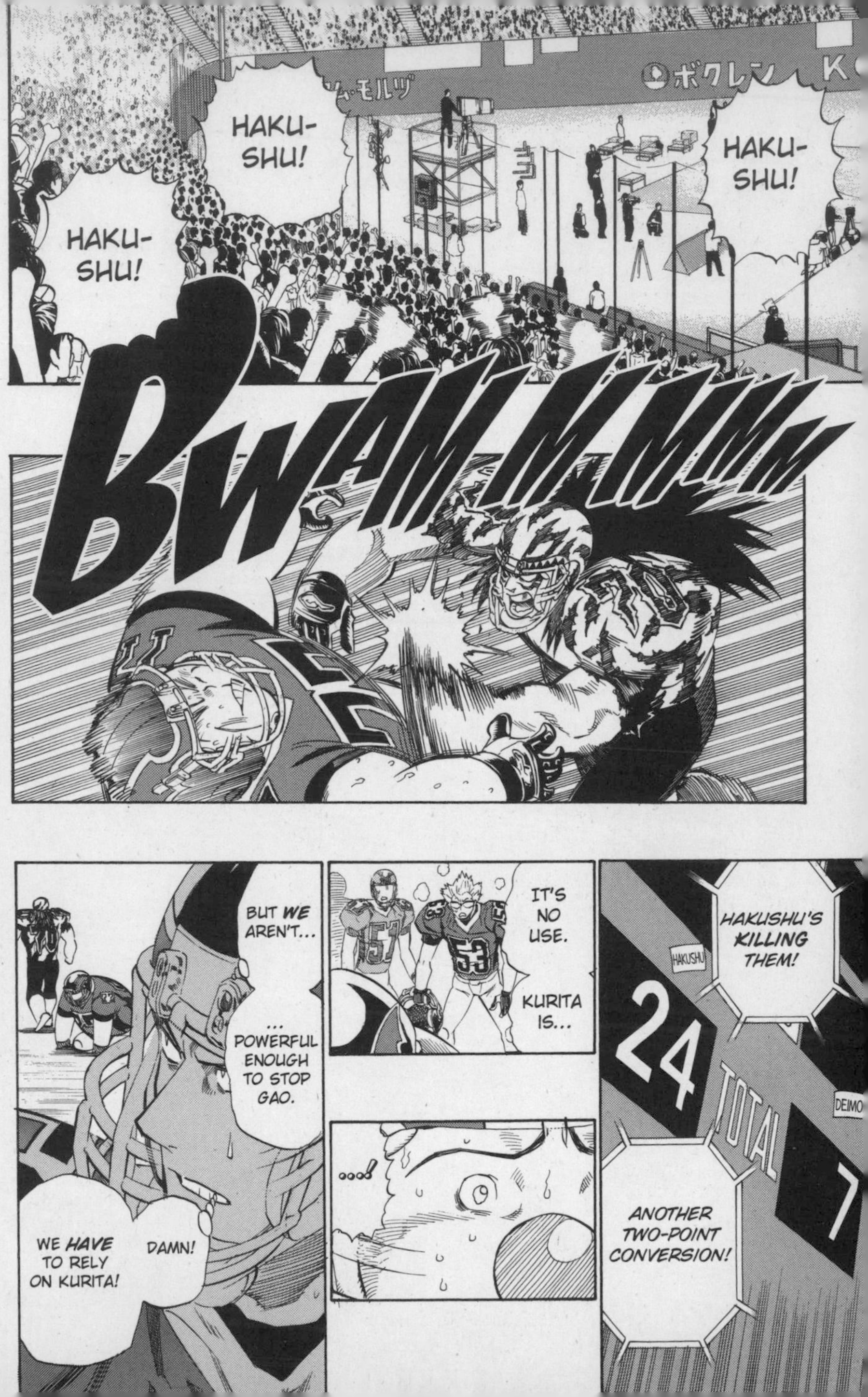
ボクレン
HAKU-SHU!
HAKU-SHU!
HAKU-SHU!
BWAMMMMM
HAKUSHU
24
TOTAL
DEIMO
7
HAKUSHU'S *KILLING* THEM!
ANOTHER TWO-POINT CONVERSION!
IT'S NO USE.
KURITA IS...
...!
BUT *WE* AREN'T...
...POWERFUL ENOUGH TO STOP GAO.
DAMN!
WE *HAVE* TO RELY ON KURITA!

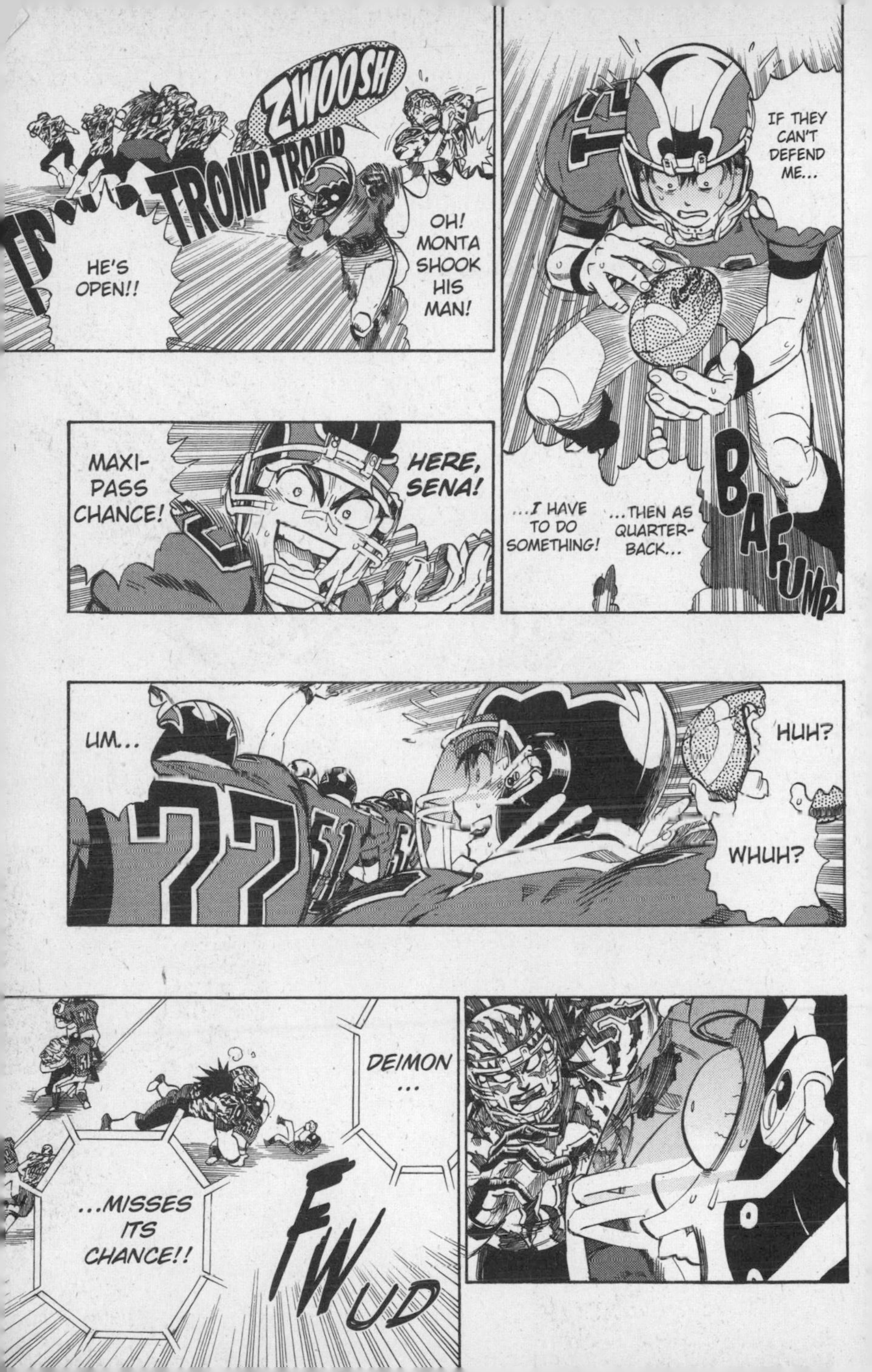
IF THEY CAN'T DEFEND ME...
...THEN AS QUARTER-BACK...
...I HAVE TO DO SOMETHING!
BAFUMP
ZWOOSH
TROMP TROMP
TP...
OH! MONTA SHOOK HIS MAN!
HE'S OPEN!!
HERE, SENA!
MAXI-PASS CHANCE!
HUH?
WHUH?
UM...
DEIMON...
...MISSES ITS CHANCE!!
FWUD

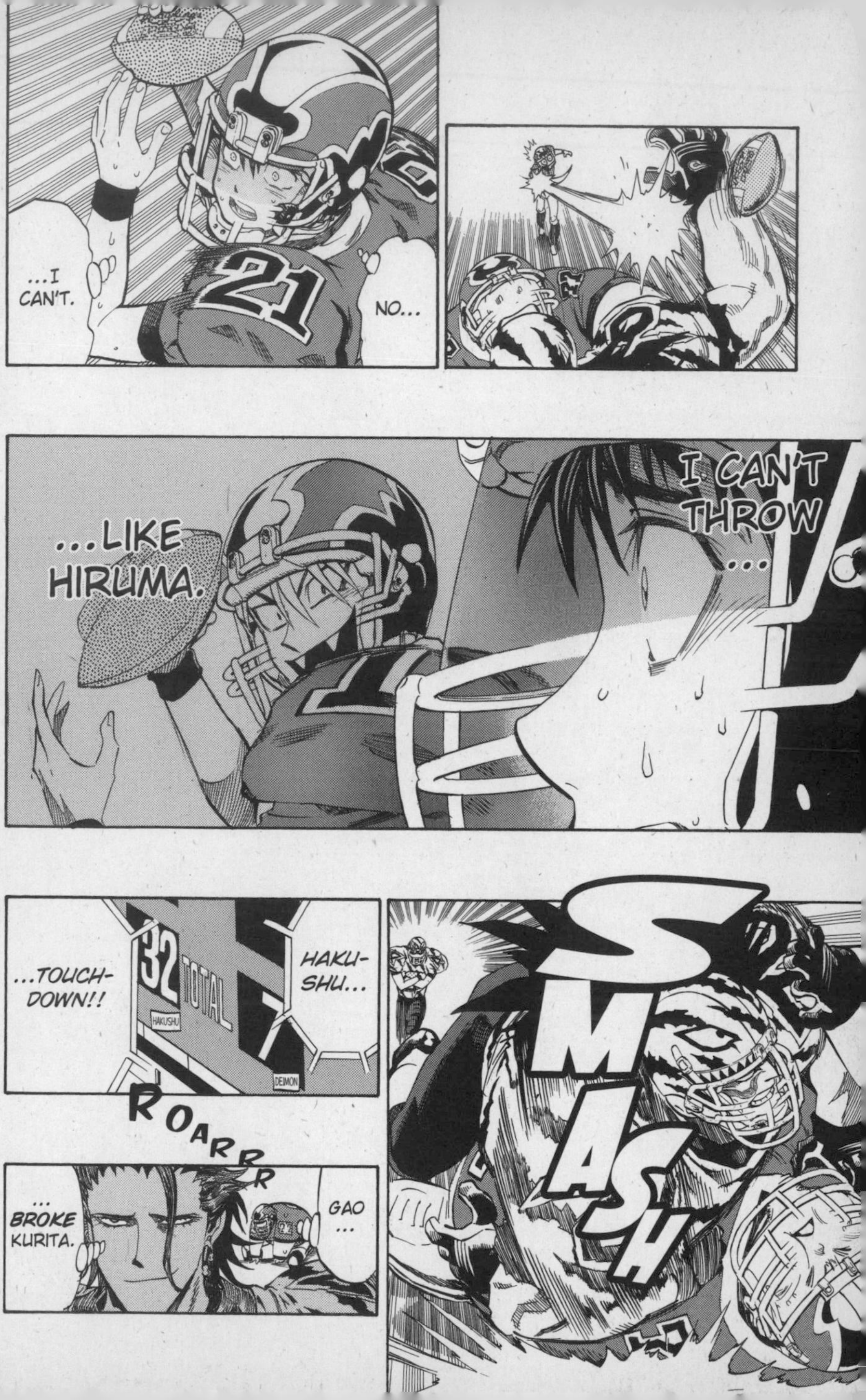
NO...
...I CAN'T.
I CAN'T THROW ...
...LIKE HIRUMA.
SMASH
HAKU-SHU...
...TOUCH-DOWN!!
32
TOTAL
HAKUSHU
DEIMON
ROARRR
GAO ...
... BROKE KURITA.

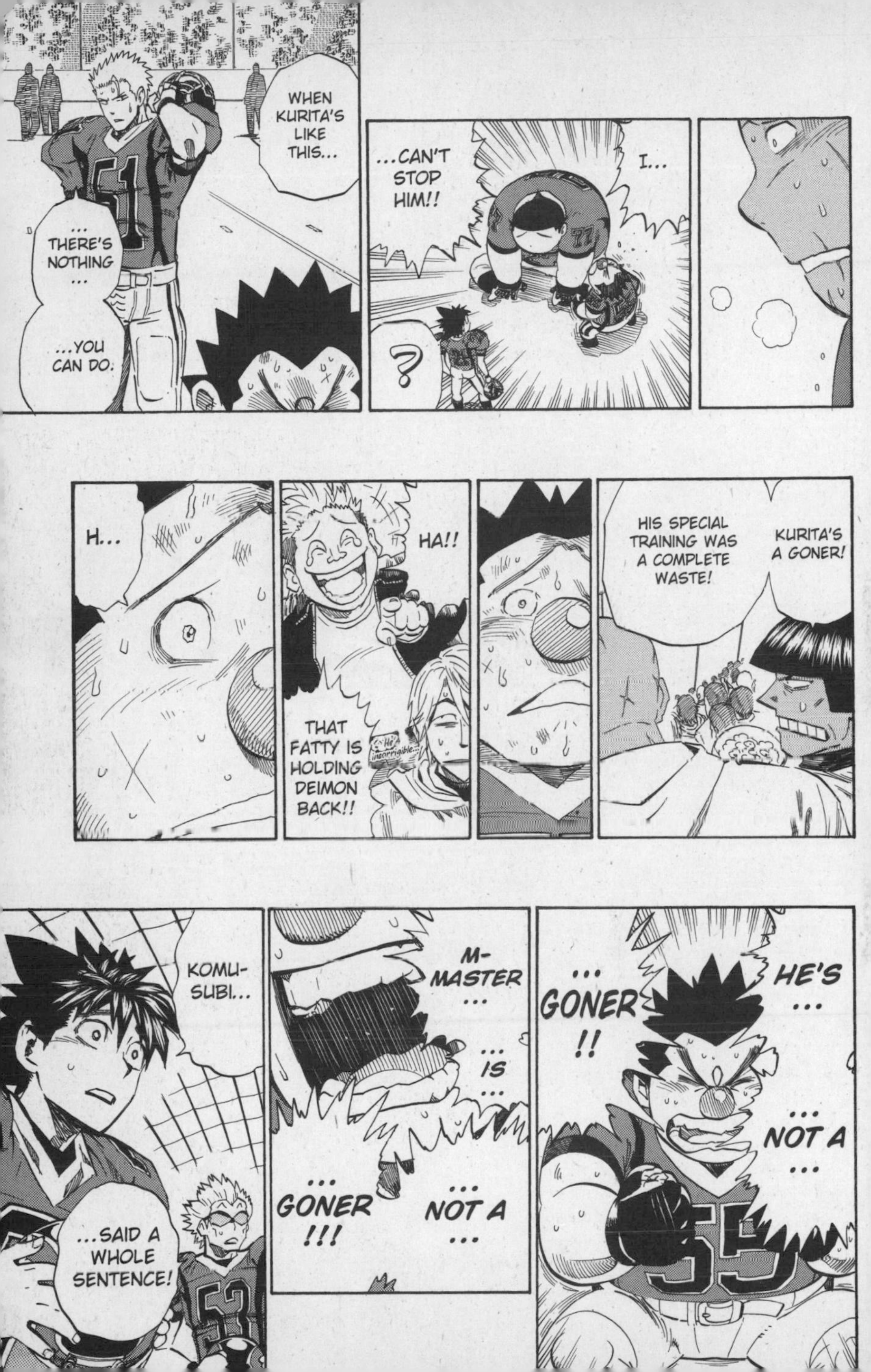
I...
...CAN'T STOP HIM!!
?
WHEN KURITA'S LIKE THIS...
... THERE'S NOTHING ...
...YOU CAN DO.
KURITA'S A GONER!
HIS SPECIAL TRAINING WAS A COMPLETE WASTE!
HA!!
THAT FATTY IS HOLDING DEIMON BACK!!
He's incorrigible...
H...
HE'S ...
... NOT A ...
... GONER !!
M-MASTER ...
... IS ...
... NOT A ...
... GONER !!!
KOMUSUBI...
...SAID A WHOLE SENTENCE!

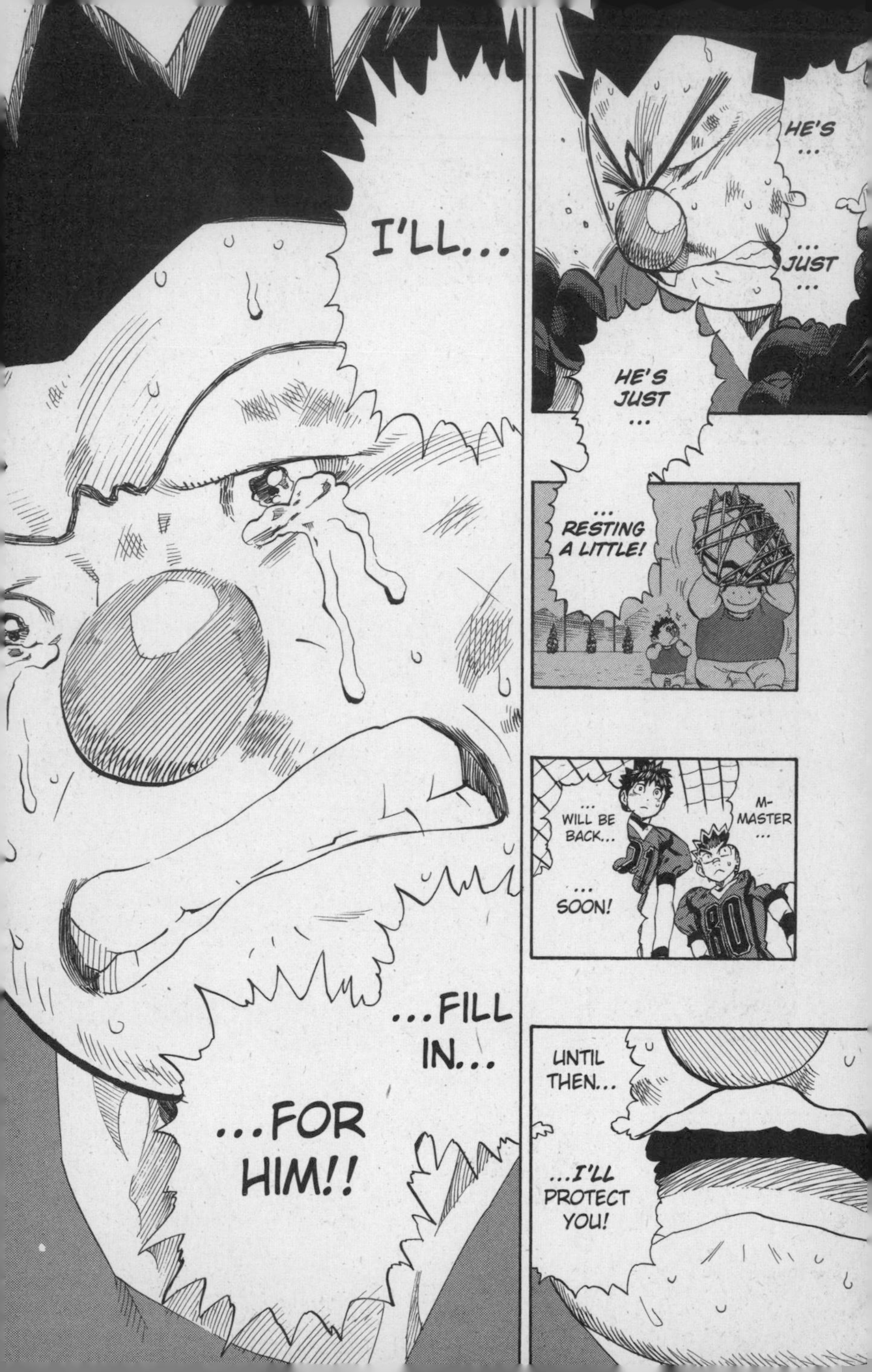
HE'S ...
... JUST ...
HE'S JUST ...
... RESTING A LITTLE!
M-MASTER ...
... WILL BE BACK...
... SOON!
UNTIL THEN...
...I'LL PROTECT YOU!
I'LL...
...FILL IN...
...FOR HIM!!

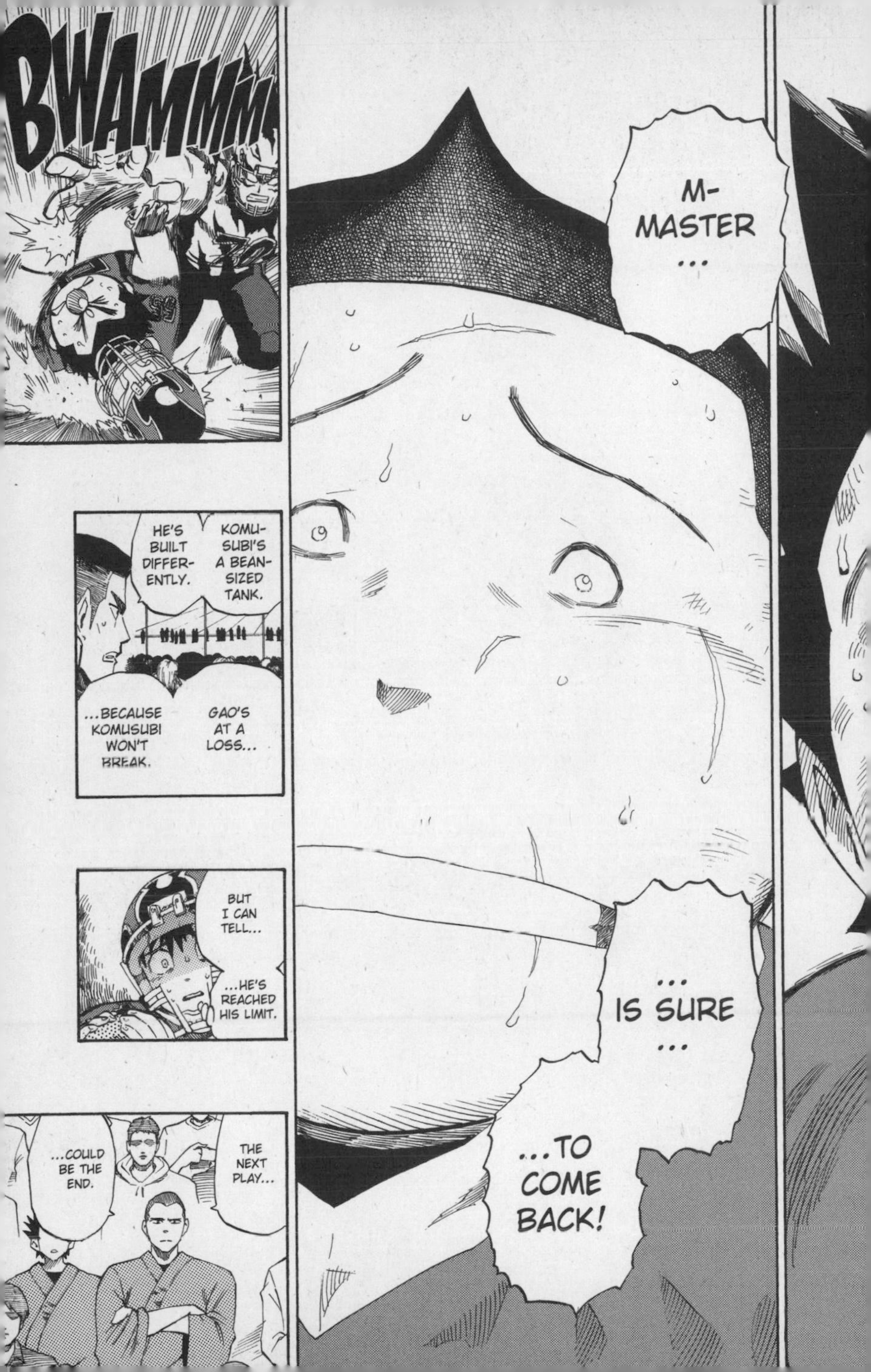
M-MASTER ...
... IS SURE ...
...TO COME BACK!
BWAMMM
KOMU-SUBI'S A BEAN-SIZED TANK.
HE'S BUILT DIFFER-ENTLY.
GAO'S AT A LOSS...
...BECAUSE KOMUSUBI WON'T BREAK.
BUT I CAN TELL...
...HE'S REACHED HIS LIMIT.
THE NEXT PLAY...
...COULD BE THE END.

... WERE HERE ...

IF HIRUMA ...

... WOULD ... HIRUMA DO?

WHAT ...

WHAT ...

...CAN I DO?

...TO OPEN UP THE CENTER.

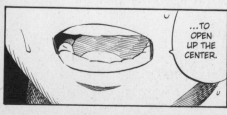

... EVERY- ONE ...

I WANT ...

...

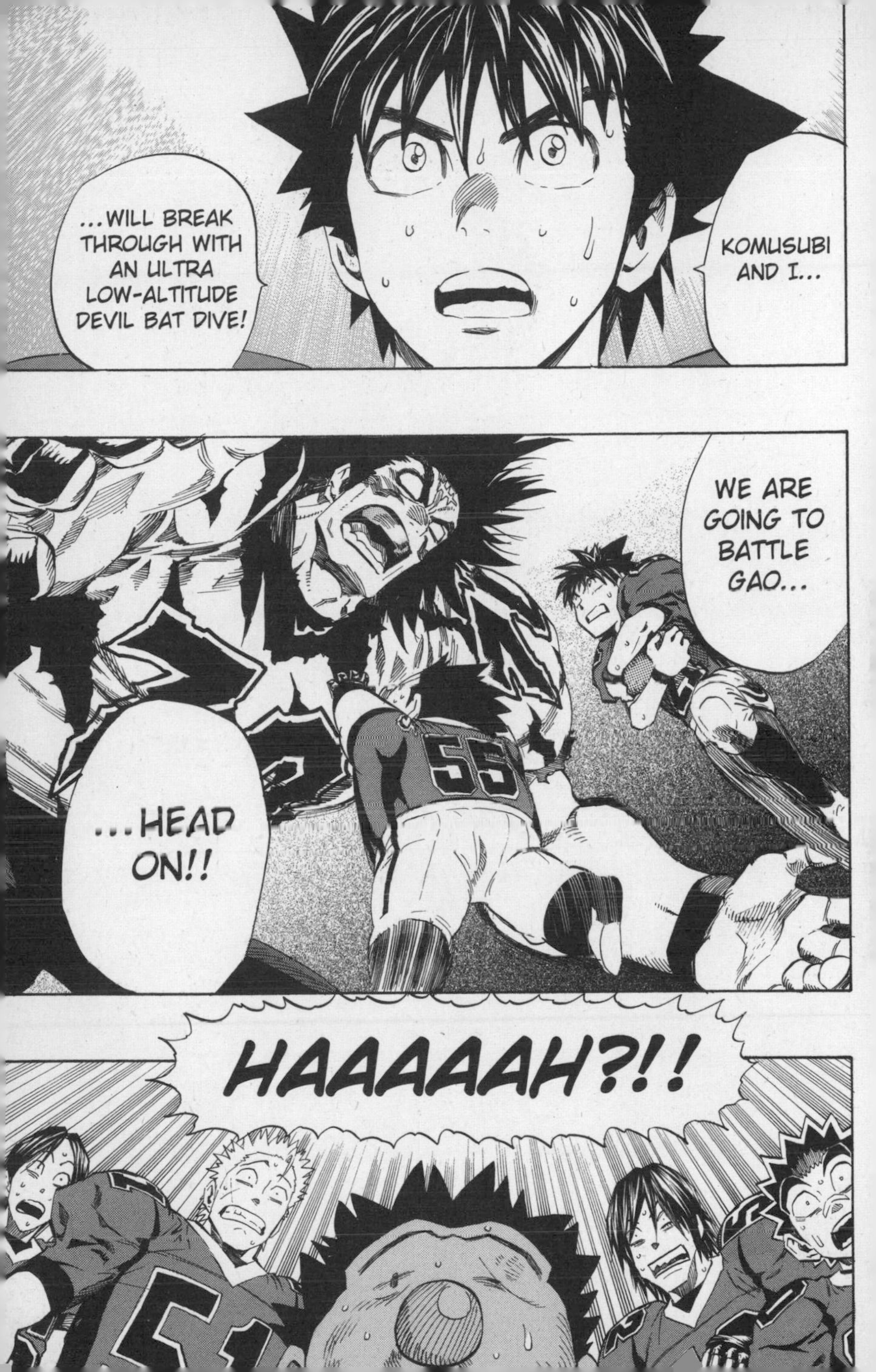
KOMUSUBI AND I...
...WILL BREAK THROUGH WITH AN ULTRA LOW-ALTITUDE DEVIL BAT DIVE!
WE ARE GOING TO BATTLE GAO...
...HEAD ON!!
HAAAAAH?!!

Eyeshield 21 Survey Corner **Devil Bat 021 SPECIAL!**

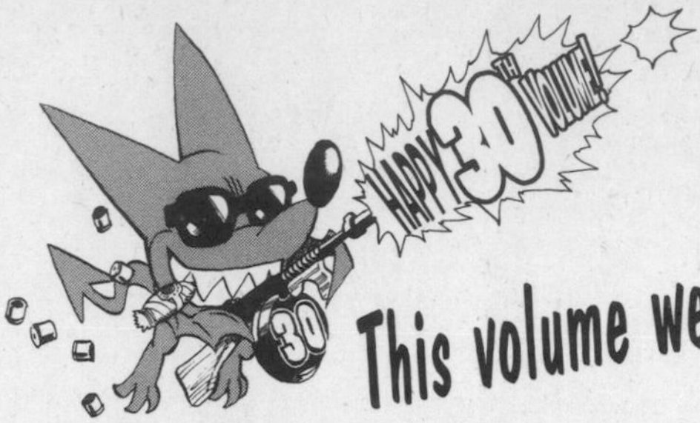
HAPPY 30TH VOLUME!
30

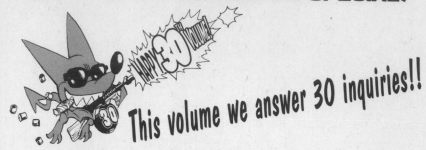

This volume we answer 30 inquiries!!

Investigation File #103

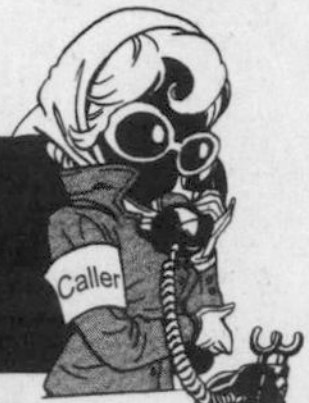
Caller

How did Gao get the scar on his forehead?

T.T. in Toyama Prefecture

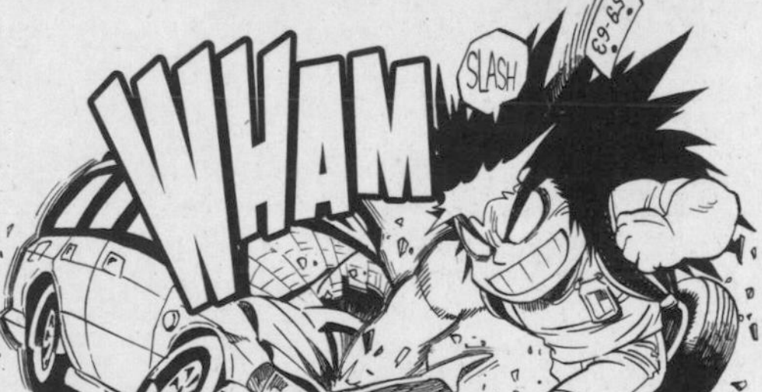
WHAM
SLASH

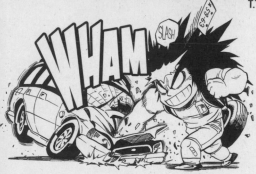

LIKE *THIS.*

Investigation File #104

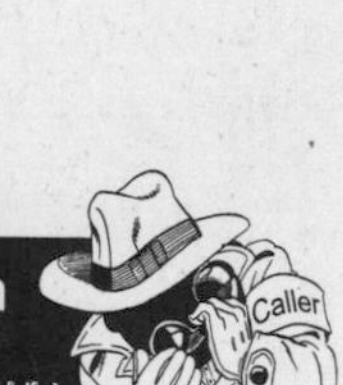
Caller

I saw Hamanasa Meat and Marusho Ham in Gao's locker. What in the world does he eat at school?!

Sho Kotsuki in Chiba Prefecture

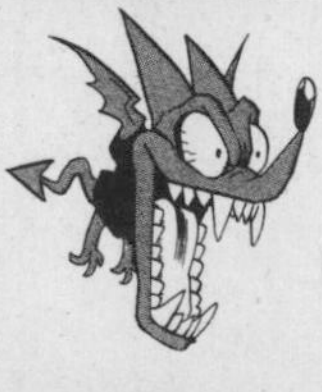

WHOLE SLABS OF RAW MEAT!
HE NEVER EATS VEGETABLES!

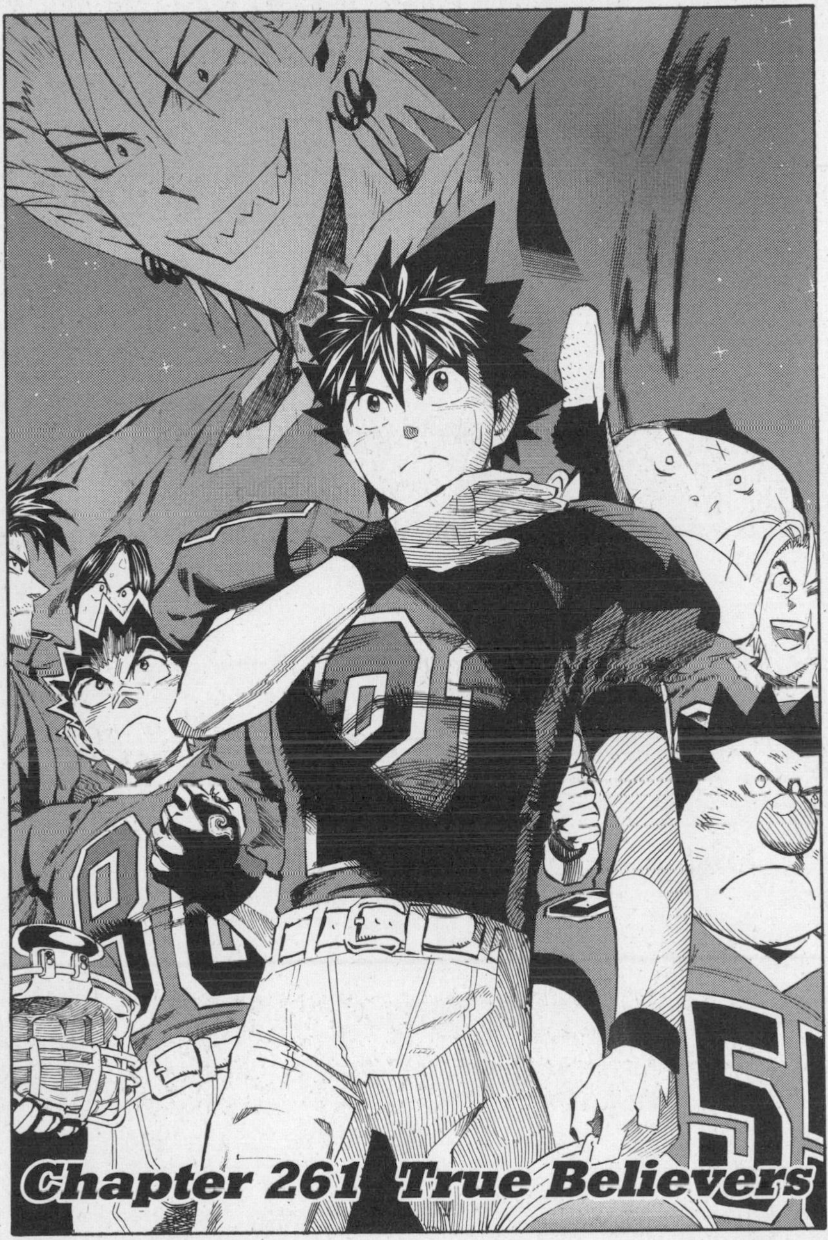
Chapter 261 True Believers

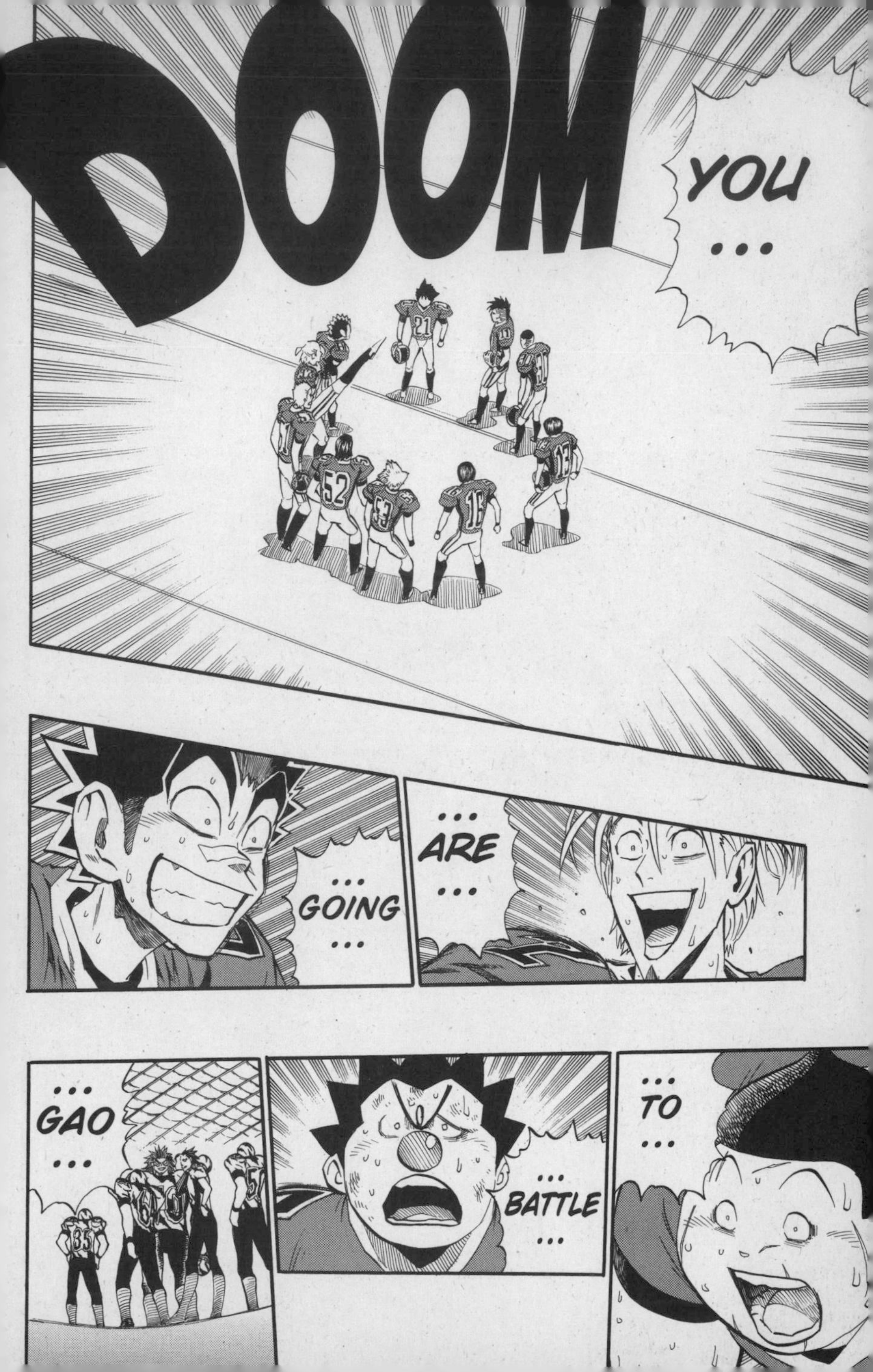
YOU ...
DOOM
... ARE ...
... GOING ...
... TO ...
... BATTLE ...
... GAO ...

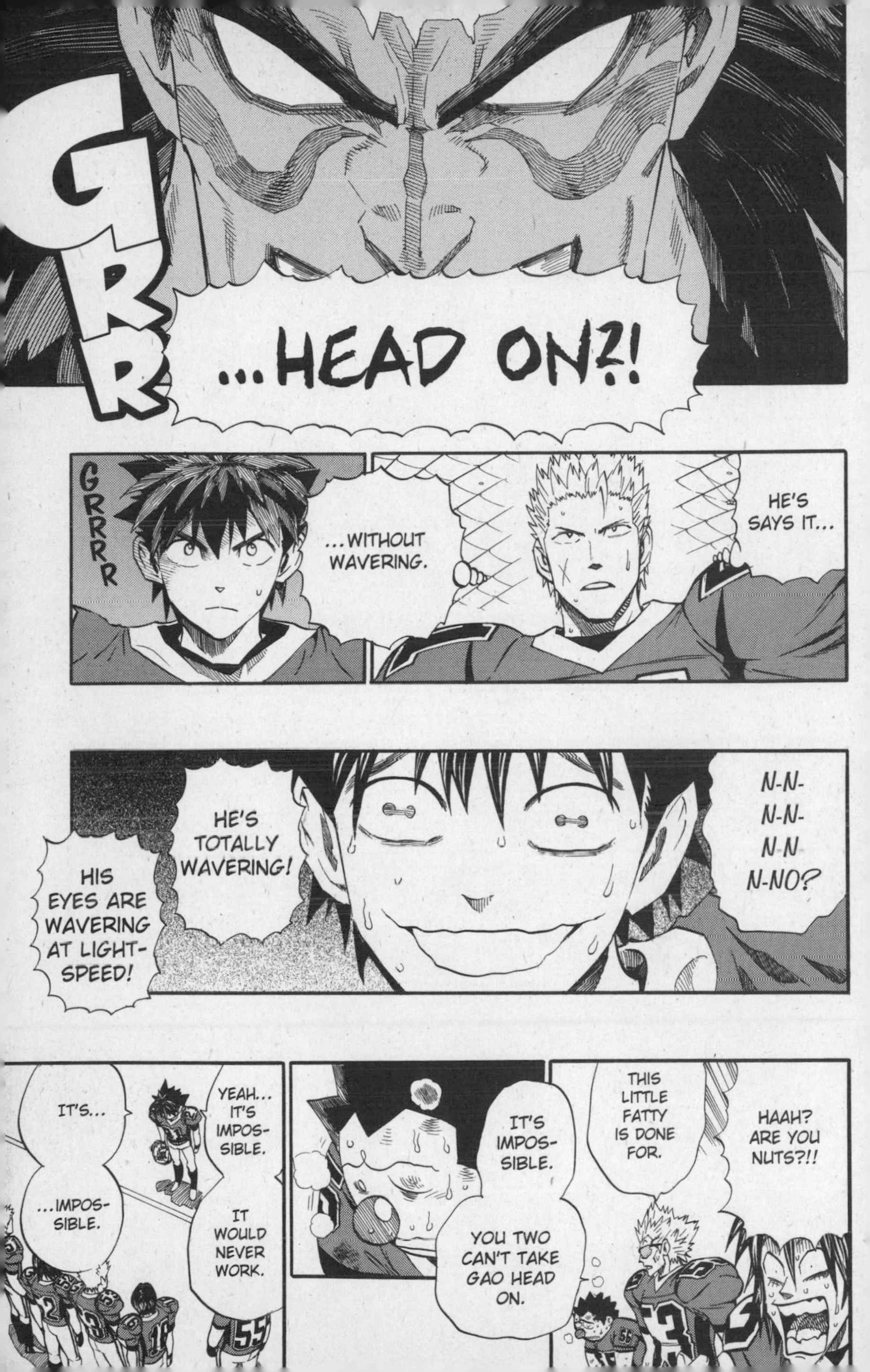
GRR
...HEAD ON?!
HE'S SAYS IT...
...WITHOUT WAVERING.
GRRRR
N-N-N-N-N-N N-NO?
HE'S TOTALLY WAVERING!
HIS EYES ARE WAVERING AT LIGHT-SPEED!
HAAH? ARE YOU NUTS?!!
THIS LITTLE FATTY IS DONE FOR.
IT'S IMPOSSIBLE.
YOU TWO CAN'T TAKE GAO HEAD ON.
YEAH... IT'S IMPOSSIBLE.
IT WOULD NEVER WORK.
IT'S...
...IMPOSSIBLE.

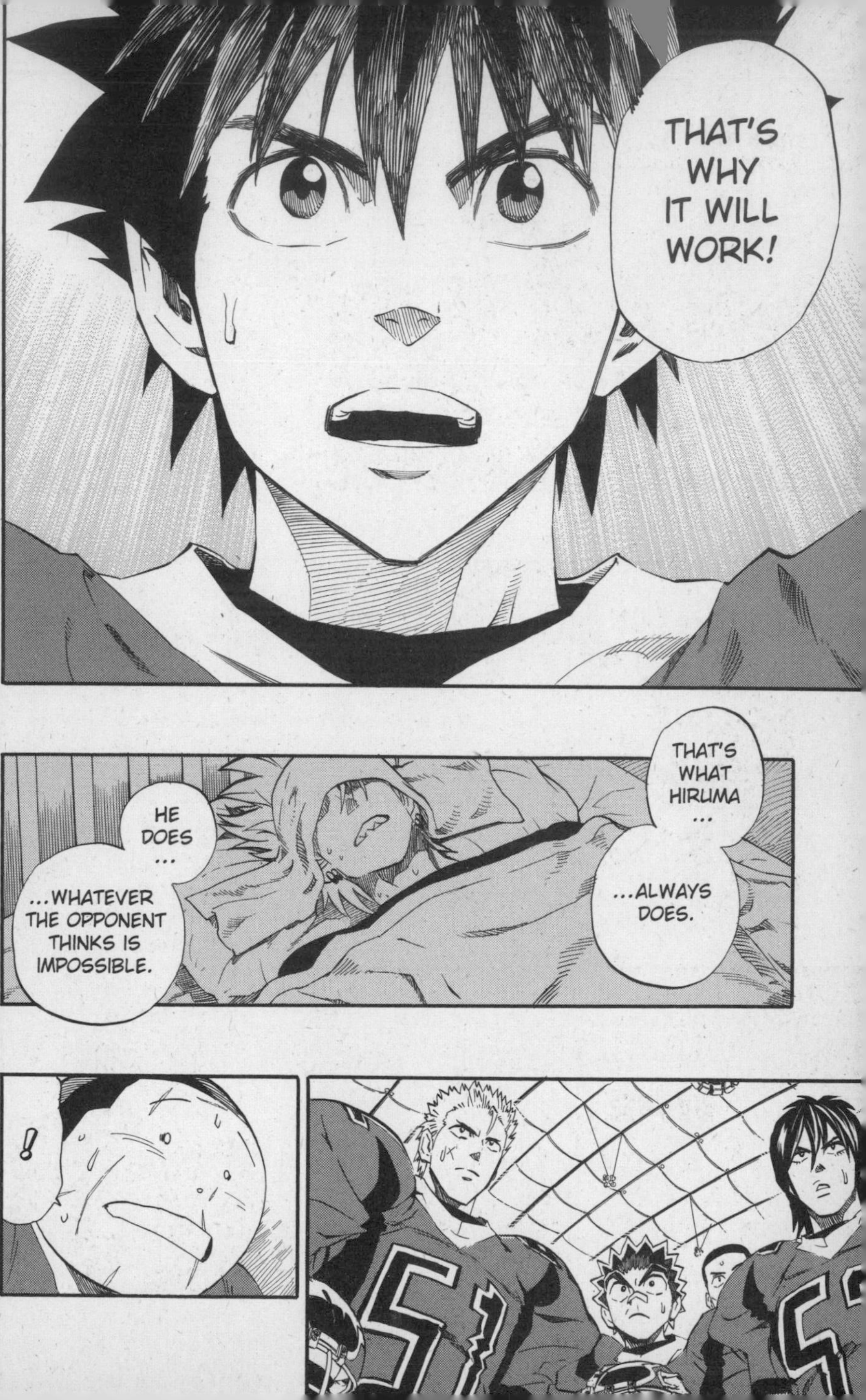
THAT'S WHY IT WILL WORK!
THAT'S WHAT HIRUMA ...
...ALWAYS DOES.
HE DOES ...
...WHATEVER THE OPPONENT THINKS IS IMPOSSIBLE.
!

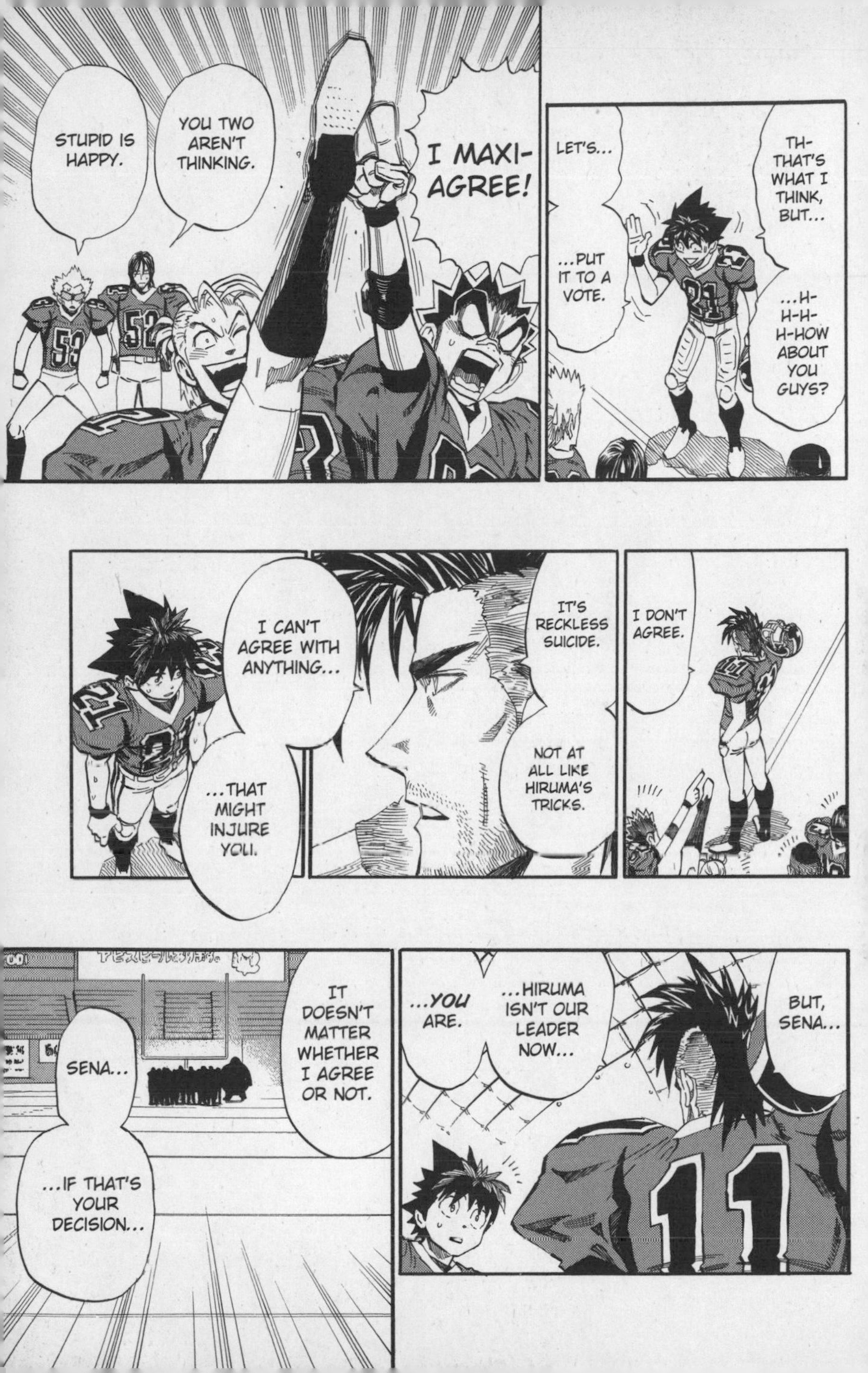
TH- THAT'S WHAT I THINK, BUT...
...H- H-H- H-HOW ABOUT YOU GUYS?
LET'S...
...PUT IT TO A VOTE.
I MAXI- AGREE!
YOU TWO AREN'T THINKING.
STUPID IS HAPPY.
I DON'T AGREE.
IT'S RECKLESS SUICIDE.
NOT AT ALL LIKE HIRUMA'S TRICKS.
I CAN'T AGREE WITH ANYTHING...
...THAT MIGHT INJURE YOU.
BUT, SENA...
...HIRUMA ISN'T OUR LEADER NOW...
...*YOU* ARE.
IT DOESN'T MATTER WHETHER I AGREE OR NOT.
SENA...
...IF THAT'S YOUR DECISION...

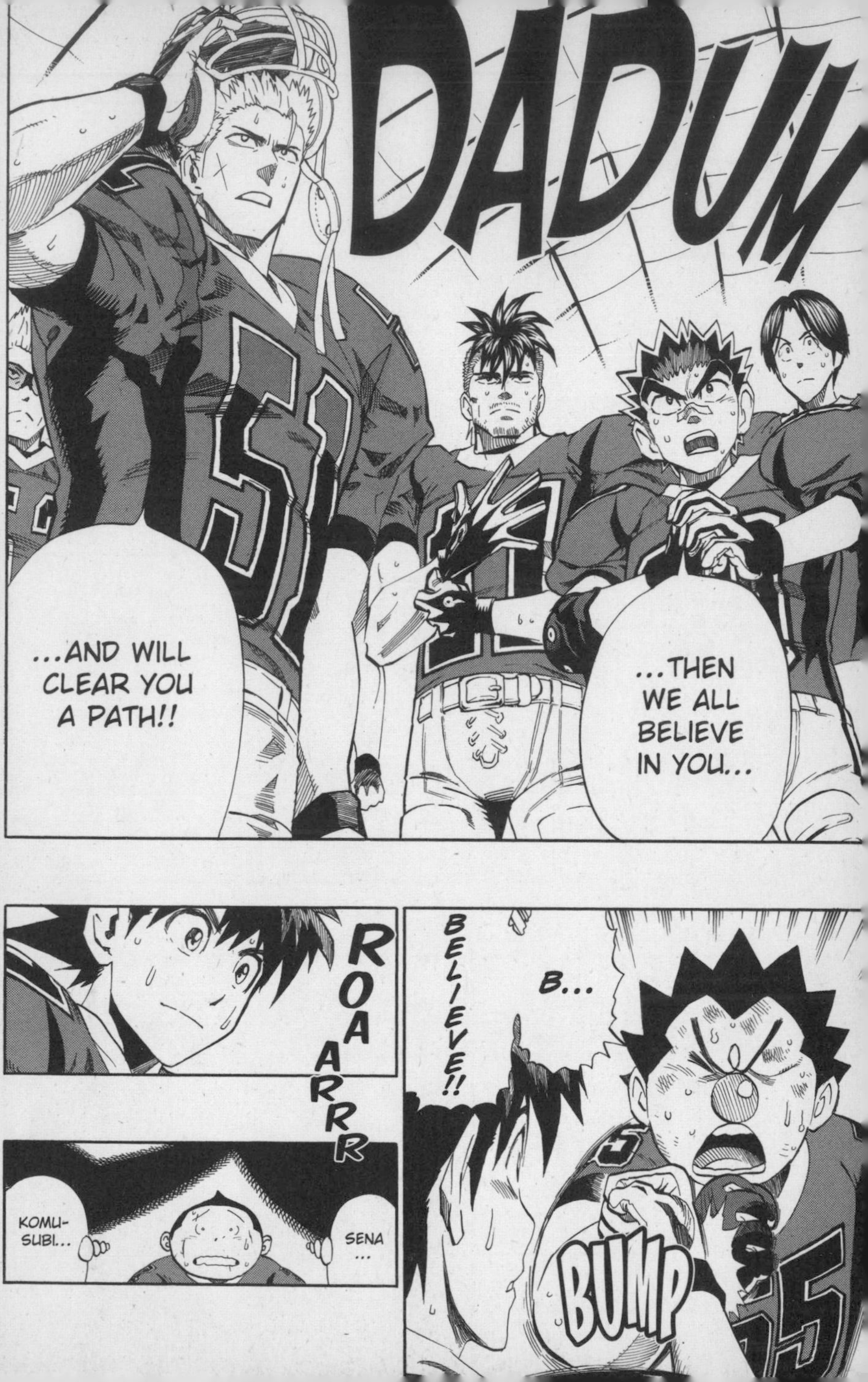
DADUM
...THEN WE ALL BELIEVE IN YOU...
...AND WILL CLEAR YOU A PATH!!
B...
BELIEVE!!
BUMP
ROAARRR
SENA ...
KOMUSUBI...

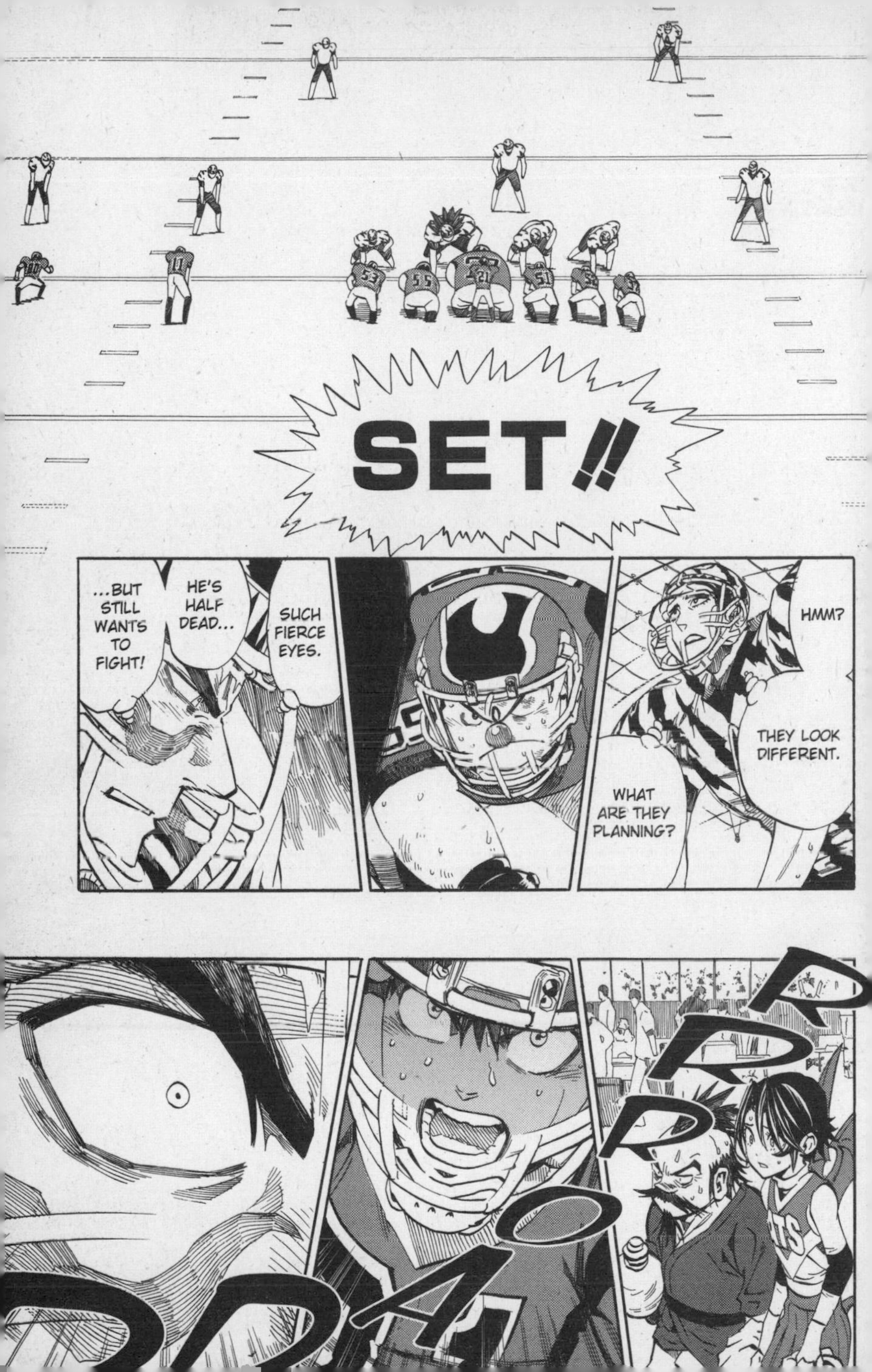
SET!!
HMM?
THEY LOOK DIFFERENT.
WHAT ARE THEY PLANNING?
SUCH FIERCE EYES.
HE'S HALF DEAD...
...BUT STILL WANTS TO FIGHT!
RRROA

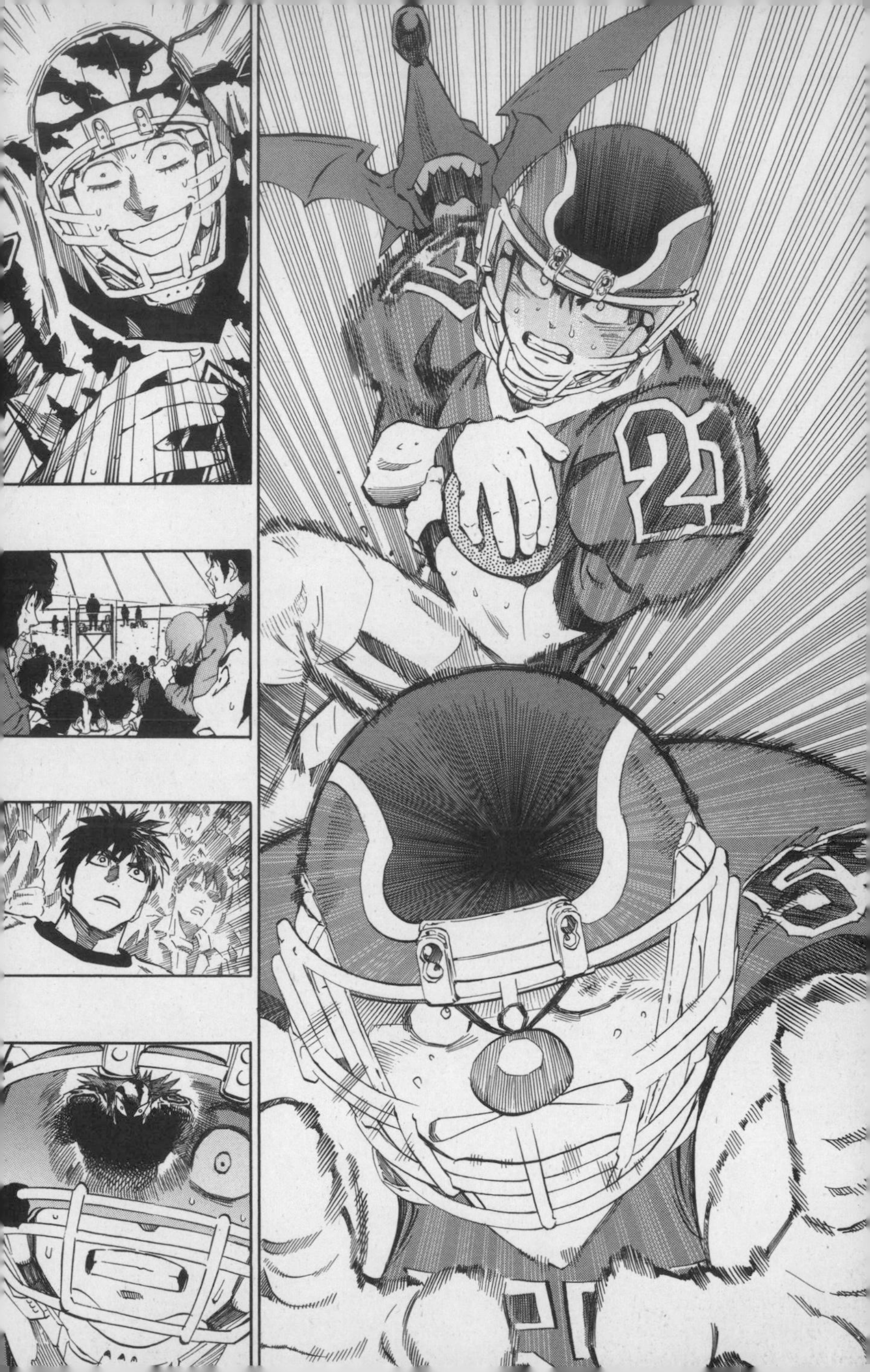

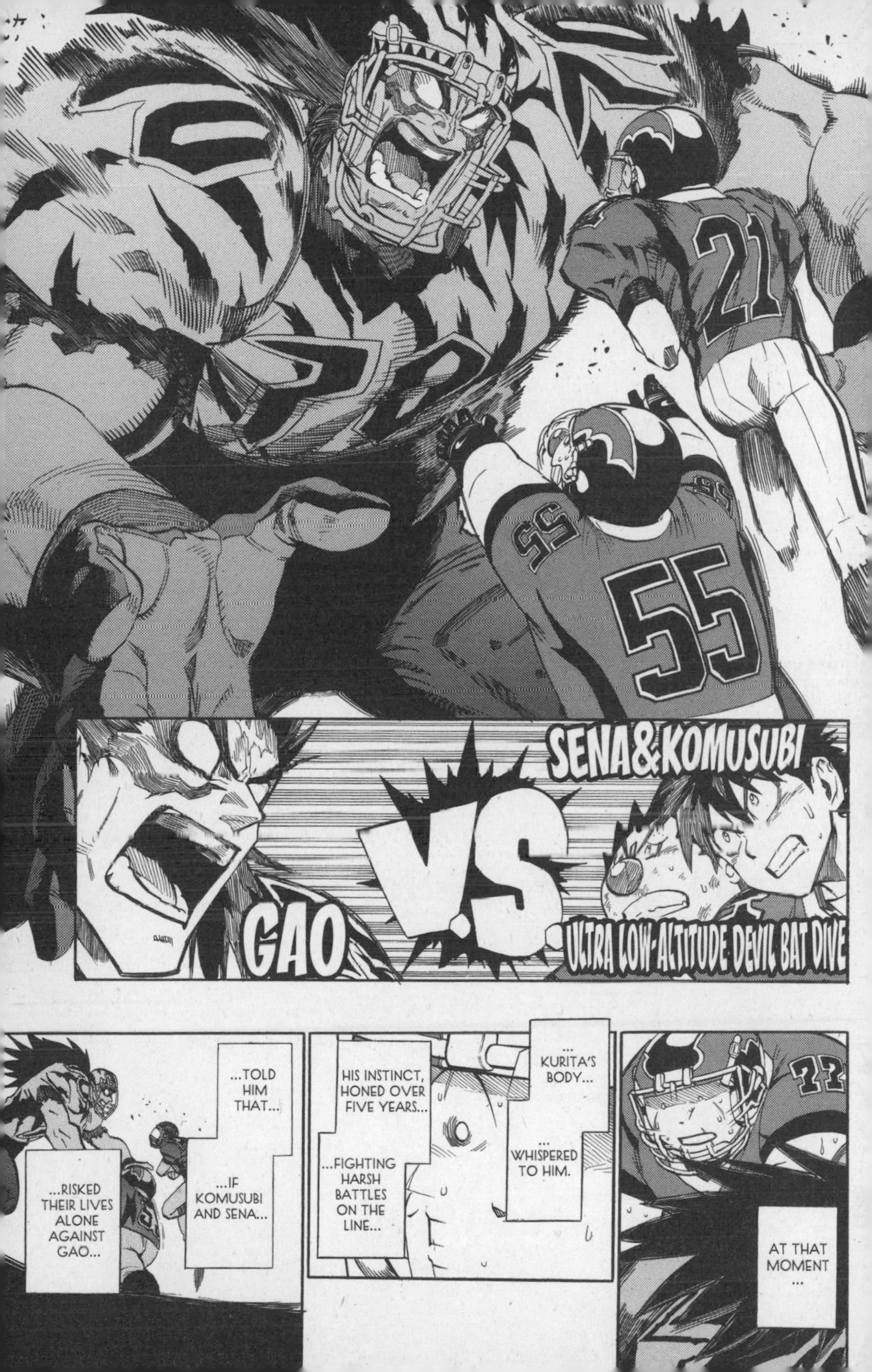
SENA&KOMUSUBI
VS
ULTRA LOW-ALTITUDE DEVIL BAT DIVE
GAO
AT THAT MOMENT ...
... KURITA'S BODY...
HIS INSTINCT, HONED OVER FIVE YEARS...
...FIGHTING HARSH BATTLES ON THE LINE...
... WHISPERED TO HIM.
...TOLD HIM THAT...
...IF KOMUSUBI AND SENA...
...RISKED THEIR LIVES ALONE AGAINST GAO...

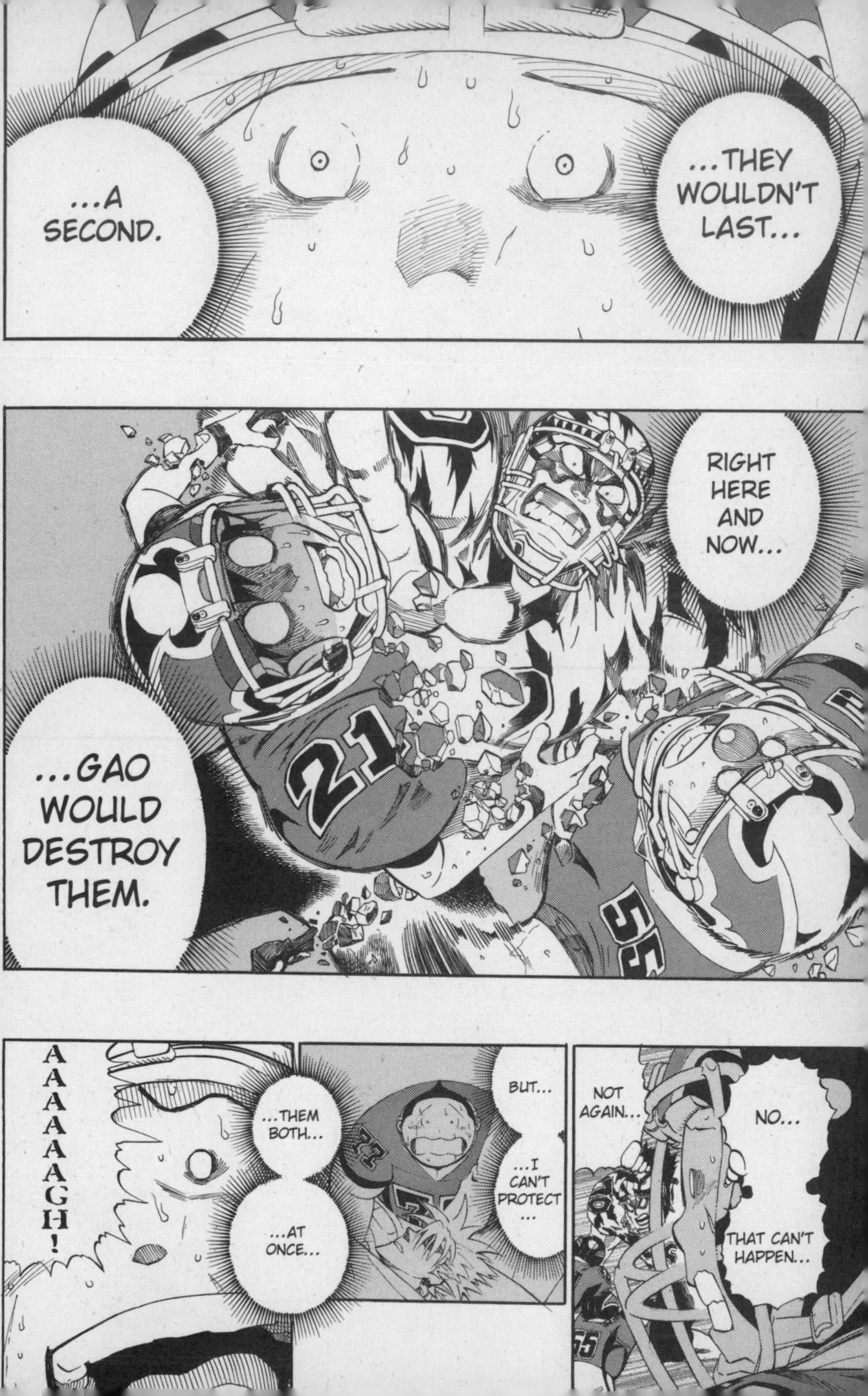

...THEY WOULDN'T LAST...
...A SECOND.
RIGHT HERE AND NOW...
...GAO WOULD DESTROY THEM.
NO...
NOT AGAIN...
THAT CAN'T HAPPEN...
BUT...
...I CAN'T PROTECT ...
...THEM BOTH...
...AT ONCE...
AAAAAAAAGH!

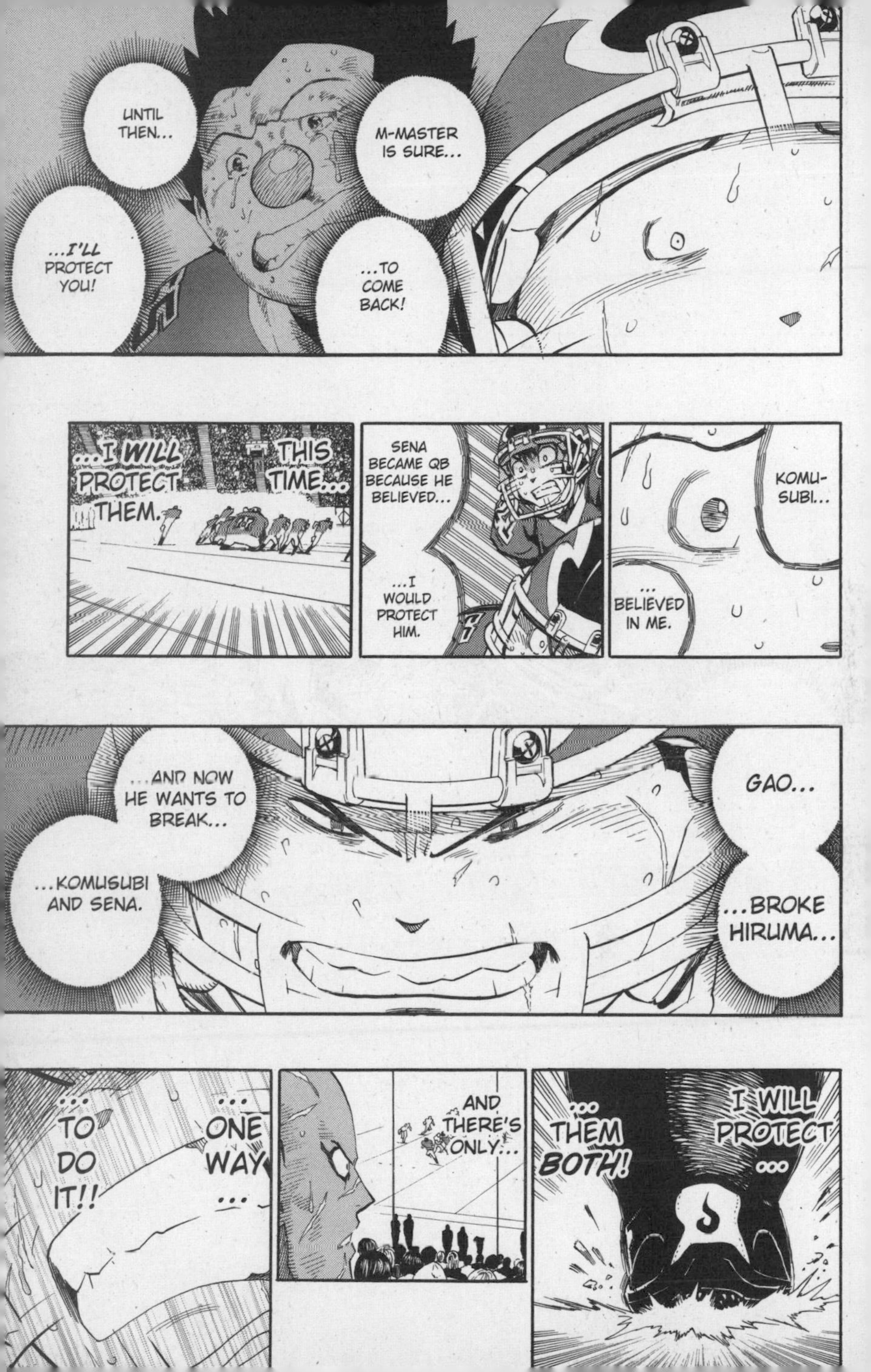
M-MASTER IS SURE...
...TO COME BACK!
UNTIL THEN...
...I'LL PROTECT YOU!
KOMU-SUBI...
...BELIEVED IN ME.
SENA BECAME QB BECAUSE HE BELIEVED...
...I WOULD PROTECT HIM.
THIS TIME...
...I WILL PROTECT THEM.
GAO...
...BROKE HIRUMA...
...AND NOW HE WANTS TO BREAK...
...KOMUSUBI AND SENA.
I WILL PROTECT...
...THEM BOTH!
AND THERE'S ONLY...
...ONE WAY...
...TO DO IT!!

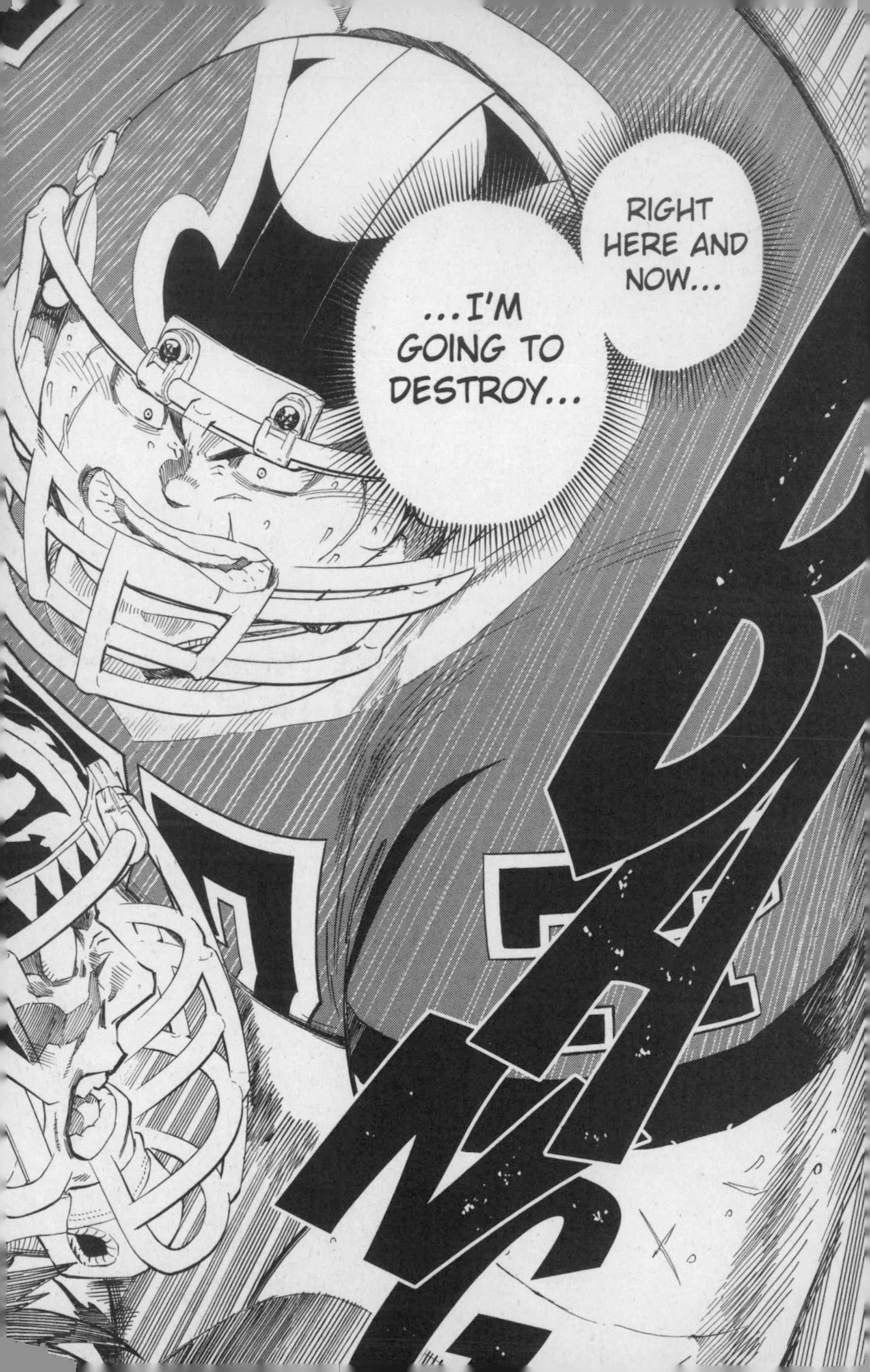
RIGHT HERE AND NOW...
...I'M GOING TO DESTROY...

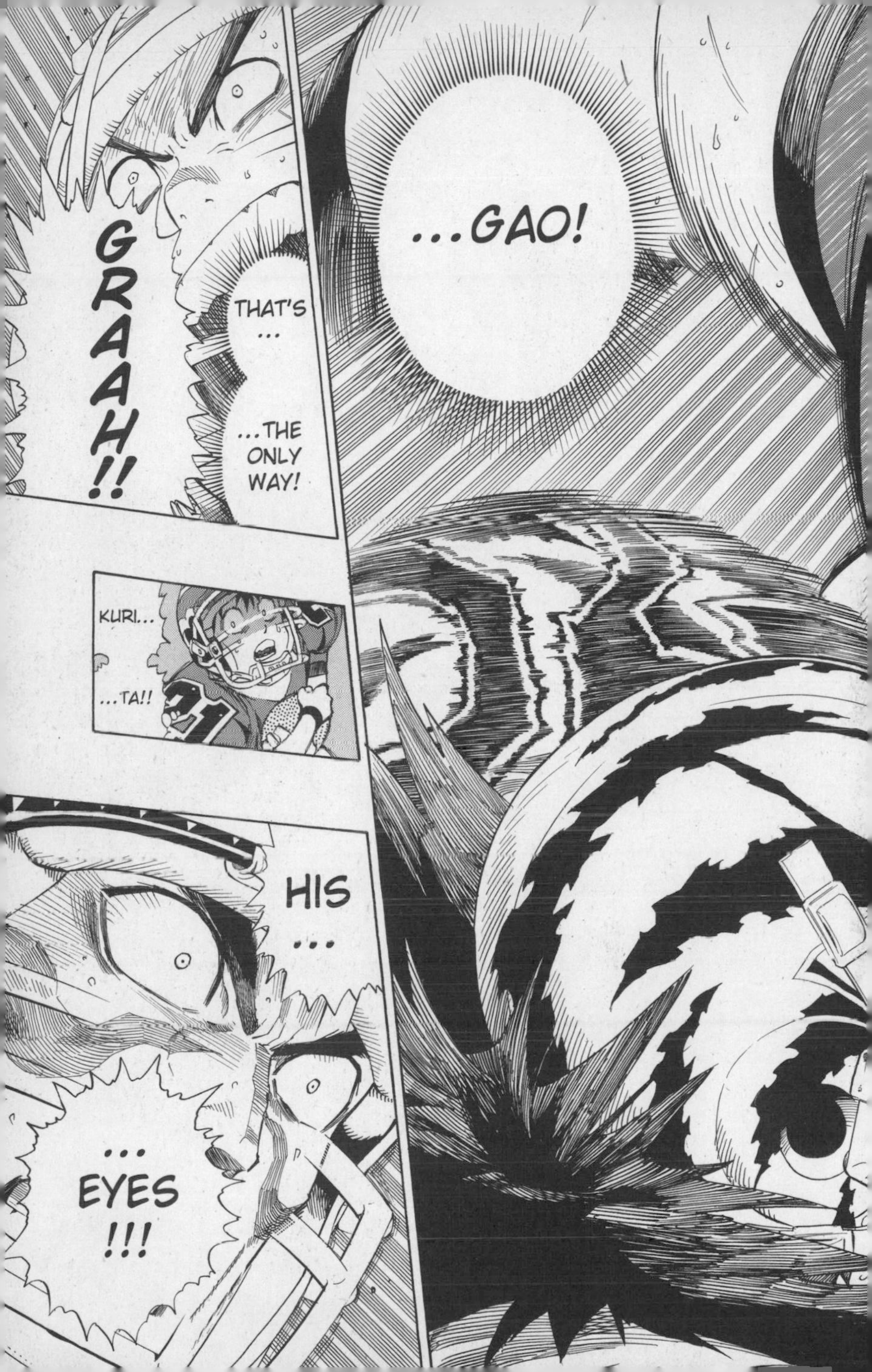
...GAO!
THAT'S ...
...THE ONLY WAY!
GRAAH!!
KURI...
...TA!!
HIS ...
... EYES !!!

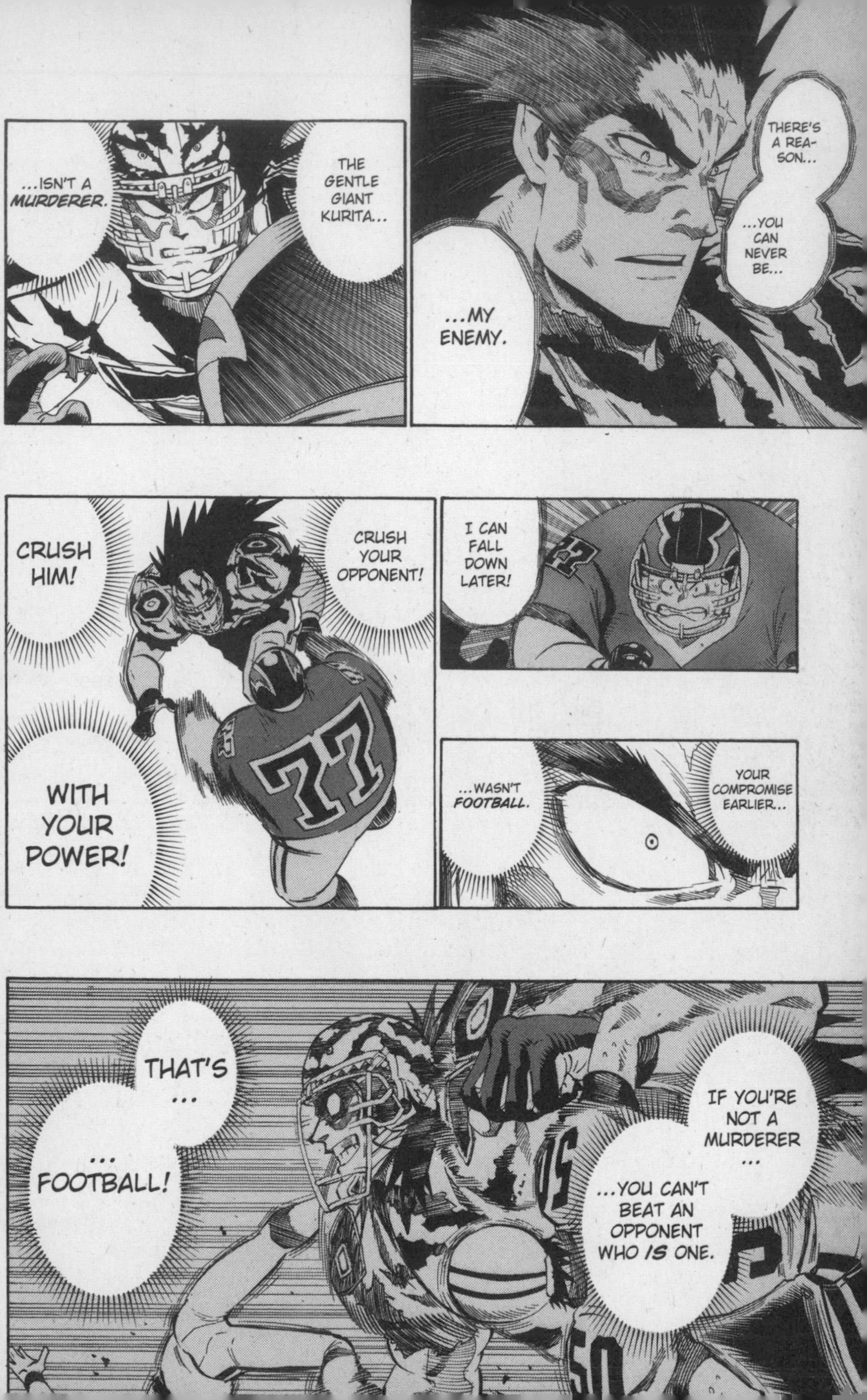
THERE'S A REASON...
...YOU CAN NEVER BE...
...MY ENEMY.
THE GENTLE GIANT KURITA...
...ISN'T A MURDERER.
I CAN FALL DOWN LATER!
YOUR COMPROMISE EARLIER...
...WASN'T FOOTBALL.
CRUSH YOUR OPPONENT!
CRUSH HIM!
WITH YOUR POWER!
IF YOU'RE NOT A MURDERER...
...YOU CAN'T BEAT AN OPPONENT WHO IS ONE.
THAT'S...
...FOOTBALL!

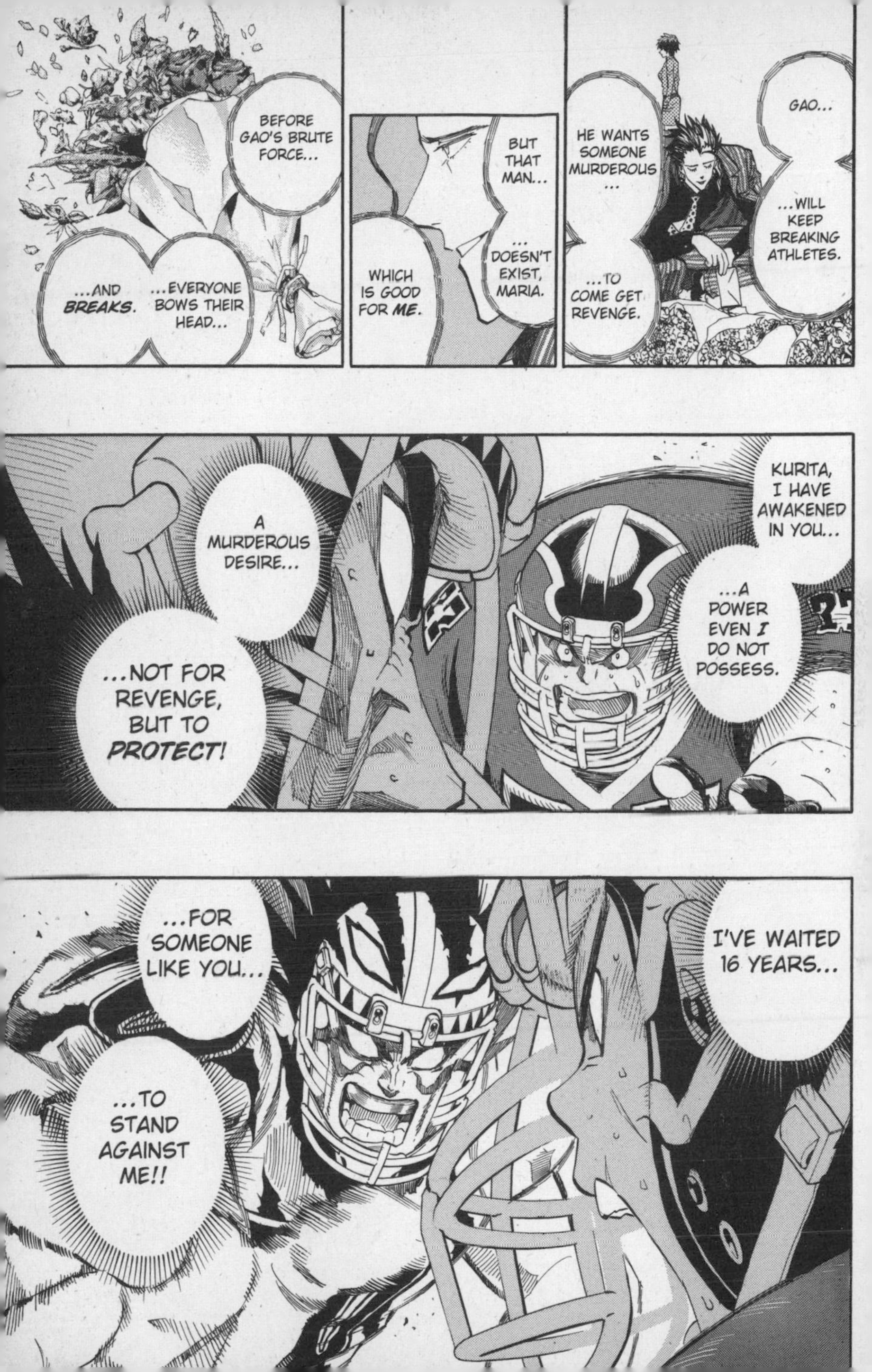
GAO...
...WILL KEEP BREAKING ATHLETES.
HE WANTS SOMEONE MURDEROUS...
...TO COME GET REVENGE.
BUT THAT MAN...
...DOESN'T EXIST, MARIA.
WHICH IS GOOD FOR *ME*.
BEFORE GAO'S BRUTE FORCE...
...EVERYONE BOWS THEIR HEAD...
...AND *BREAKS*.
KURITA, I HAVE AWAKENED IN YOU...
...A POWER EVEN *I* DO NOT POSSESS.
A MURDEROUS DESIRE...
...NOT FOR REVENGE, BUT TO *PROTECT*!
I'VE WAITED 16 YEARS...
...FOR SOMEONE LIKE YOU...
...TO STAND AGAINST ME!!

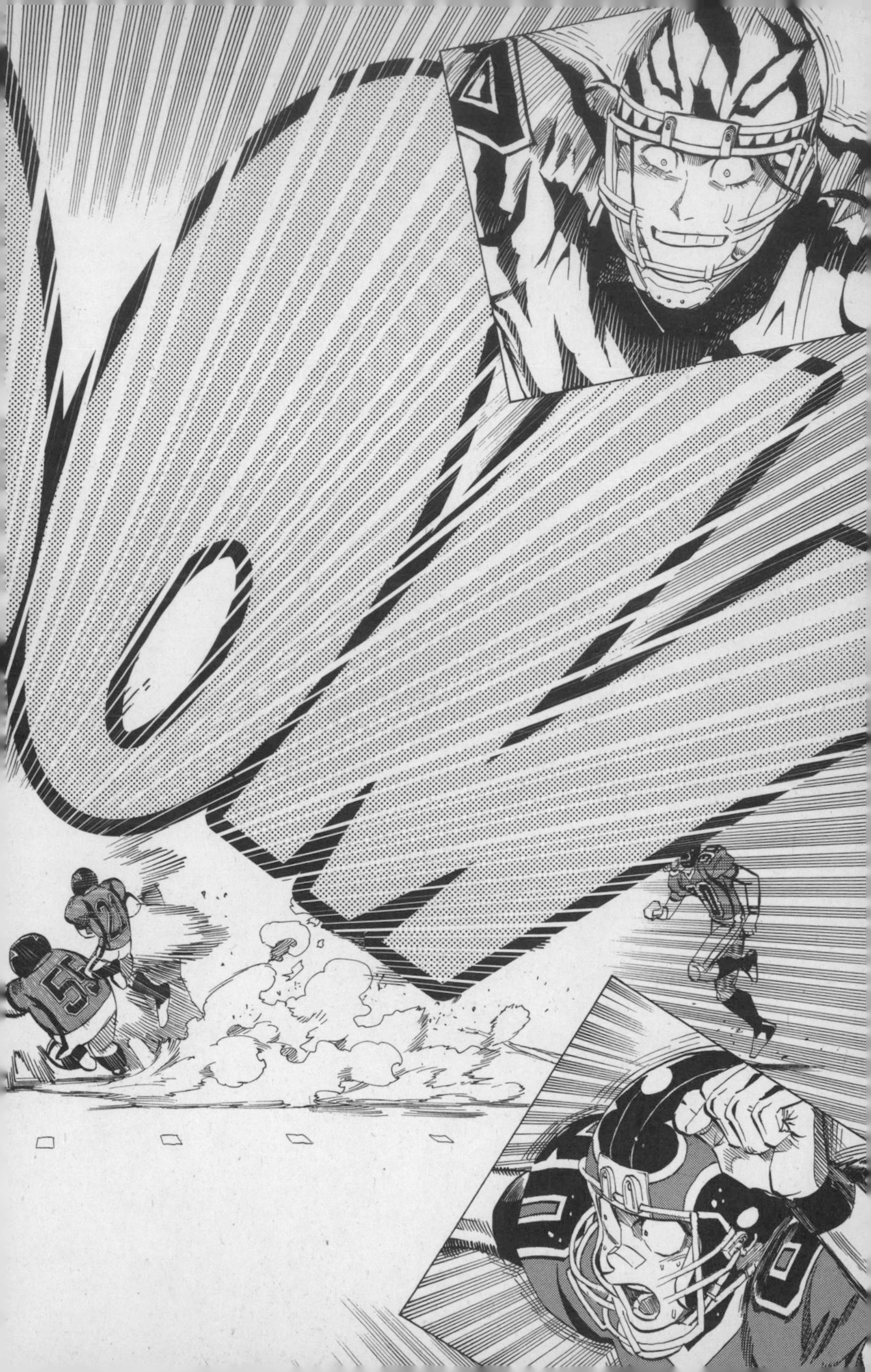

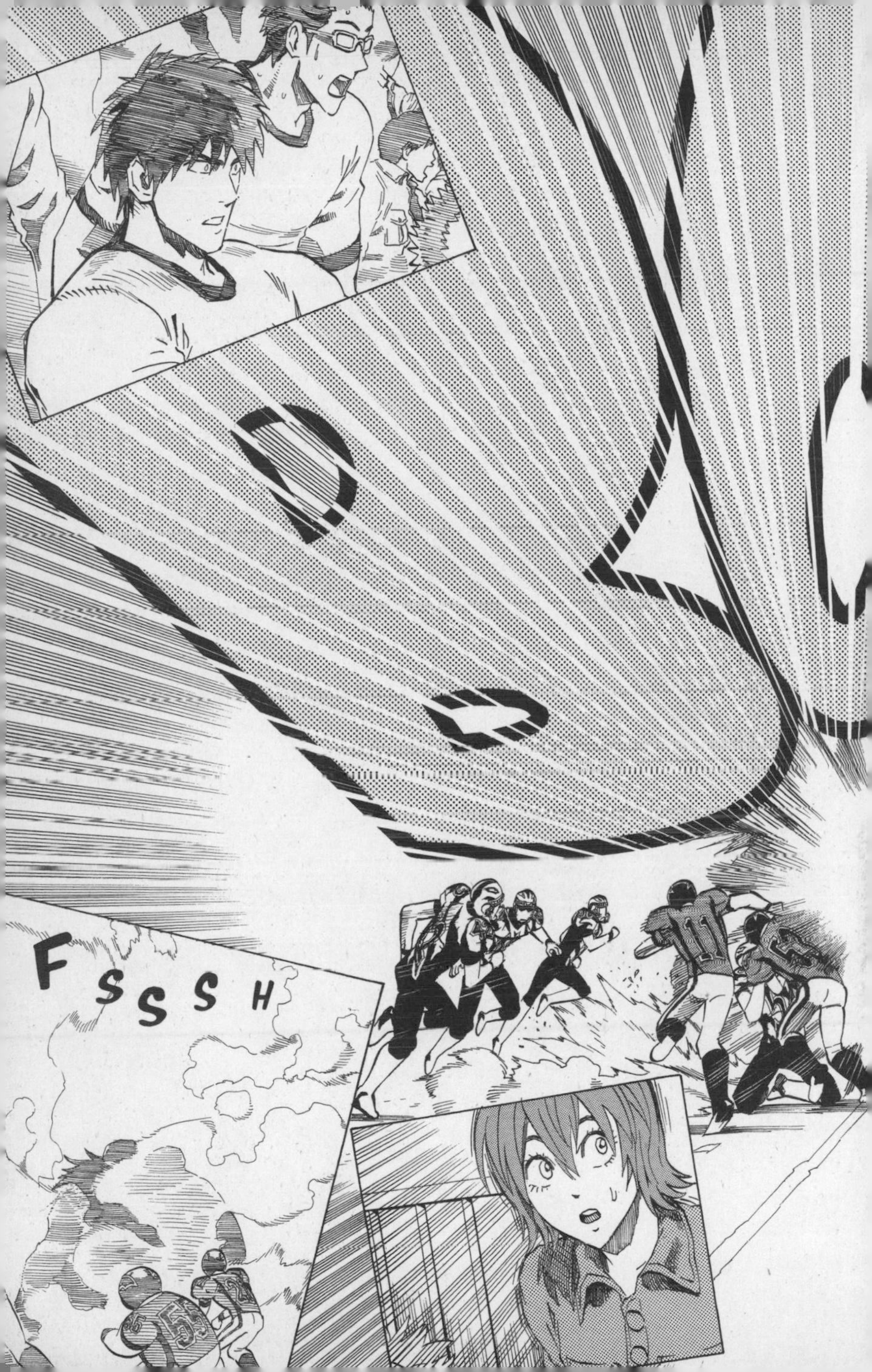
FSSSH

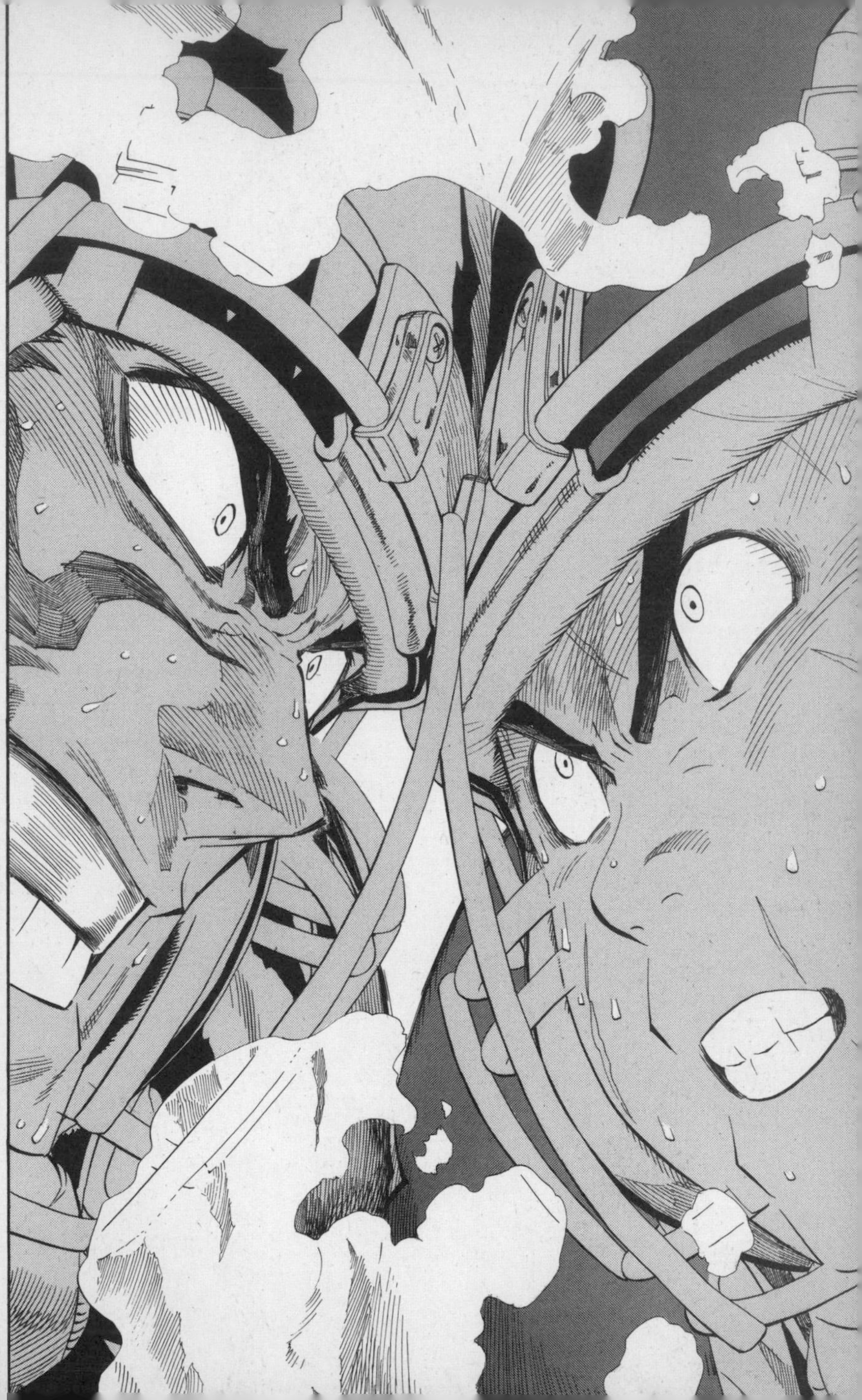

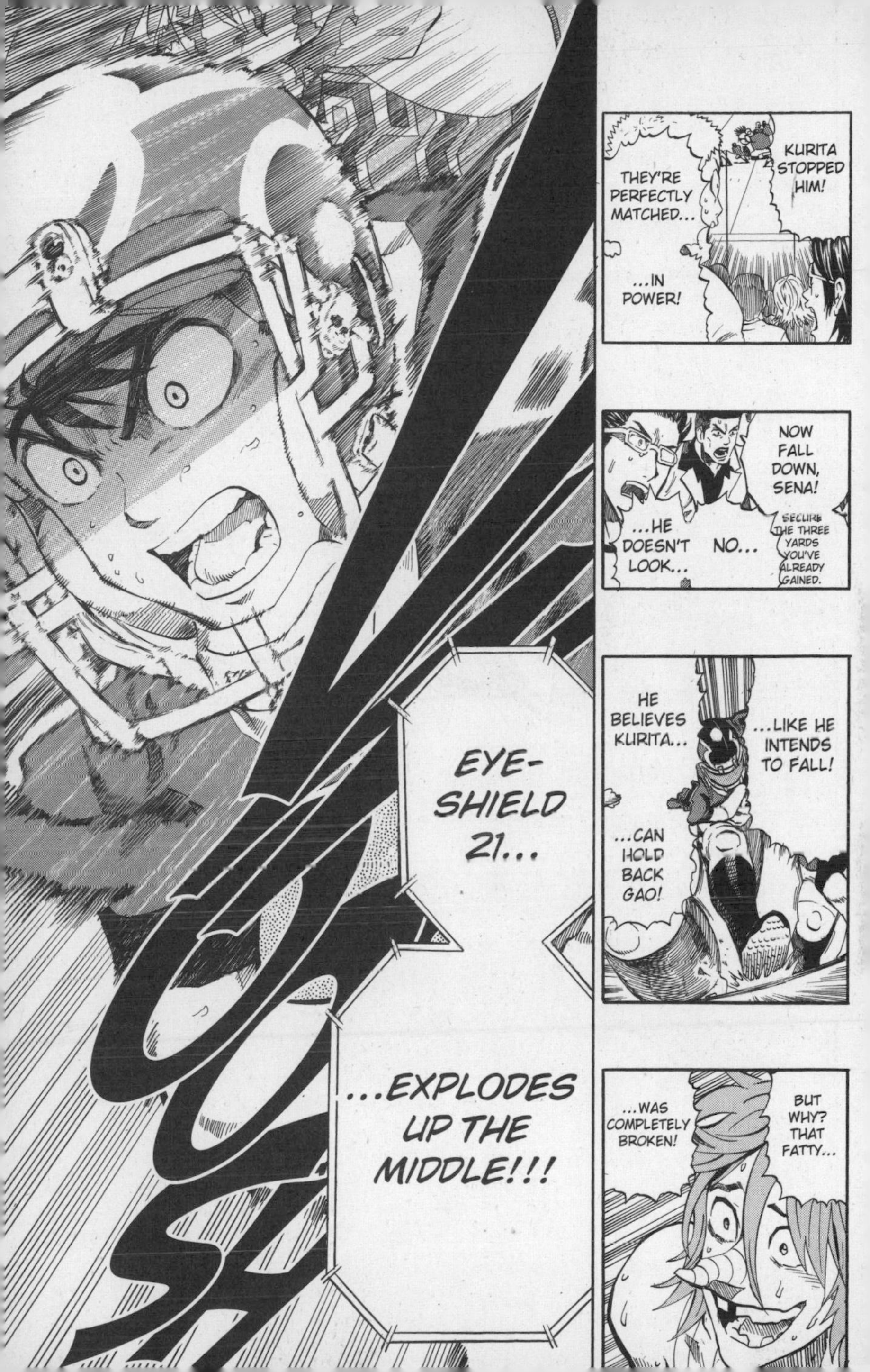
KURITA STOPPED HIM!
THEY'RE PERFECTLY MATCHED...
...IN POWER!
NOW FALL DOWN, SENA!
SECURE THE THREE YARDS YOU'VE ALREADY GAINED.
NO...
...HE DOESN'T LOOK...
...LIKE HE INTENDS TO FALL!
HE BELIEVES KURITA...
...CAN HOLD BACK GAO!
BUT WHY? THAT FATTY...
...WAS COMPLETELY BROKEN!
EYE-SHIELD 21...
...EXPLODES UP THE MIDDLE!!!

Investigation File #105

What do Marco's parents do?

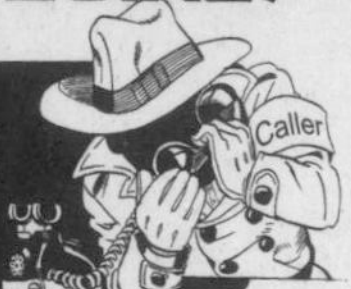
Caller

S.H. in Shizuoka Prefecture

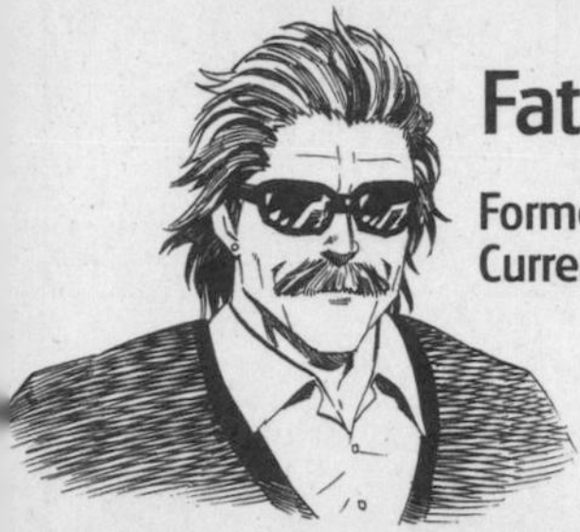

Father

Former mafia member
Currently an investor

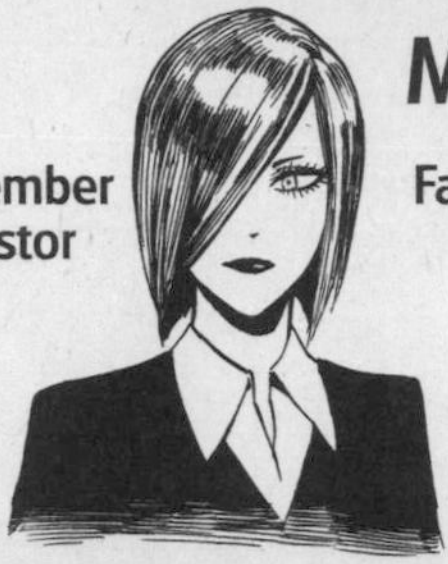

Mother

Fashion designer

Investigation File #106

How many decimal points of pi can Hiruma remember?

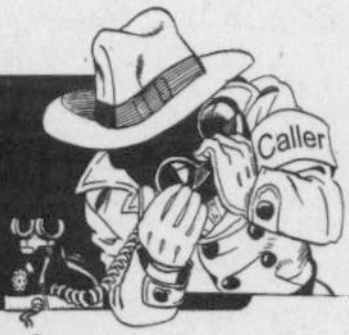
Caller

Mr. D in Chiba Prefecture

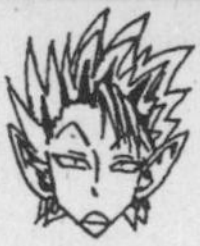

UP TO 3.141592. LIKE EVERYONE.

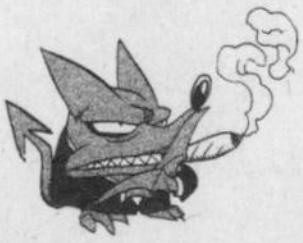

HE DOESN'T MEMORIZE ANYTHING THAT ISN'T USEFUL.

Investigation File #107

Do Mizumachi and Otawara take off their clothes even in the winter?

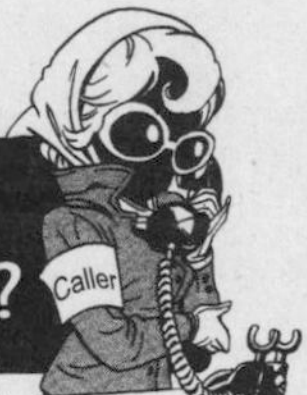
Caller

Natsuki in Kumamoto Prefecture

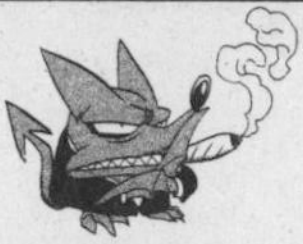

YOU BETCHA. IDIOTS DON'T CATCH C—

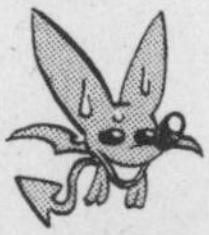

SHH!

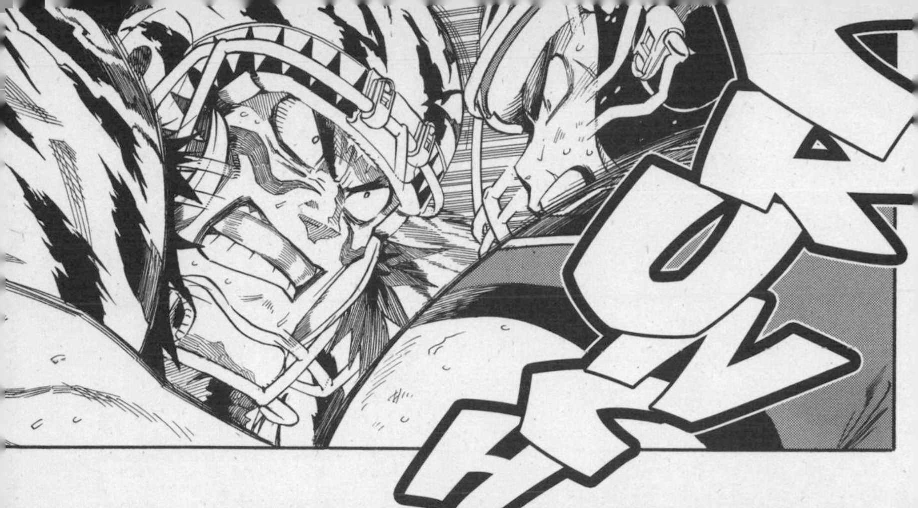

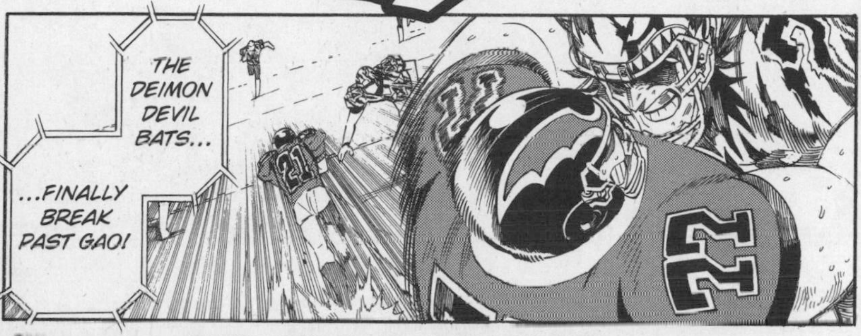
THE DEIMON DEVIL BATS...
...FINALLY BREAK PAST GAO!

Chapter 262 This Is Football

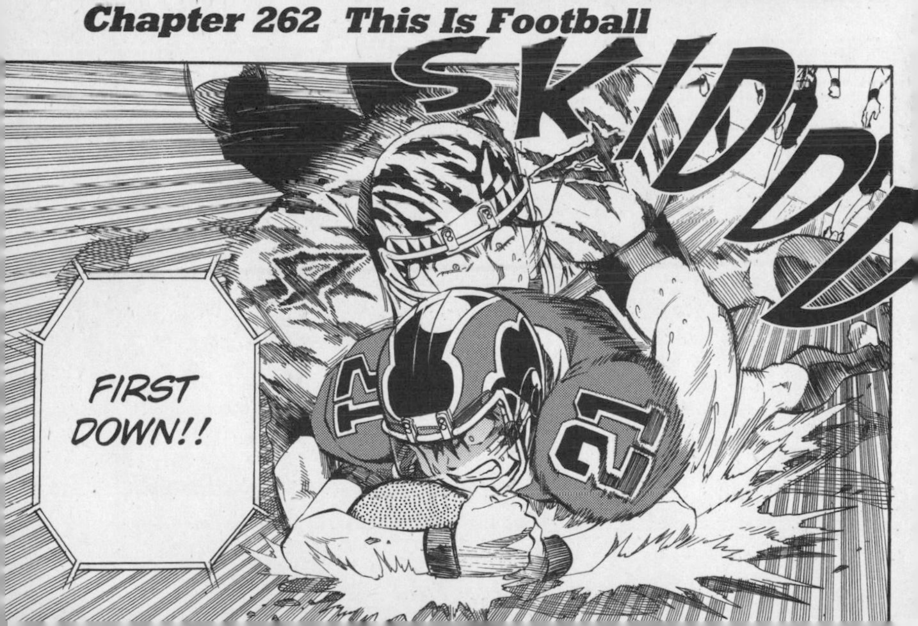
FIRST DOWN!!

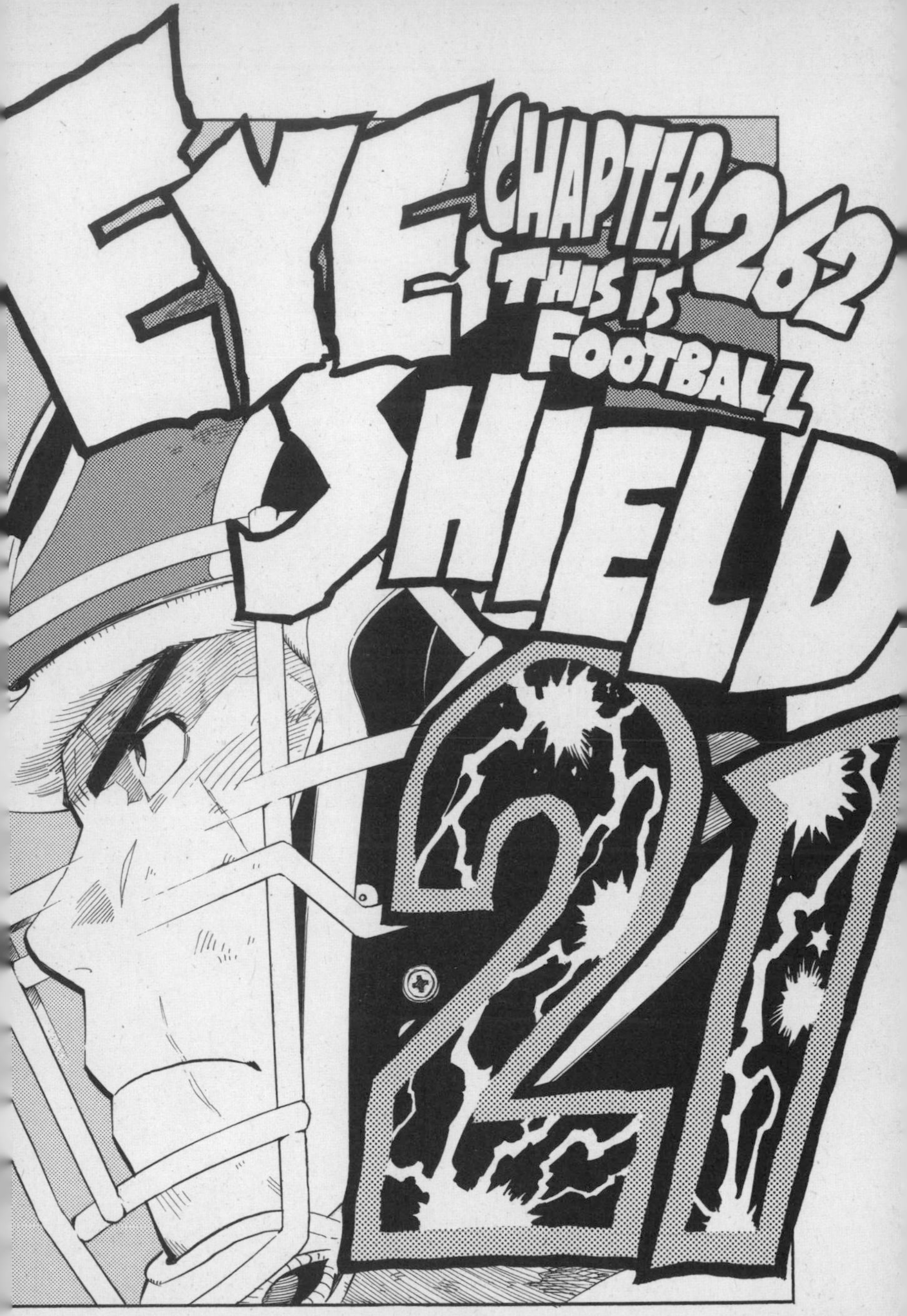
EYESHIELD 21
CHAPTER 262
THIS IS FOOTBALL

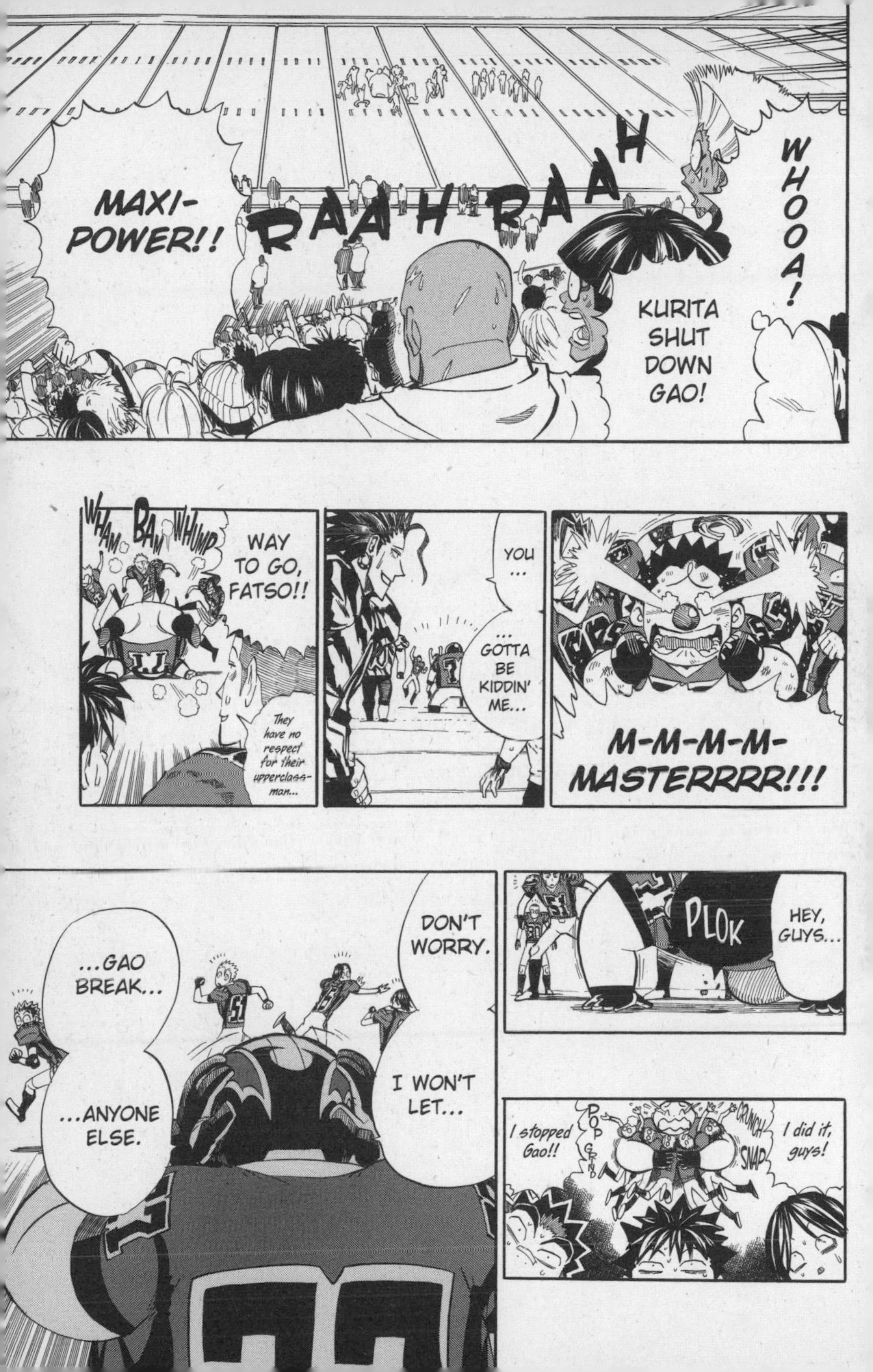

WHOOA!
KURITA SHUT DOWN GAO!
RAAH RAAH
MAXI-POWER!!
M-M-M-M-MASTERRRR!!!
YOU ...
... GOTTA BE KIDDIN' ME...
WHAM BAM WHUMP
WAY TO GO, FATSO!!
They have no respect for their upperclassman...
HEY, GUYS...
PLOK
I did it, guys!
CRUNCH SNAP
POP GRIND
I stopped Gao!!
DON'T WORRY.
I WON'T LET...
...GAO BREAK...
...ANYONE ELSE.

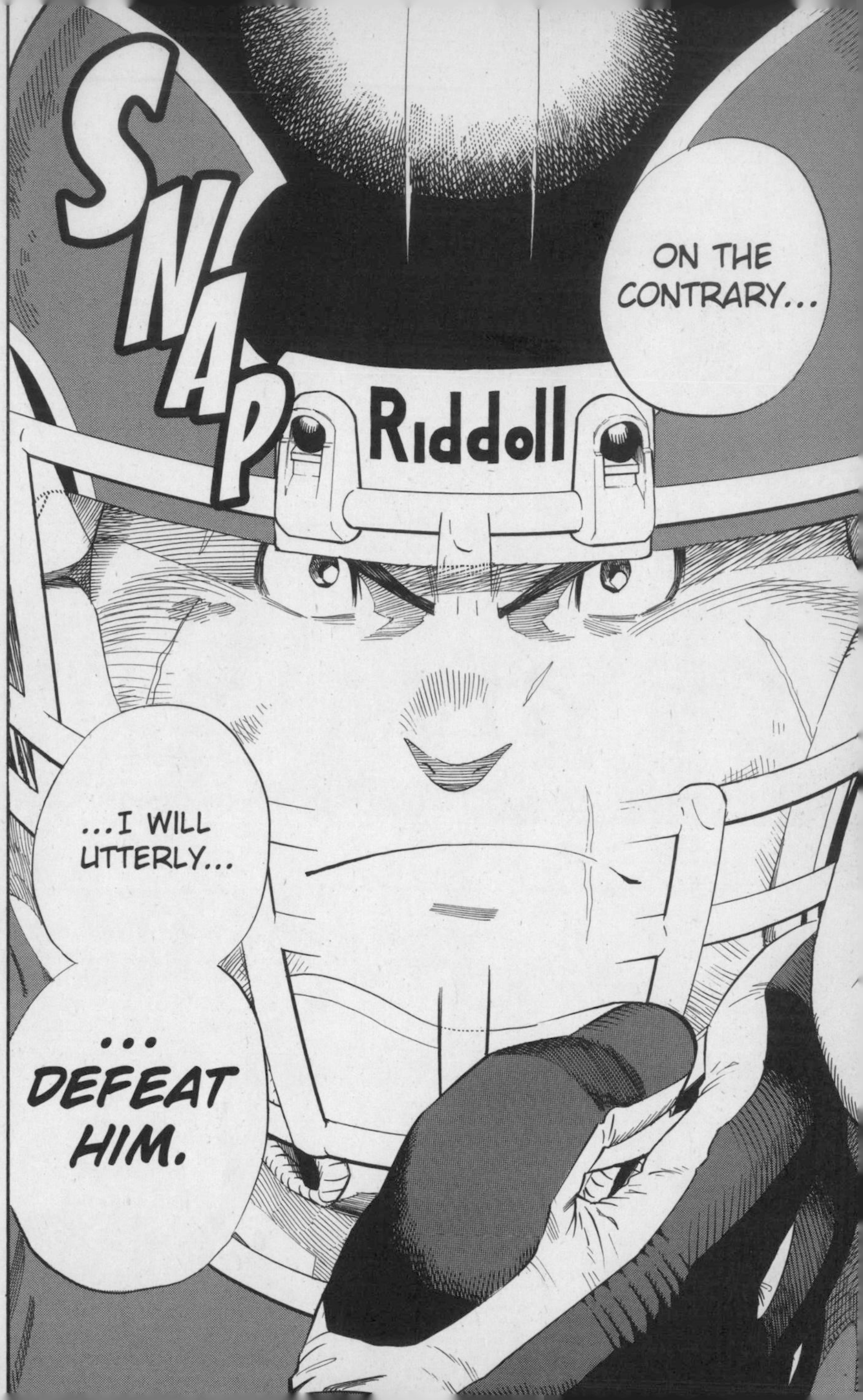
SNAP
Riddoll
ON THE CONTRARY...
...I WILL UTTERLY...
...DEFEAT HIM.

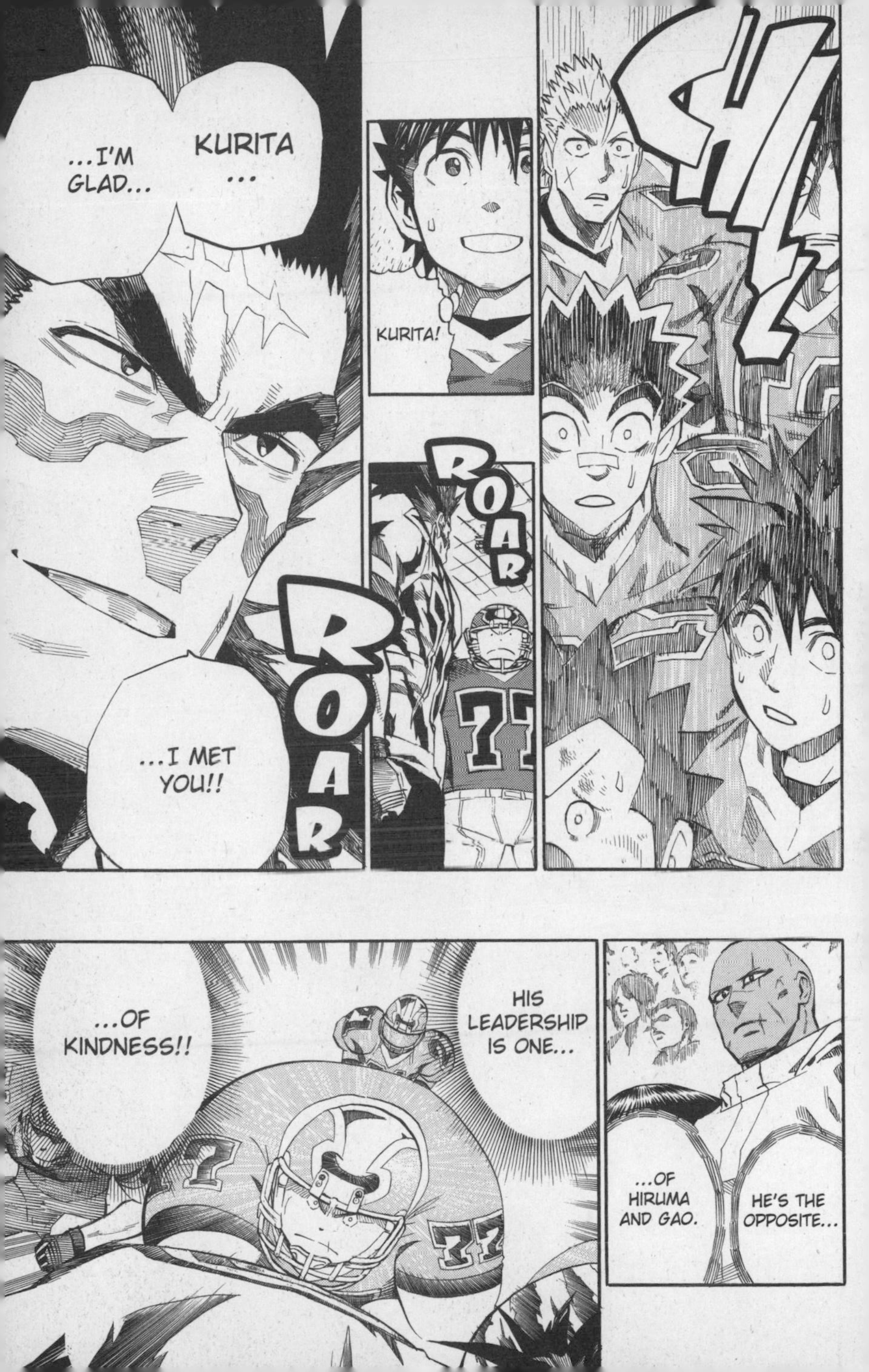
KURITA!
ROAR
KURITA...
...I'M GLAD...
ROAR
...I MET YOU!!
HE'S THE OPPOSITE...
...OF HIRUMA AND GAO.
HIS LEADERSHIP IS ONE...
...OF KINDNESS!!

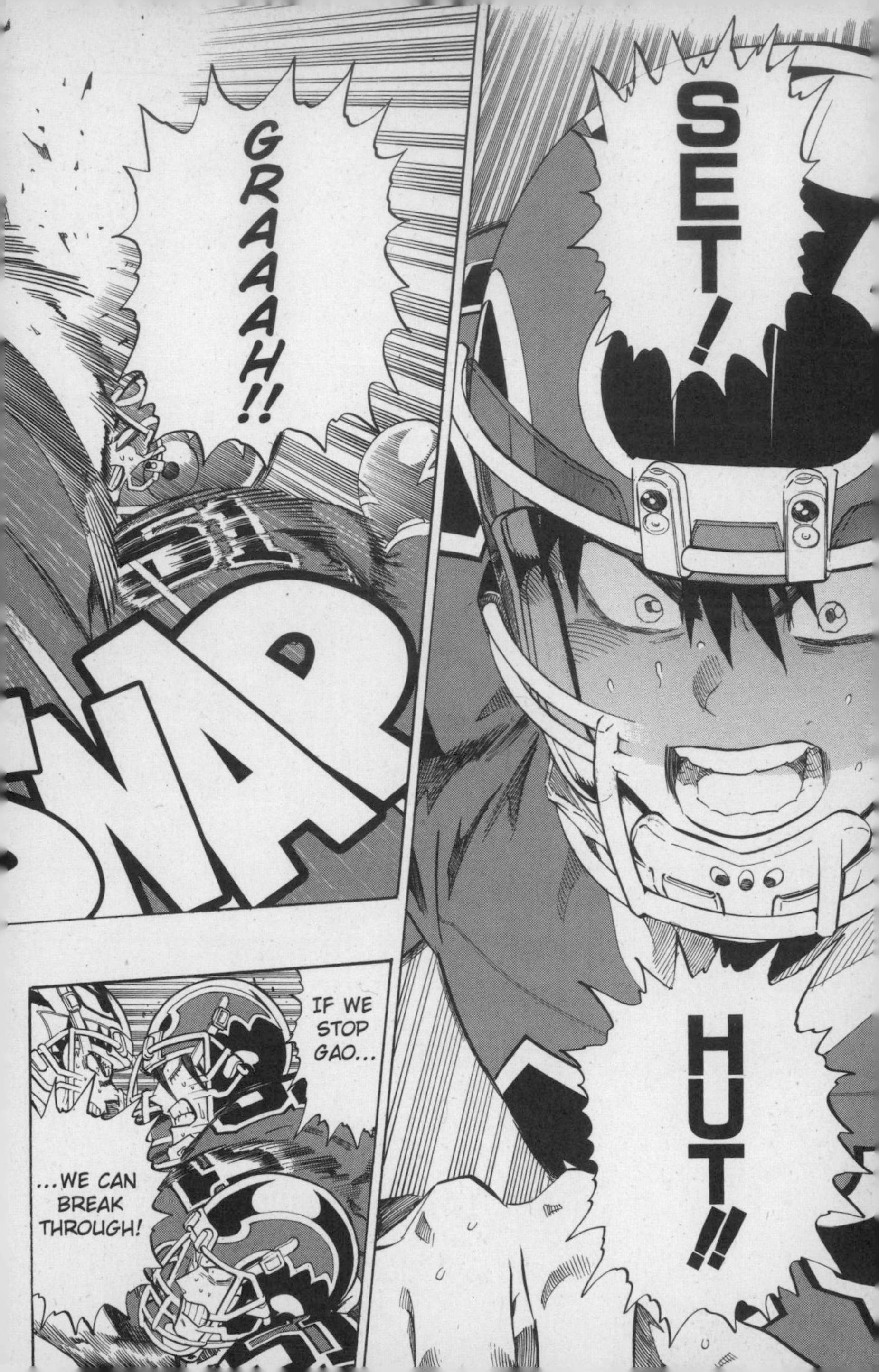
SET!
HUT!!
GRAAAAH!!
IF WE STOP GAO...
...WE CAN BREAK THROUGH!

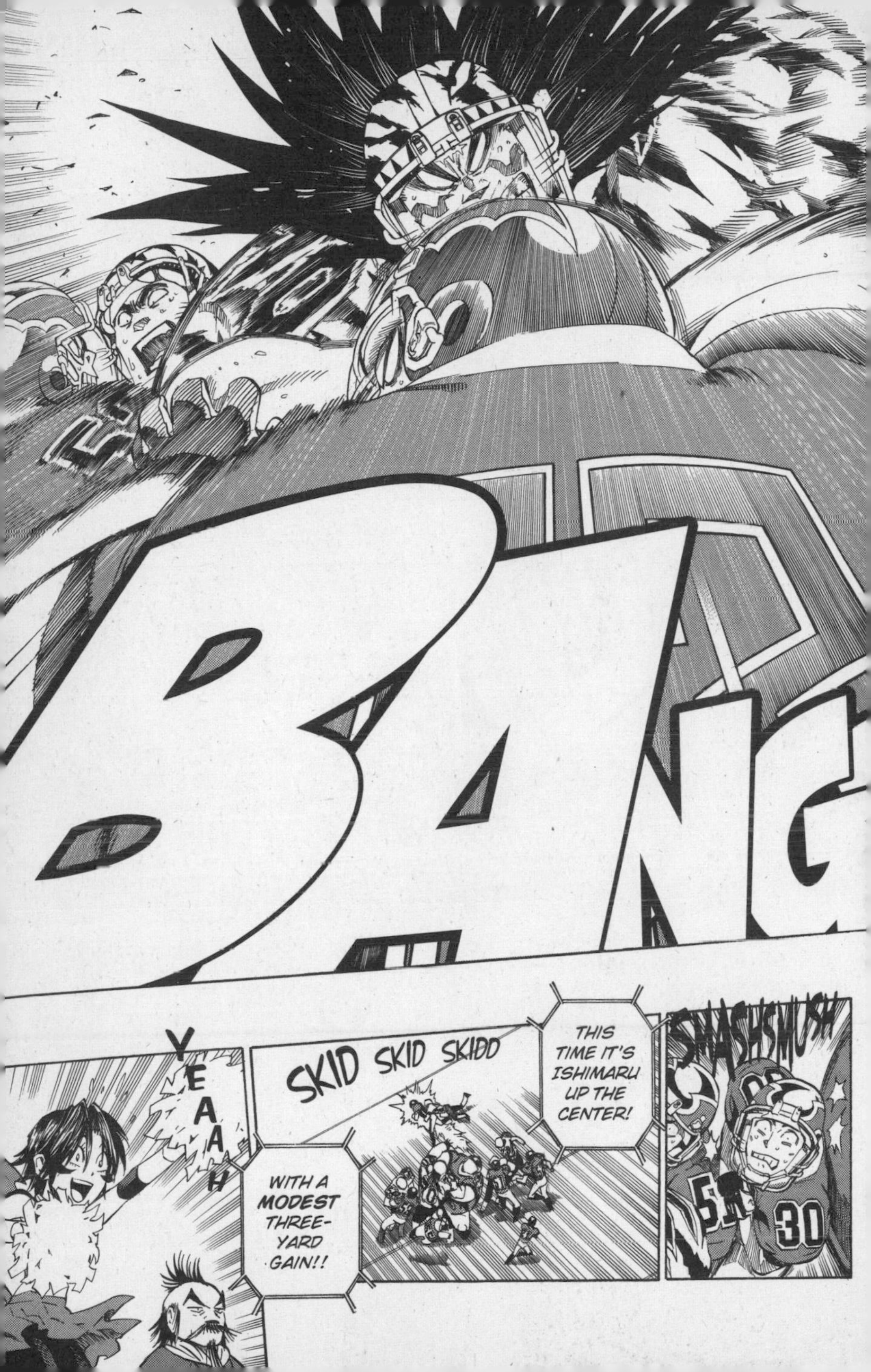
BANG
SHASHSMUSH
THIS TIME IT'S ISHIMARU UP THE CENTER!
SKID SKID SKIDD
WITH A MODEST THREE-YARD GAIN!!
YEAAAH

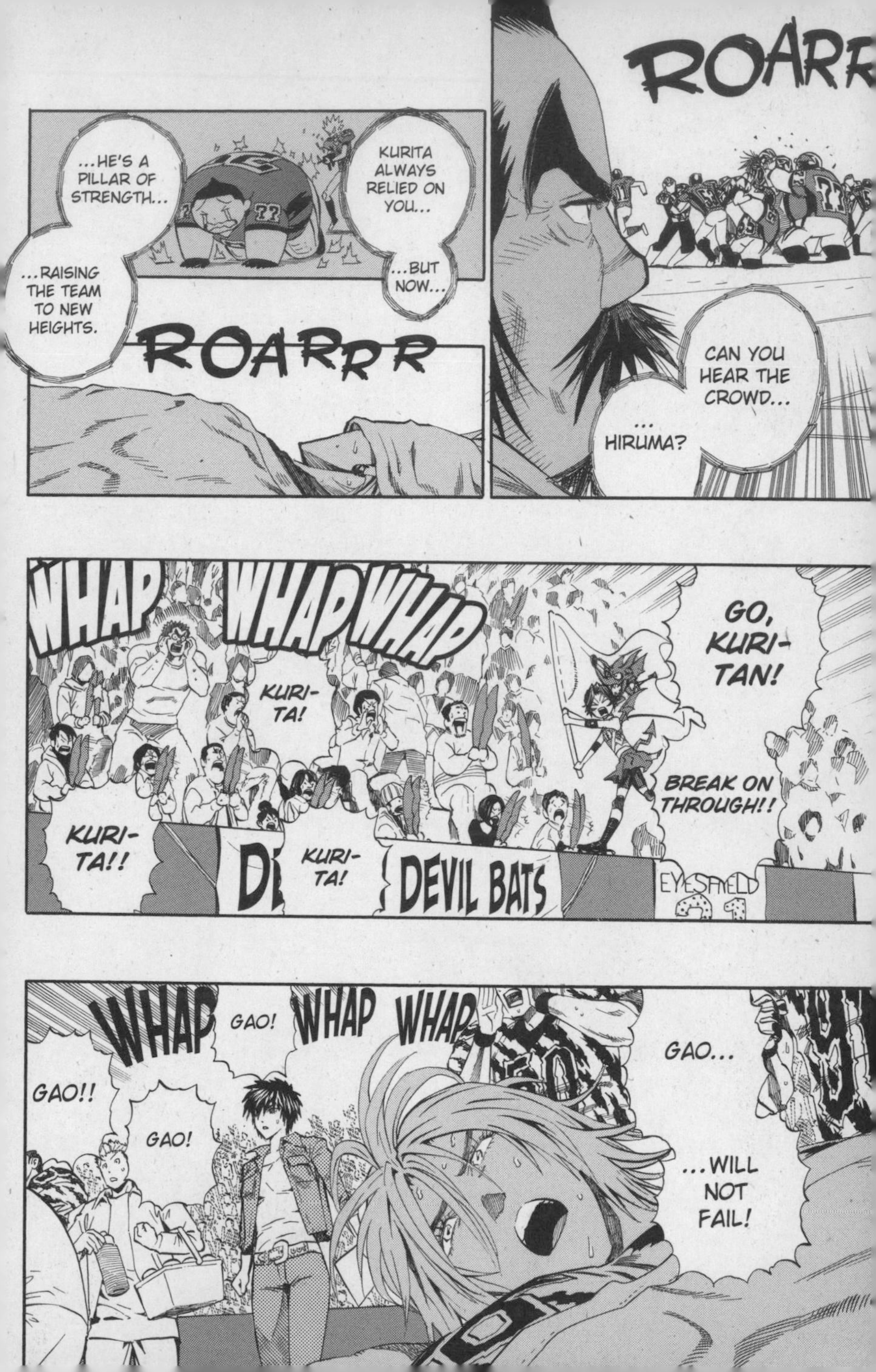
ROARR
CAN YOU HEAR THE CROWD...
...HIRUMA?
KURITA ALWAYS RELIED ON YOU...
...BUT NOW...
...HE'S A PILLAR OF STRENGTH...
...RAISING THE TEAM TO NEW HEIGHTS.
ROARRR
GO, KURI-TAN!
BREAK ON THROUGH!!
WHAP WHAP WHAP
WHAP
KURI-TA!
KURI-TA!
KURI-TA!!
DEVIL BATS
EYESHIELD 21
GAO...
...WILL NOT FAIL!
WHAP
WHAP
GAO!
WHAP
GAO!!
GAO!

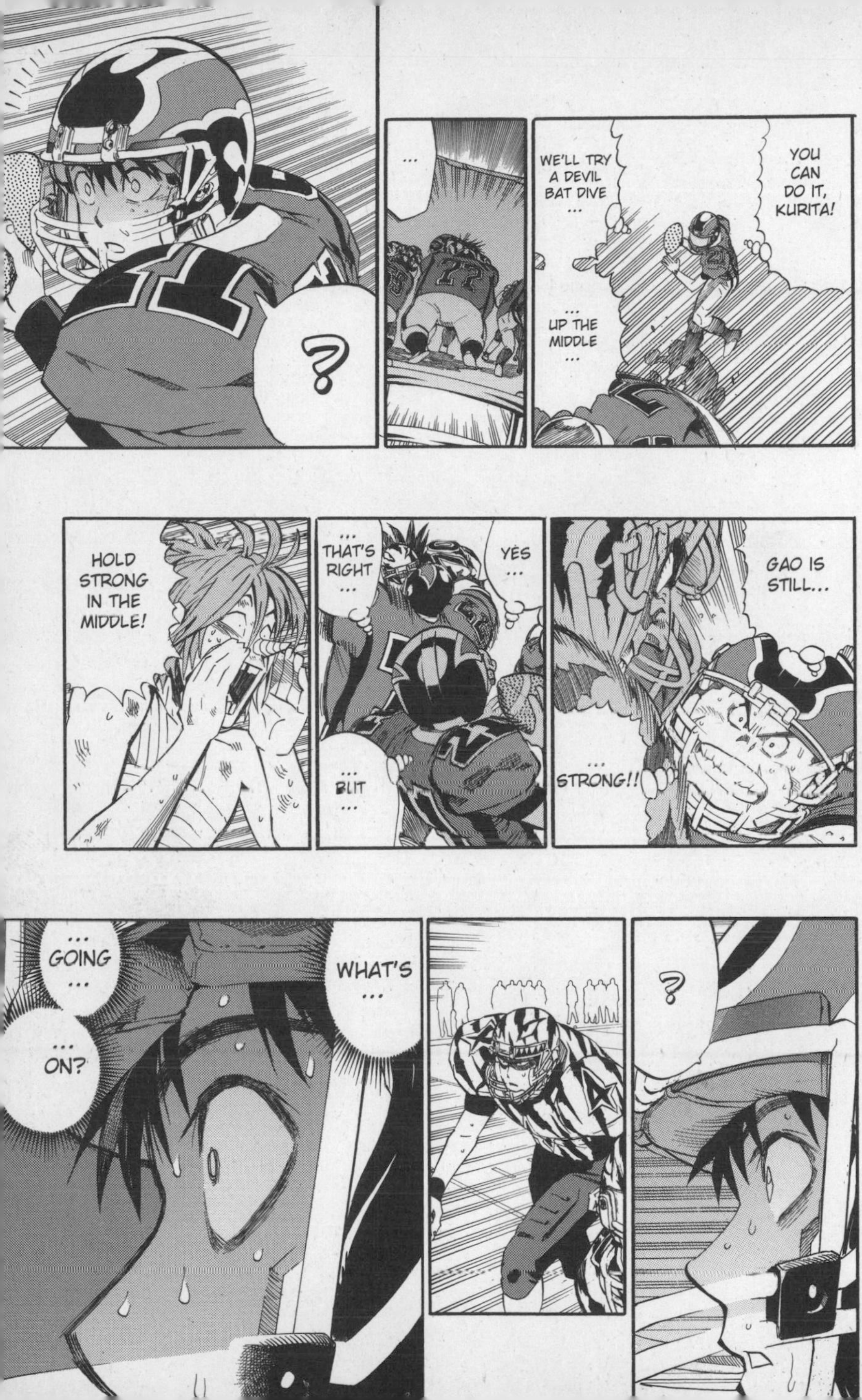
YOU CAN DO IT, KURITA!
WE'LL TRY A DEVIL BAT DIVE ...
... UP THE MIDDLE ...
...
?
GAO IS STILL...
... STRONG!!
YES ...
... THAT'S RIGHT ...
... BUT ...
HOLD STRONG IN THE MIDDLE!
?
WHAT'S ...
... GOING ...
... ON?

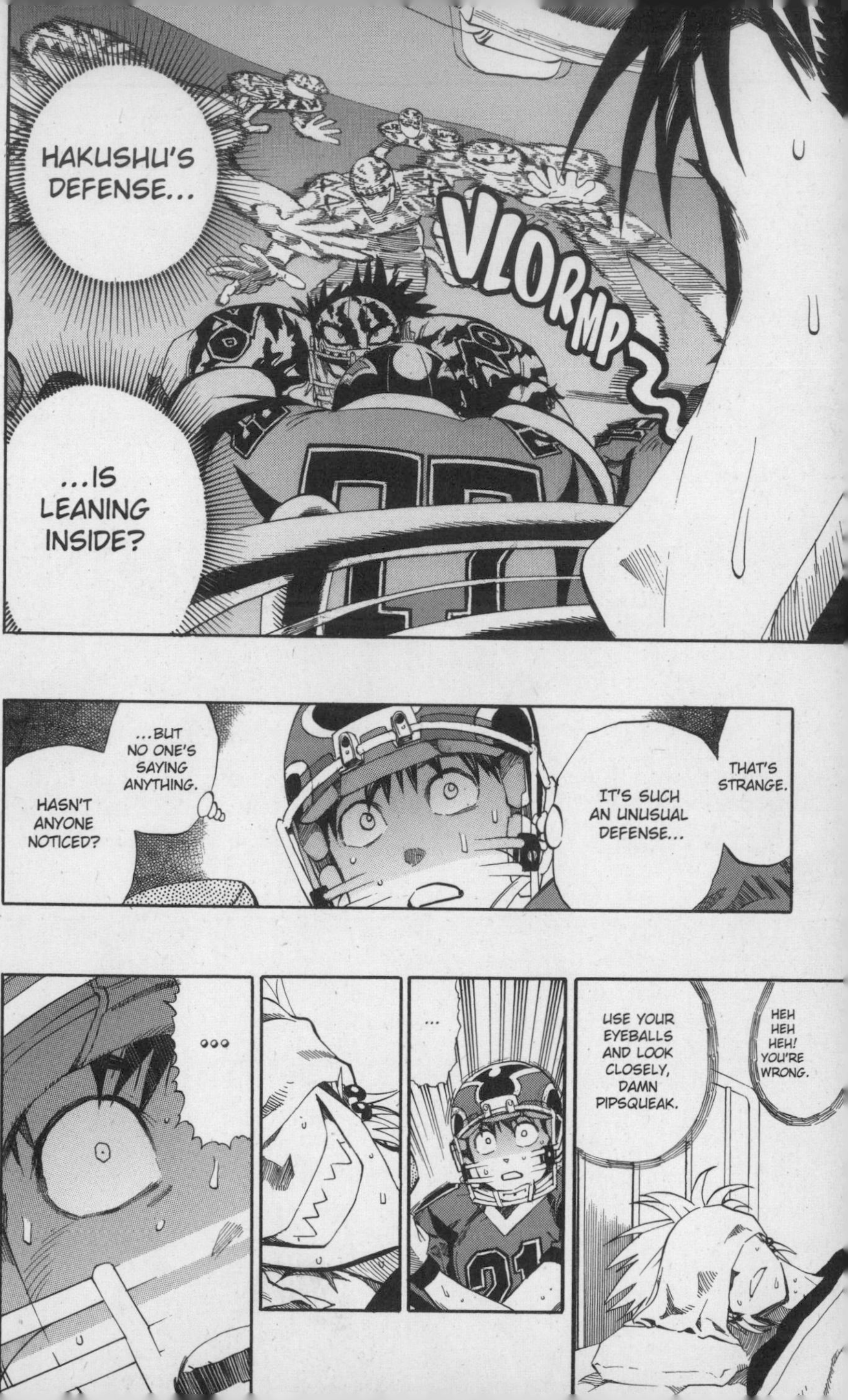
HAKUSHU'S DEFENSE...
VLORMP
...IS LEANING INSIDE?
THAT'S STRANGE.
IT'S SUCH AN UNUSUAL DEFENSE...
...BUT NO ONE'S SAYING ANYTHING.
HASN'T ANYONE NOTICED?
HEH HEH HEH! YOU'RE WRONG.
USE YOUR EYEBALLS AND LOOK CLOSELY, DAMN PIPSQUEAK.
...
...

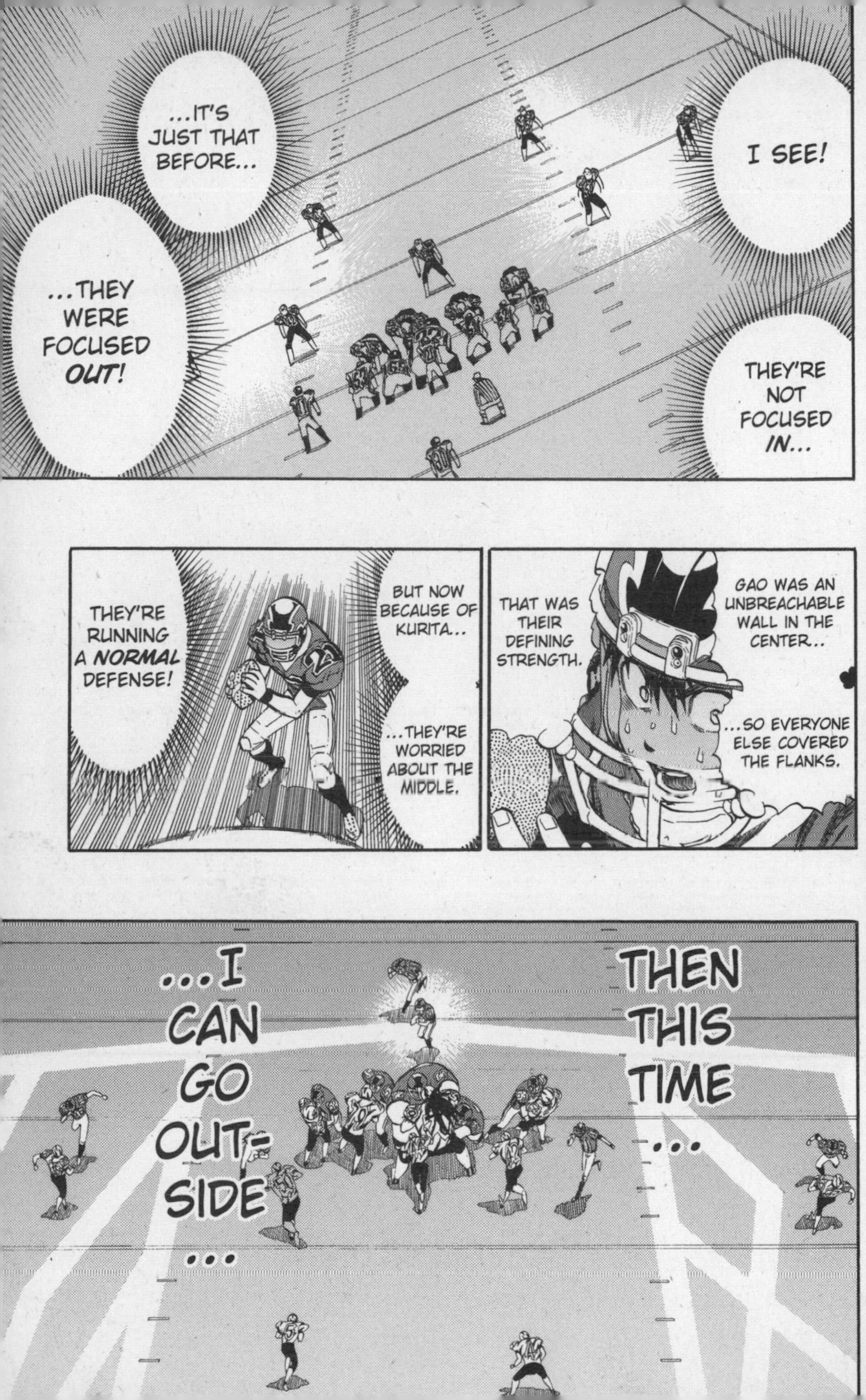
I SEE!
THEY'RE NOT FOCUSED IN...
...IT'S JUST THAT BEFORE...
...THEY WERE FOCUSED OUT!
GAO WAS AN UNBREACHABLE WALL IN THE CENTER...
THAT WAS THEIR DEFINING STRENGTH.
...SO EVERYONE ELSE COVERED THE FLANKS.
BUT NOW BECAUSE OF KURITA...
...THEY'RE WORRIED ABOUT THE MIDDLE.
THEY'RE RUNNING A NORMAL DEFENSE!
THEN THIS TIME...
...I CAN GO OUT-SIDE...

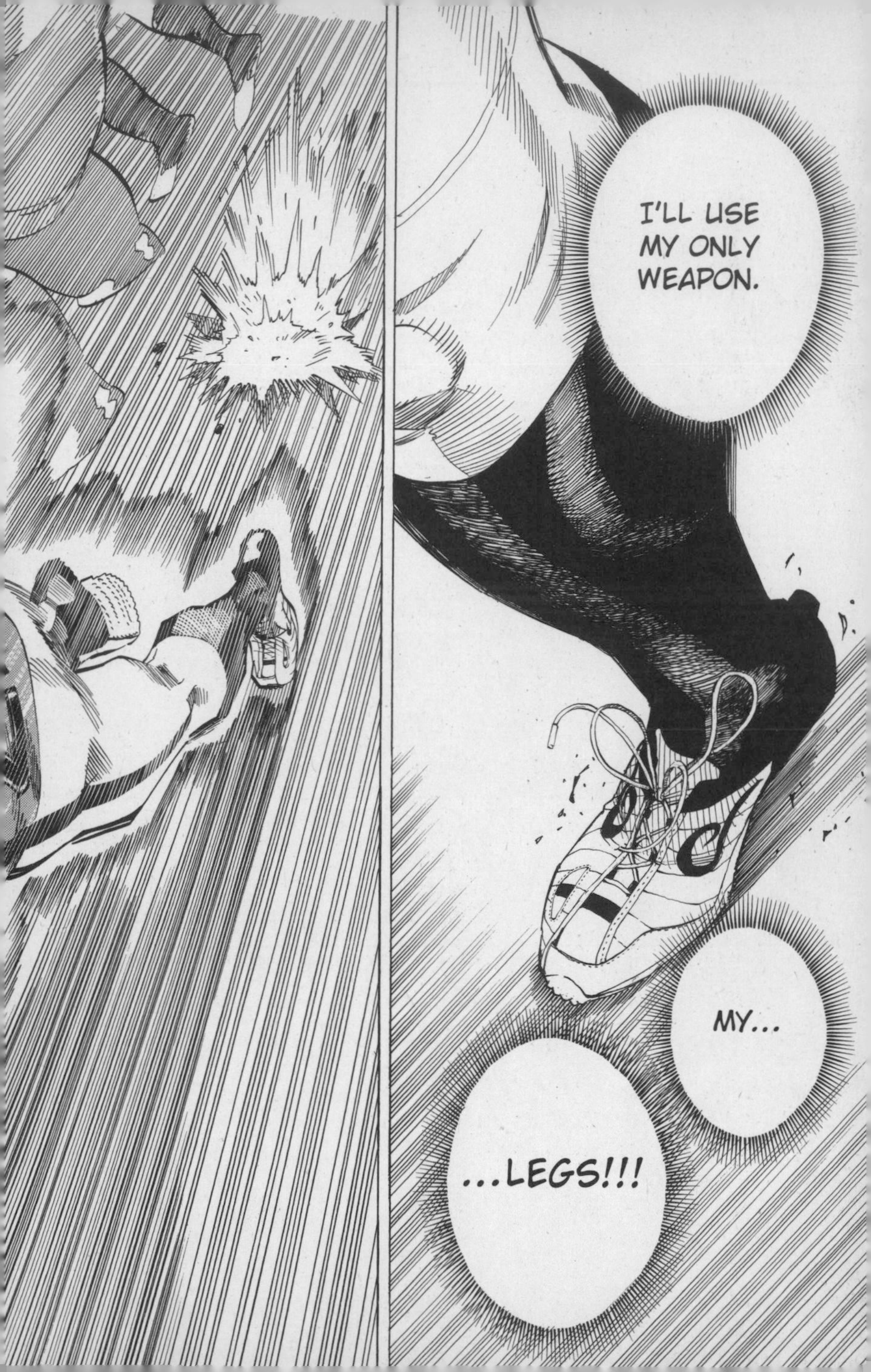
I'LL USE MY ONLY WEAPON.
MY...
...LEGS!!!

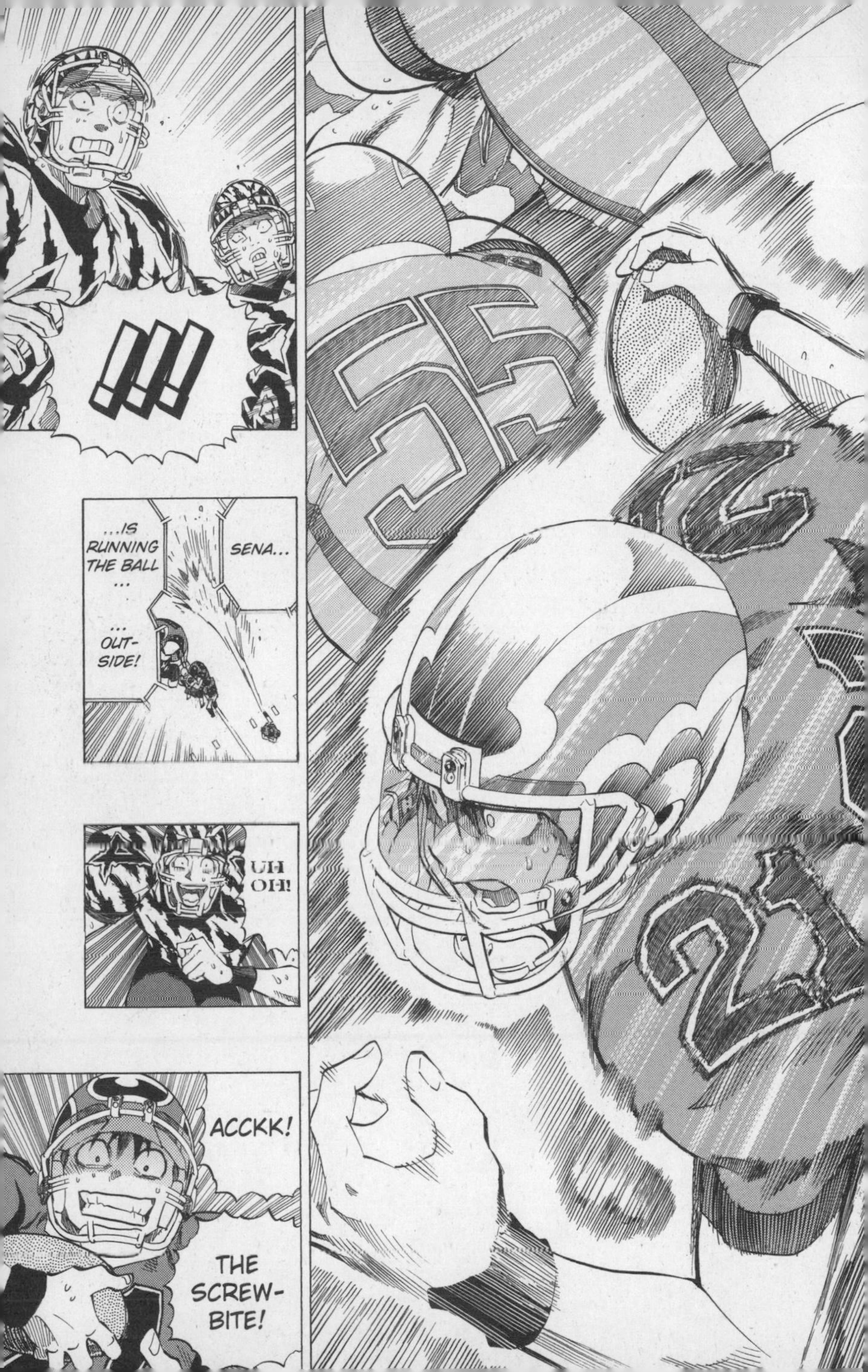
!!!
SENA...
...IS RUNNING THE BALL ...
... OUT-SIDE!
UH OH!
ACCKK!
THE SCREW-BITE!

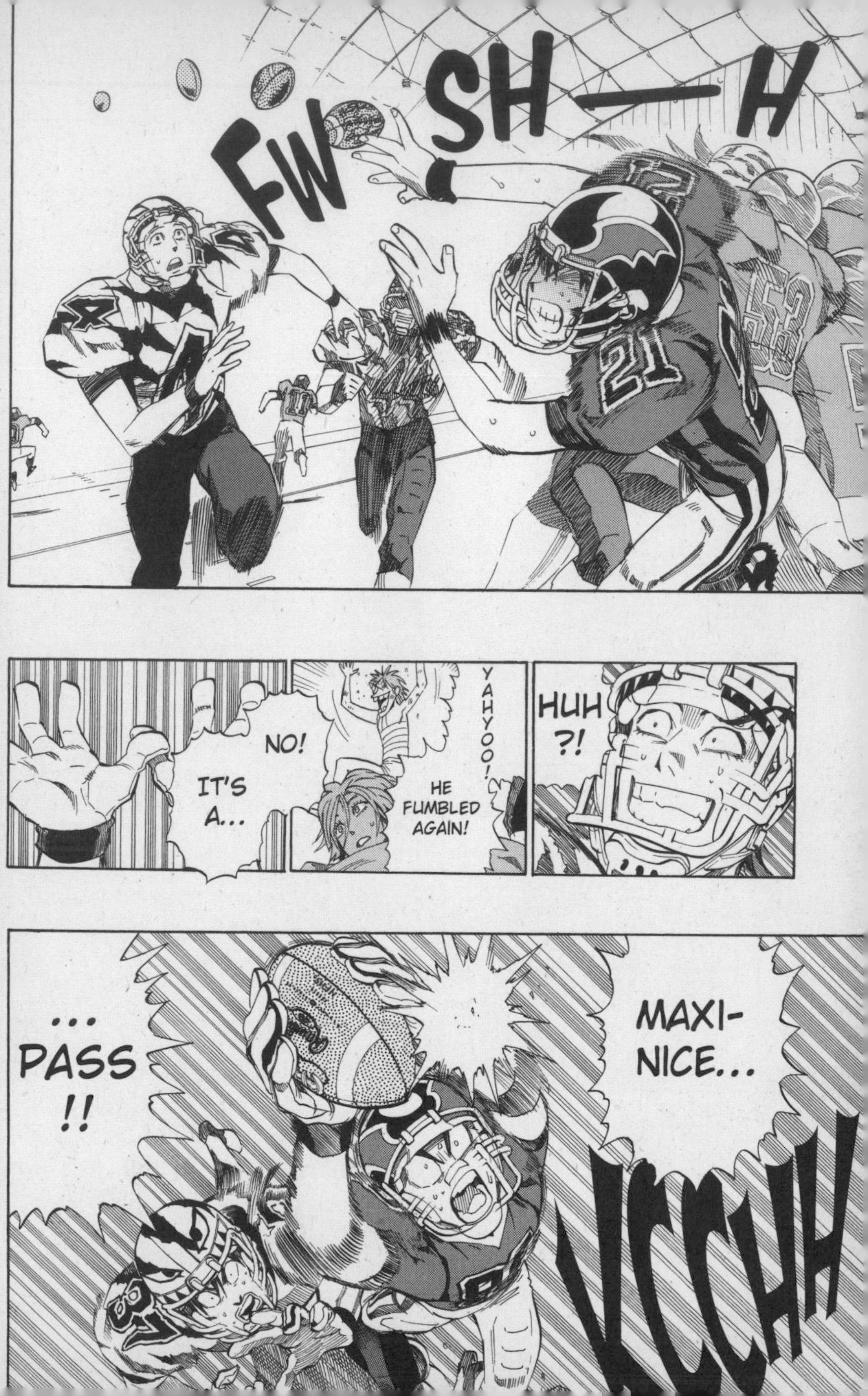
FWSH—H
HUH ?!
YAHYOO!
HE FUMBLED AGAIN!
NO!
IT'S A...
MAXI-NICE...
... PASS !!

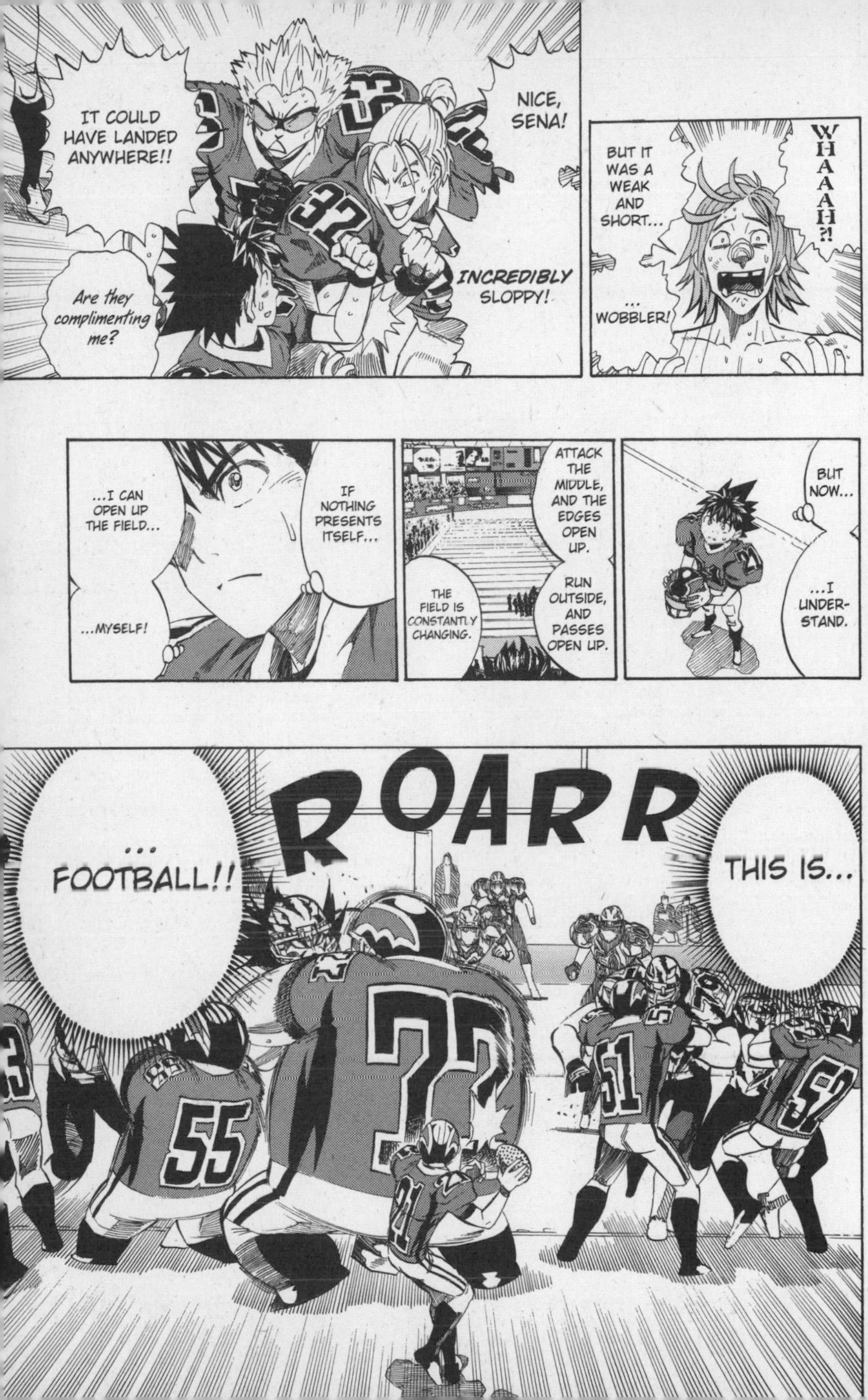
WHAAAAH?!
BUT IT WAS A WEAK AND SHORT...
... WOBBLER!
NICE, SENA!
IT COULD HAVE LANDED ANYWHERE!!
INCREDIBLY SLOPPY!
Are they complimenting me?
BUT NOW...
...I UNDERSTAND.
ATTACK THE MIDDLE, AND THE EDGES OPEN UP.
RUN OUTSIDE, AND PASSES OPEN UP.
THE FIELD IS CONSTANTLY CHANGING.
IF NOTHING PRESENTS ITSELF...
...I CAN OPEN UP THE FIELD...
...MYSELF!
THIS IS...
ROARR
... FOOTBALL!!

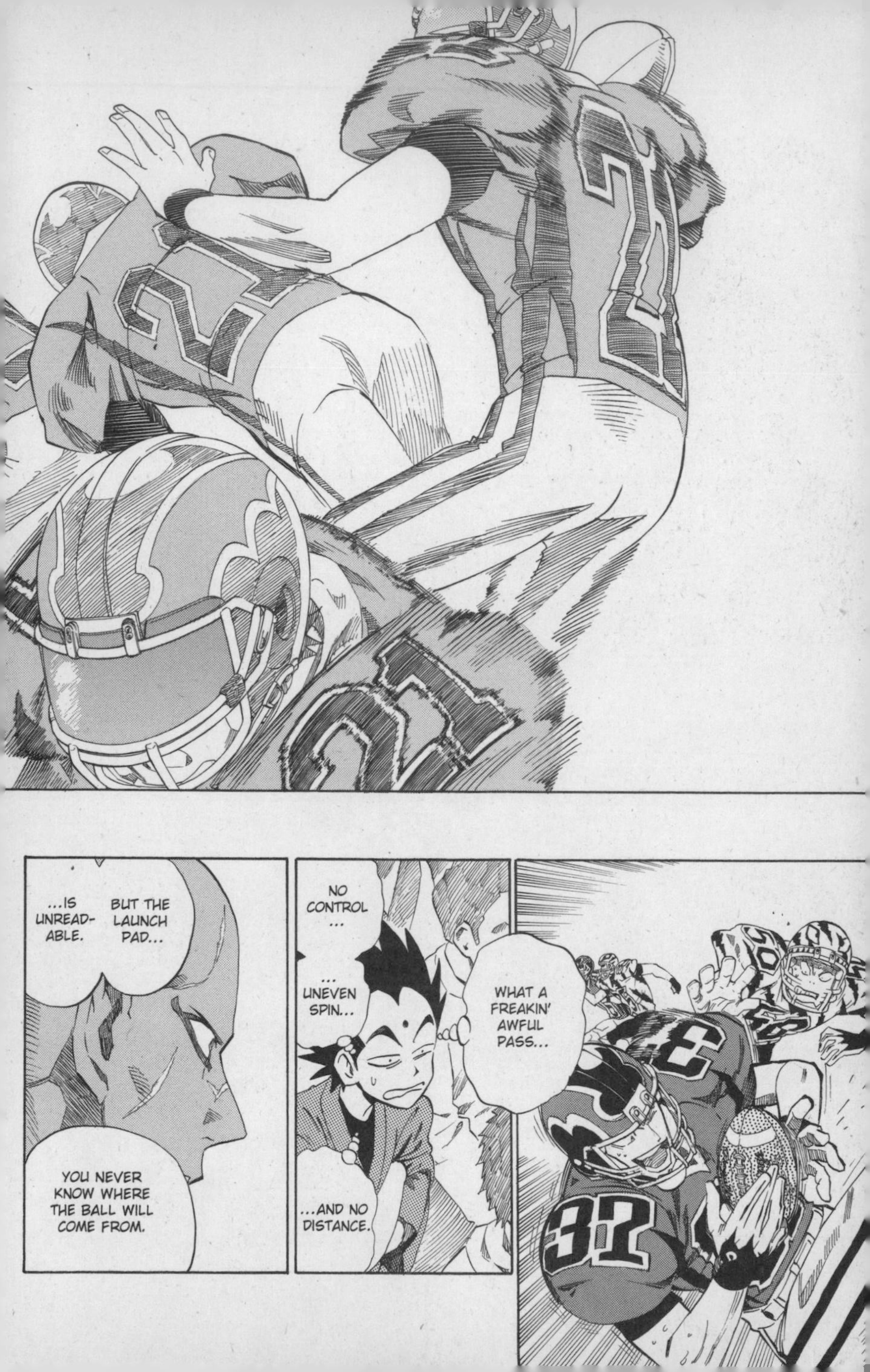
WHAT A FREAKIN' AWFUL PASS...
NO CONTROL ...
... UNEVEN SPIN...
...AND NO DISTANCE.
BUT THE LAUNCH PAD...
...IS UNREAD-ABLE.
YOU NEVER KNOW WHERE THE BALL WILL COME FROM.

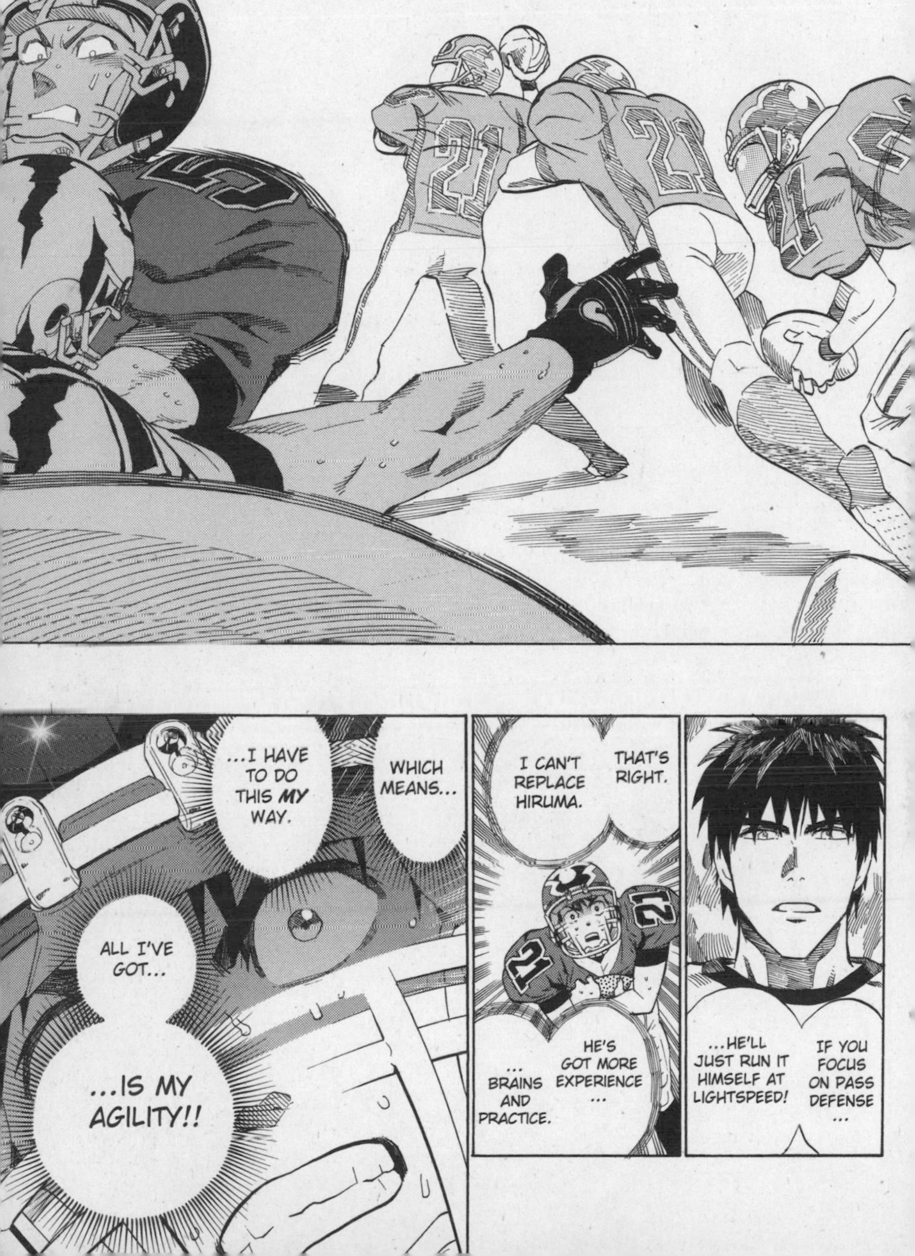
IF YOU FOCUS ON PASS DEFENSE ...
...HE'LL JUST RUN IT HIMSELF AT LIGHTSPEED!
THAT'S RIGHT.
I CAN'T REPLACE HIRUMA.
HE'S GOT MORE EXPERIENCE ...
... BRAINS AND PRACTICE.
WHICH MEANS...
...I HAVE TO DO THIS *MY* WAY.
ALL I'VE GOT...
...IS MY AGILITY!!

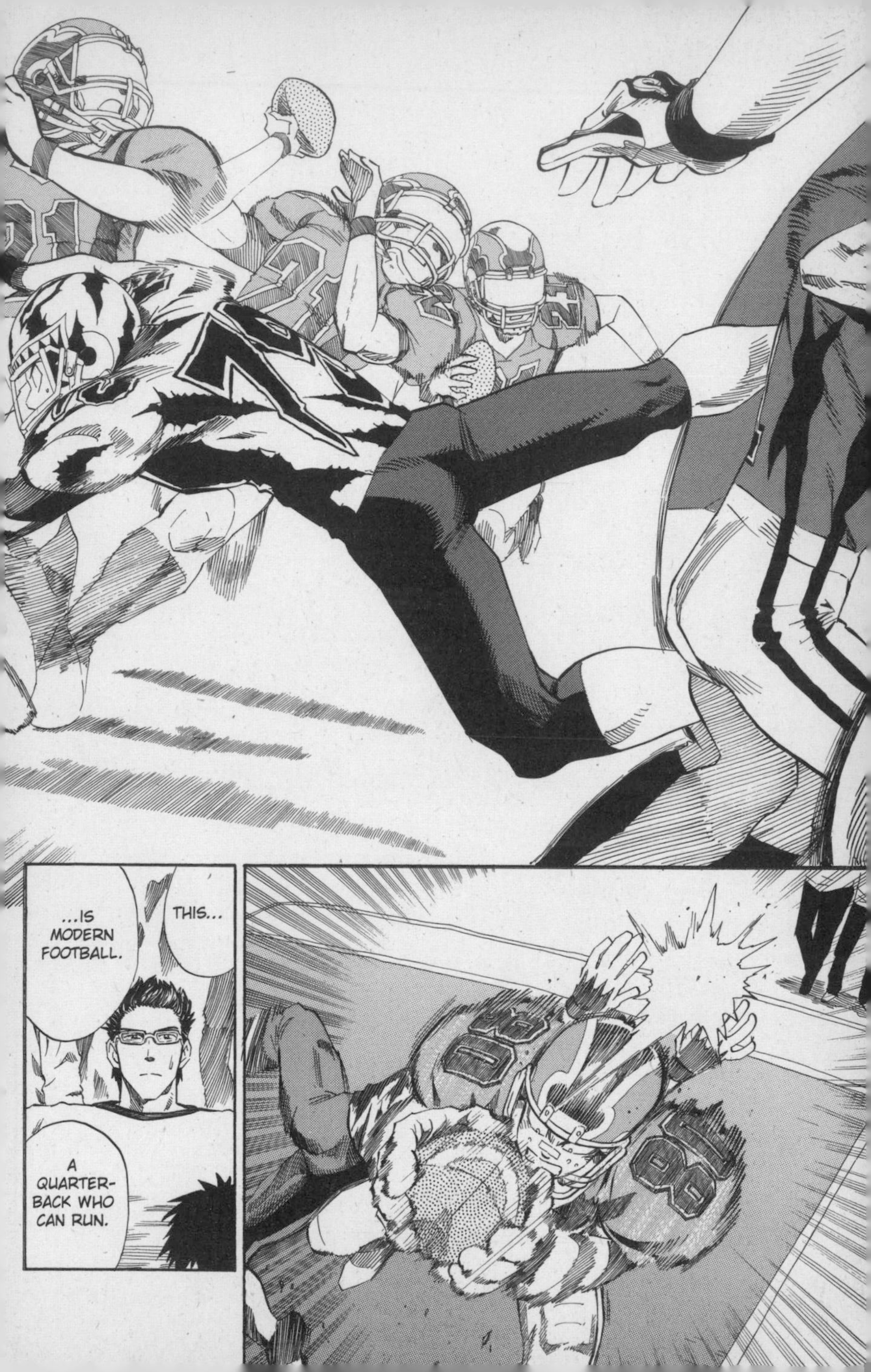
THIS...
...IS MODERN FOOTBALL.
A QUARTER-BACK WHO CAN RUN.

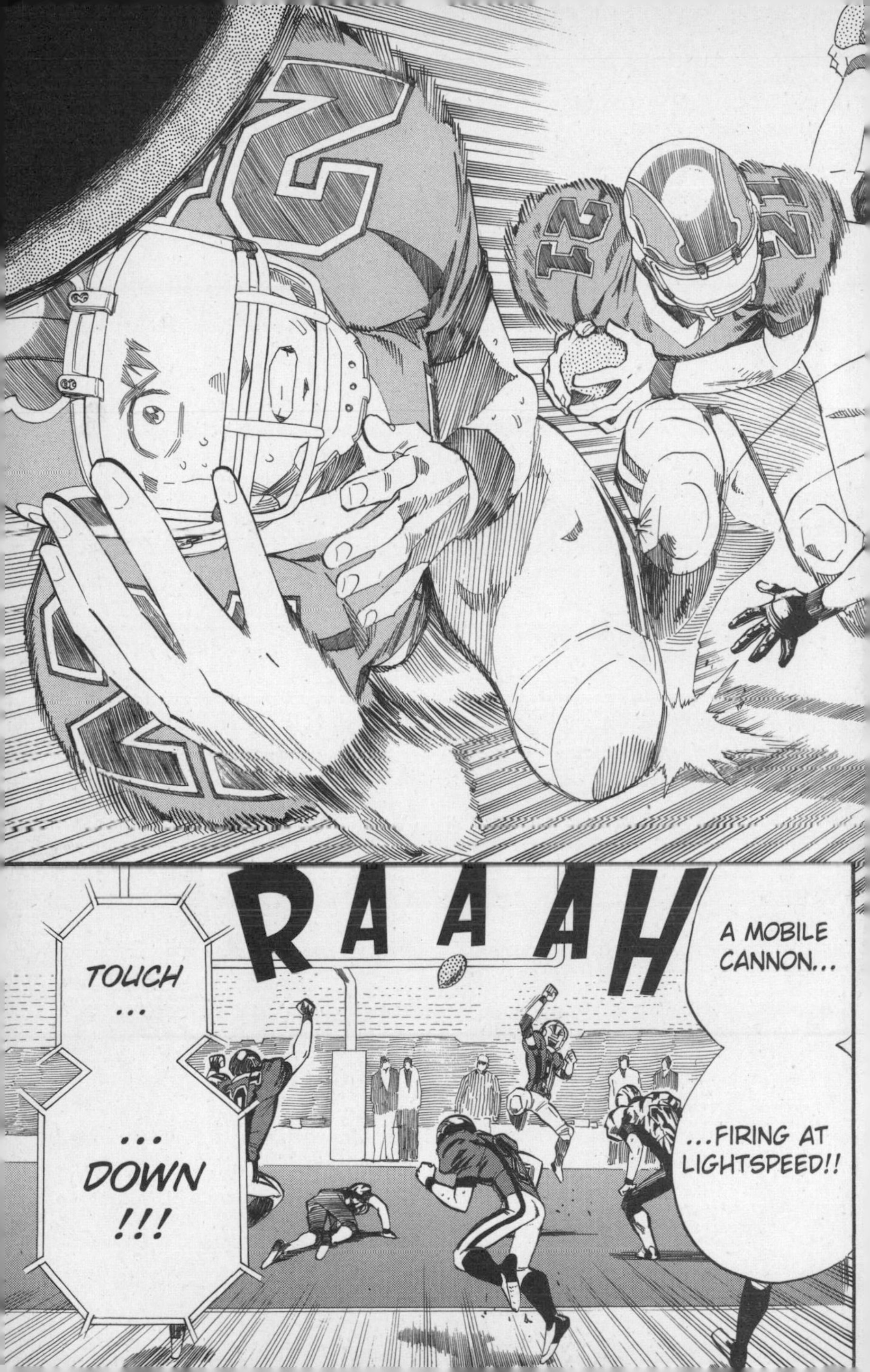
A MOBILE CANNON...
...FIRING AT LIGHTSPEED!!
RAAAH
TOUCH ...
... DOWN !!!

Eyeshield 21 Survey Corner **Devil Bat 021 SPECIAL!**

#108

Is all the soda Marco gave Deimon gone? If not, give me some!

T.O. in Gifu Prefecture

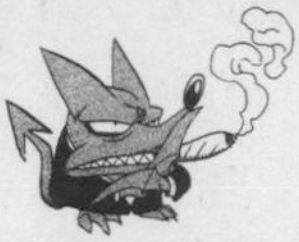

CERBERUS DRANK IT ALL IN AN INSTANT.

#109

What breed is Cerberus? A new breed?

H.I. in Kumamoto Prefecture, and many others

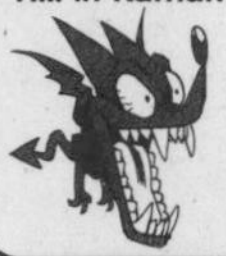

HE'S A PUREBRED *MUTT!*

#110

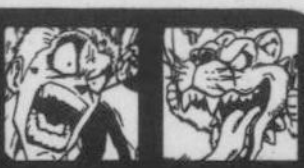

So who won the battle between Ikari and Cerberus?

Jo Burinkurin in Osaka Prefecture, and others

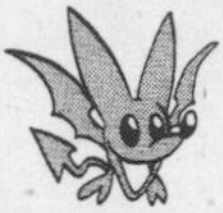

THESE TWO WILD MEN EXCHANGED BLOWS AND FORMED A LIGHT FRIENDSHIP!

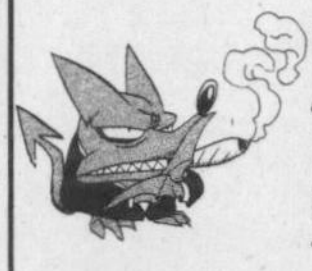

BUT THREE SECONDS AFTER THE GAME RE-STARTED, THEY FORGOT ALL ABOUT THAT FRIENDSHIP.

#111

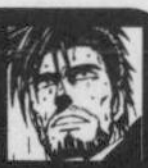

What can Musashi do besides kick?

Makkuro in Hyogo Prefecture

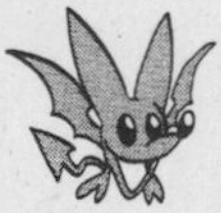

HE PLAYS DEFENSE, BUT JUST PRACTICES KICKING DURING OFFENSE!

#112

What does Hiruma's "Ya-ha" mean?

Doragaa in Shiga Prefecture, and many others

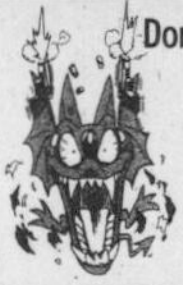

THERE'S NO MEANING! IT'S JUST A REBEL YELL! YA-HA!

#113

Hiruma always calls people "damn" something. What does he call Suzuna?

K.N. in Niigata Prefecture, and many others

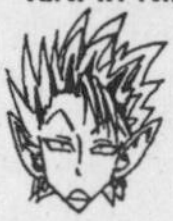

DAMN CHEER.

#114

What was everyone drinking after the Bando game? They're all underage, but it looked like alcohol!!

Matt in Osaka Prefecture

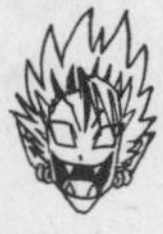

A CARBONATED BEVERAGE THAT STARTS WITH A "B." HEH HEH HEH!

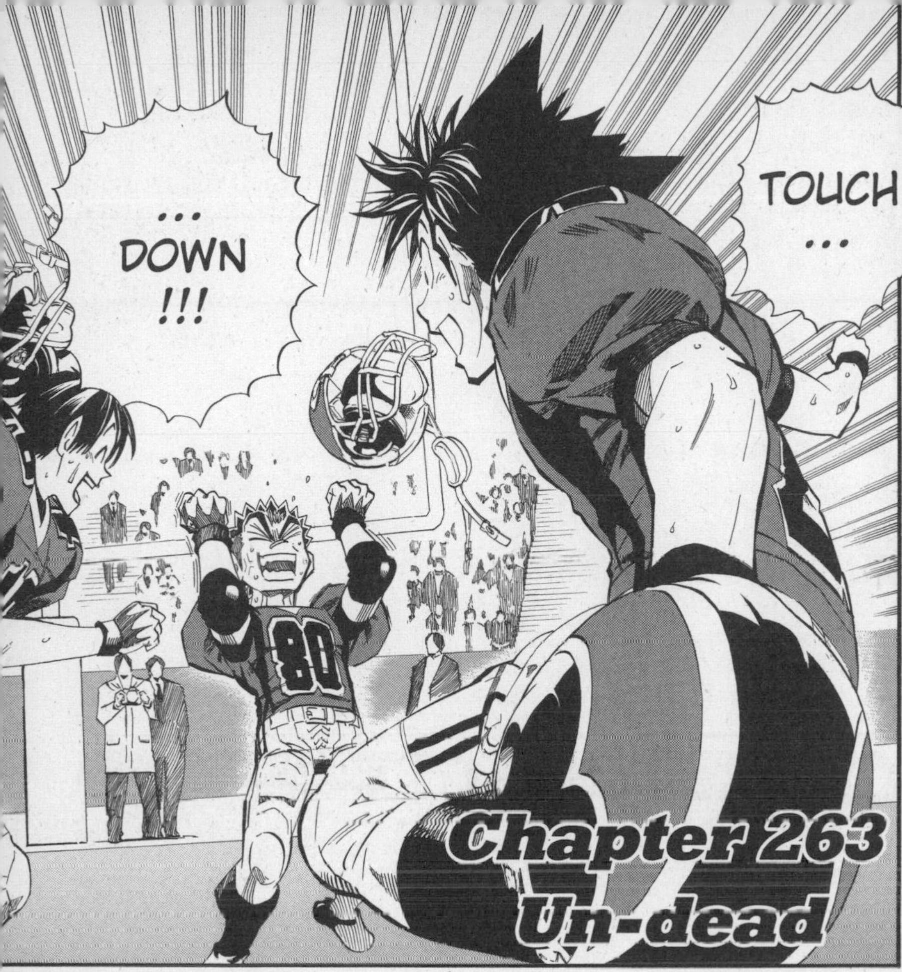
TOUCH ...
... DOWN !!!
Chapter 263
Un-dead

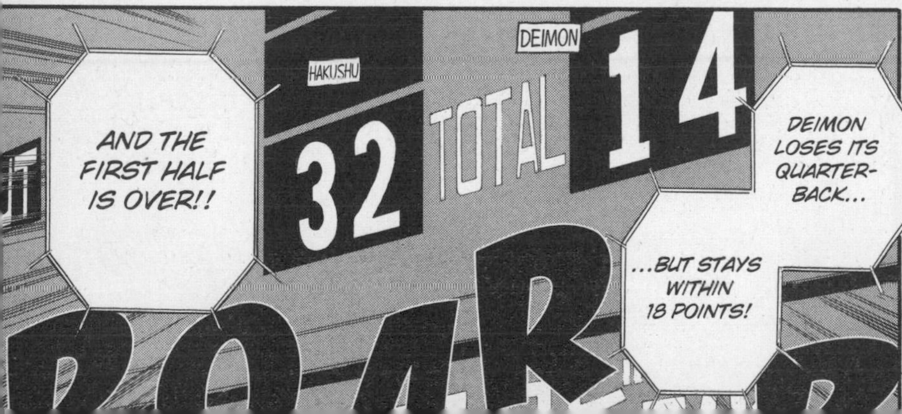
DEIMON LOSES ITS QUARTER-BACK...
...BUT STAYS WITHIN 18 POINTS!
DEIMON
14
TOTAL
HAKUSHU
32
AND THE FIRST HALF IS OVER!!
ROAR

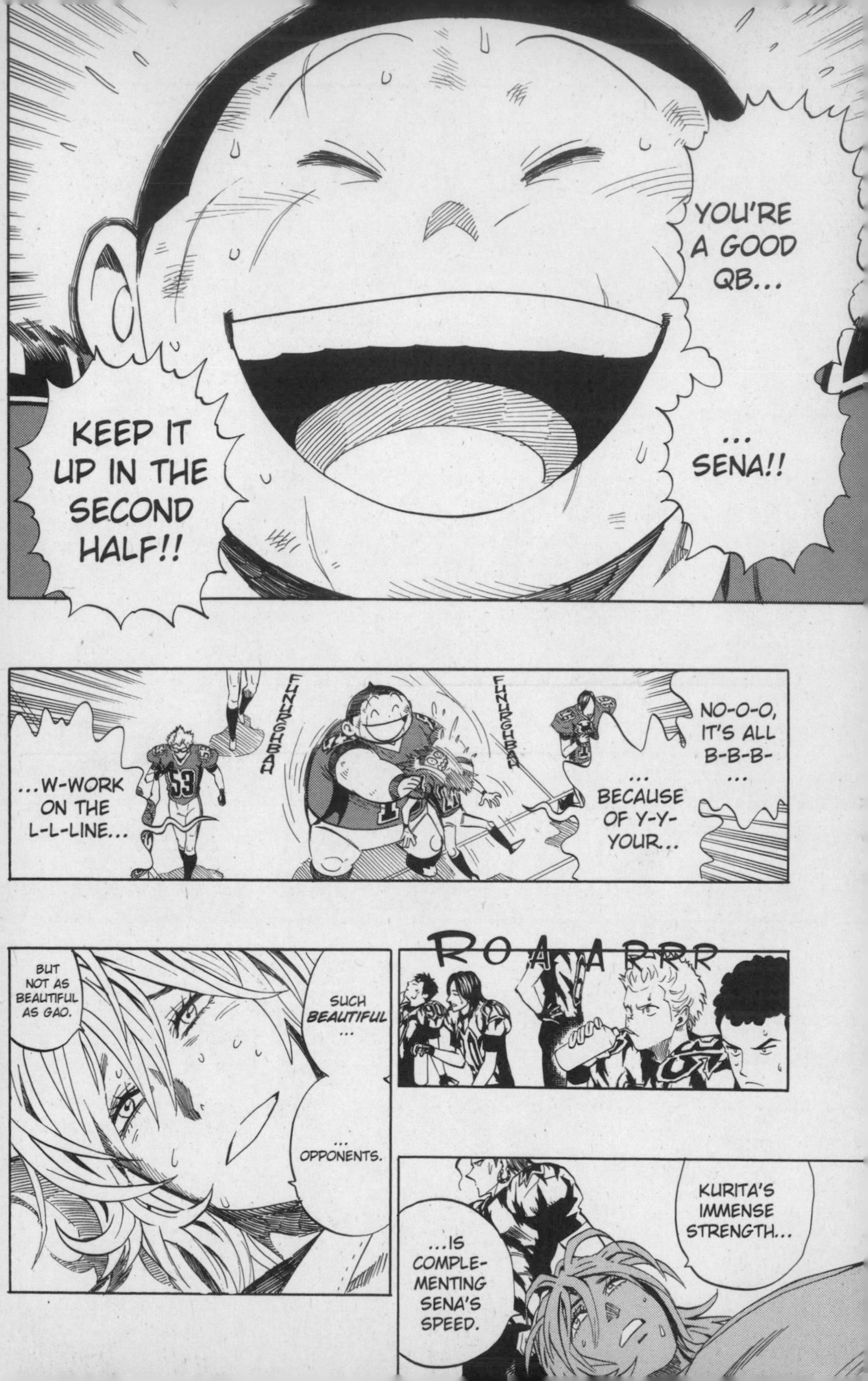
YOU'RE A GOOD QB...
...SENA!!
KEEP IT UP IN THE SECOND HALF!!
NO-O-O, IT'S ALL B-B-B-...
...BECAUSE OF Y-Y-YOUR...
FUNURGHBAH
FUNURGHBAH
...W-WORK ON THE L-L-LINE...
ROAARRR
KURITA'S IMMENSE STRENGTH...
...IS COMPLEMENTING SENA'S SPEED.
SUCH *BEAUTIFUL* ...
...OPPONENTS.
BUT NOT AS BEAUTIFUL AS GAO.

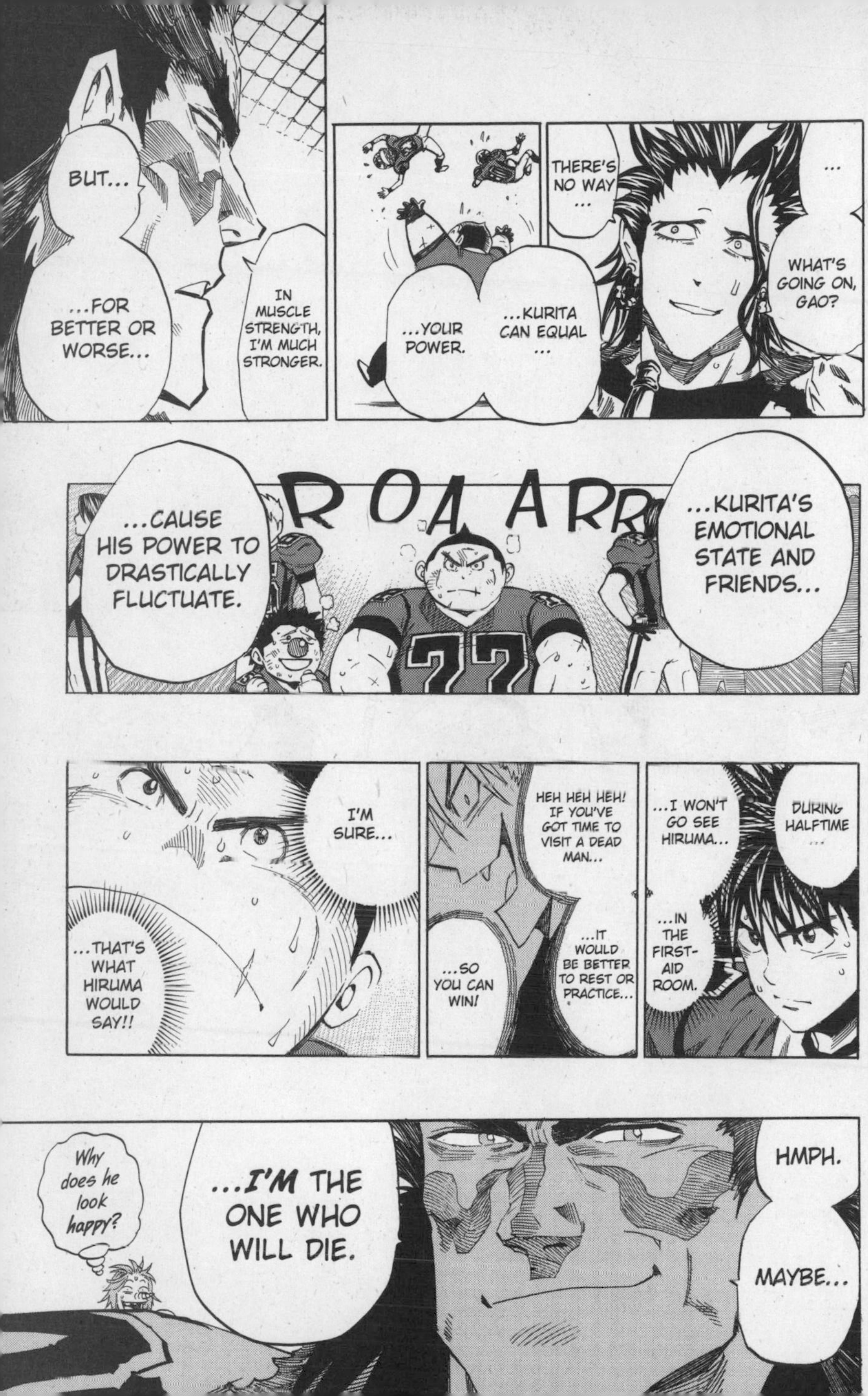
...
WHAT'S GOING ON, GAO?
THERE'S NO WAY...
...KURITA CAN EQUAL...
...YOUR POWER.
IN MUSCLE STRENGTH, I'M MUCH STRONGER.
BUT...
...FOR BETTER OR WORSE...
...KURITA'S EMOTIONAL STATE AND FRIENDS...
ROAARR
...CAUSE HIS POWER TO DRASTICALLY FLUCTUATE.
DURING HALFTIME...
...I WON'T GO SEE HIRUMA...
...IN THE FIRST-AID ROOM.
HEH HEH HEH! IF YOU'VE GOT TIME TO VISIT A DEAD MAN...
...IT WOULD BE BETTER TO REST OR PRACTICE...
...SO YOU CAN WIN!
I'M SURE...
...THAT'S WHAT HIRUMA WOULD SAY!!
HMPH.
MAYBE...
...*I'M* THE ONE WHO WILL DIE.
Why does he look happy?

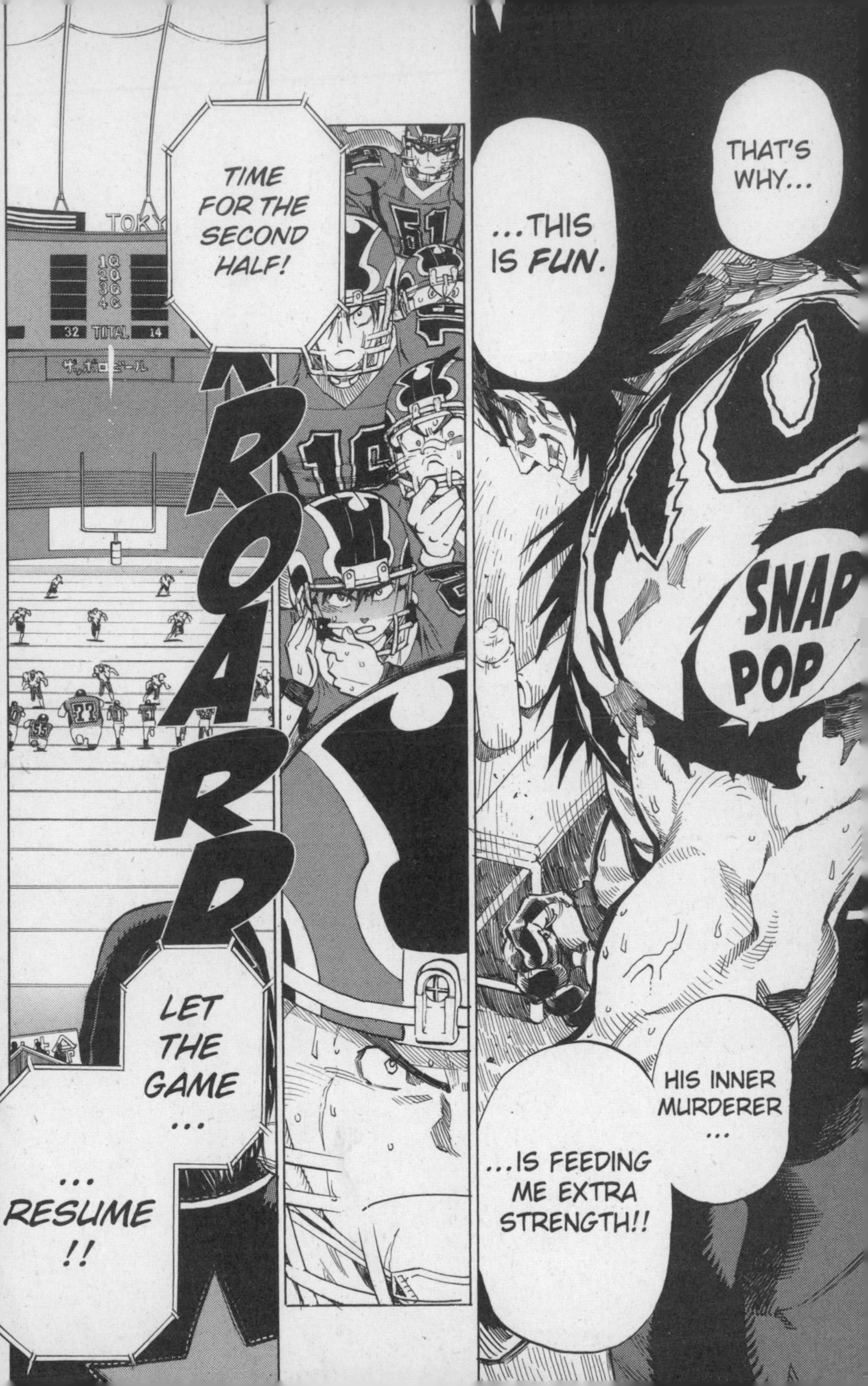
THAT'S WHY...
...THIS IS FUN.
SNAP POP
HIS INNER MURDERER ...
...IS FEEDING ME EXTRA STRENGTH!!
TIME FOR THE SECOND HALF!
ROARR
LET THE GAME ...
... RESUME !!

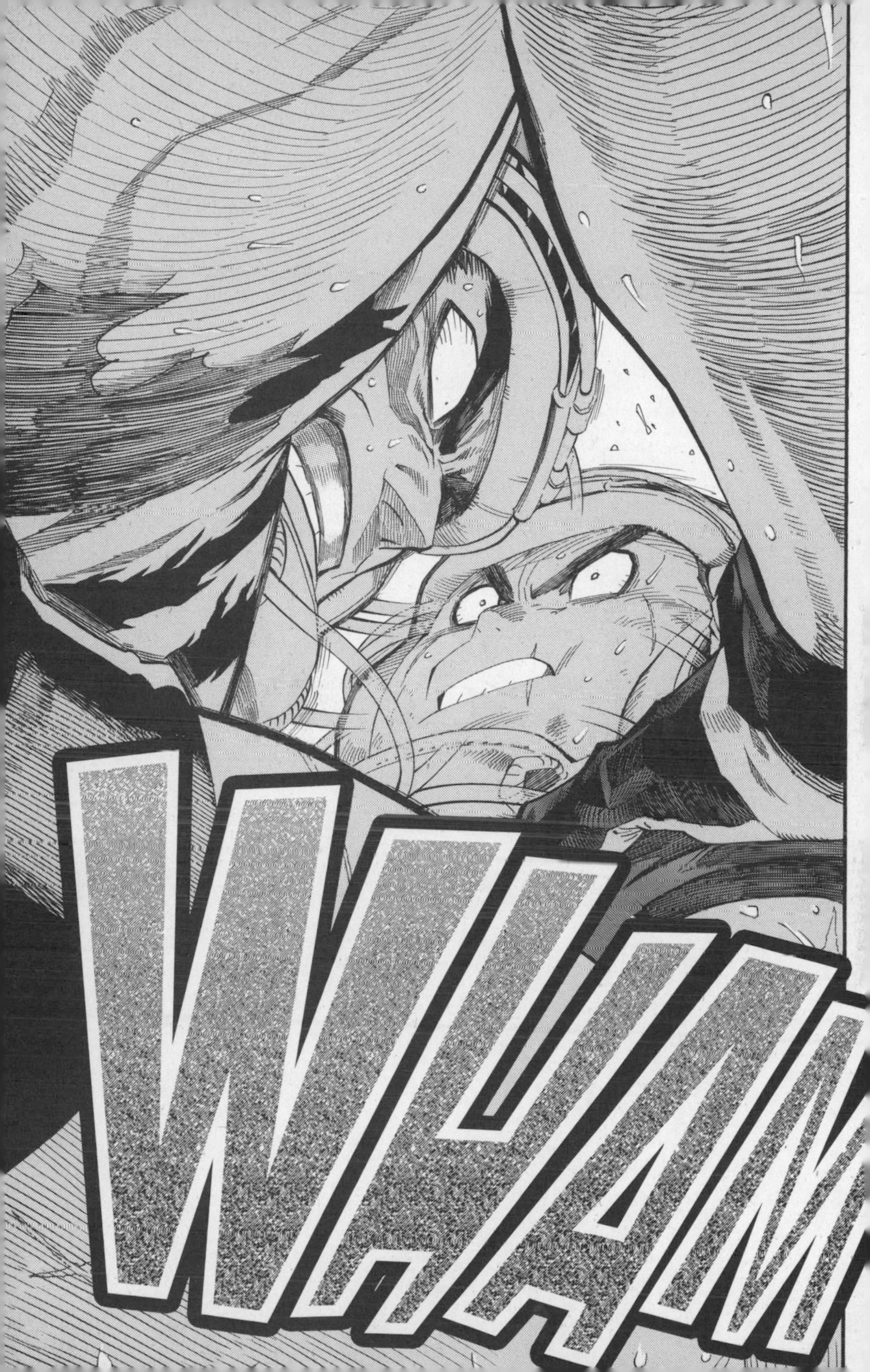
WHAM

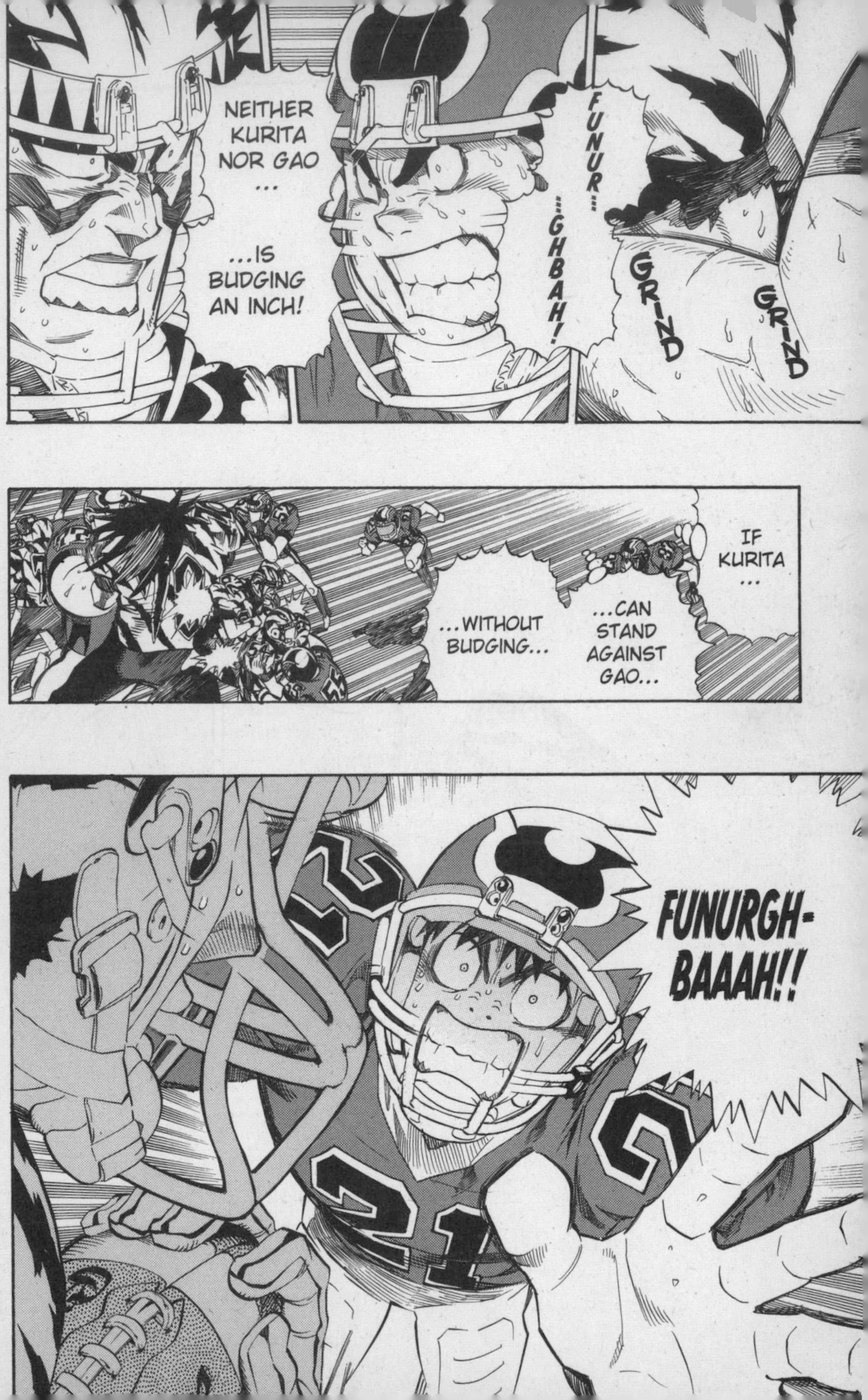
GRIND
GRIND
FUNUR...
...GHBAH!
NEITHER KURITA NOR GAO ...
...IS BUDGING AN INCH!
IF KURITA ...
...CAN STAND AGAINST GAO...
...WITHOUT BUDGING...
FUNURGH-BAAAH!!

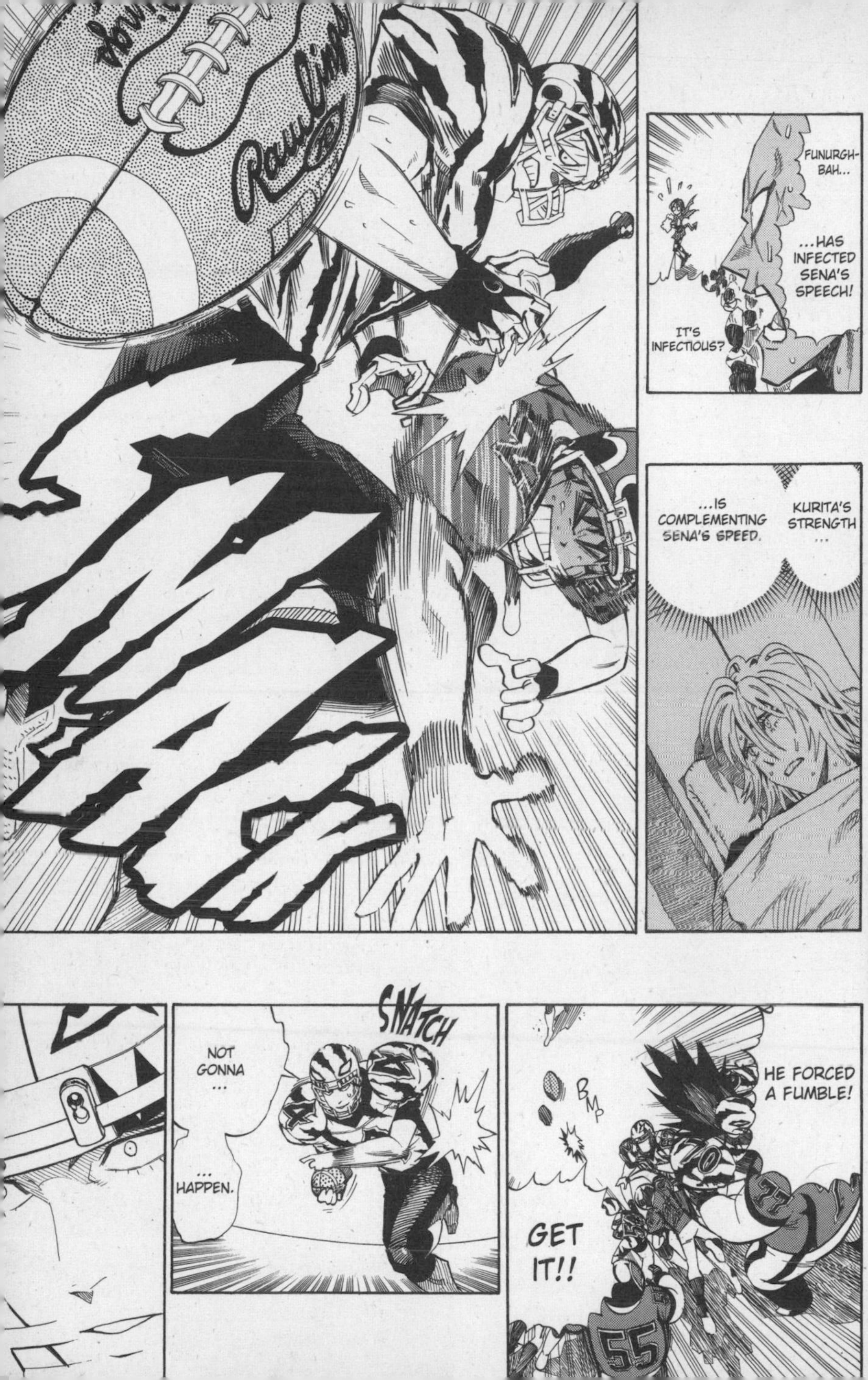
FUNURGH-BAH...
...HAS INFECTED SENA'S SPEECH!
IT'S INFECTIOUS?
KURITA'S STRENGTH ...
...IS COMPLEMENTING SENA'S SPEED.
HE FORCED A FUMBLE!
BMP
GET IT!!
SNATCH
NOT GONNA ...
... HAPPEN.

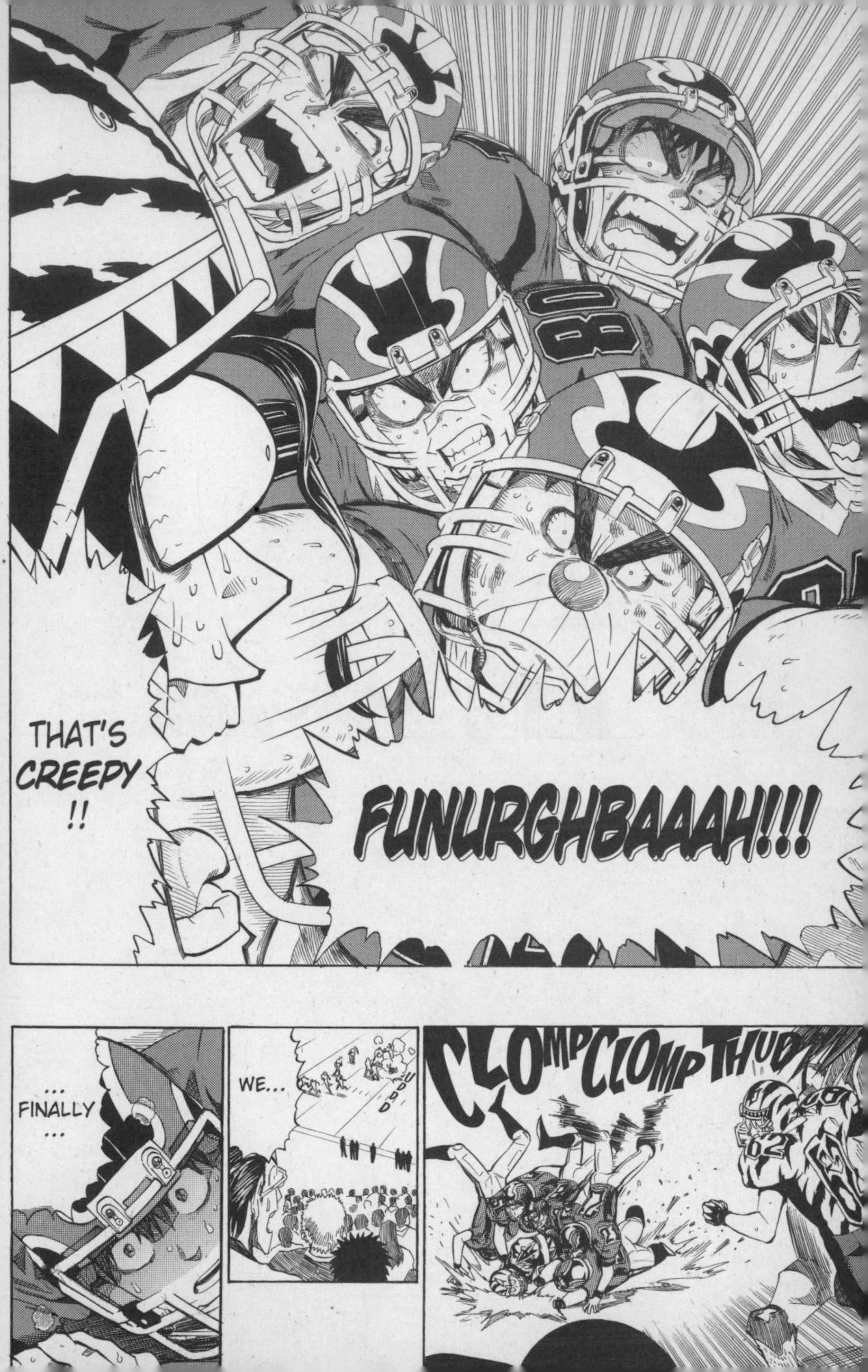
FUNURGHBAAAH!!!
THAT'S CREEPY !!
CLOMP CLOMP THUD
WE...
... FINALLY ...

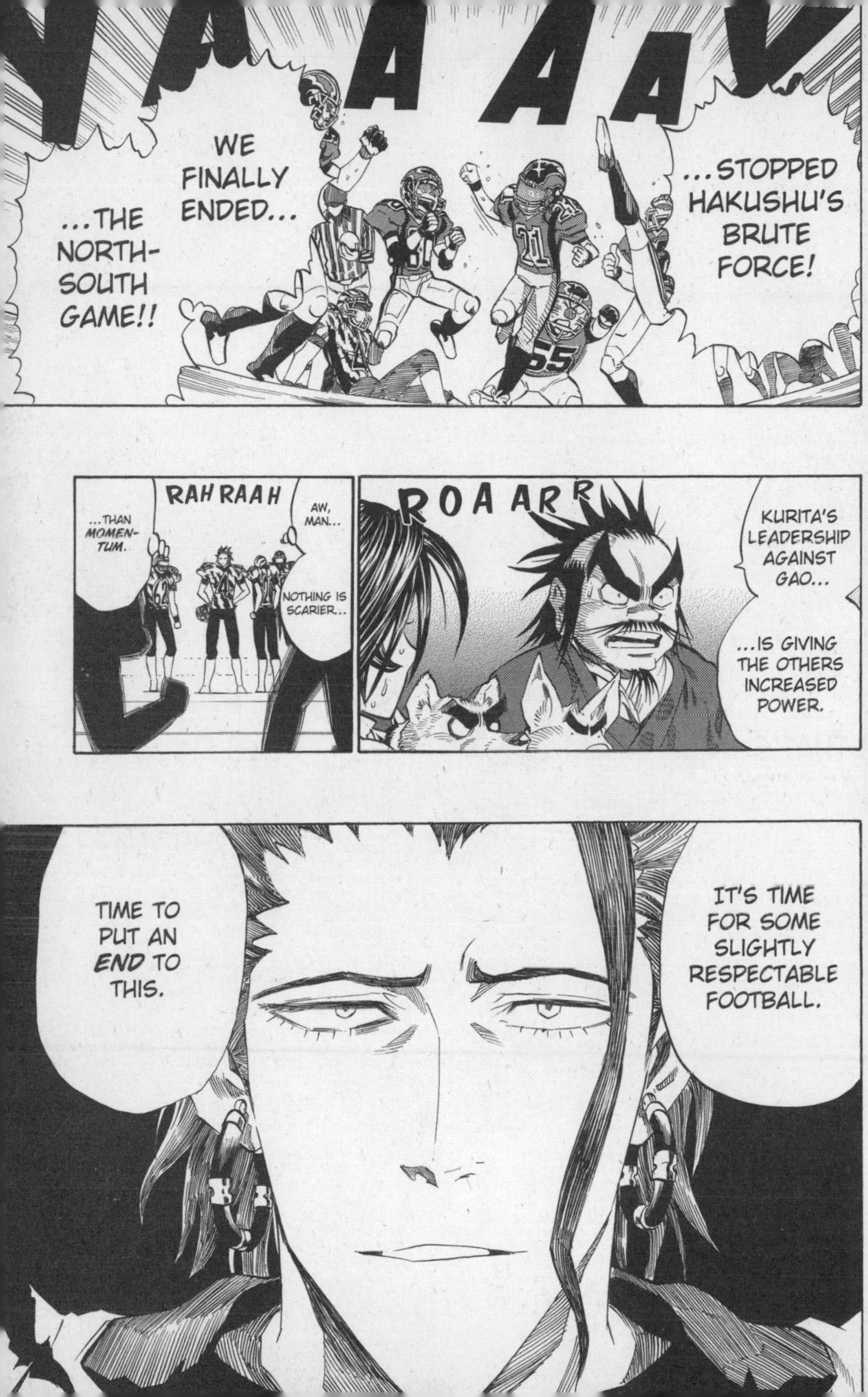
YAAAAY
...STOPPED HAKUSHU'S BRUTE FORCE!
WE FINALLY ENDED...
...THE NORTH-SOUTH GAME!!
ROAARR
KURITA'S LEADERSHIP AGAINST GAO...
...IS GIVING THE OTHERS INCREASED POWER.
RAH RAAH
AW, MAN...
NOTHING IS SCARIER...
...THAN *MOMENTUM*.
IT'S TIME FOR SOME SLIGHTLY RESPECTABLE FOOTBALL.
TIME TO PUT AN ***END*** TO THIS.

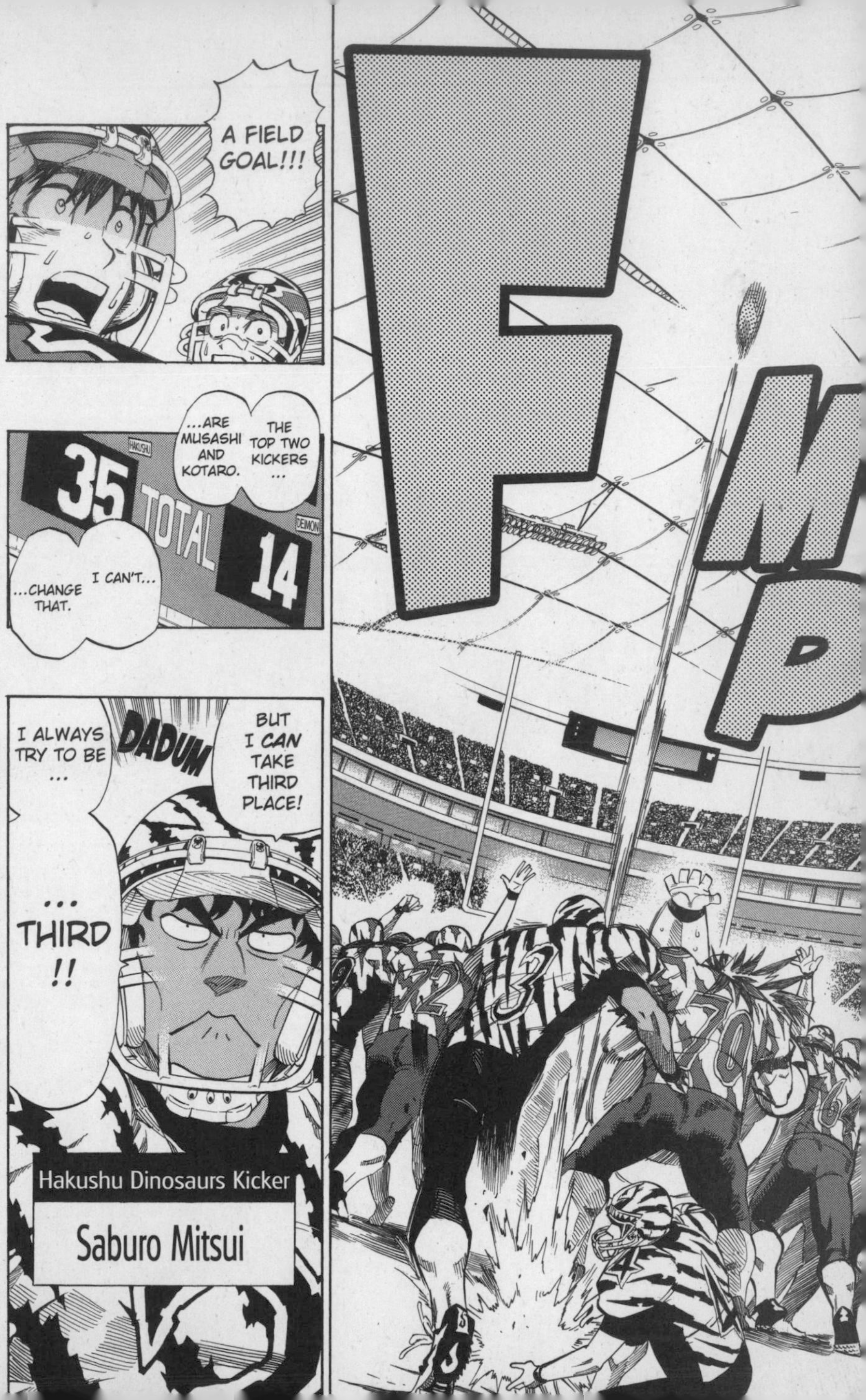
FMP
A FIELD GOAL!!!
THE TOP TWO KICKERS ...
...ARE MUSASHI AND KOTARO.
HAKUSHU
35
TOTAL
DEIMON
14
I CAN'T...
...CHANGE THAT.
BUT I CAN TAKE THIRD PLACE!
DADUM
I ALWAYS TRY TO BE ...
... THIRD !!
Hakushu Dinosaurs Kicker
Saburo Mitsui

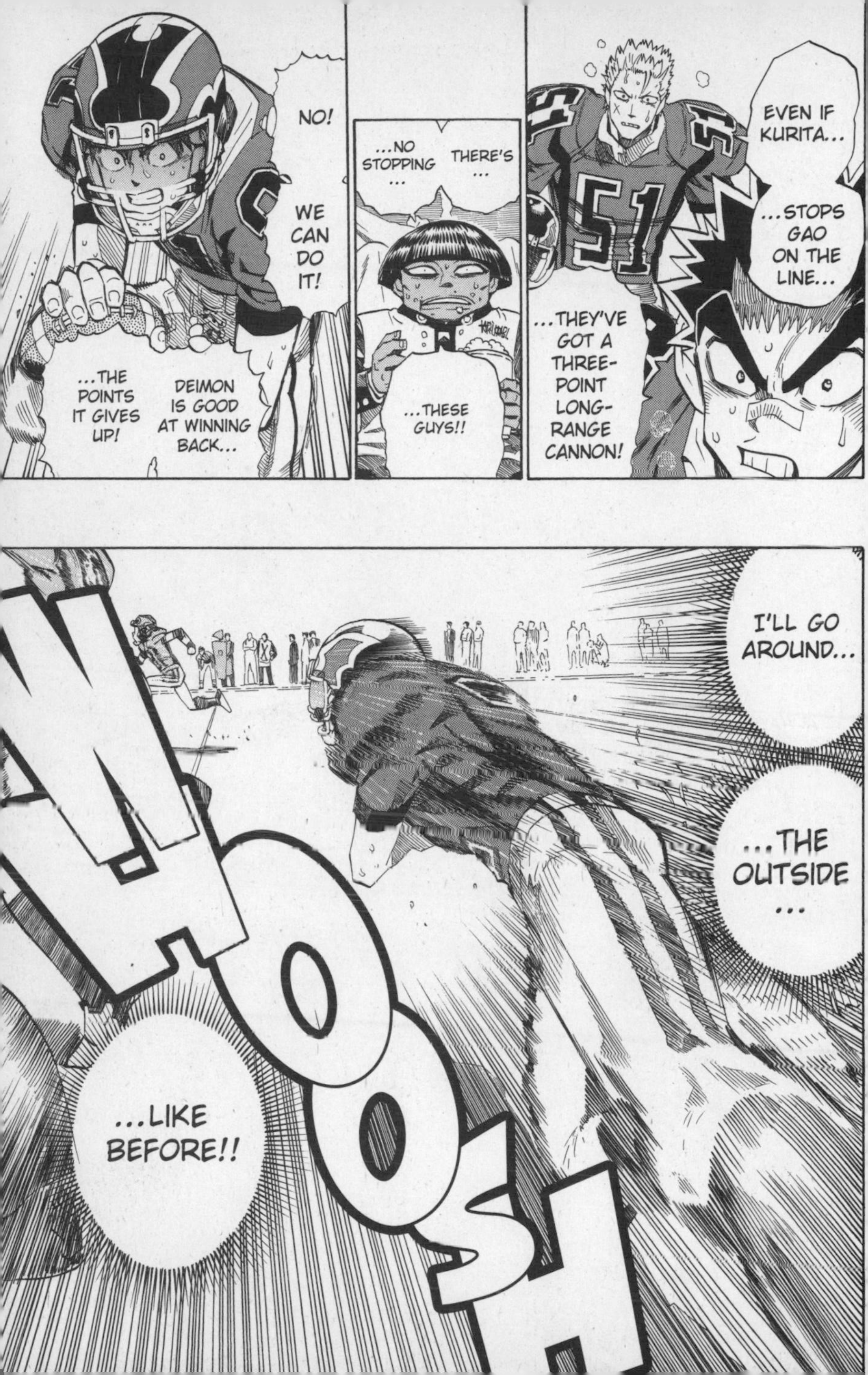
EVEN IF KURITA...
...STOPS GAO ON THE LINE...
...THEY'VE GOT A THREE-POINT LONG-RANGE CANNON!
THERE'S ...
...NO STOPPING ...
...THESE GUYS!!
NO!
WE CAN DO IT!
DEIMON IS GOOD AT WINNING BACK...
...THE POINTS IT GIVES UP!
I'LL GO AROUND...
...THE OUTSIDE ...
...LIKE BEFORE!!
WHOOSH!

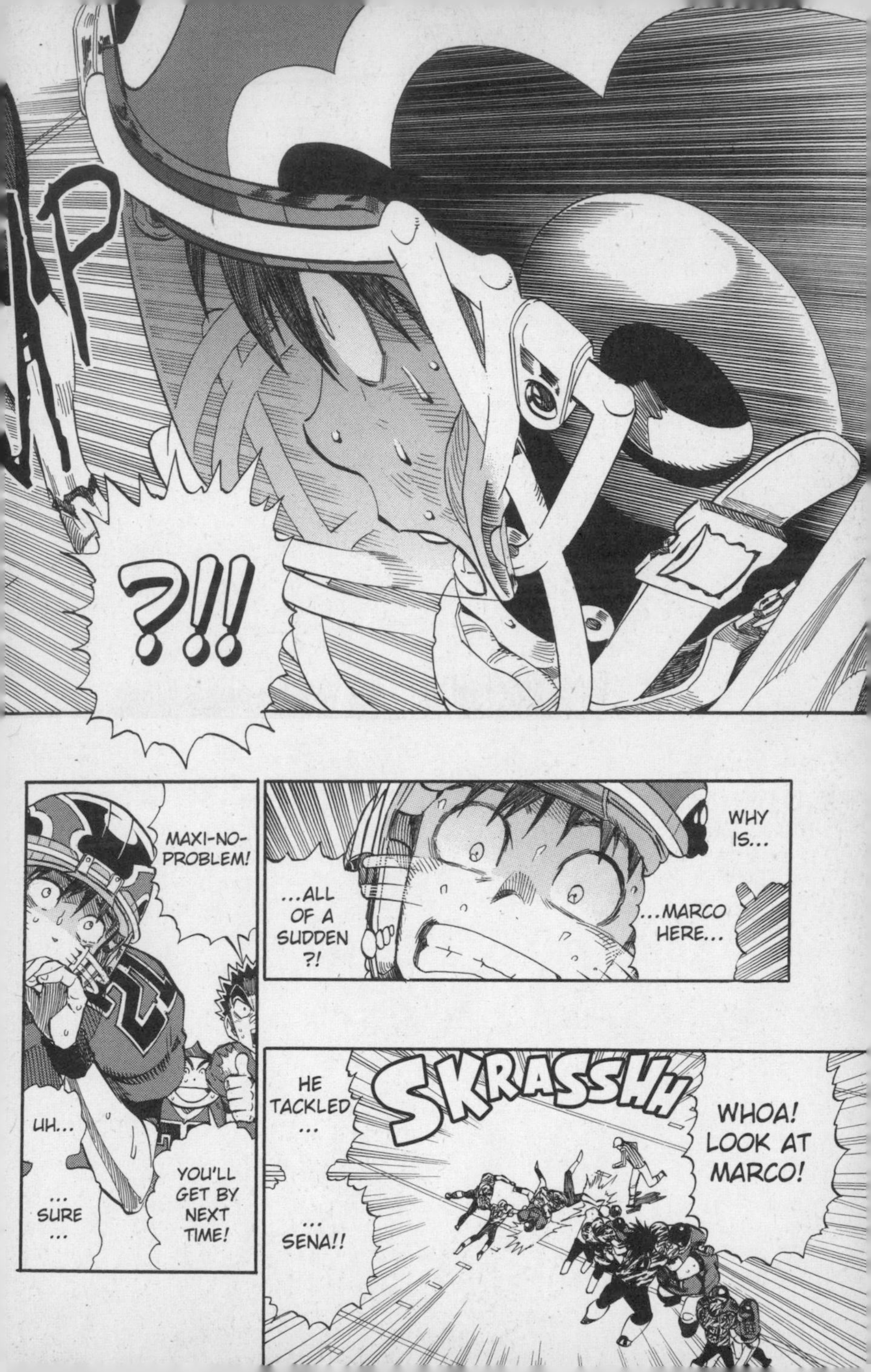
?!!
WHY IS...
...MARCO HERE...
...ALL OF A SUDDEN?!
SKRASSHH
WHOA! LOOK AT MARCO!
HE TACKLED ...
... SENA!!
MAXI-NO-PROBLEM!
YOU'LL GET BY NEXT TIME!
UH...
... SURE ...

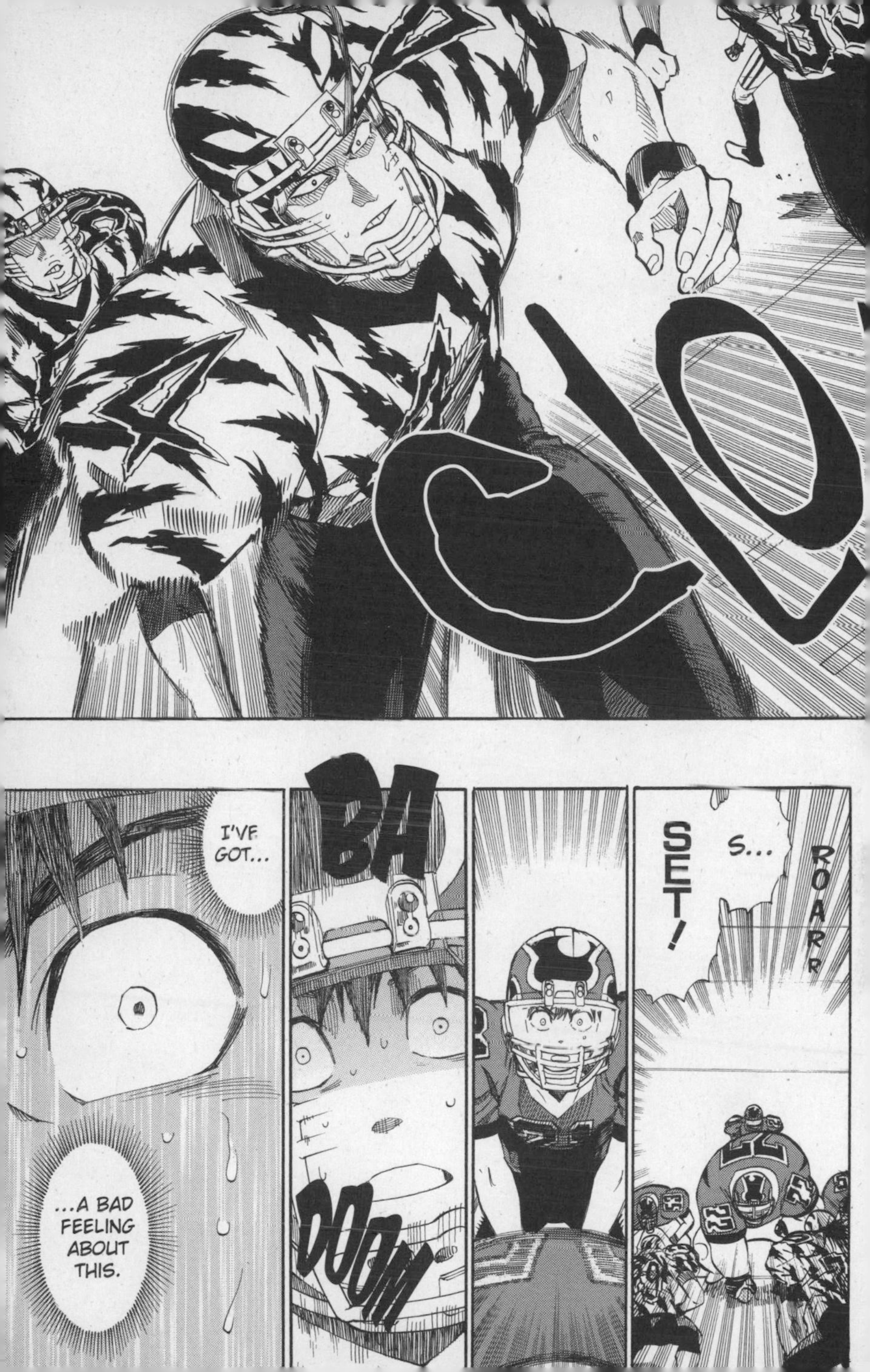
ROARR
S...
SET!
BA
DOOM
I'VE GOT...
...A BAD FEELING ABOUT THIS.

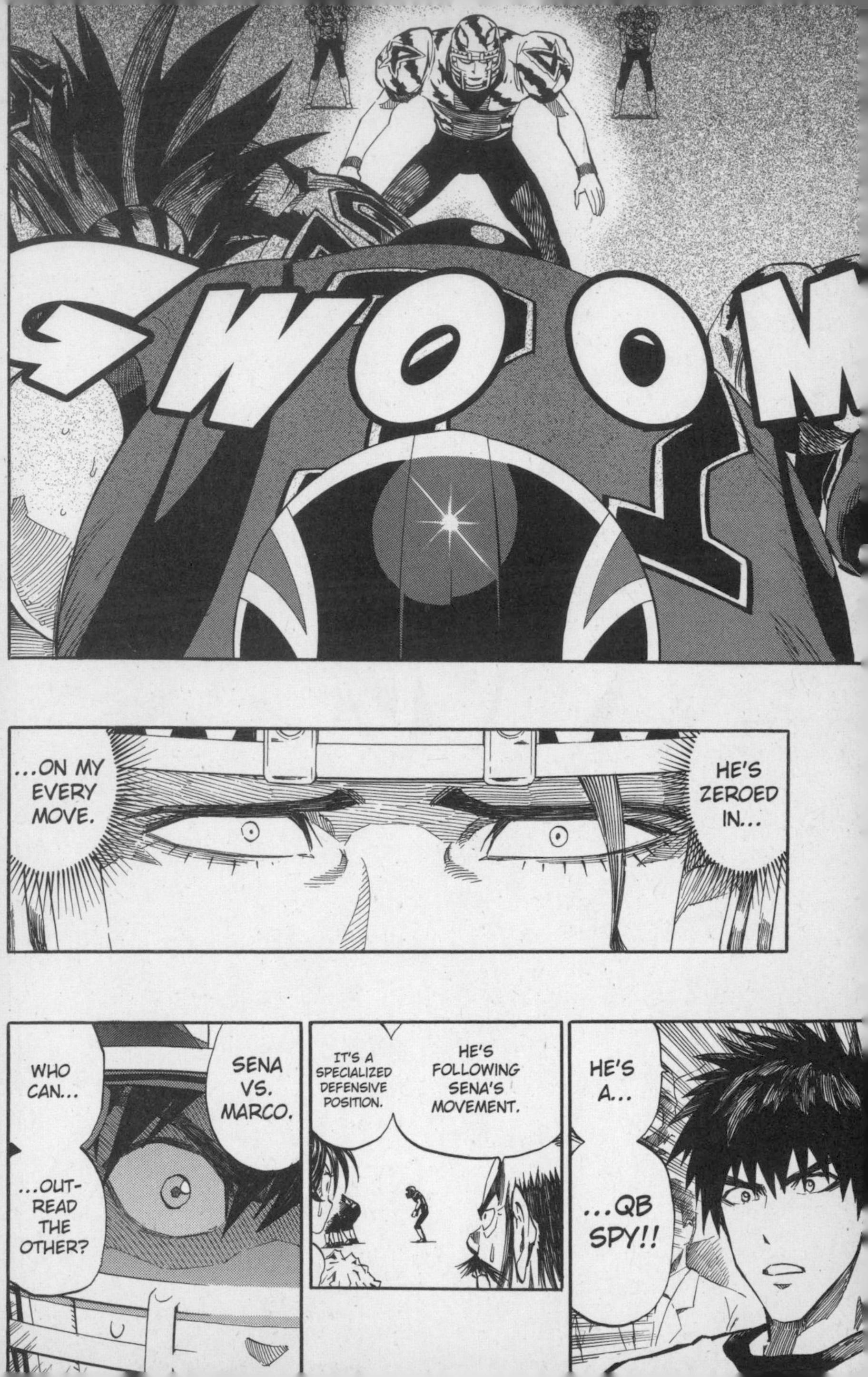
SWOOM
HE'S ZEROED IN...
...ON MY EVERY MOVE.
HE'S A...
...QB SPY!!
HE'S FOLLOWING SENA'S MOVEMENT.
IT'S A SPECIALIZED DEFENSIVE POSITION.
SENA VS. MARCO.
WHO CAN...
...OUT-READ THE OTHER?

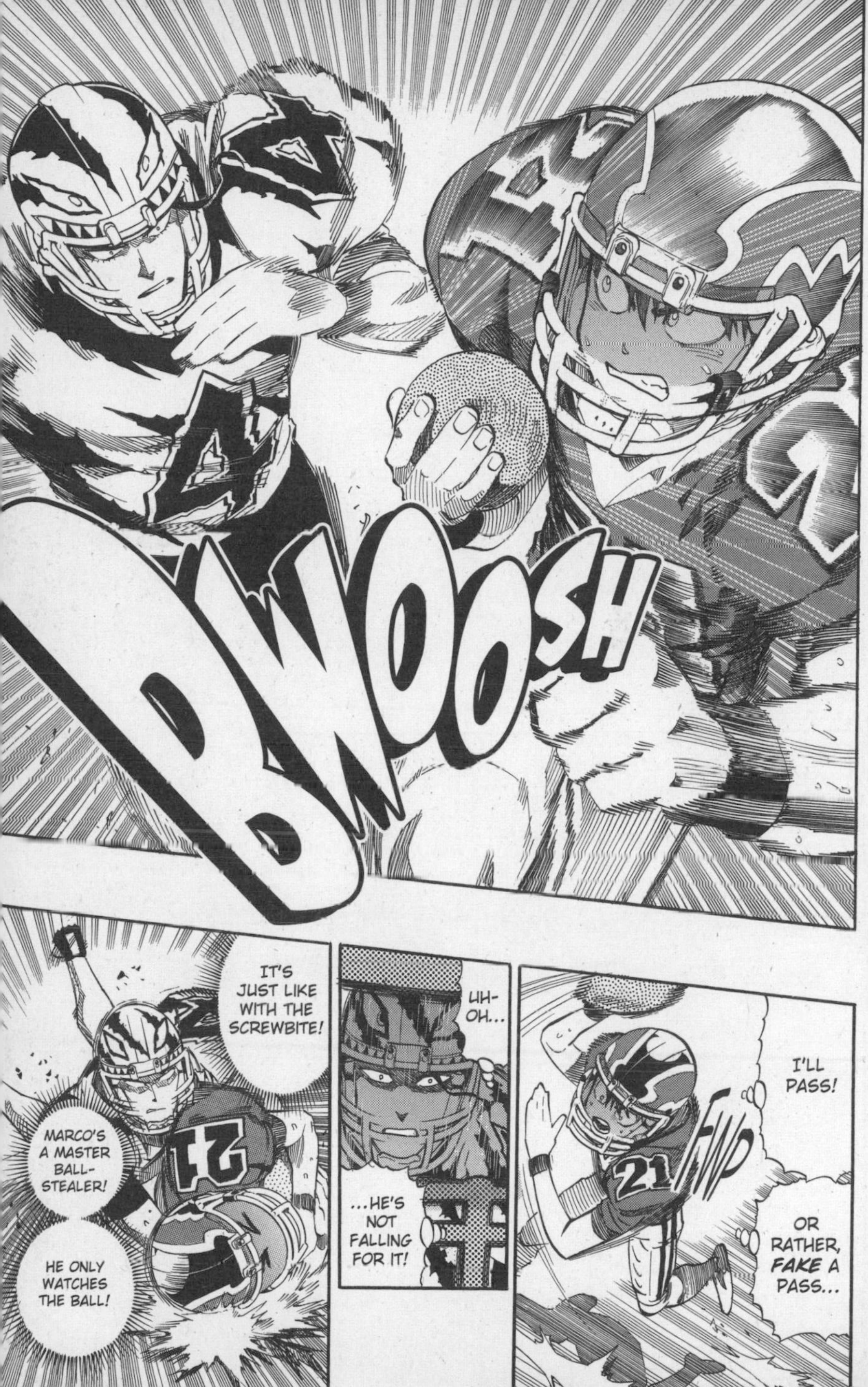
BWOOSH
I'LL PASS!
OR RATHER, FAKE A PASS...
UH-OH...
...HE'S NOT FALLING FOR IT!
IT'S JUST LIKE WITH THE SCREWBITE!
MARCO'S A MASTER BALL-STEALER!
HE ONLY WATCHES THE BALL!

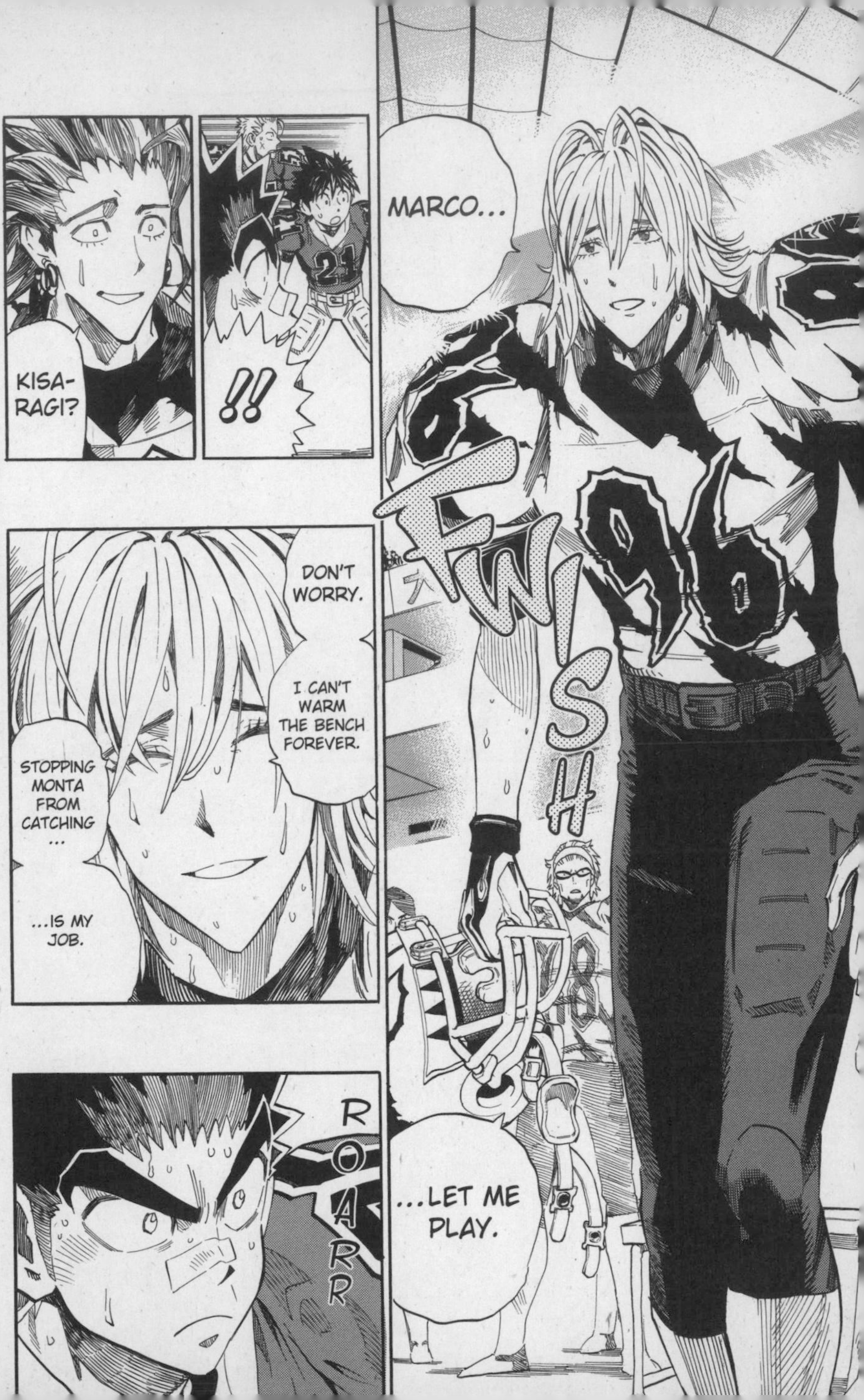

MARCO...
FWISH
...LET ME PLAY.
!!
KISA-RAGI?
DON'T WORRY.
I CAN'T WARM THE BENCH FOREVER.
STOPPING MONTA FROM CATCHING...
...IS MY JOB.
ROARR

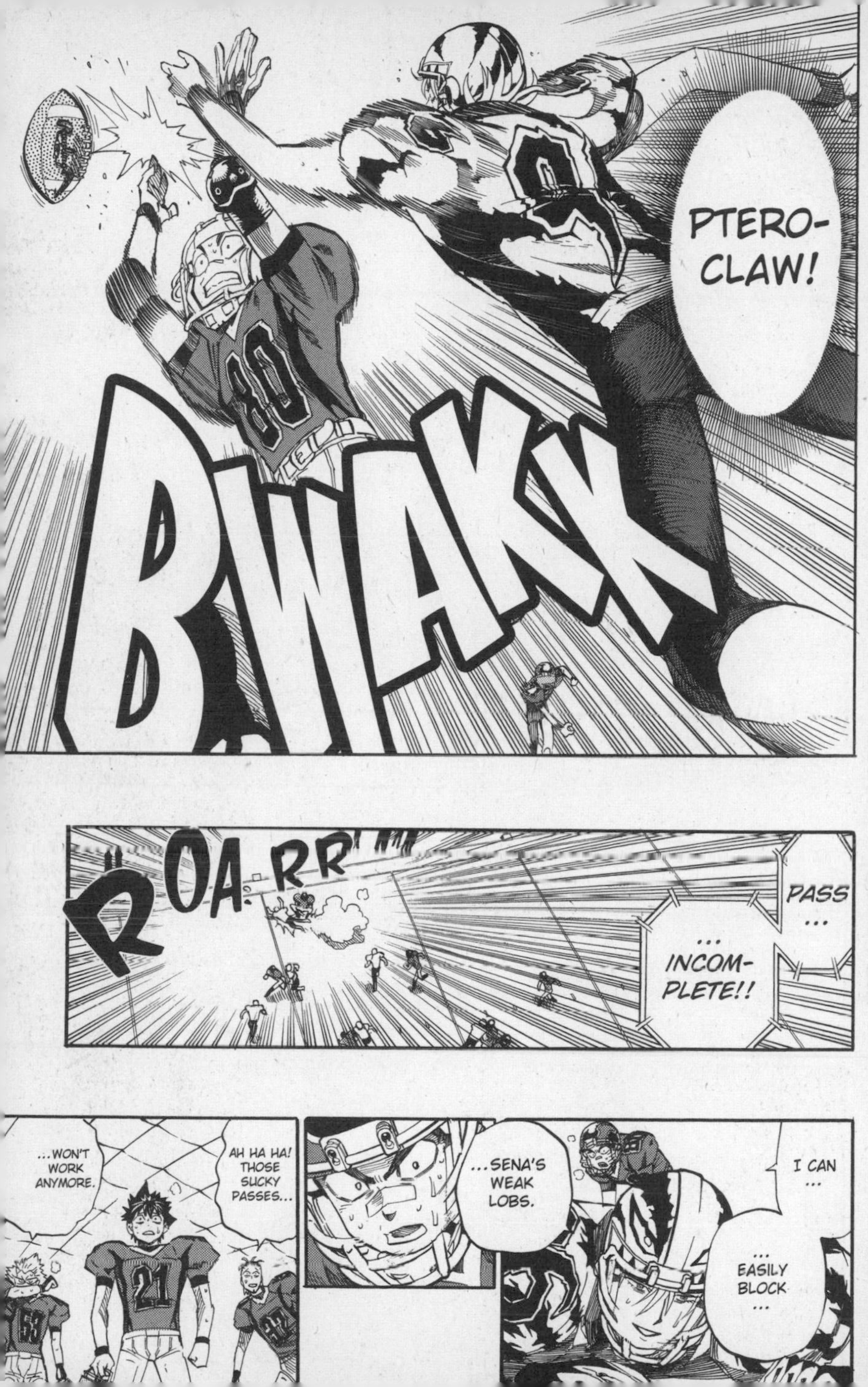
PTERO-CLAW!
BWAKK!
PASS ...
... INCOMPLETE!!
ROARR
I CAN ...
... EASILY BLOCK ...
...SENA'S WEAK LOBS.
AH HA HA! THOSE SUCKY PASSES...
...WON'T WORK ANYMORE.

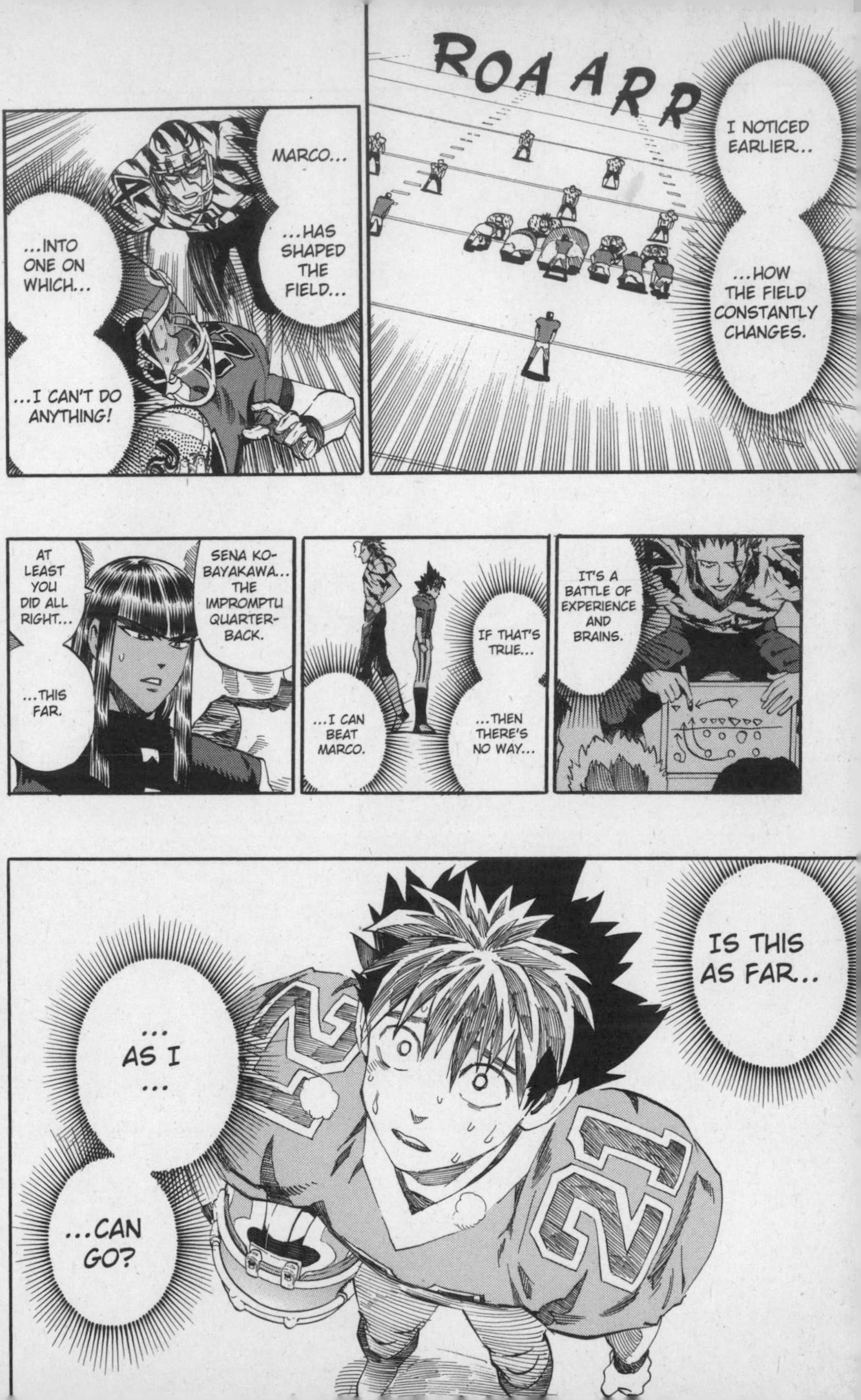
ROAARR
I NOTICED EARLIER...
...HOW THE FIELD CONSTANTLY CHANGES.
MARCO...
...HAS SHAPED THE FIELD...
...INTO ONE ON WHICH...
...I CAN'T DO ANYTHING!
IT'S A BATTLE OF EXPERIENCE AND BRAINS.
IF THAT'S TRUE...
...THEN THERE'S NO WAY...
...I CAN BEAT MARCO.
SENA KOBAYAKAWA... THE IMPROMPTU QUARTERBACK.
AT LEAST YOU DID ALL RIGHT...
...THIS FAR.
IS THIS AS FAR...
...AS I...
...CAN GO?

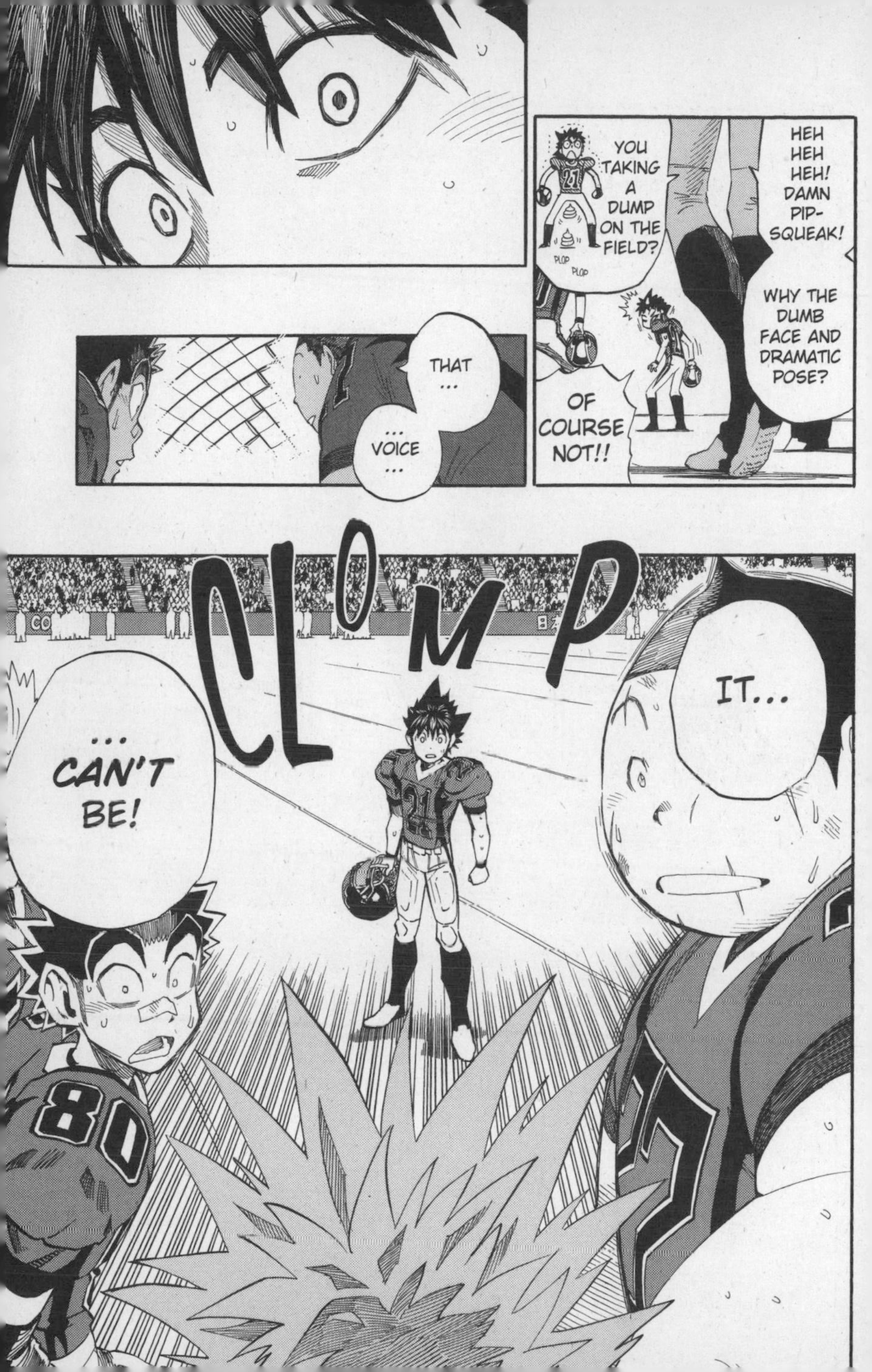
HEH HEH HEH! DAMN PIP-SQUEAK!
YOU TAKING A DUMP ON THE FIELD?
PLOP
PLOP
WHY THE DUMB FACE AND DRAMATIC POSE?
OF COURSE NOT!!
THAT ...
... VOICE ...
CLOMP
IT...
... CAN'T BE!

Eyeshield 21 Survey Corner **Devil Bat 021 SPECIAL!**

Investigation File #115

Kisaragi equates strength with beauty. Based on that, show me how everyone looks!

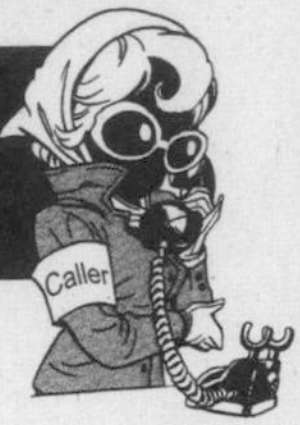
Caller

Yoru in Chiba Prefecture

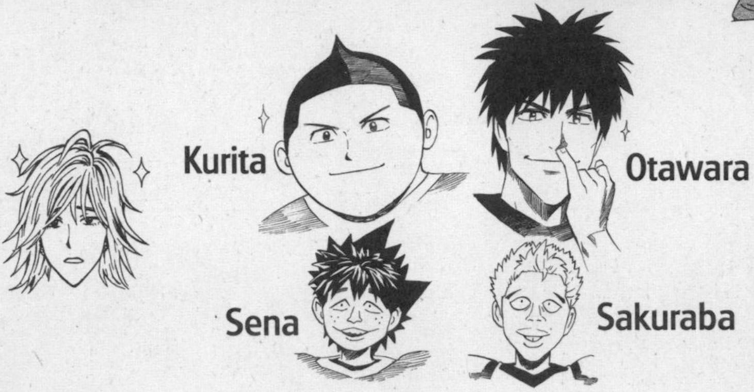
Kurita
Otawara
Sena
Sakuraba

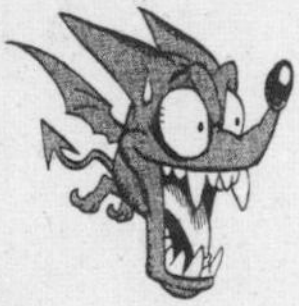

THEIR HANDSOMENESS IS PROPORTIONATE TO THEIR STRENGTH...

Investigation File #116

Kisaragi admires Gao, but he likes girls not boys, right?

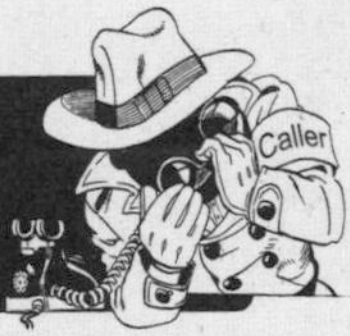
Caller

Big Leaguer Jiro in Akita Prefecture

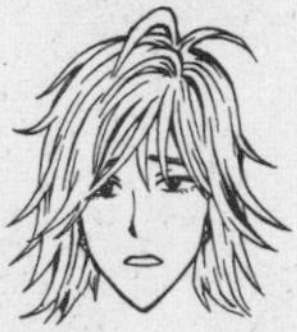

I LIKE STRONG GIRLS.

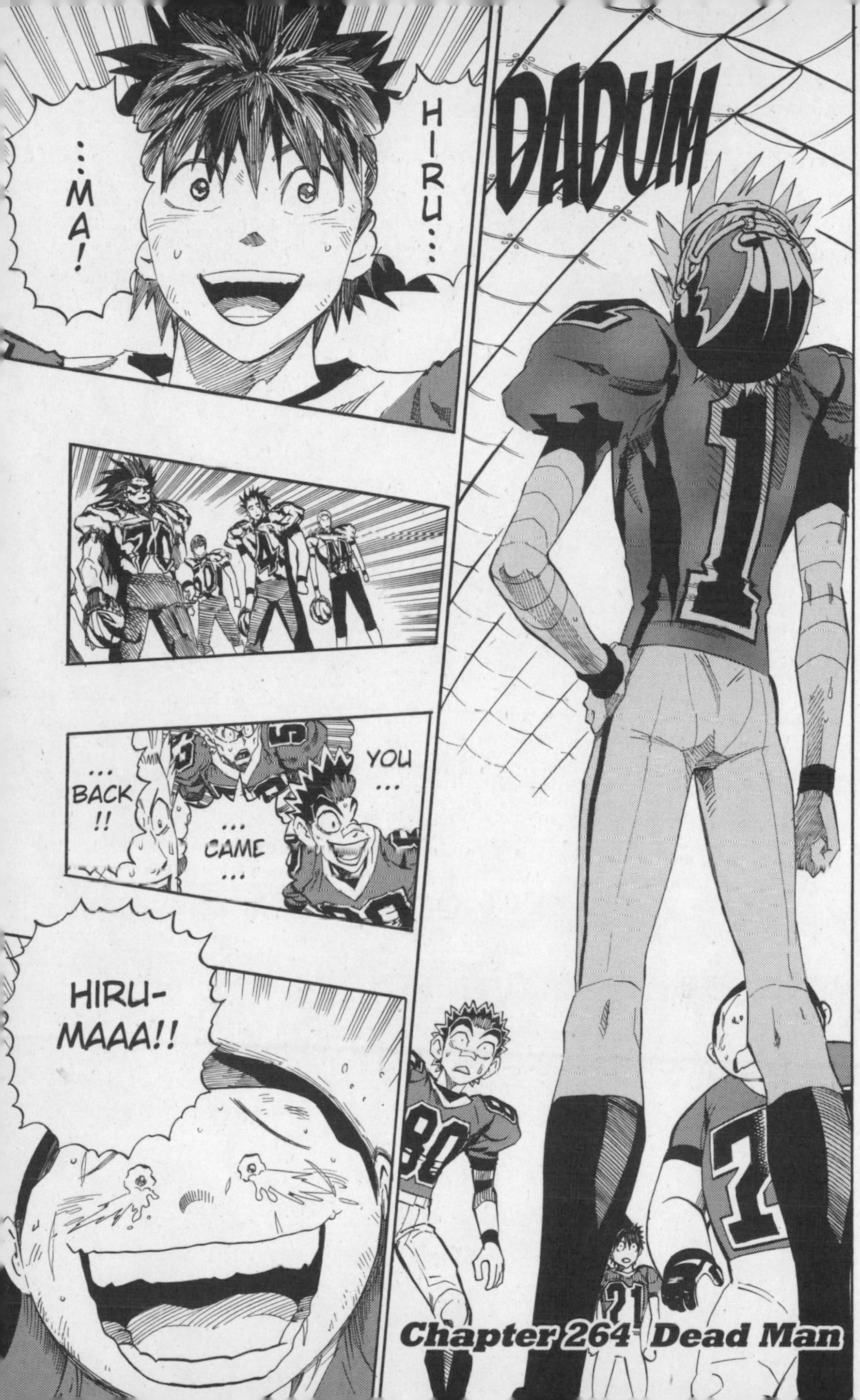
DADUM
Chapter 264 Dead Man
HIRU...
...MA!
YOU...
...CAME...
...BACK!!
HIRU-MAAA!!

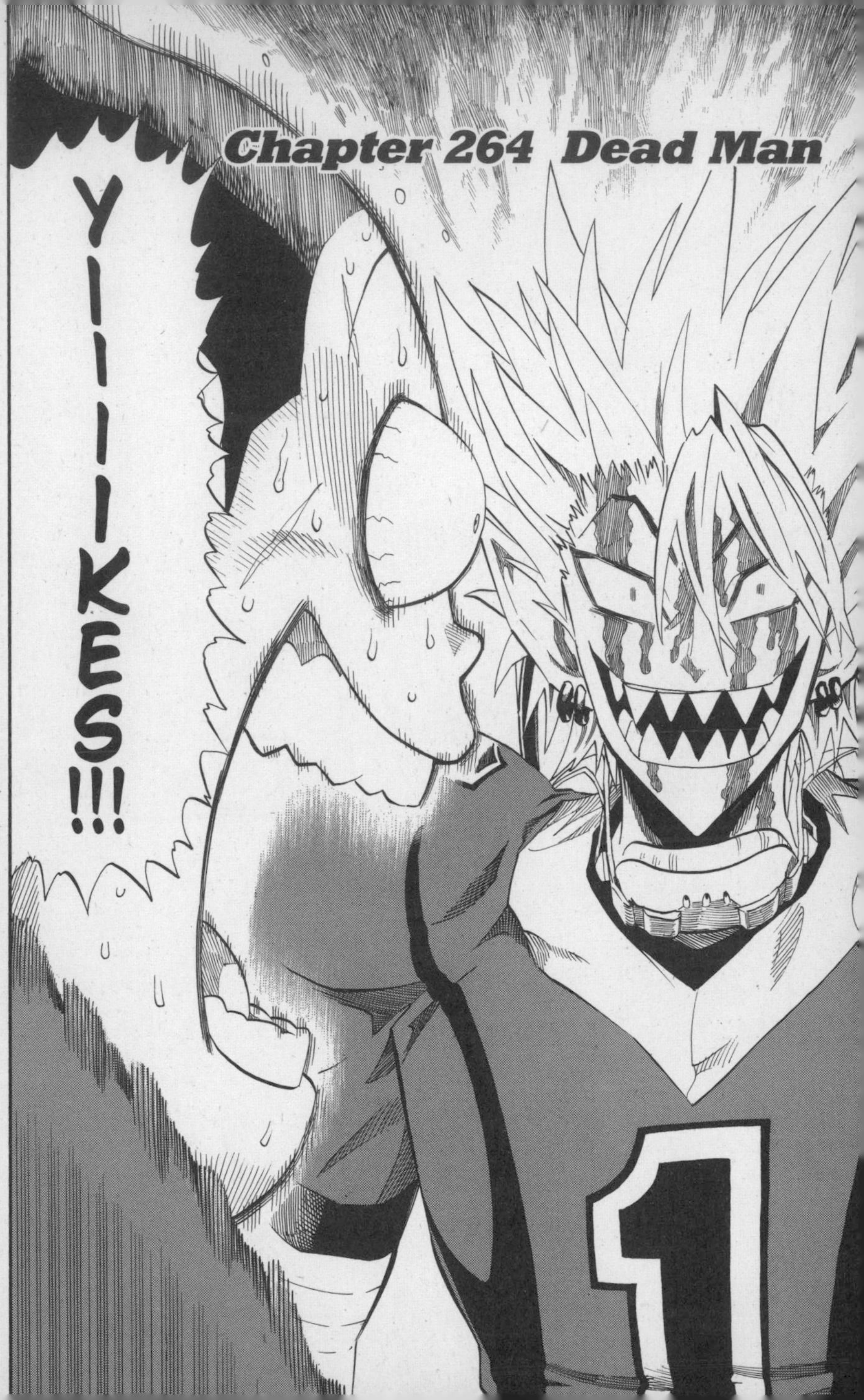
Chapter 264 Dead Man
YIIIIKES!!!

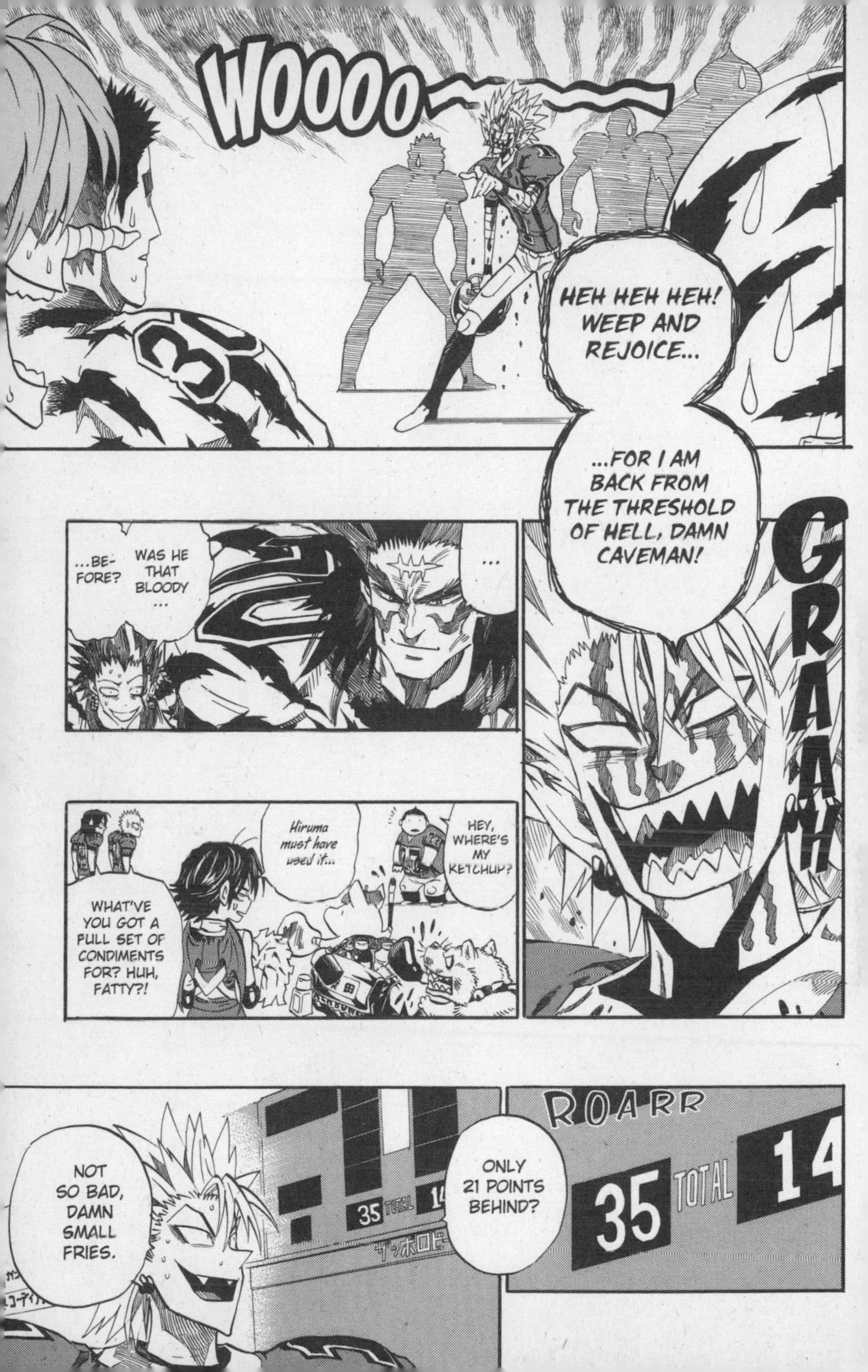
WOOOO~
HEH HEH HEH! WEEP AND REJOICE...
...FOR I AM BACK FROM THE THRESHOLD OF HELL, DAMN CAVEMAN!
GRAAH
...
WAS HE THAT BLOODY ...
...BE-FORE?
HEY, WHERE'S MY KETCHUP?
Hiruma must have used it...
WHAT'VE YOU GOT A FULL SET OF CONDIMENTS FOR? HUH, FATTY?!
ROARR
35 TOTAL 14
ONLY 21 POINTS BEHIND?
NOT SO BAD, DAMN SMALL FRIES.

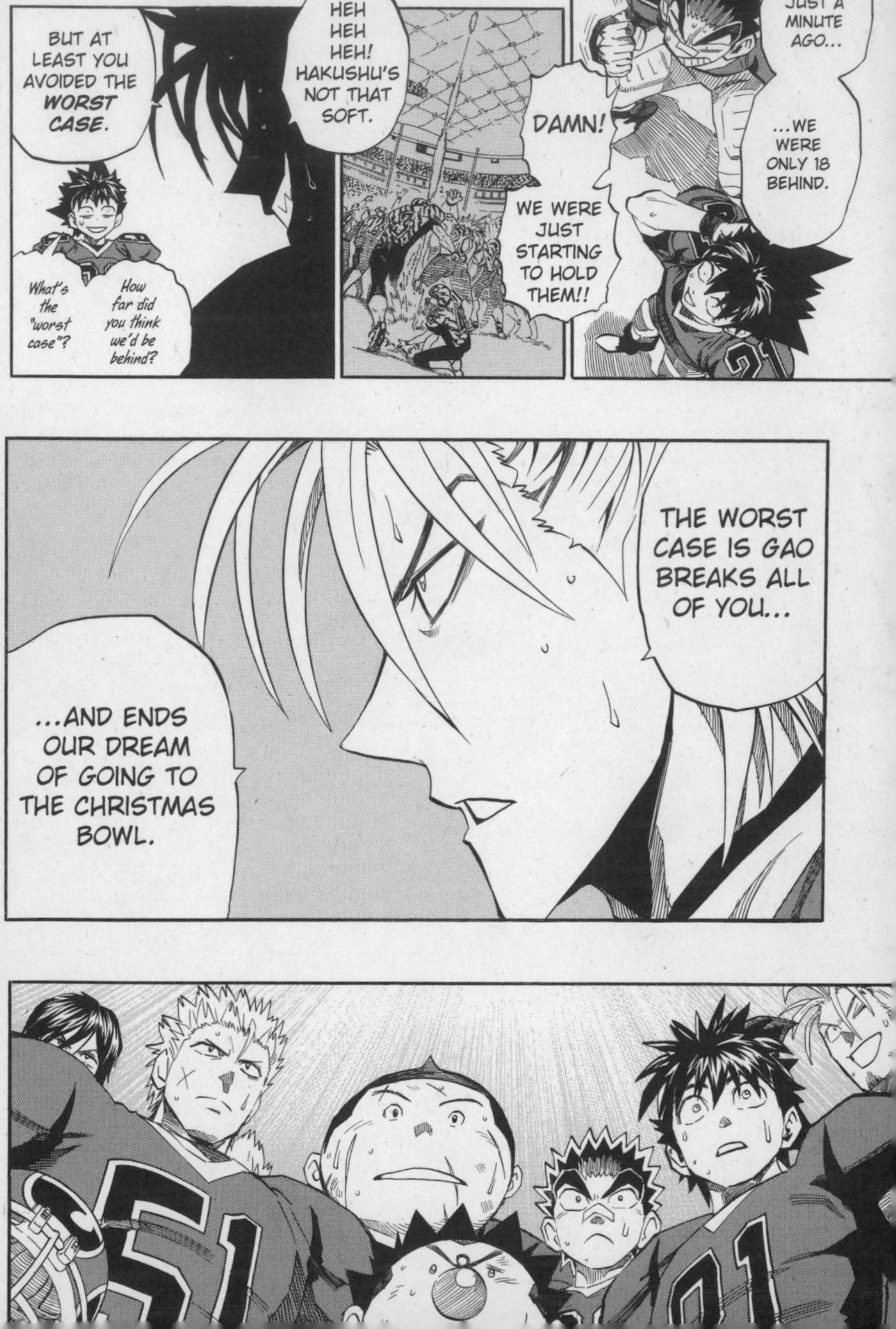
UNTIL JUST A MINUTE AGO...
...WE WERE ONLY 18 BEHIND.
DAMN!
WE WERE JUST STARTING TO HOLD THEM!!
HEH HEH HEH! HAKUSHU'S NOT THAT SOFT.
BUT AT LEAST YOU AVOIDED THE WORST CASE.
How far did you think we'd be behind?
What's the "worst case"?
THE WORST CASE IS GAO BREAKS ALL OF YOU...
...AND ENDS OUR DREAM OF GOING TO THE CHRISTMAS BOWL.

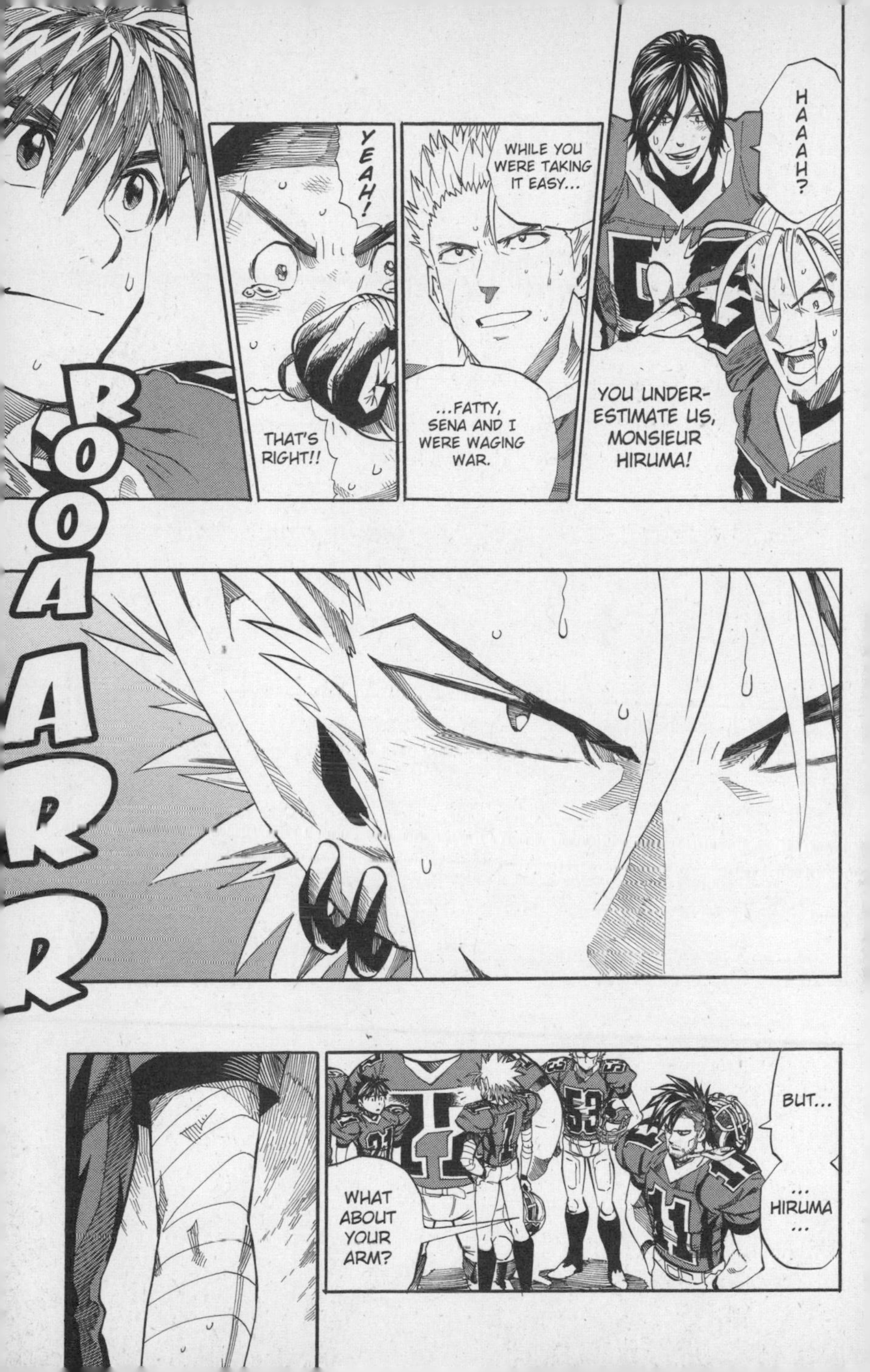
HAAAH?
YOU UNDER-ESTIMATE US, MONSIEUR HIRUMA!
WHILE YOU WERE TAKING IT EASY...
...FATTY, SENA AND I WERE WAGING WAR.
YEAH!
THAT'S RIGHT!!
ROOAARR
BUT...
...HIRUMA...
WHAT ABOUT YOUR ARM?

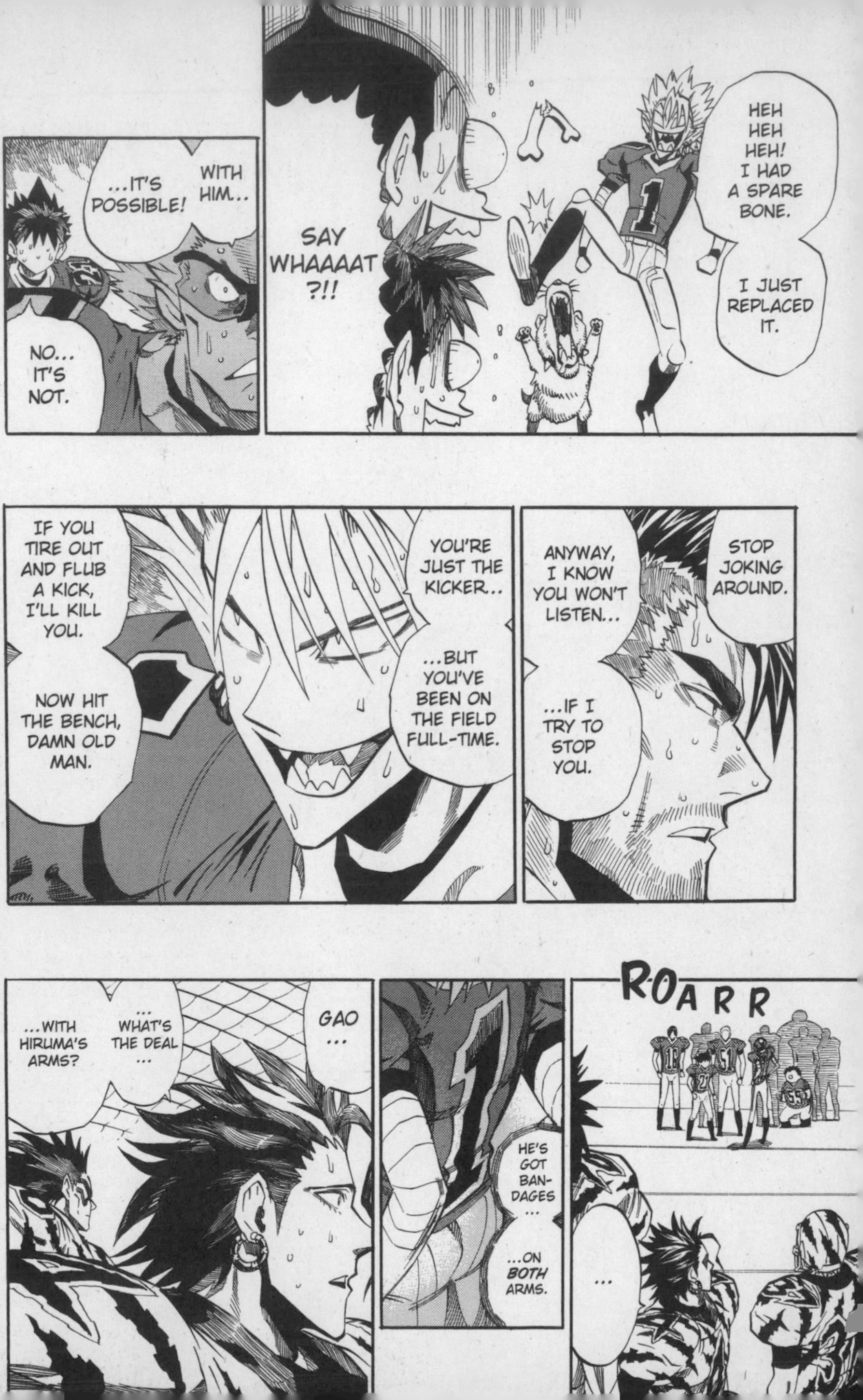
HEH HEH HEH! I HAD A SPARE BONE.
I JUST REPLACED IT.
SAY WHAAAAT ?!!
WITH HIM...
...IT'S POSSIBLE!
NO... IT'S NOT.
STOP JOKING AROUND.
ANYWAY, I KNOW YOU WON'T LISTEN...
...IF I TRY TO STOP YOU.
YOU'RE JUST THE KICKER...
...BUT YOU'VE BEEN ON THE FIELD FULL-TIME.
IF YOU TIRE OUT AND FLUB A KICK, I'LL KILL YOU.
NOW HIT THE BENCH, DAMN OLD MAN.
ROARR
...
HE'S GOT BAN-DAGES...
...ON *BOTH* ARMS.
GAO...
...WHAT'S THE DEAL...
...WITH HIRUMA'S ARMS?

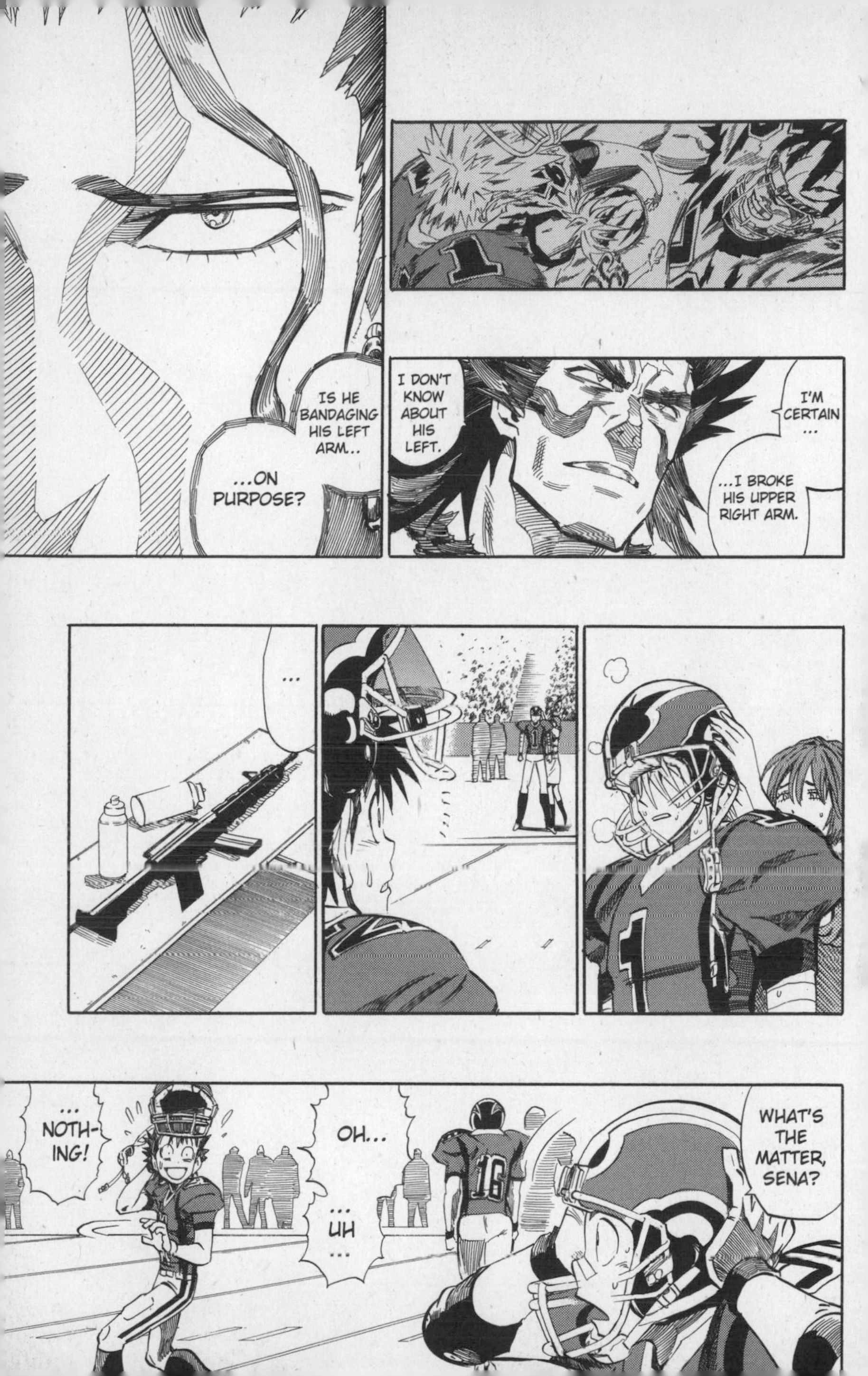
I'M CERTAIN...
...I BROKE HIS UPPER RIGHT ARM.
I DON'T KNOW ABOUT HIS LEFT.
IS HE BANDAGING HIS LEFT ARM...
...ON PURPOSE?
...
WHAT'S THE MATTER, SENA?
OH...
...UH...
...NOTH-ING!

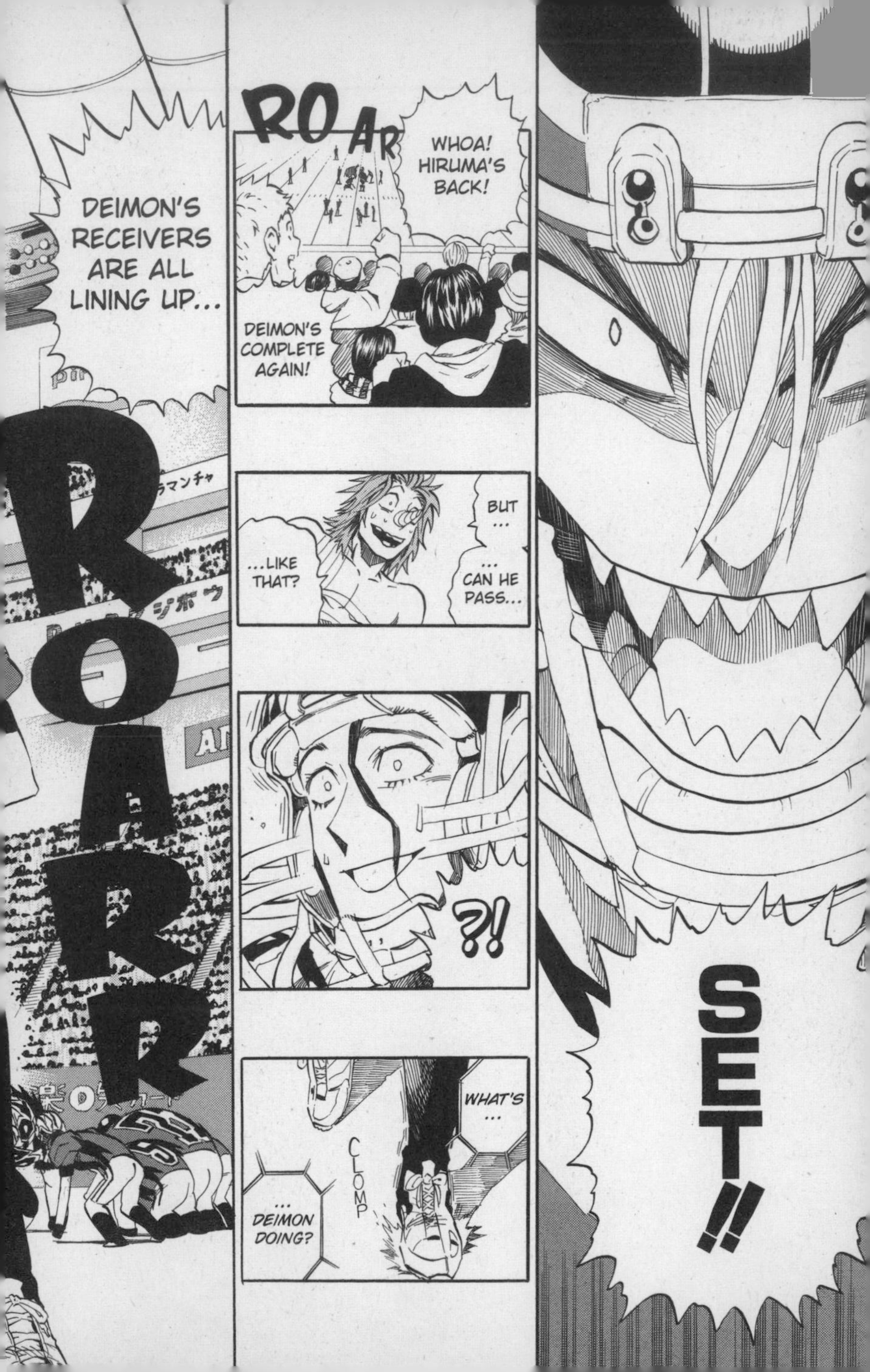
SET!!
ROAR
WHOA! HIRUMA'S BACK!
DEIMON'S COMPLETE AGAIN!
BUT...
...CAN HE PASS...
...LIKE THAT?
?!
WHAT'S...
...DEIMON DOING?
CLOMP
DEIMON'S RECEIVERS ARE ALL LINING UP...
ROARR

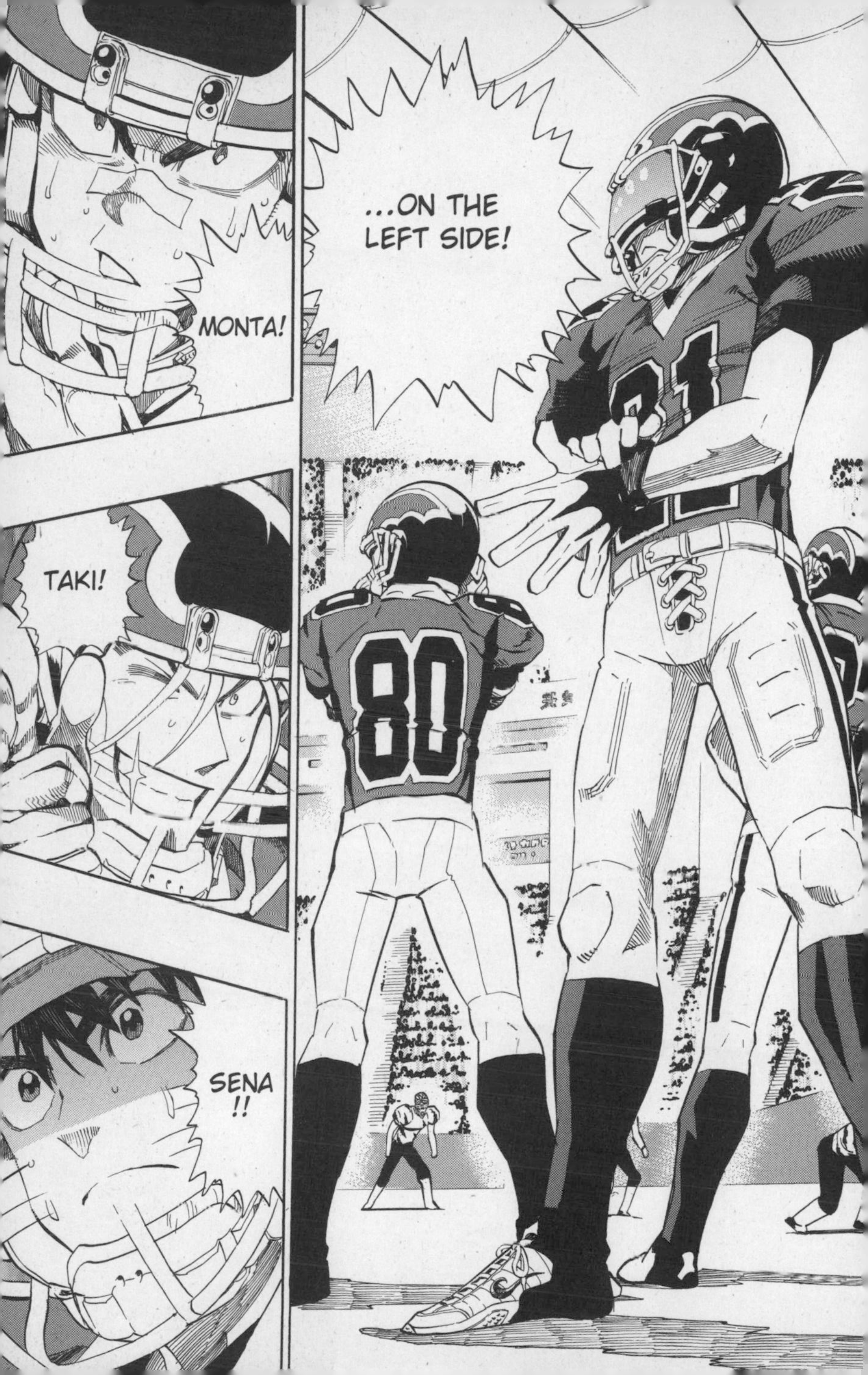
...ON THE LEFT SIDE!
MONTA!
TAKI!
SENA !!

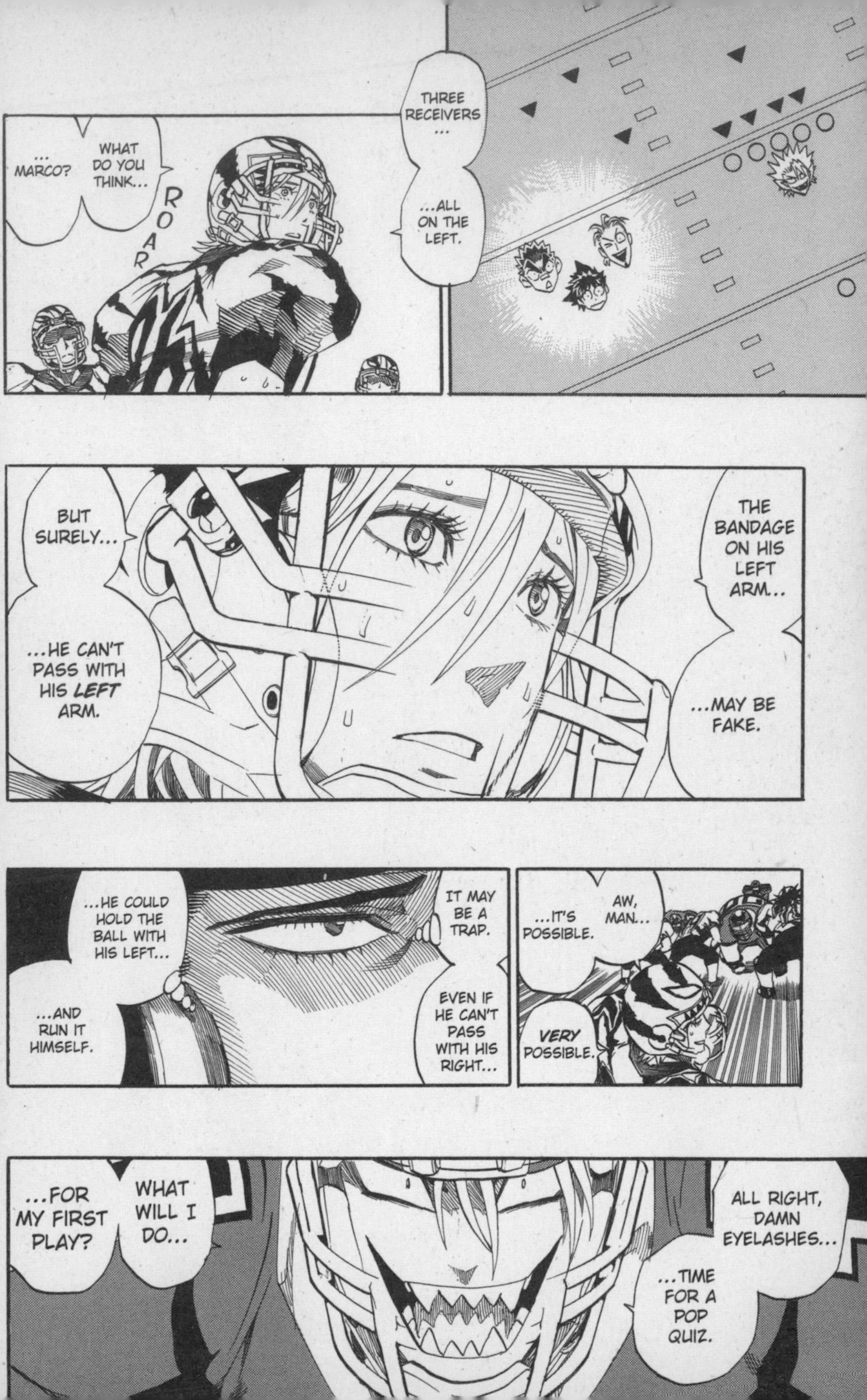
THREE RECEIVERS...
...ALL ON THE LEFT.
WHAT DO YOU THINK...
...MARCO?
ROAR
THE BANDAGE ON HIS LEFT ARM...
...MAY BE FAKE.
BUT SURELY...
...HE CAN'T PASS WITH HIS *LEFT* ARM.
AW, MAN...
...IT'S POSSIBLE.
VERY POSSIBLE.
IT MAY BE A TRAP.
EVEN IF HE CAN'T PASS WITH HIS RIGHT...
...HE COULD HOLD THE BALL WITH HIS LEFT...
...AND RUN IT HIMSELF.
ALL RIGHT, DAMN EYELASHES...
...TIME FOR A POP QUIZ.
WHAT WILL I DO...
...FOR MY FIRST PLAY?

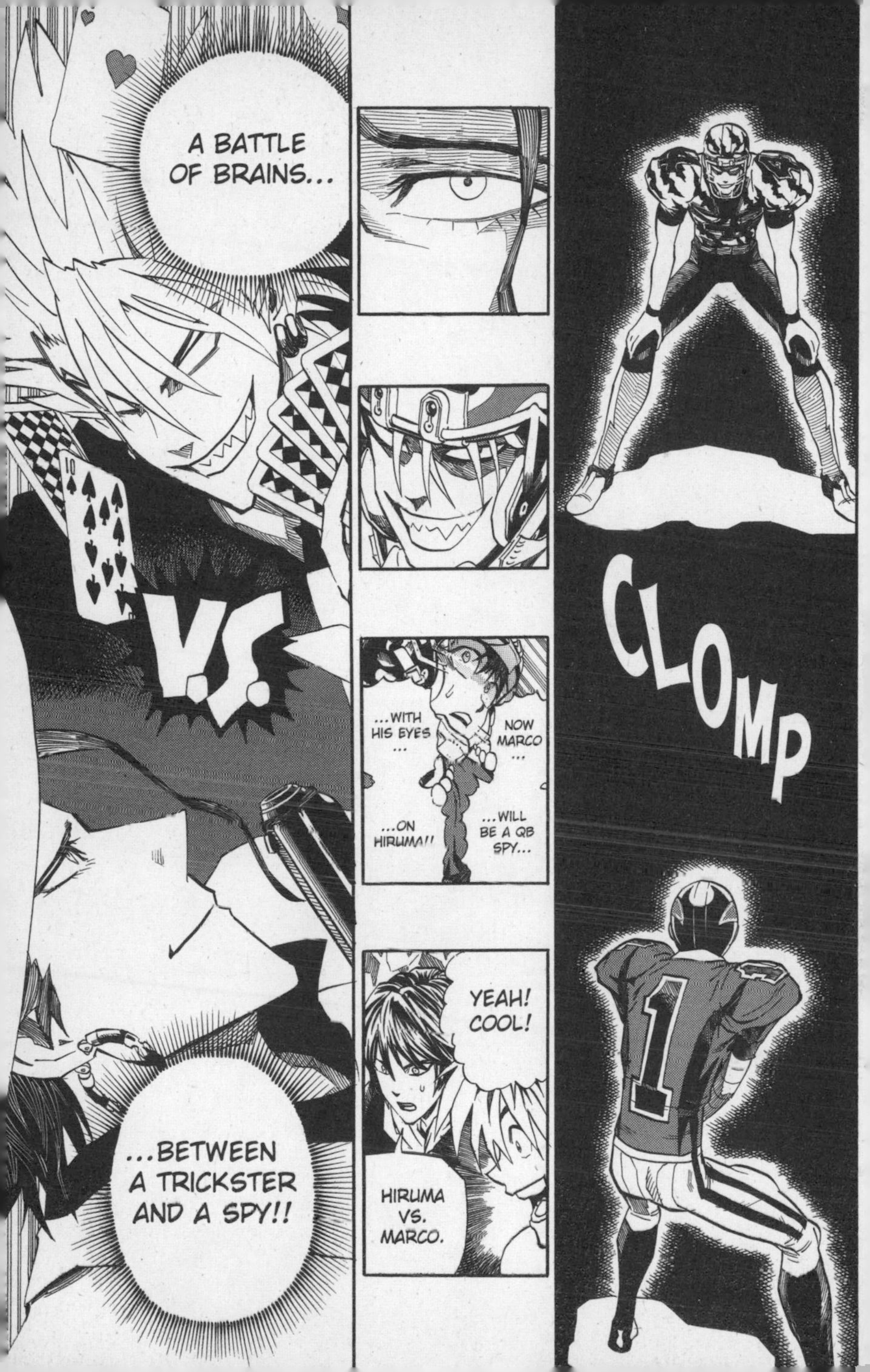
CLOMP
NOW MARCO ...
...WILL BE A QB SPY...
...WITH HIS EYES ...
...ON HIRUMA!!
YEAH! COOL!
HIRUMA VS. MARCO.
A BATTLE OF BRAINS...
V.S.
...BETWEEN A TRICKSTER AND A SPY!!

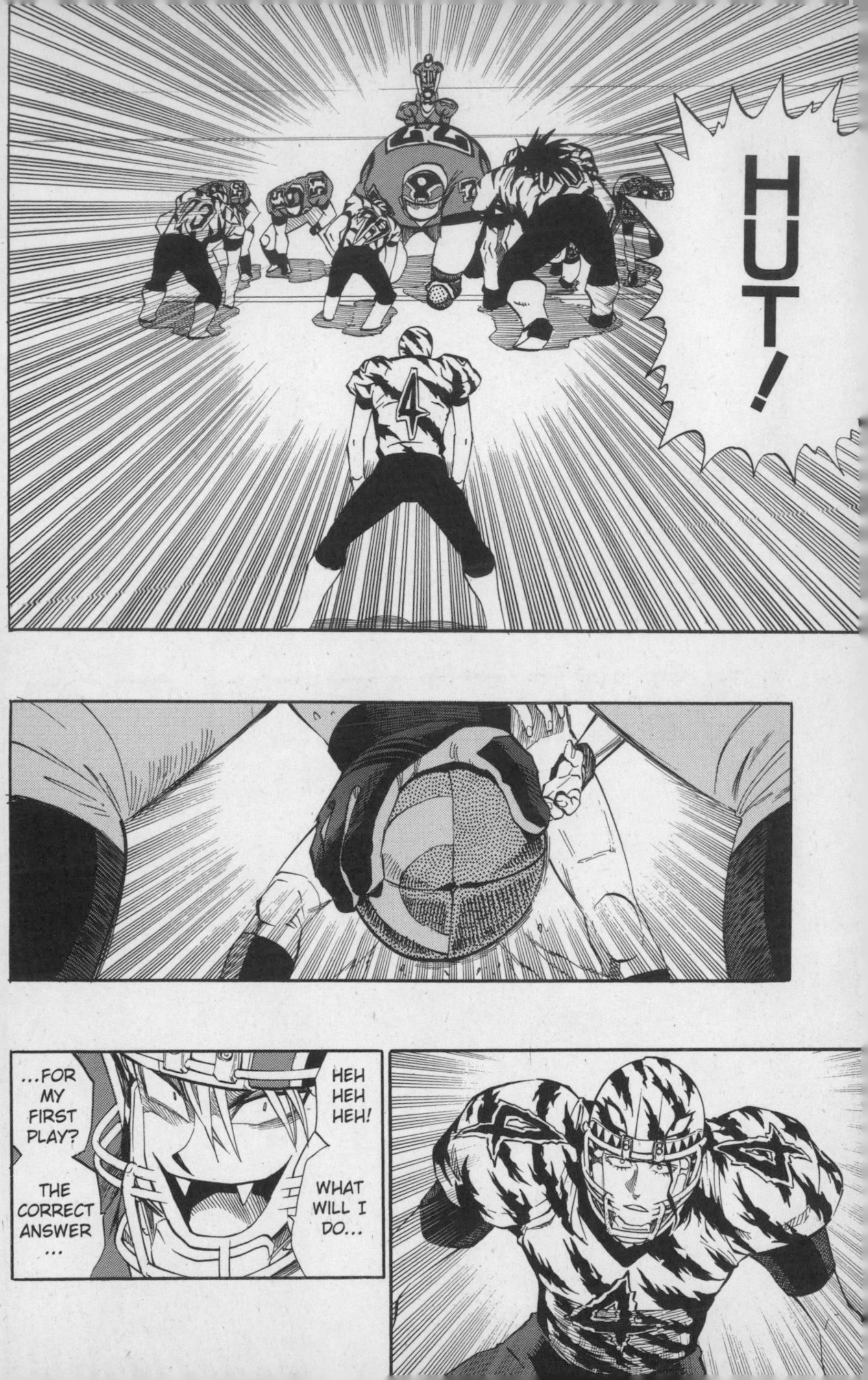
HUT!
HEH HEH HEH!
...FOR MY FIRST PLAY?
WHAT WILL I DO...
THE CORRECT ANSWER ...

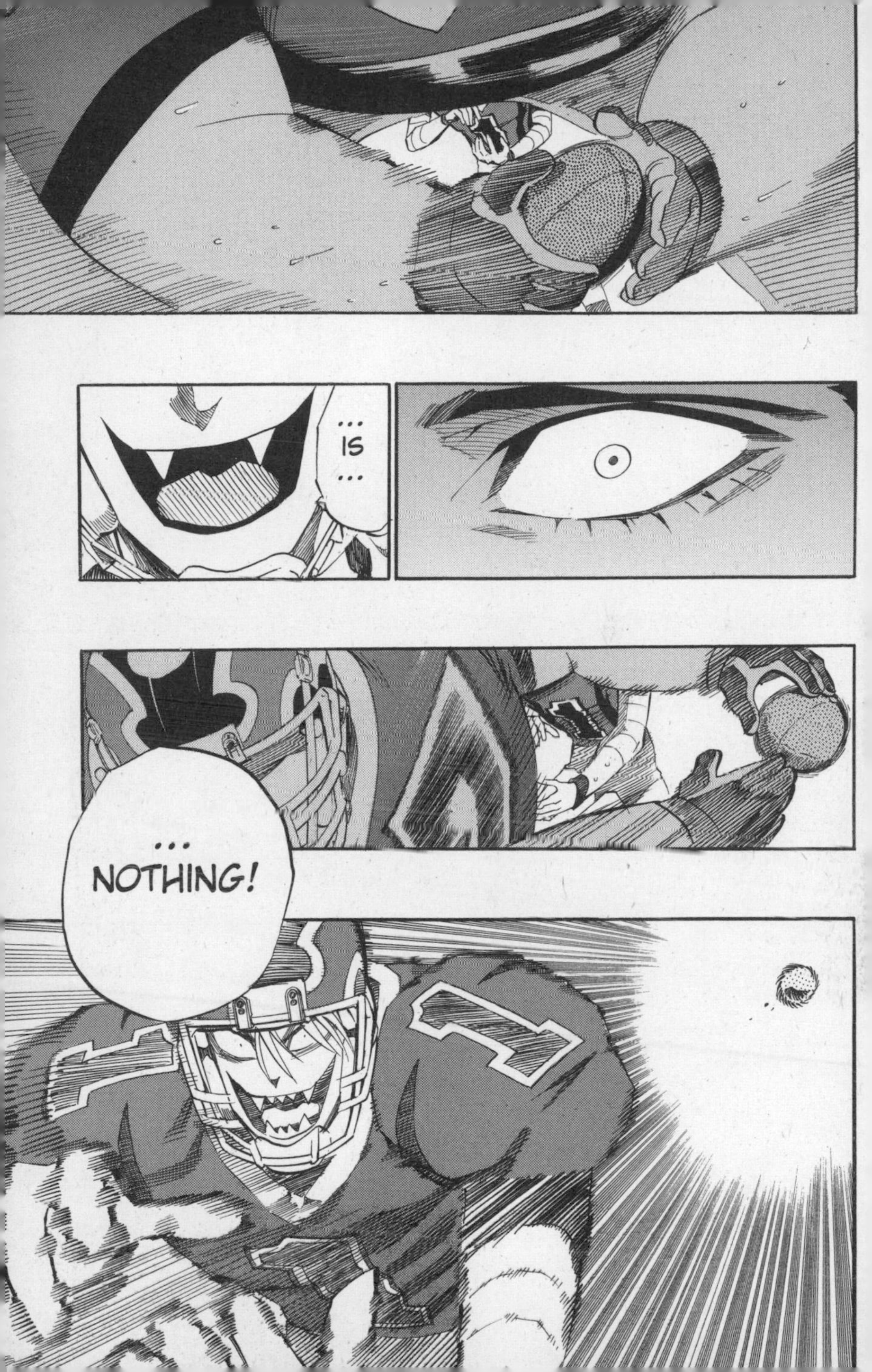
... IS ...
... NOTHING!

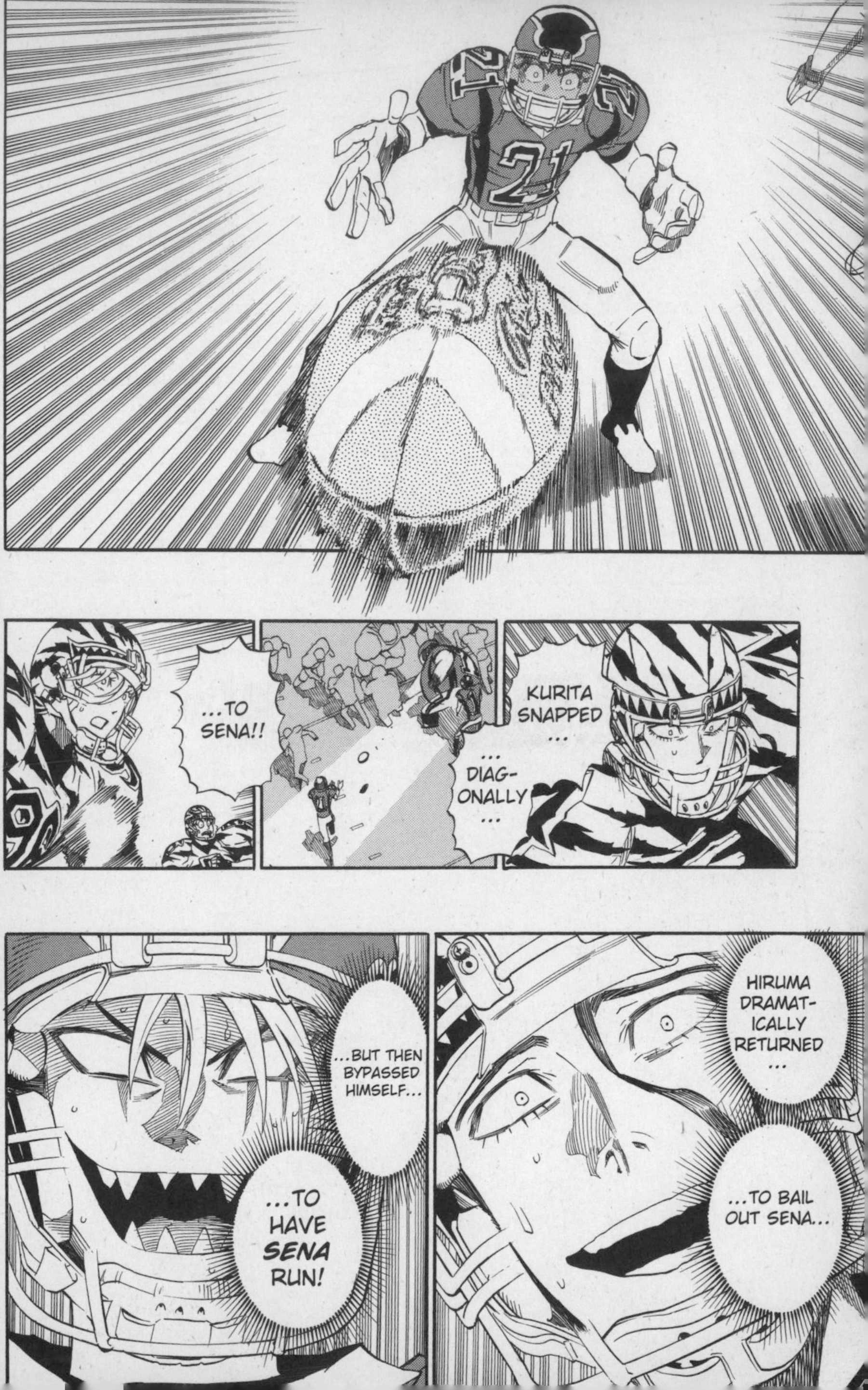
KURITA SNAPPED ...
... DIAGONALLY ...
...TO SENA!!
HIRUMA DRAMATICALLY RETURNED ...
...TO BAIL OUT SENA...
...BUT THEN BYPASSED HIMSELF...
...TO HAVE SENA RUN!

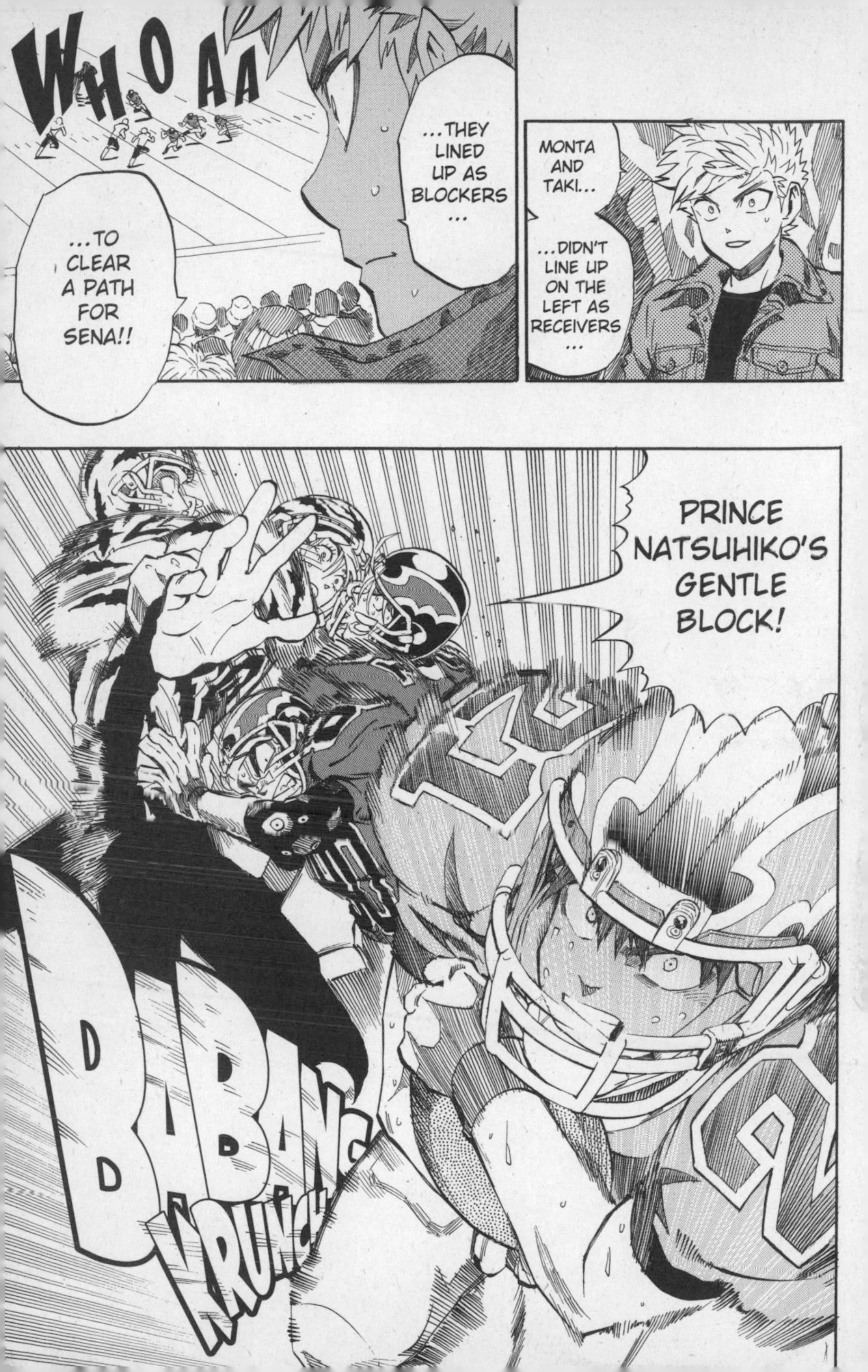
MONTA AND TAKI...
...DIDN'T LINE UP ON THE LEFT AS RECEIVERS...
...THEY LINED UP AS BLOCKERS...
WHOAA
...TO CLEAR A PATH FOR SENA!!
PRINCE NATSUHIKO'S GENTLE BLOCK!
DBDBANG
CRUNCH

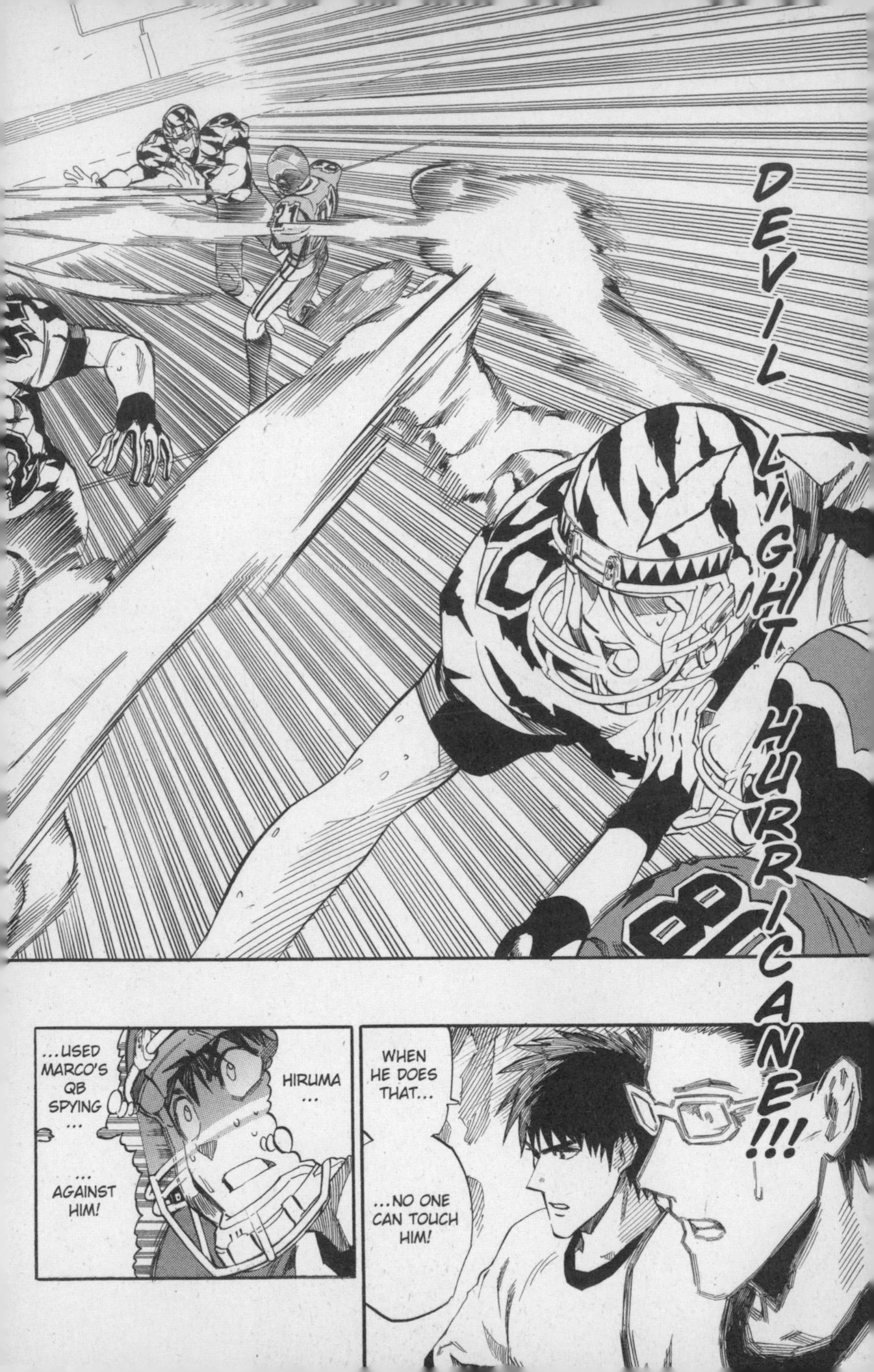
DEVIL LIGHT HURRICANE!!!
WHEN HE DOES THAT...
...NO ONE CAN TOUCH HIM!
HIRUMA ...
...USED MARCO'S QB SPYING ...
... AGAINST HIM!

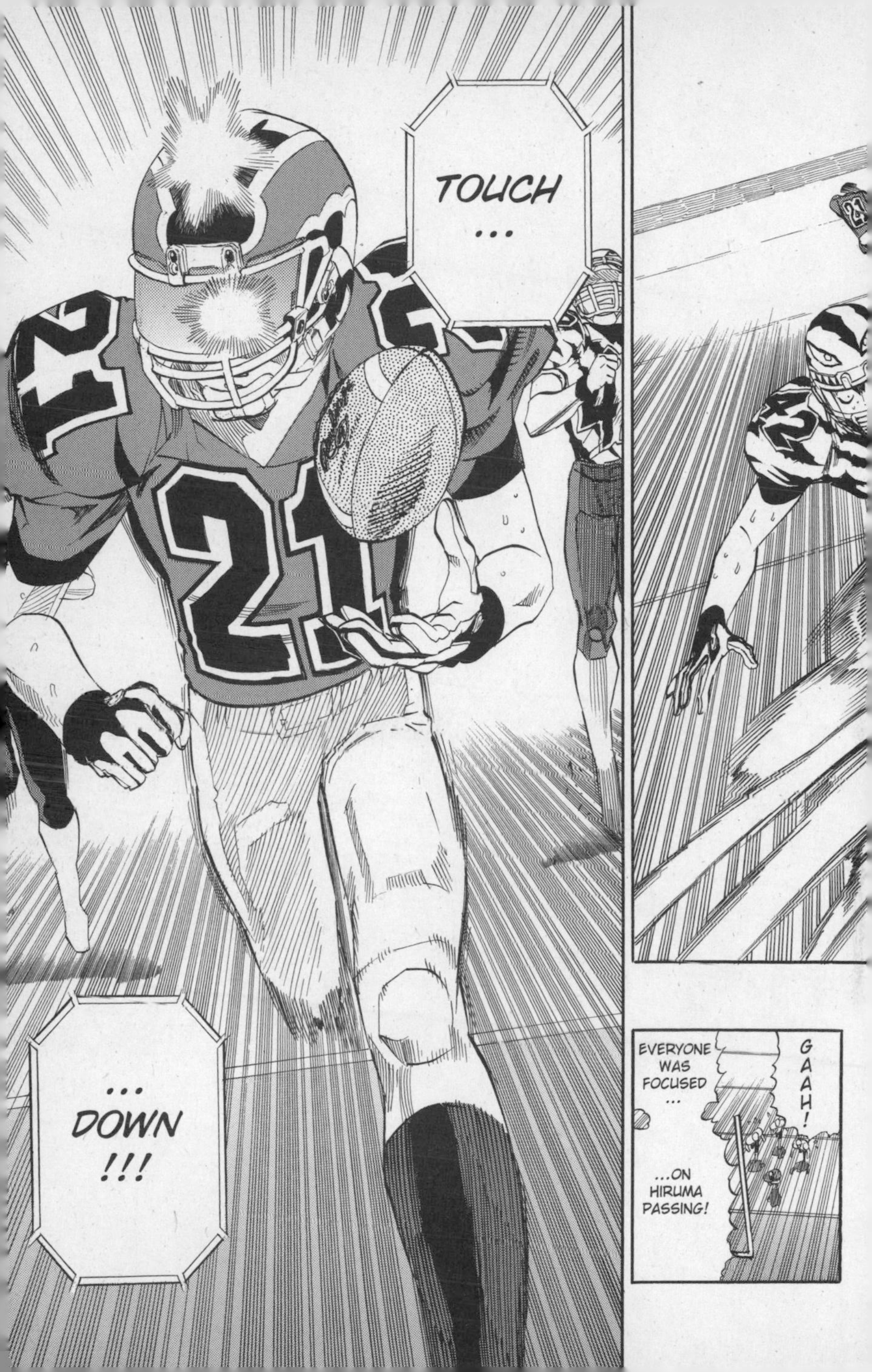
GAAH!
EVERYONE WAS FOCUSED...
...ON HIRUMA PASSING!
TOUCH...
...DOWN!!!

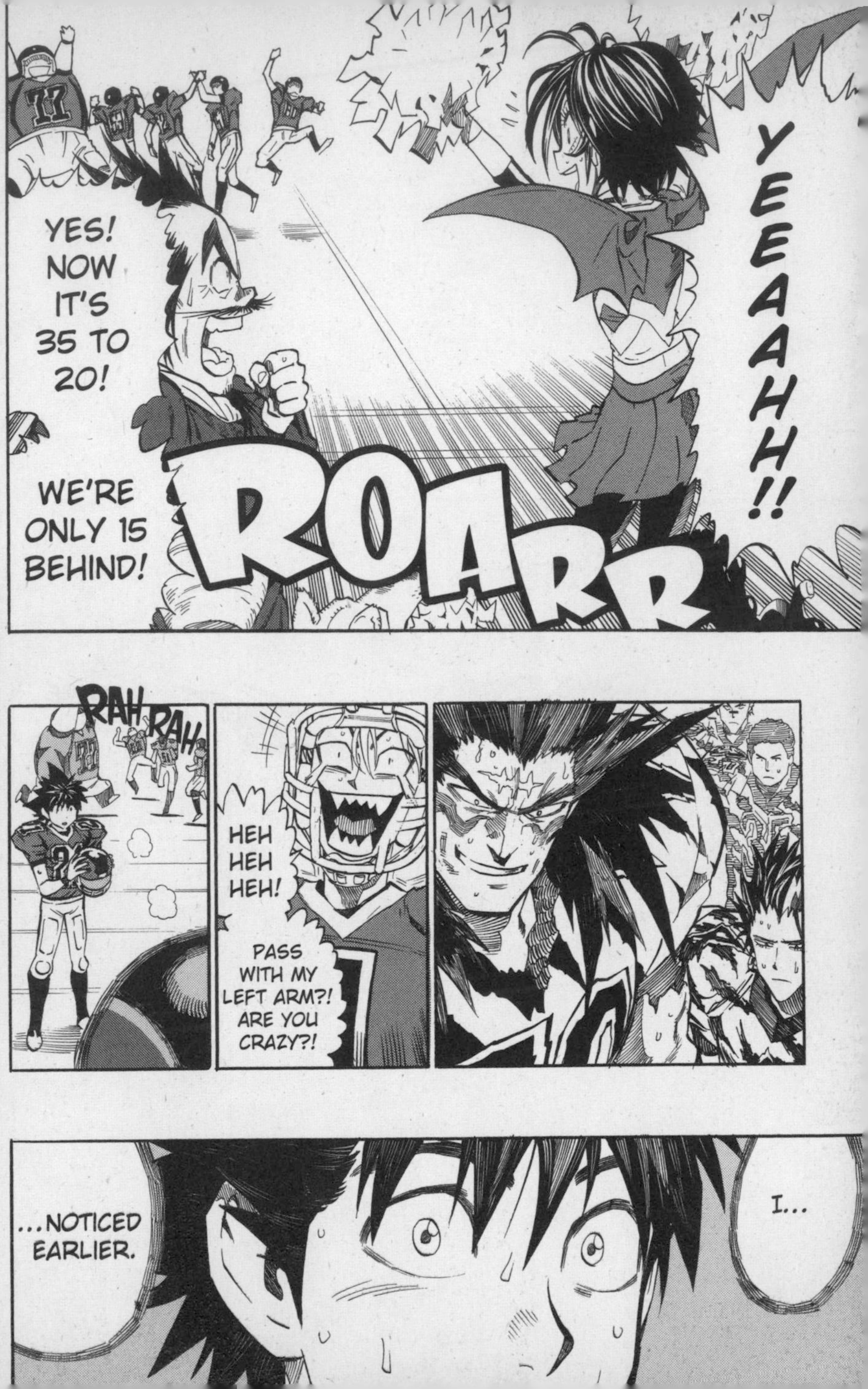
YEEAAHH!!
YES! NOW IT'S 35 TO 20!
ROARR
WE'RE ONLY 15 BEHIND!
HEH HEH HEH!
PASS WITH MY LEFT ARM?! ARE YOU CRAZY?!
RAH RAH
I...
...NOTICED EARLIER.

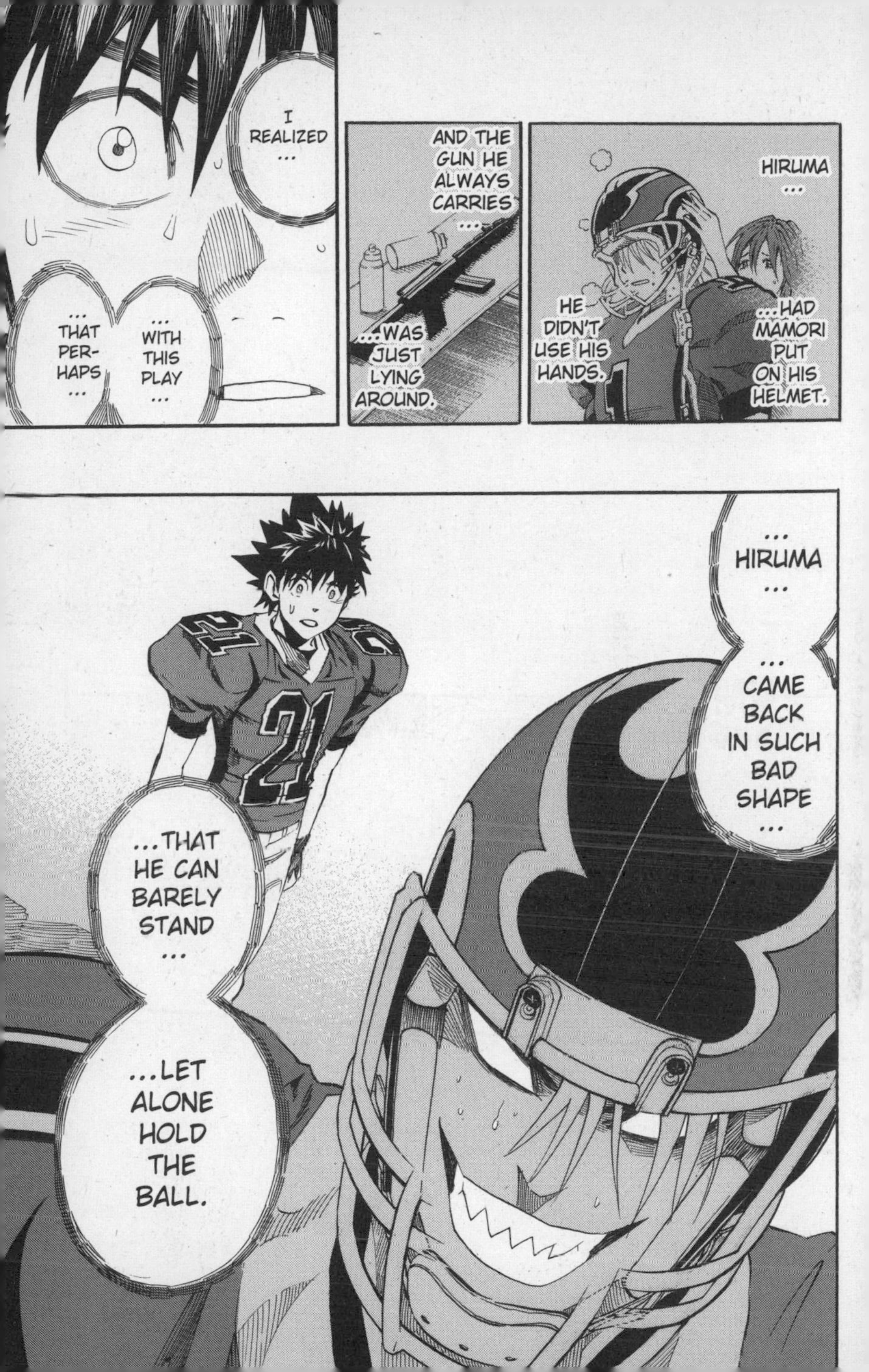
HIRUMA ...
...HAD MAMORI PUT ON HIS HELMET.
HE DIDN'T USE HIS HANDS.
AND THE GUN HE ALWAYS CARRIES ...
...WAS JUST LYING AROUND.
I REALIZED ...
... WITH THIS PLAY ...
... THAT PER-HAPS ...
... HIRUMA ...
... CAME BACK IN SUCH BAD SHAPE ...
...THAT HE CAN BARELY STAND ...
...LET ALONE HOLD THE BALL.

#117

How many kilometers does Shin run each day?

R.T. in Fukui Prefecture, and others

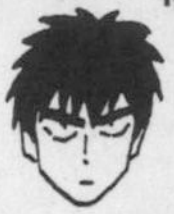

ABOUT 10 KILOMETERS, DEPENDING ON THE DAY'S TRAINING SCHEDULE.

#118

Shin is bad with machines, so he doesn't have a cell phone, right? How do people get in touch with him?

Nana in Nakano Ward

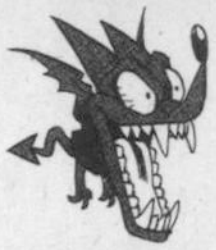

HE SHOWS UP FOR PRACTICE EVERY DAY NO MORE THAN FIVE MINUTES LATE, SO YOU CAN TALK TO HIM THEN!

#119

Shin's good at cooking, but no good with machines. How does he use a gas stove?

H.W. in Ehime Prefecture

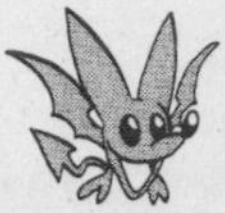

A GAS STOVE ISN'T REALLY A MACHINE, SO HE JUST BARELY MANAGES!

#120

Who would win in a fight between Gao and Agon?

Ucchii GEANA in Tokyo Prefecture

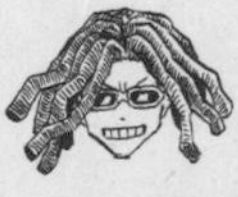

HEH HEH HEH! NO ONE'S STUPID ENOUGH TO ATTACK SUCH STUPID STRENGTH HEAD ON. I'D CATCH HIM BY SURPRISE!

#121

Musashi's 60-yard Magnum is just a bluff, but how far can he really kick?

Mr. D in Chiba Prefecture

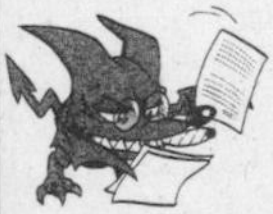

ACCORDING TO OFFICIAL RECORDS, 50 YARDS IN THE BANDO GAME.

IN PRACTICES, HE'S PUT IT IN FROM 55 YARDS!

#122

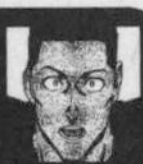

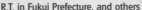

In Volume 10, Jimmy Simard, who looks like Ishimaru, took the pro test. How did that turn out? I'm a little worried because he's so plain.

T.Y. in Shizuoka Prefecture

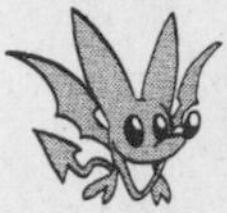

UNFORTUNATELY, HE FAILED THE SECOND TEST. BUT HE HASN'T GIVEN UP YET!

#123

I once accidentally wrote "Kakei" when I meant to write "khaki."

Hina Takase in Osaka Prefecture

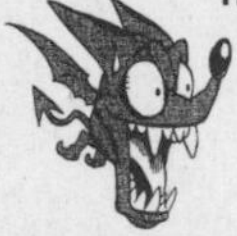

I CAN'T HELP YA, BUB.

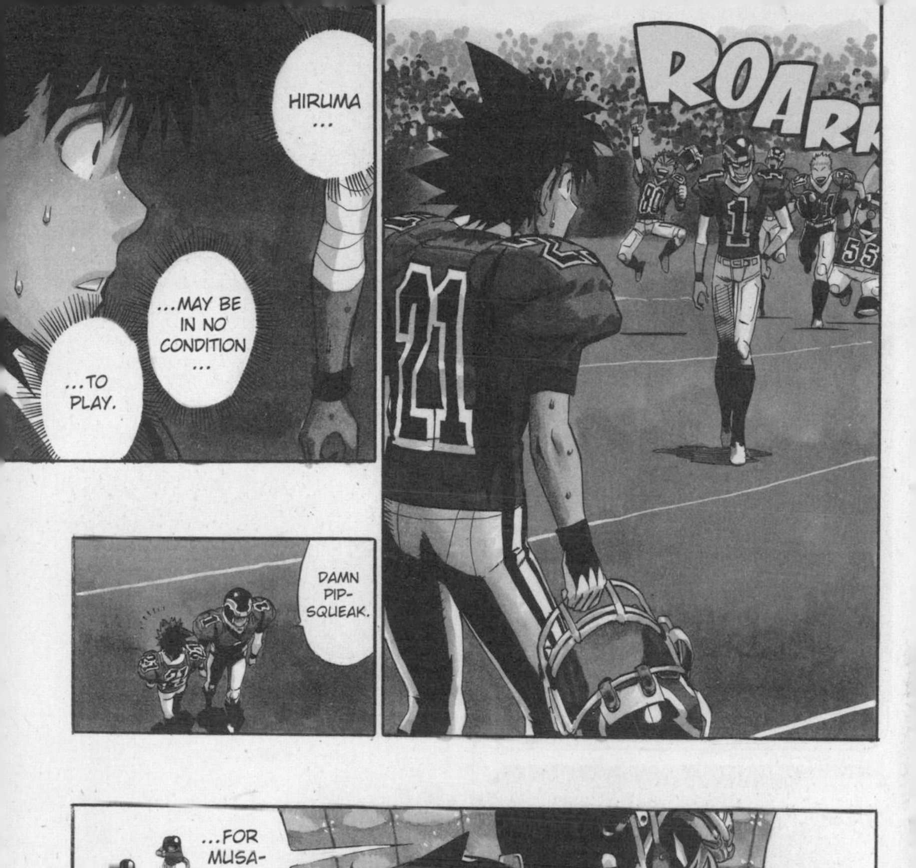
ROARK
HIRUMA ...
...MAY BE IN NO CONDITION ...
...TO PLAY.
DAMN PIP-SQUEAK.
HOLD THE BALL
...FOR MUSASHI'S NEXT KICK.

Chapter 265 Stone Gargoyle

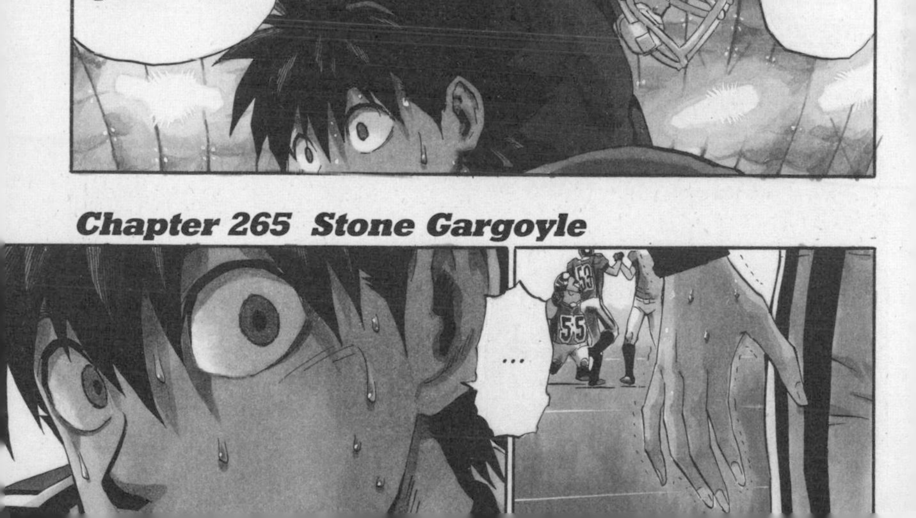
...

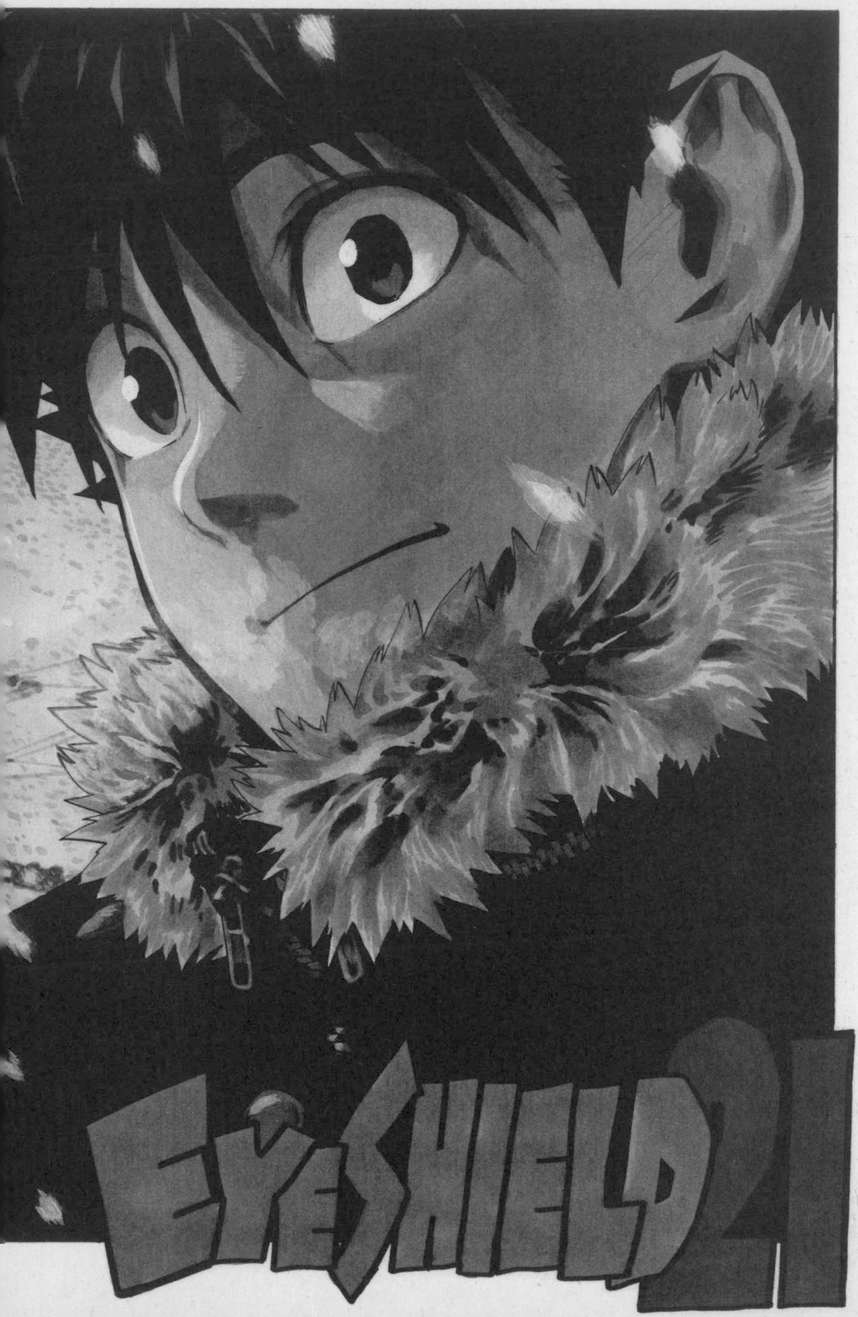
EYESHIELD 21

Chapter 265 Stone Gargoyle

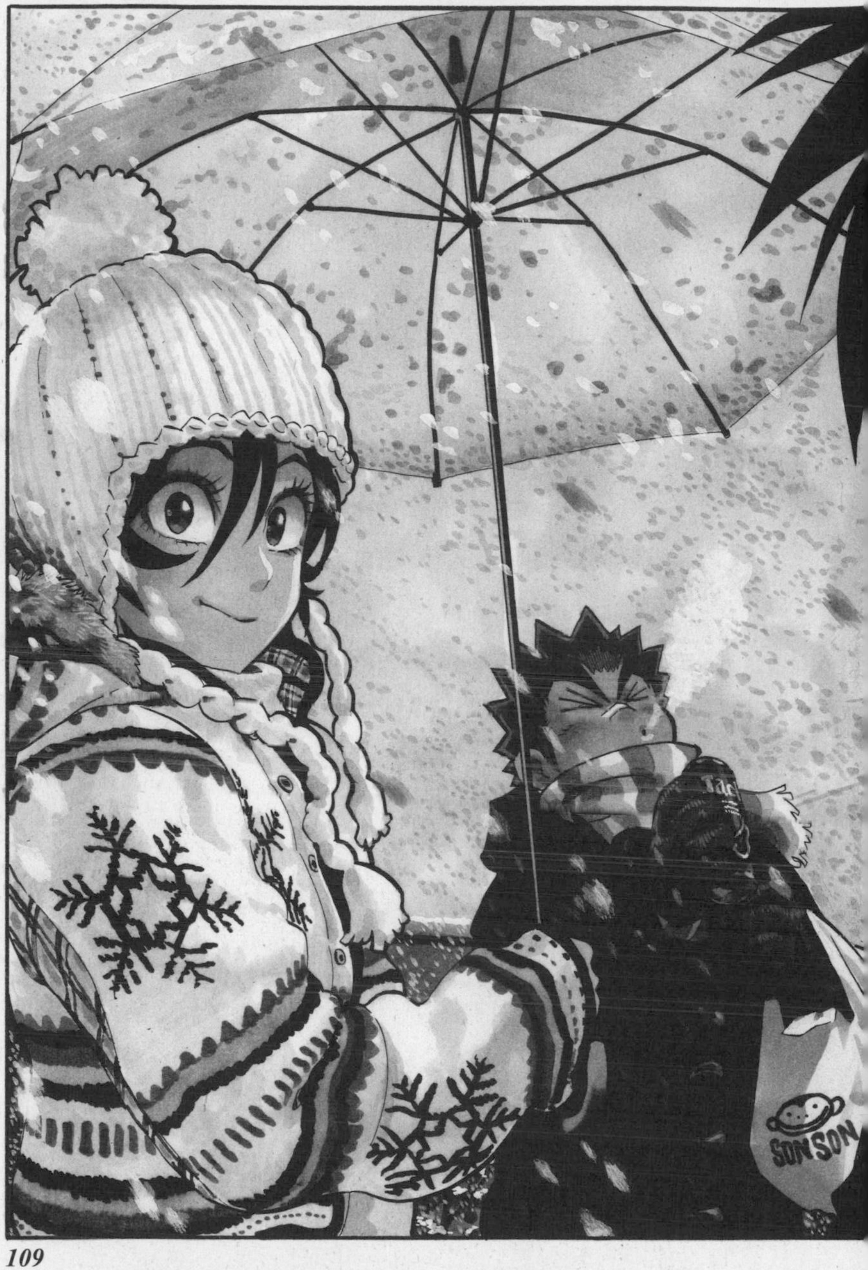
SONSON

Investigation File #124

I've heard that quarterbacks are popular with women. Is that true for Deimon's quarterback and the others?

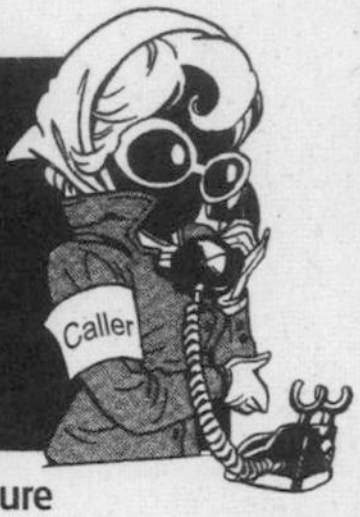
Caller

Akigon in Oita Prefecture

QB Popularity with Women Graph

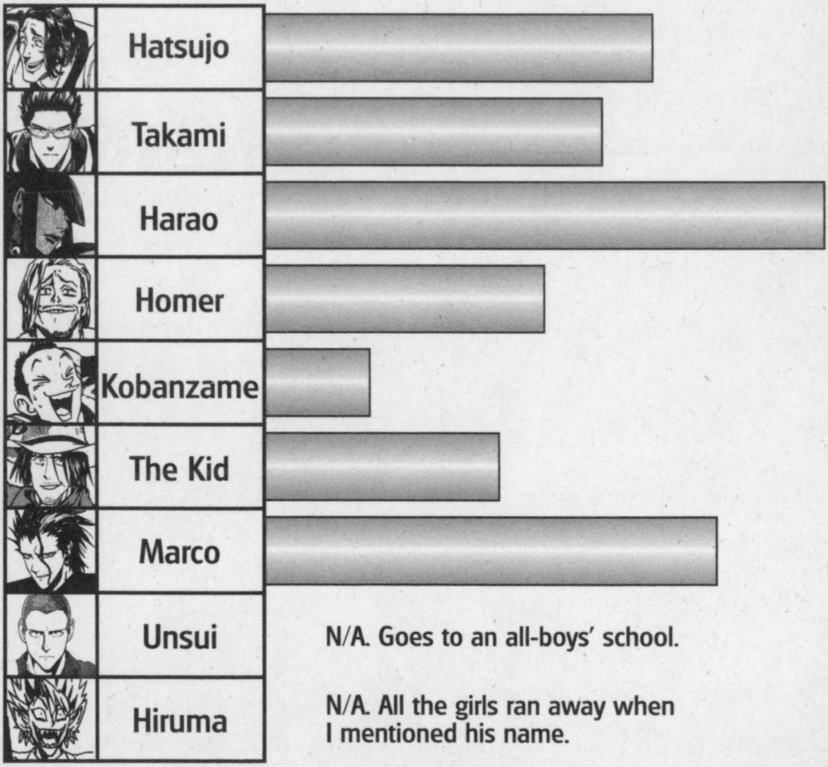
Hatsujo
Takami
Harao
Homer
Kobanzame
The Kid
Marco
Unsui
N/A. Goes to an all-boys' school.
Hiruma
N/A. All the girls ran away when I mentioned his name.

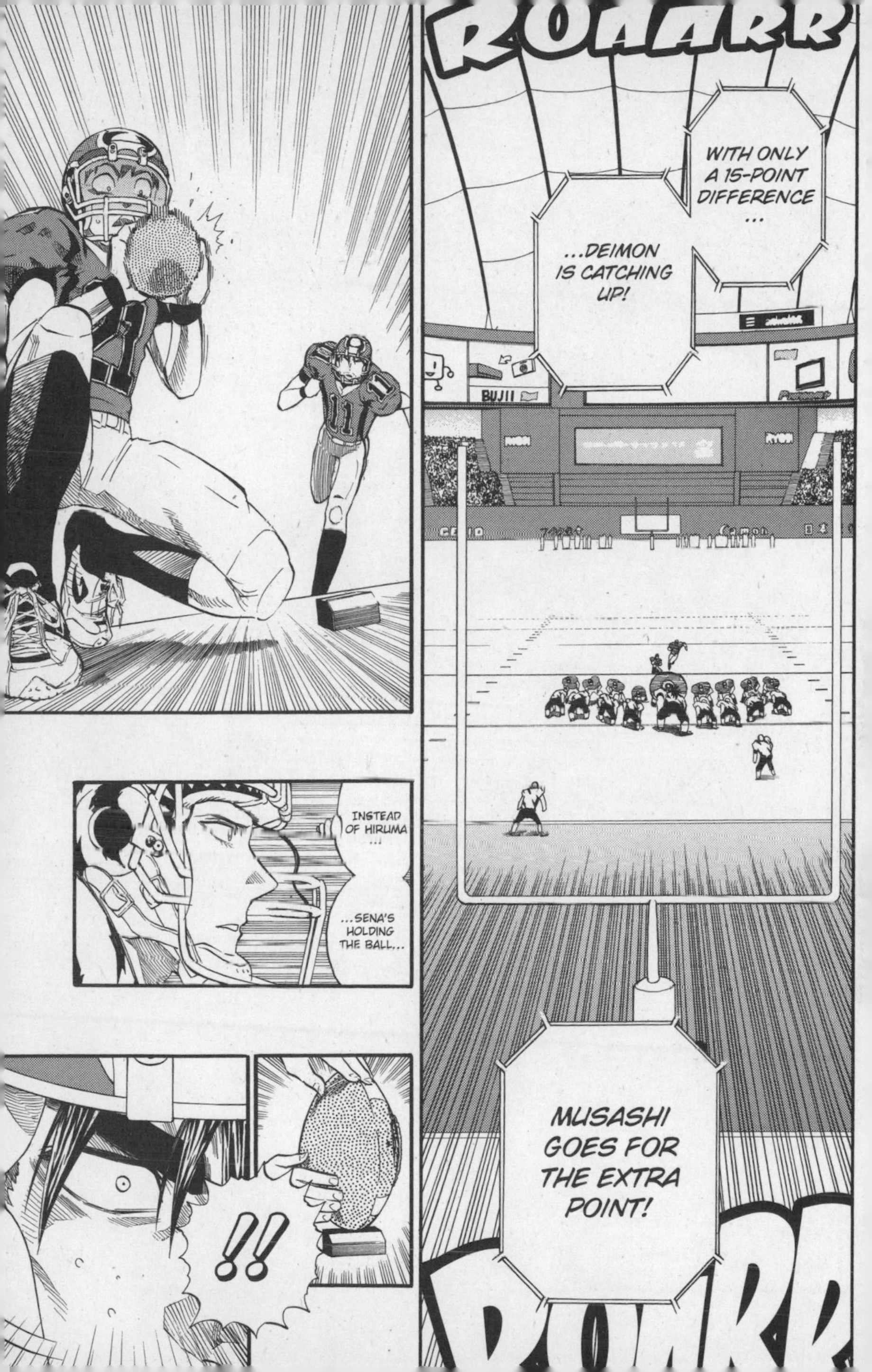
ROAARR
WITH ONLY A 15-POINT DIFFERENCE ...
...DEIMON IS CATCHING UP!
MUSASHI GOES FOR THE EXTRA POINT!
INSTEAD OF HIRUMA ...
...SENA'S HOLDING THE BALL...
!!

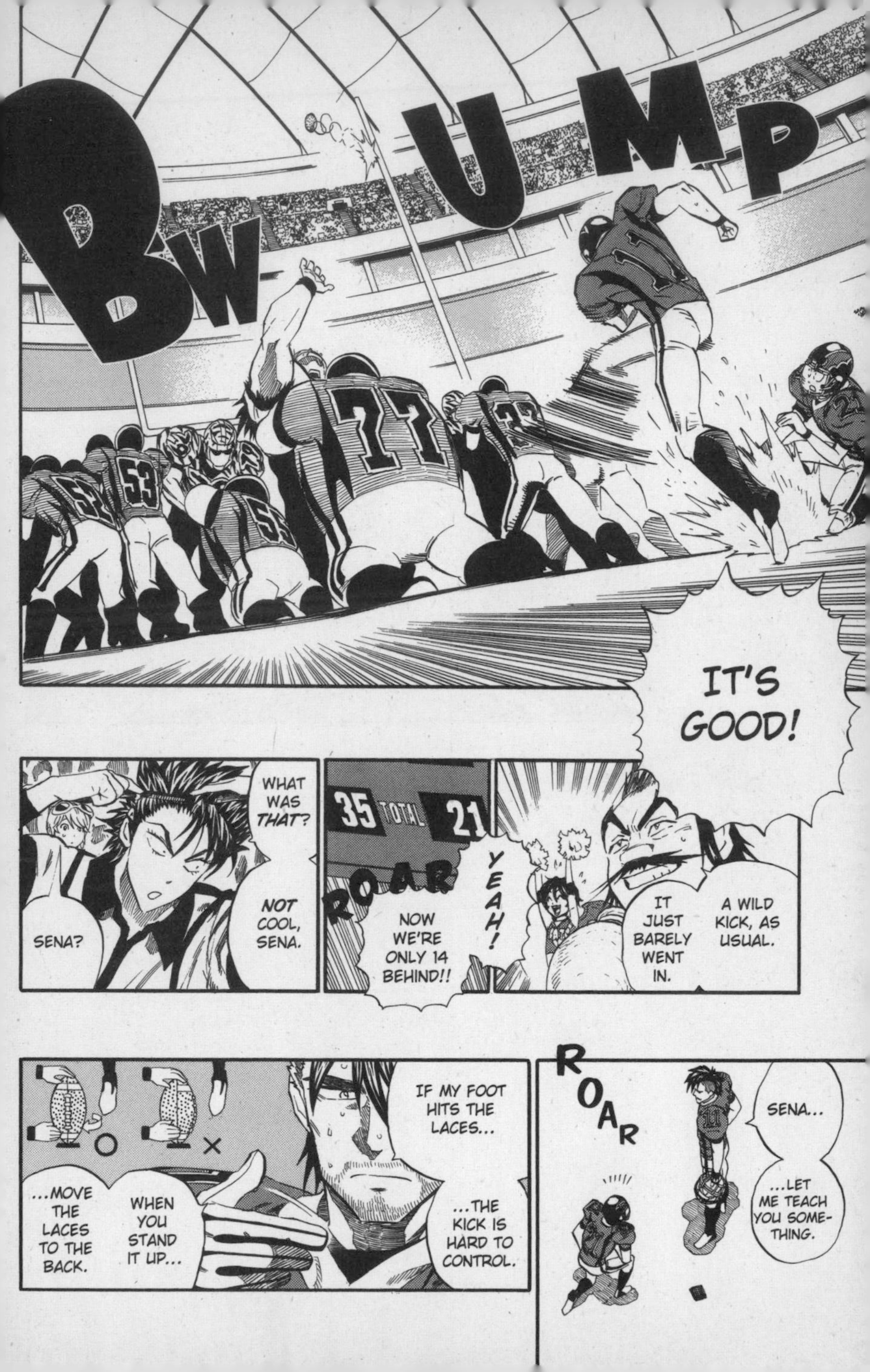
BWUMP
IT'S GOOD!
A WILD KICK, AS USUAL.
IT JUST BARELY WENT IN.
35 TOTAL 21
YEAH!
ROAR
NOW WE'RE ONLY 14 BEHIND!!
WHAT WAS *THAT*?
NOT COOL, SENA.
SENA?
ROAR
SENA...
...LET ME TEACH YOU SOME-THING.
IF MY FOOT HITS THE LACES...
...THE KICK IS HARD TO CONTROL.
WHEN YOU STAND IT UP...
...MOVE THE LACES TO THE BACK.

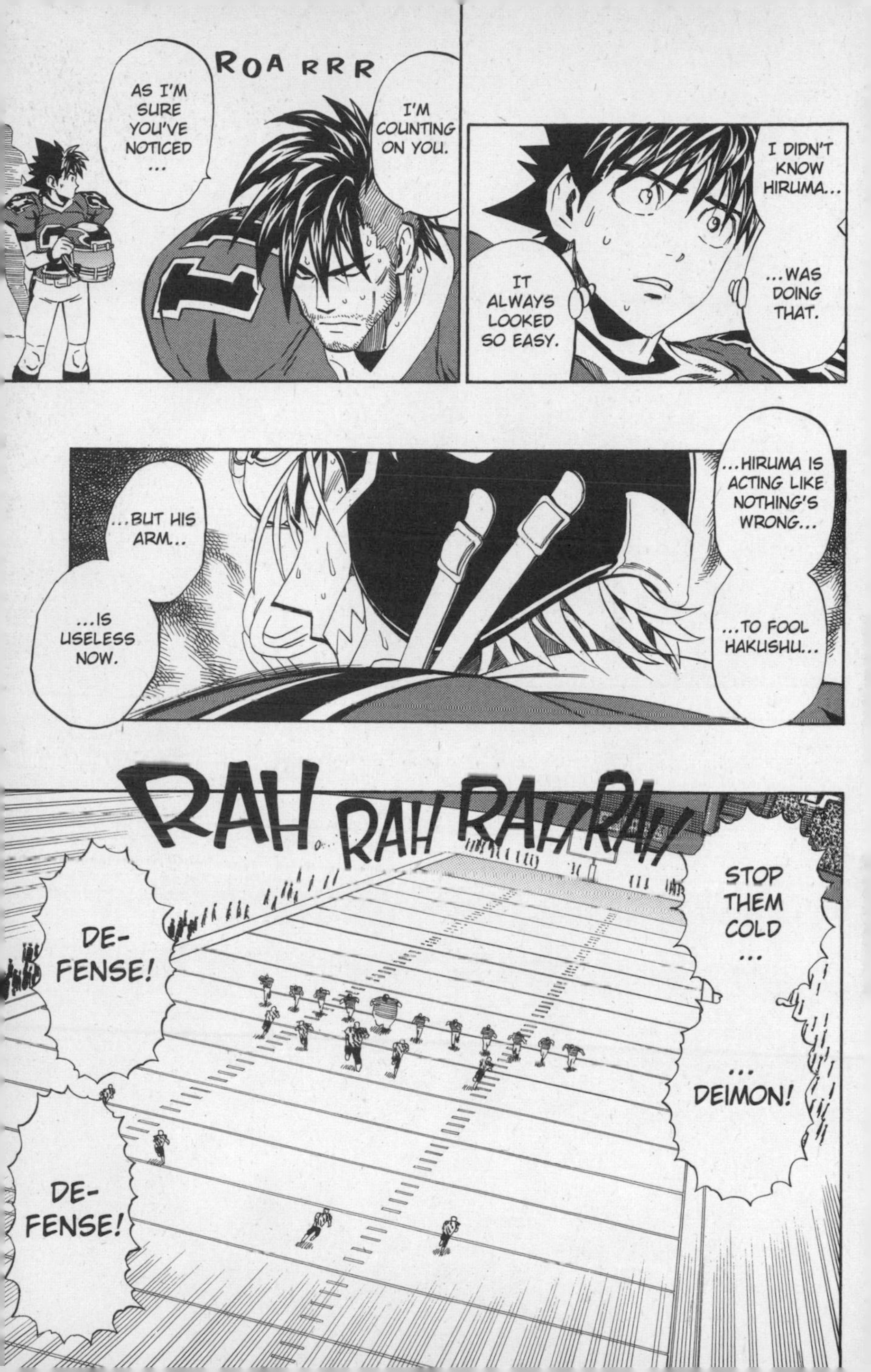
I DIDN'T KNOW HIRUMA...
...WAS DOING THAT.
IT ALWAYS LOOKED SO EASY.
I'M COUNTING ON YOU.
ROA RRR
AS I'M SURE YOU'VE NOTICED...
...HIRUMA IS ACTING LIKE NOTHING'S WRONG...
...TO FOOL HAKUSHU...
...BUT HIS ARM...
...IS USELESS NOW.
RAH RAH RAH RAH
STOP THEM COLD...
...DEIMON!
DE-FENSE!
DE-FENSE!

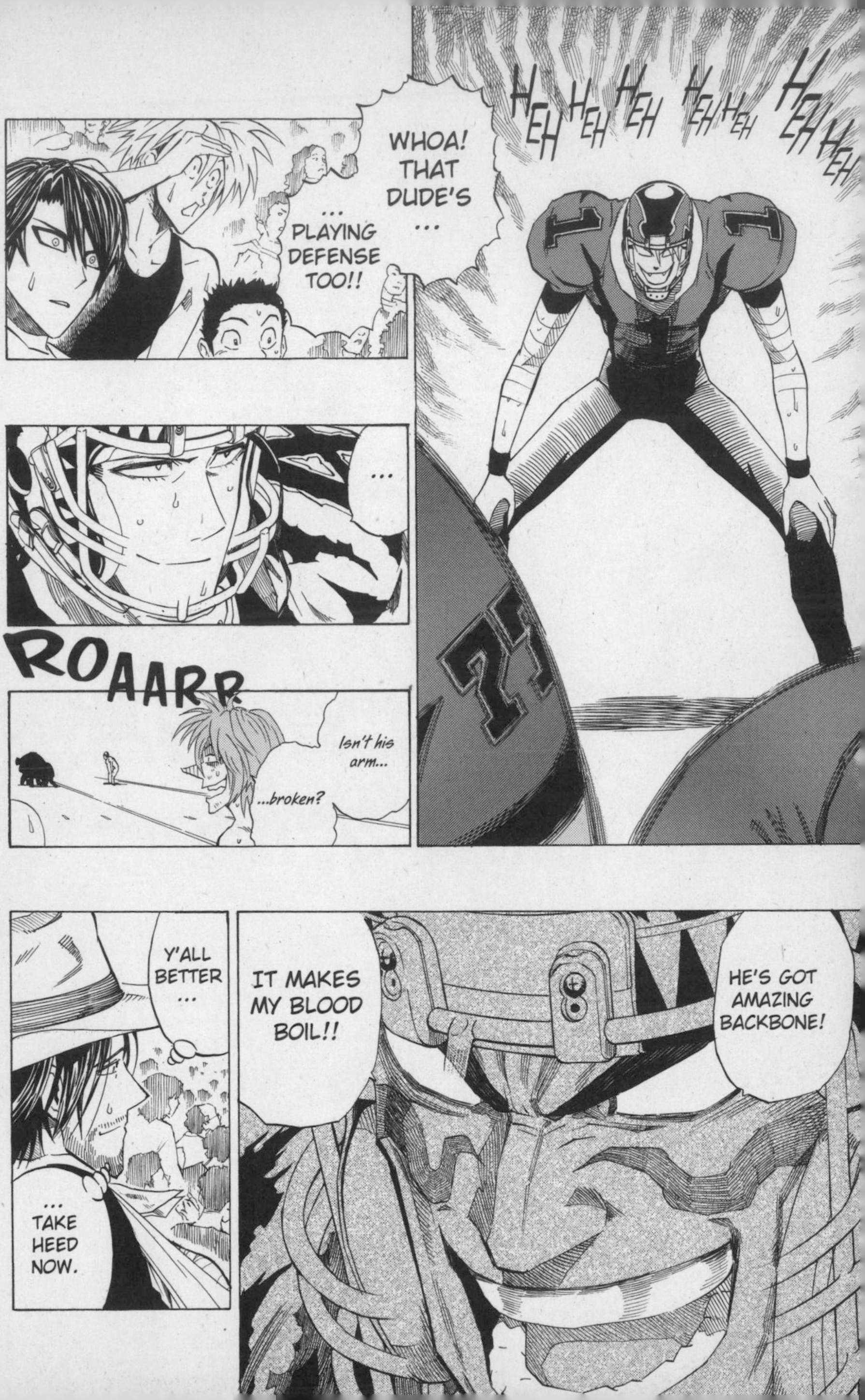
HEH HEH HEH HEH HEH HEH HEH
WHOA! THAT DUDE'S ...
... PLAYING DEFENSE TOO!!
...
ROAARR
Isn't his arm...
...broken?
HE'S GOT AMAZING BACKBONE!
IT MAKES MY BLOOD BOIL!!
Y'ALL BETTER ...
... TAKE HEED NOW.

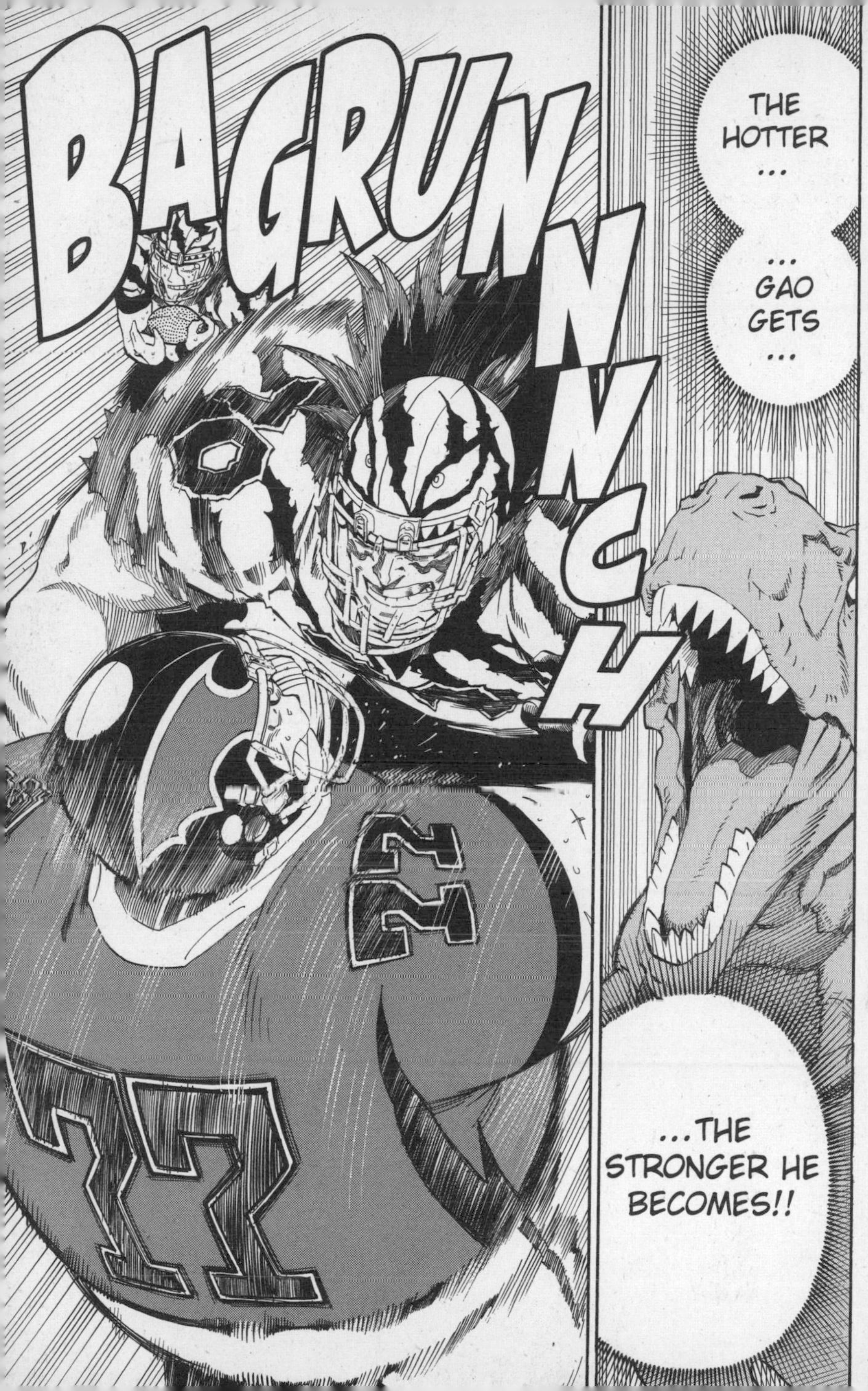
THE HOTTER ...
... GAO GETS ...
...THE STRONGER HE BECOMES!!
BAGRUNNNNCH

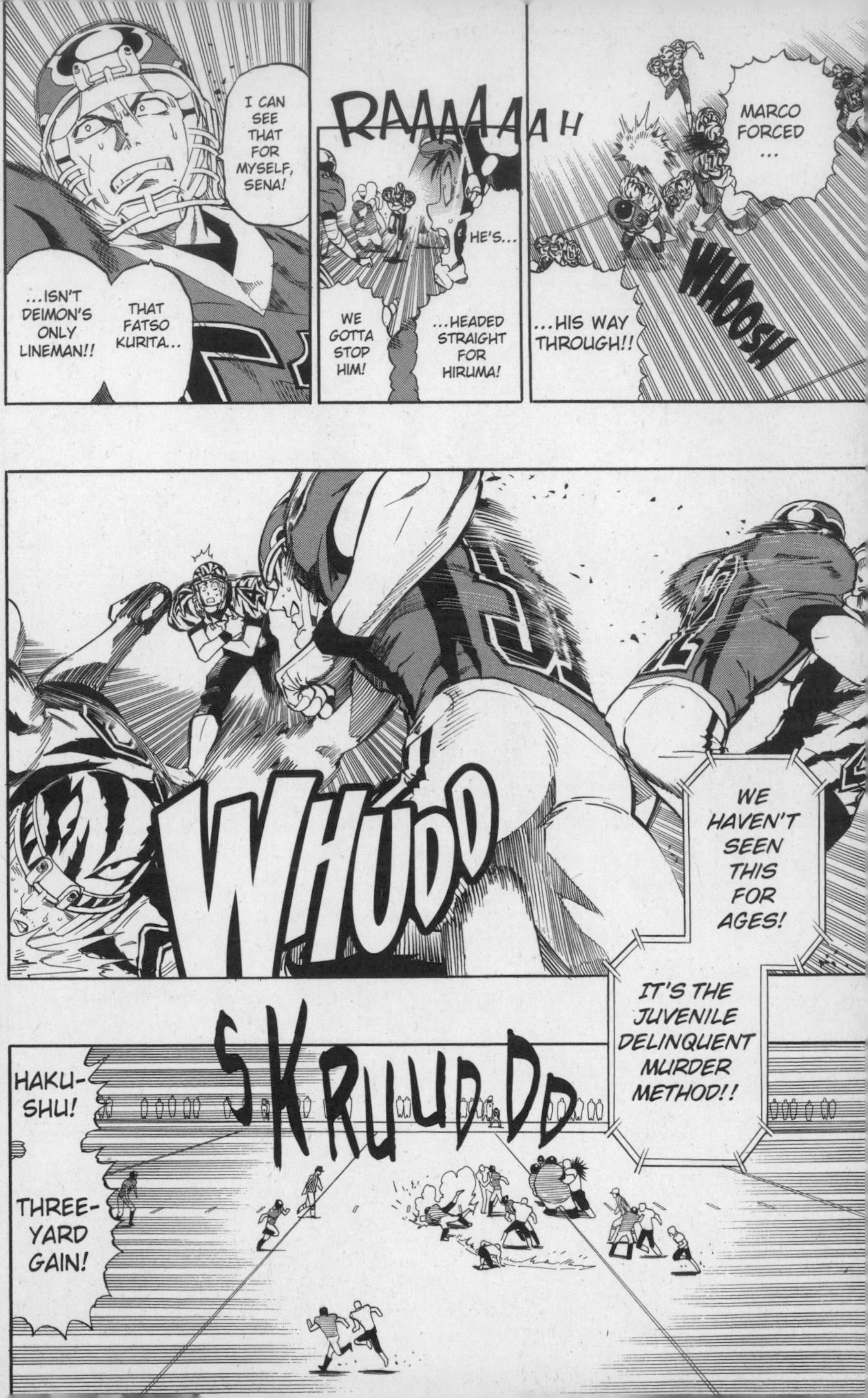
MARCO FORCED ...
...HIS WAY THROUGH!!
WHOOSH
RAAAAAAH
HE'S...
...HEADED STRAIGHT FOR HIRUMA!
WE GOTTA STOP HIM!
I CAN SEE THAT FOR MYSELF, SENA!
THAT FATSO KURITA...
...ISN'T DEIMON'S ONLY LINEMAN!!
WE HAVEN'T SEEN THIS FOR AGES!
WHUDD
IT'S THE JUVENILE DELINQUENT MURDER METHOD!!
SKRUUDDD
HAKU-SHU!
THREE-YARD GAIN!

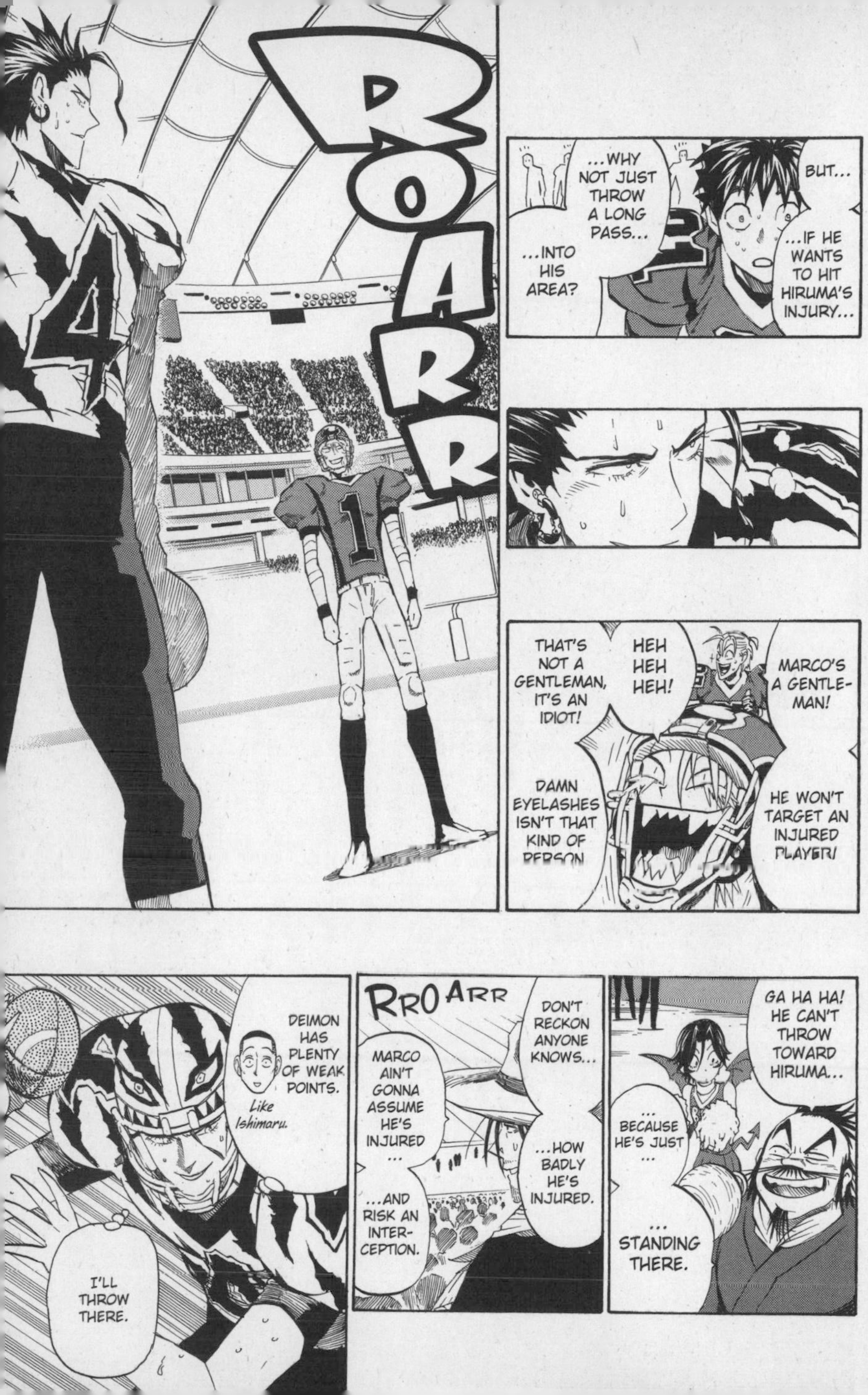
BUT...
...IF HE WANTS TO HIT HIRUMA'S INJURY...
...WHY NOT JUST THROW A LONG PASS...
...INTO HIS AREA?
MARCO'S A GENTLEMAN!
HE WON'T TARGET AN INJURED PLAYER!
HEH HEH HEH!
THAT'S NOT A GENTLEMAN, IT'S AN IDIOT!
DAMN EYELASHES ISN'T THAT KIND OF PERSON
ROARR
GA HA HA! HE CAN'T THROW TOWARD HIRUMA...
...BECAUSE HE'S JUST...
...STANDING THERE.
DON'T RECKON ANYONE KNOWS...
...HOW BADLY HE'S INJURED.
MARCO AIN'T GONNA ASSUME HE'S INJURED...
...AND RISK AN INTERCEPTION.
RROARR
DEIMON HAS PLENTY OF WEAK POINTS.
Like Ishimaru.
I'LL THROW THERE.

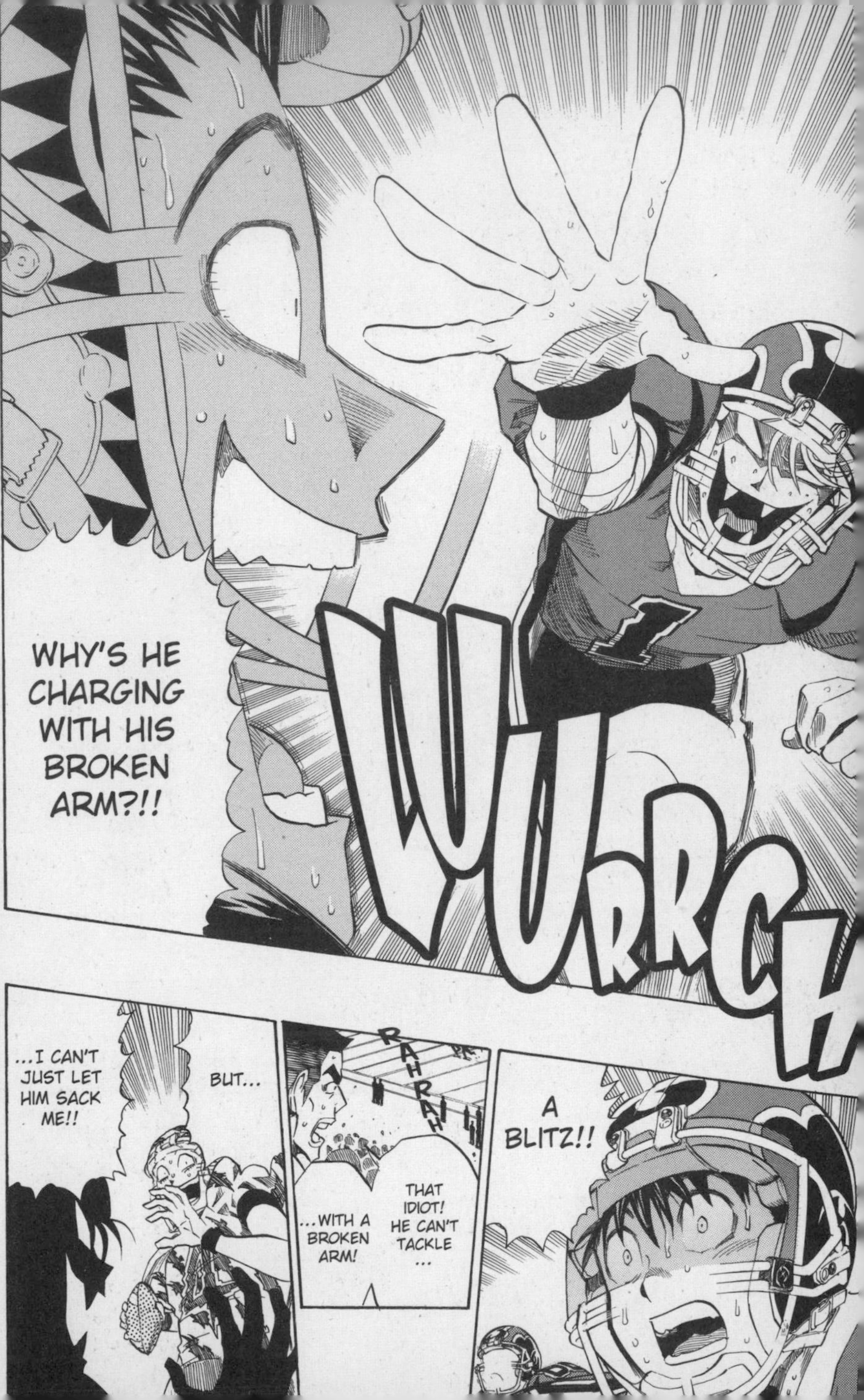
WHY'S HE CHARGING WITH HIS BROKEN ARM?!!
WURRCH
A BLITZ!!
RAHRAH
THAT IDIOT! HE CAN'T TACKLE ...
...WITH A BROKEN ARM!
BUT...
...I CAN'T JUST LET HIM SACK ME!!

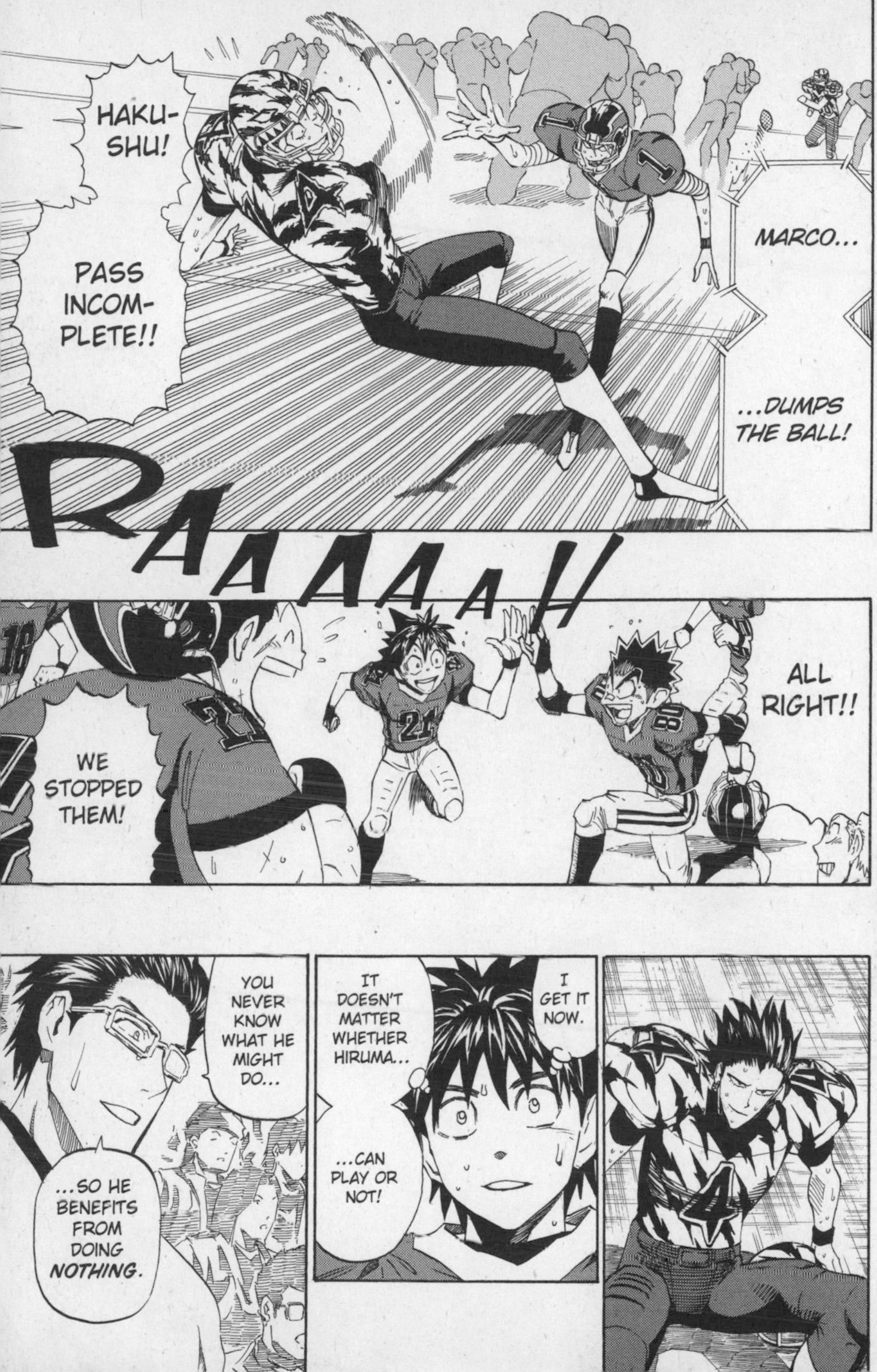
MARCO...
...DUMPS THE BALL!
HAKU-SHU!
PASS INCOMPLETE!!
RAAAAAH
ALL RIGHT!!
WE STOPPED THEM!
I GET IT NOW.
IT DOESN'T MATTER WHETHER HIRUMA...
...CAN PLAY OR NOT!
YOU NEVER KNOW WHAT HE MIGHT DO...
...SO HE BENEFITS FROM DOING *NOTHING*.

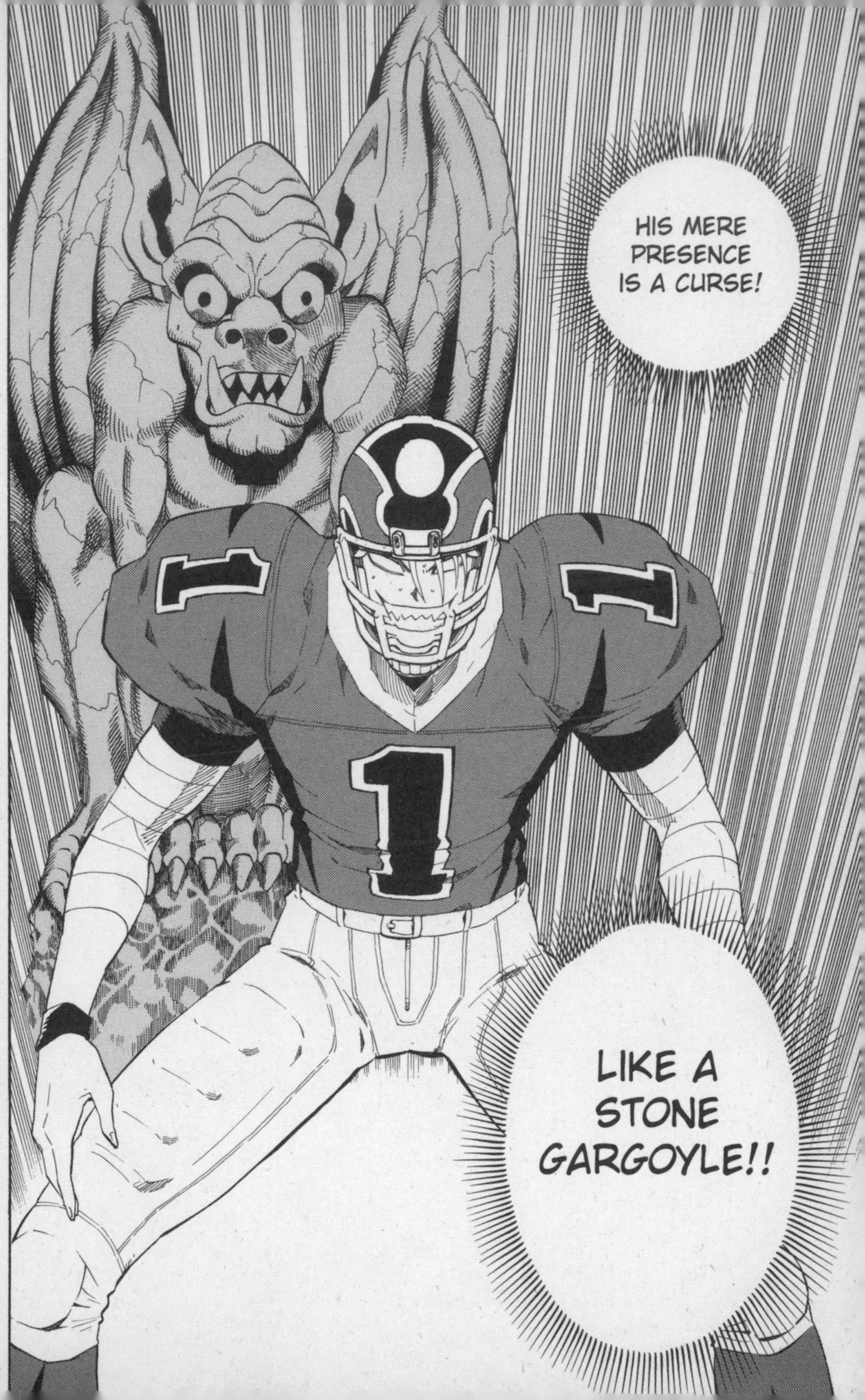
HIS MERE PRESENCE IS A CURSE!
LIKE A STONE GARGOYLE!!

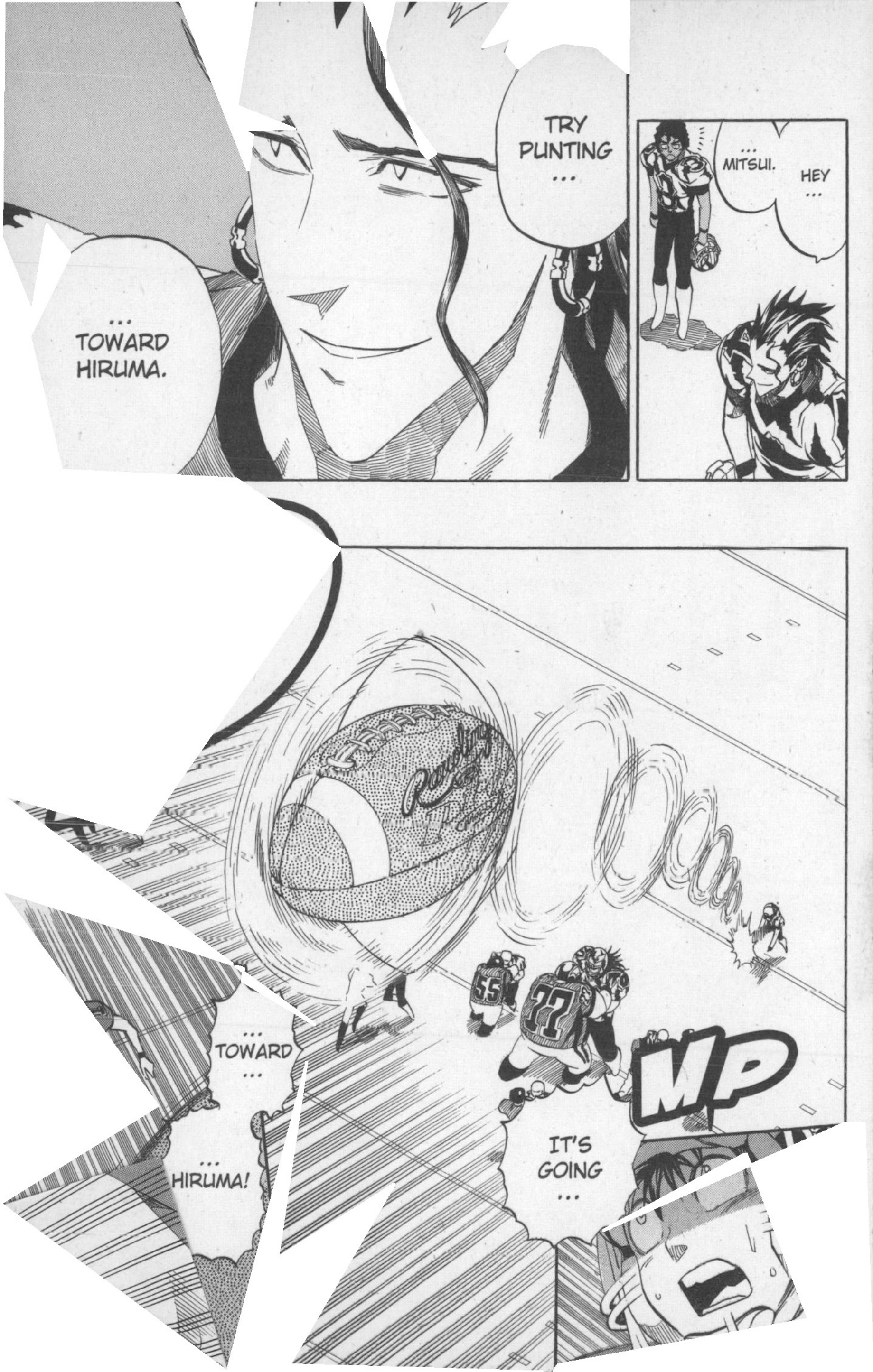
HEY ...
... MITSUI.
TRY PUNTING ...
... TOWARD HIRUMA.
MP
IT'S GOING ...
... TOWARD ...
... HIRUMA!

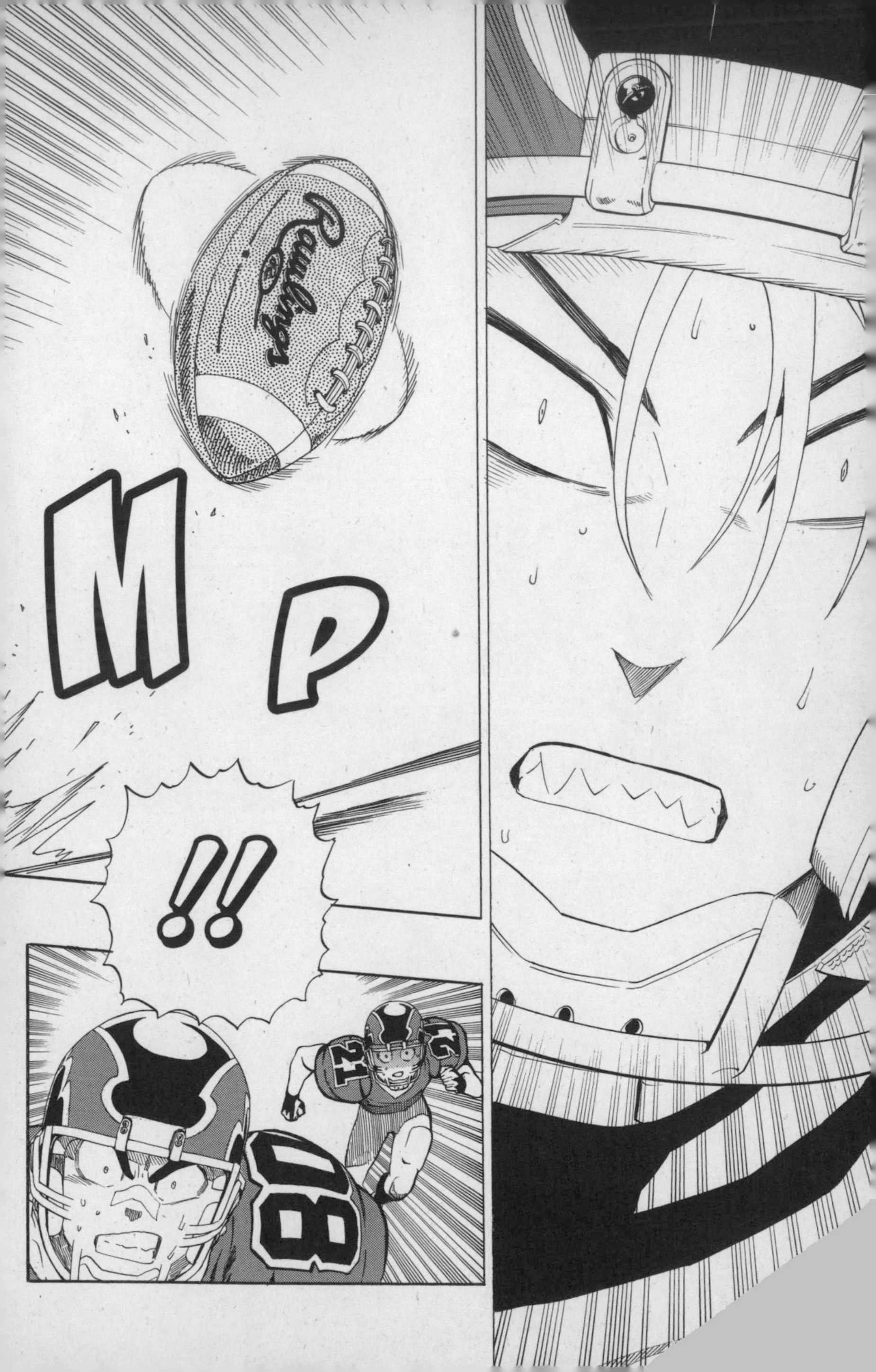
Rawlings
MP
!!

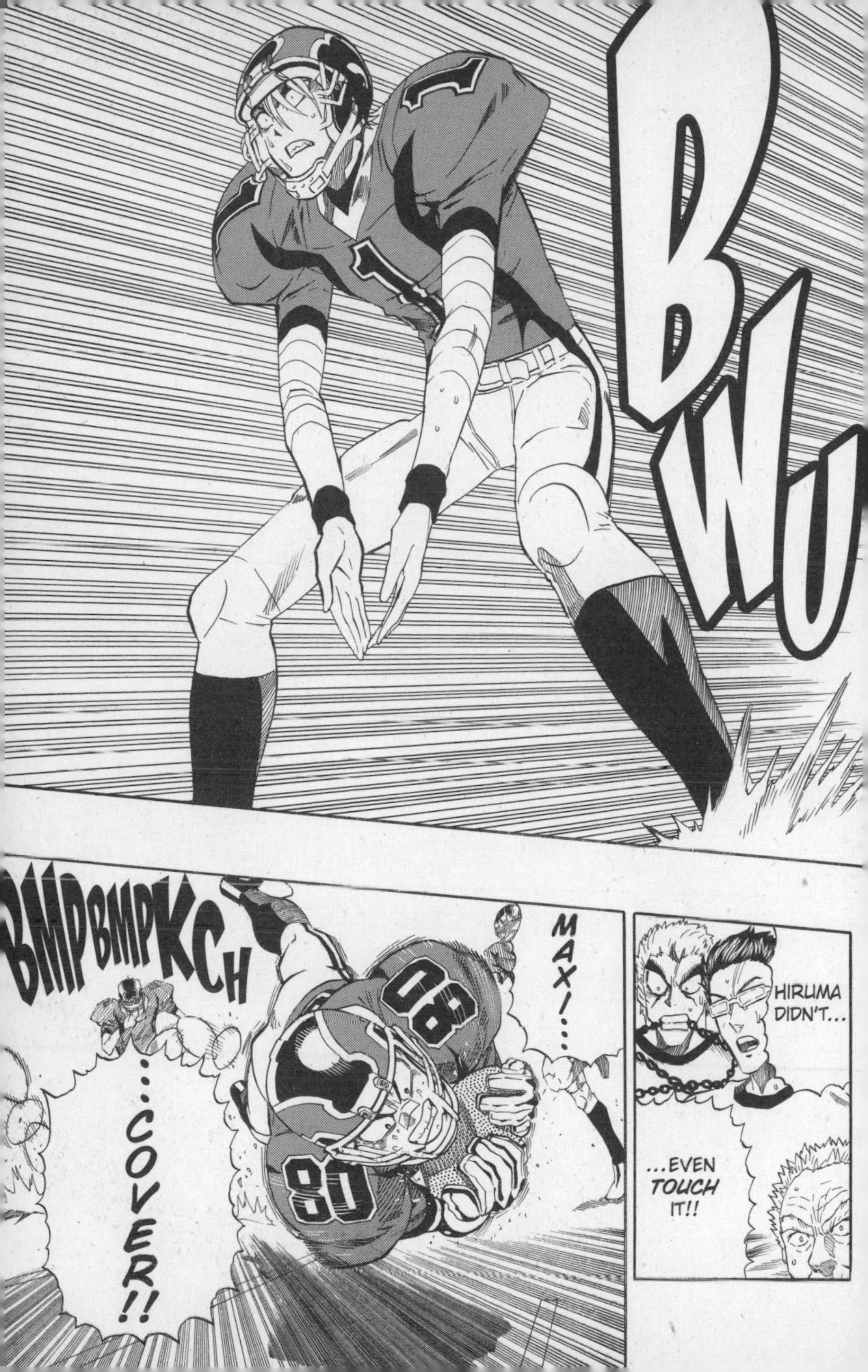
BWU
HIRUMA DIDN'T...
...EVEN TOUCH IT!!
MAX!...
BMPBMPKCH
...COVER!!

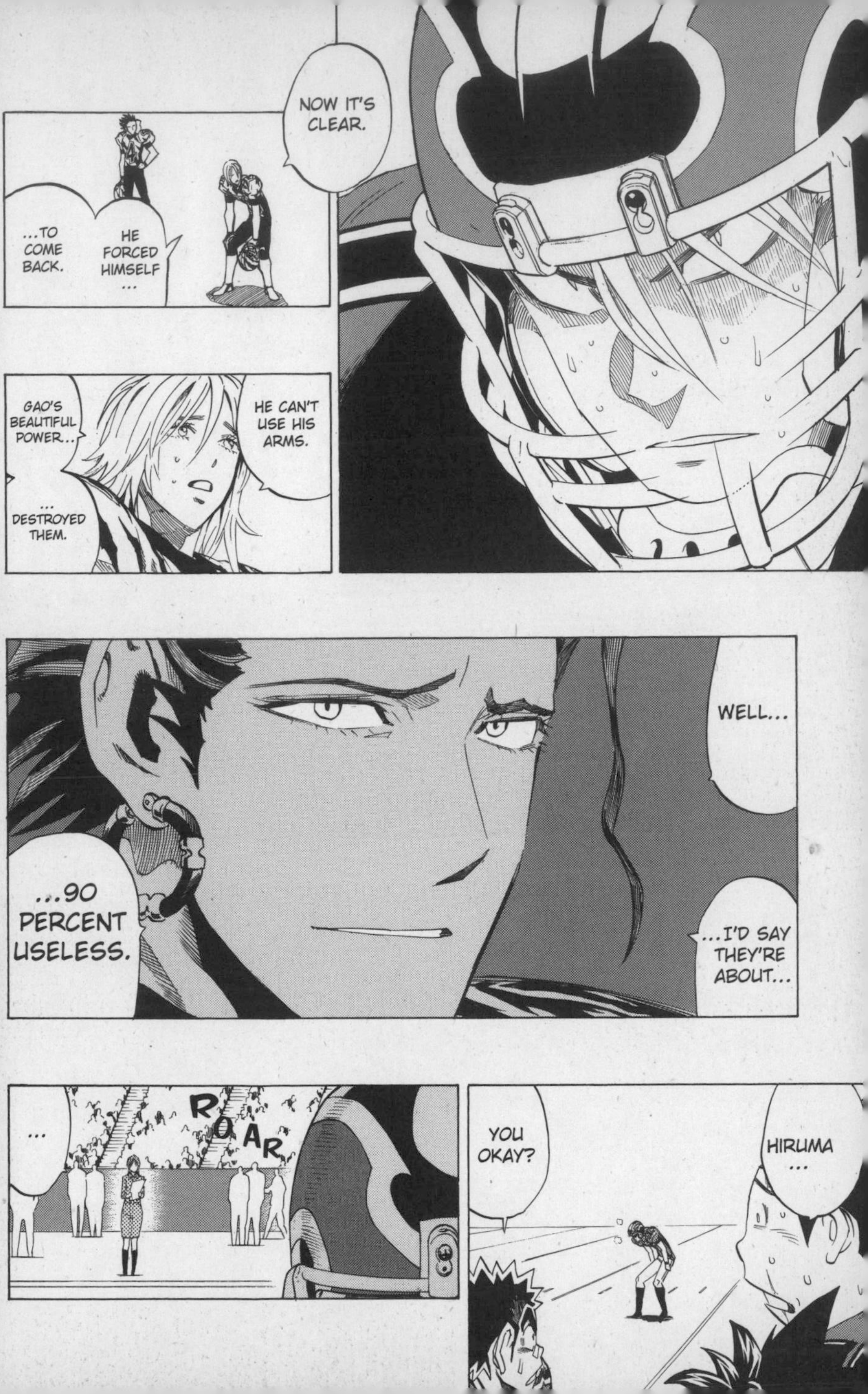
NOW IT'S CLEAR.
HE FORCED HIMSELF ...
...TO COME BACK.
HE CAN'T USE HIS ARMS.
GAO'S BEAUTIFUL POWER...
... DESTROYED THEM.
WELL...
...I'D SAY THEY'RE ABOUT...
...90 PERCENT USELESS.
HIRUMA ...
YOU OKAY?
ROAR
...

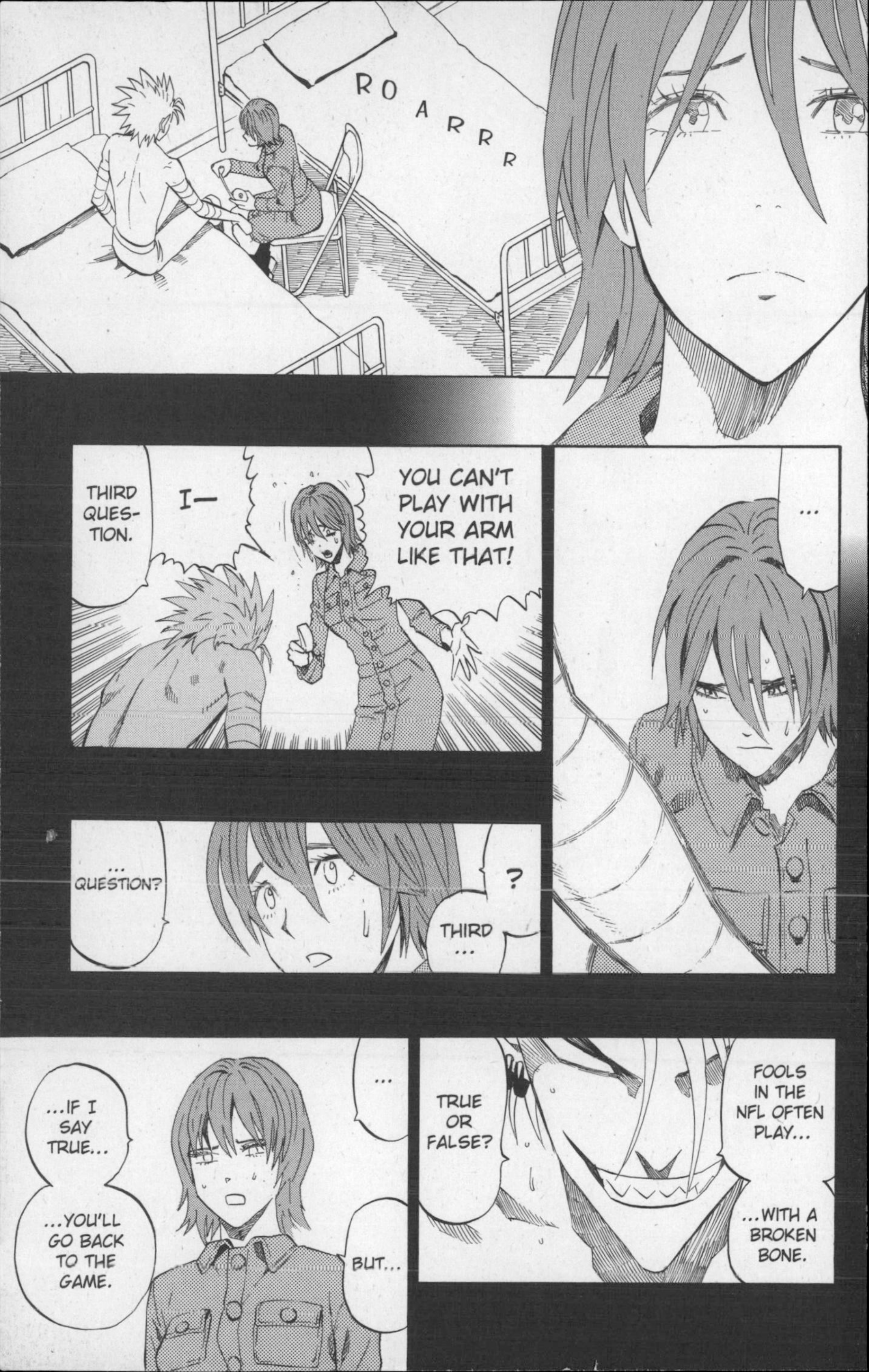
ROARRR
...
YOU CAN'T PLAY WITH YOUR ARM LIKE THAT!
I—
THIRD QUES-TION.
?
THIRD ...
... QUESTION?
FOOLS IN THE NFL OFTEN PLAY...
...WITH A BROKEN BONE.
TRUE OR FALSE?
...
BUT...
...IF I SAY TRUE...
...YOU'LL GO BACK TO THE GAME.

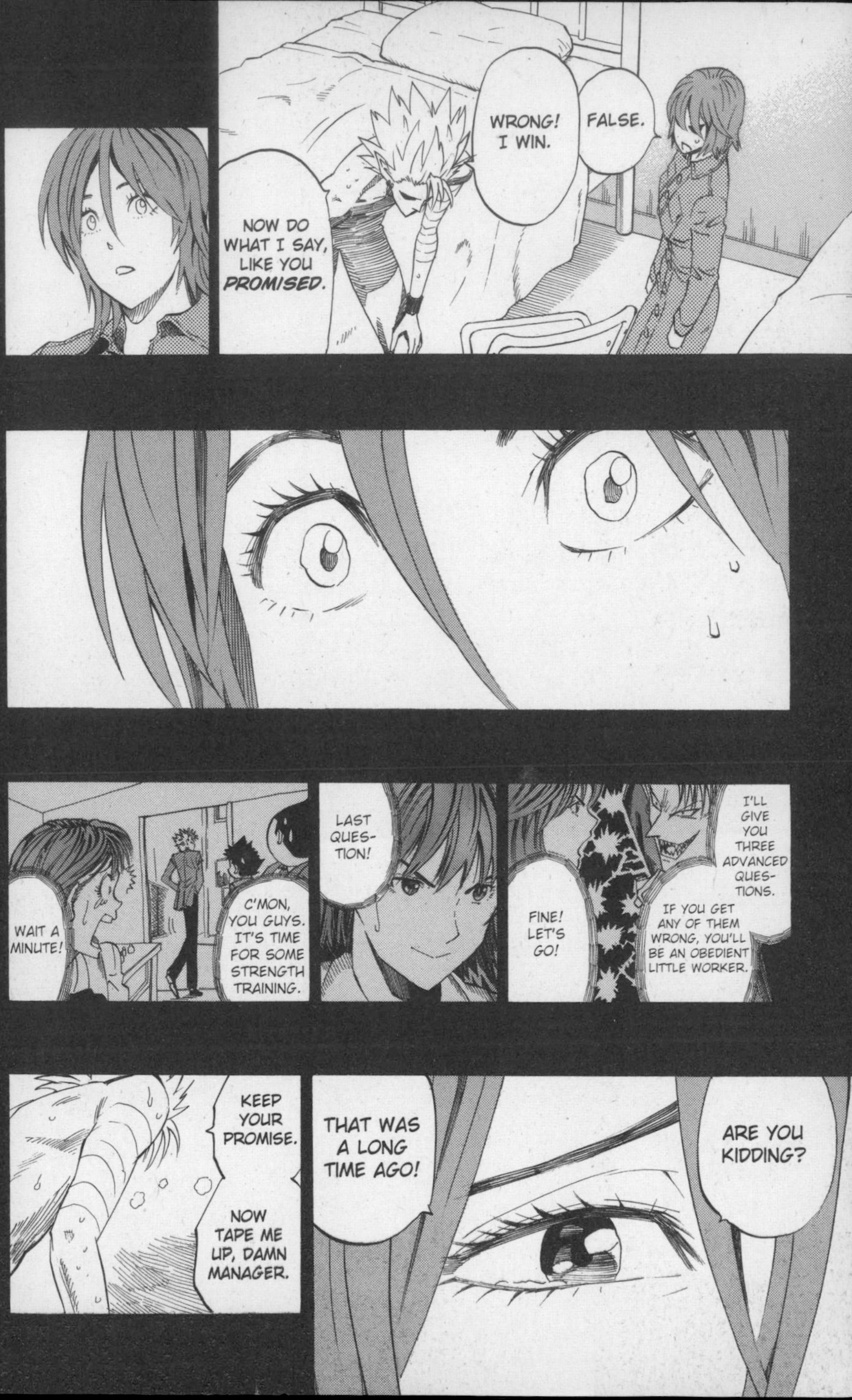
FALSE.
WRONG! I WIN.
NOW DO WHAT I SAY, LIKE YOU *PROMISED*.
I'LL GIVE YOU THREE ADVANCED QUES-TIONS.
IF YOU GET ANY OF THEM WRONG, YOU'LL BE AN OBEDIENT LITTLE WORKER.
FINE! LET'S GO!
LAST QUES-TION!
C'MON, YOU GUYS. IT'S TIME FOR SOME STRENGTH TRAINING.
WAIT A MINUTE!
ARE YOU KIDDING?
THAT WAS A LONG TIME AGO!
KEEP YOUR PROMISE.
NOW TAPE ME UP, DAMN MANAGER.

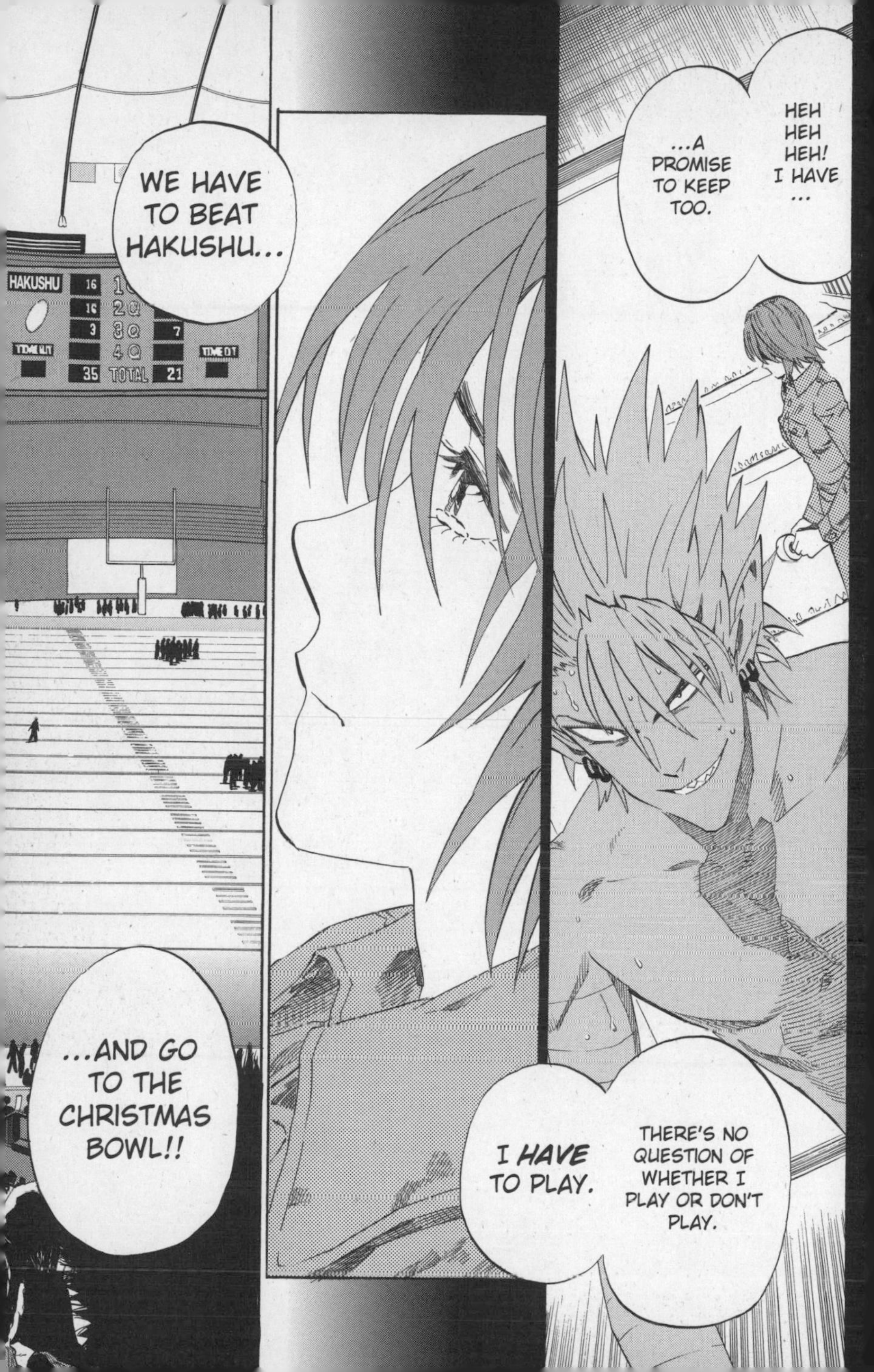
HEH HEH HEH! I HAVE ...
...A PROMISE TO KEEP TOO.
THERE'S NO QUESTION OF WHETHER I PLAY OR DON'T PLAY.
I *HAVE* TO PLAY.
WE HAVE TO BEAT HAKUSHU...
...AND GO TO THE CHRISTMAS BOWL!!

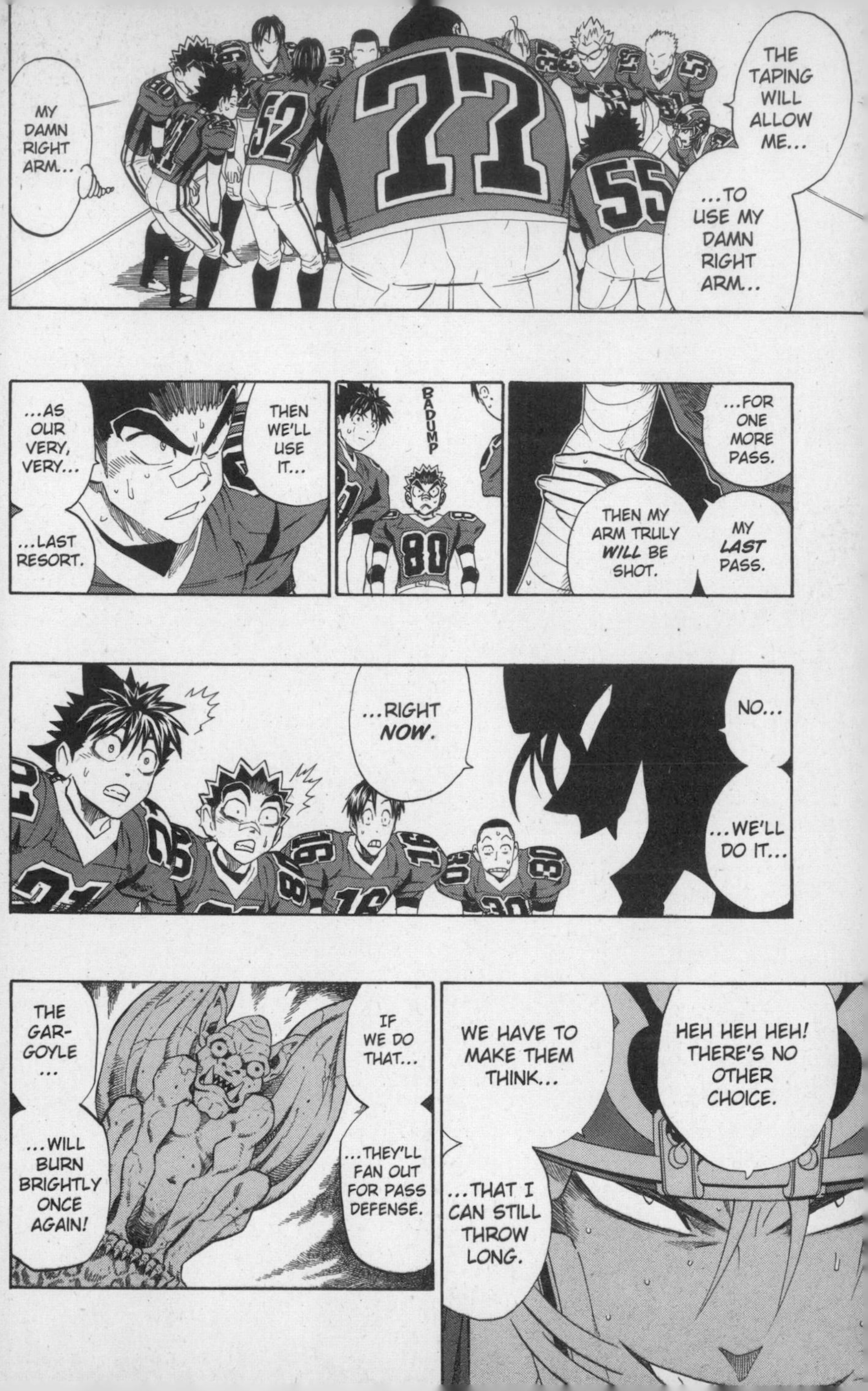
THE TAPING WILL ALLOW ME...
...TO USE MY DAMN RIGHT ARM...
MY DAMN RIGHT ARM...
...FOR ONE MORE PASS.
MY *LAST* PASS.
THEN MY ARM TRULY *WILL* BE SHOT.
BADUMP
THEN WE'LL USE IT...
...AS OUR VERY, VERY...
...LAST RESORT.
NO...
...WE'LL DO IT...
...RIGHT *NOW*.
HEH HEH HEH! THERE'S NO OTHER CHOICE.
WE HAVE TO MAKE THEM THINK...
...THAT I CAN STILL THROW LONG.
IF WE DO THAT...
...THEY'LL FAN OUT FOR PASS DEFENSE.
THE GAR-GOYLE...
...WILL BURN BRIGHTLY ONCE AGAIN!

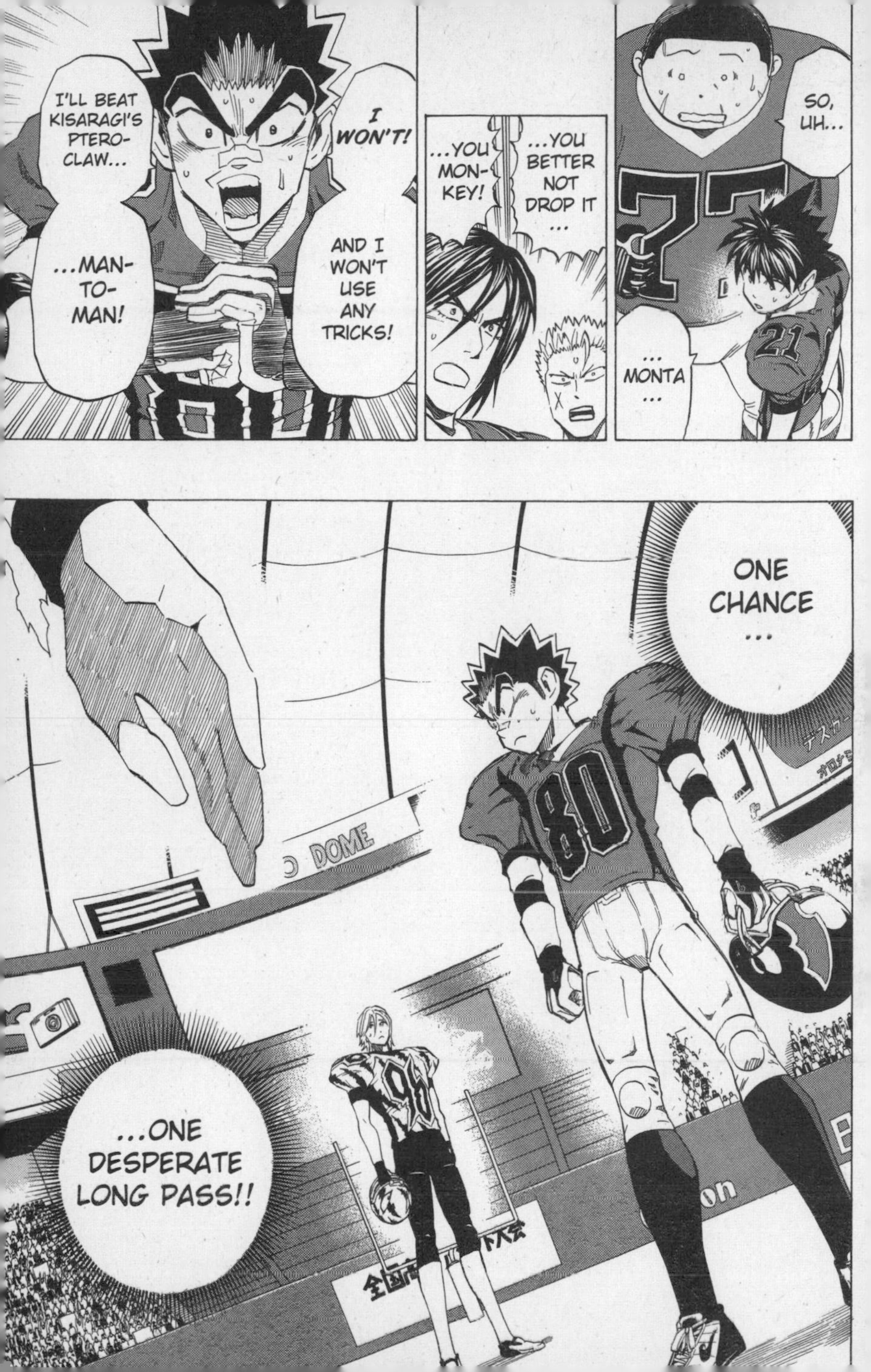
SO, UH...
... MONTA ...
...YOU BETTER NOT DROP IT ...
...YOU MON-KEY!
I WON'T!
I'LL BEAT KISARAGI'S PTERO-CLAW...
...MAN-TO-MAN!
AND I WON'T USE ANY TRICKS!
ONE CHANCE ...
DOME
...ONE DESPERATE LONG PASS!!

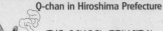

#125

Is the Fake Sena  who appeared in Volume 23 still alive?

T.S. in Saitama Prefecture

OF COURSE!!

#126

How much does Hiruma pay each month in cell phone bills?

Q-chan in Hiroshima Prefecture

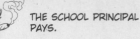

THE SCHOOL PRINCIPAL PAYS.

#127

Hiruma promised the principal to build extensions every time the Devil Bats won. What has he built since the Yuhi Guts game?

T.H. in Shizuoka Prefecture, and many others

SECRET WEAPONS LOCKERS ALL OVER THE SCHOOL!

#128

Komusubi even writes in Powerspeak. What are his school notes like?

T.H. in Mie Prefecture

DURING CLASSES HE'S BUSY DOING AIR SQUATS, SO HE DOESN'T TAKE ANY NOTES!

#129

How did Komusubi cry when he was born?

Han! in Saga Prefecture

UMPH! · *UMPH!*

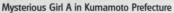

#130

When does Suzuna's antenna pop up?

Mysterious Girl A in Kumamoto Prefecture

WHENEVER SHE SENSES SOMETHING ROMANTIC!

#131

Why does Monta look like a monkey?

Kaho in Hiroshima Prefecture

WHOOEE! I DON'T LOOK LIKE A MONKEY!

YOU JUST *DID.*

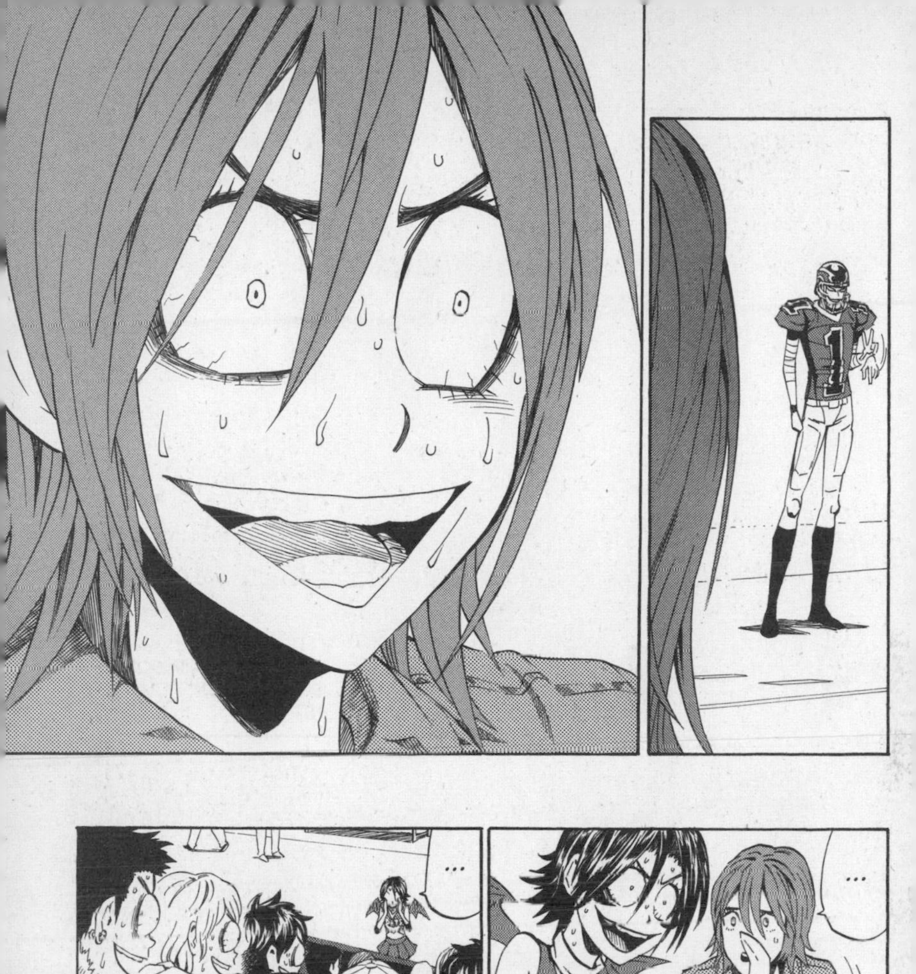
...
...

Chapter 266 A Desperate Long Pass

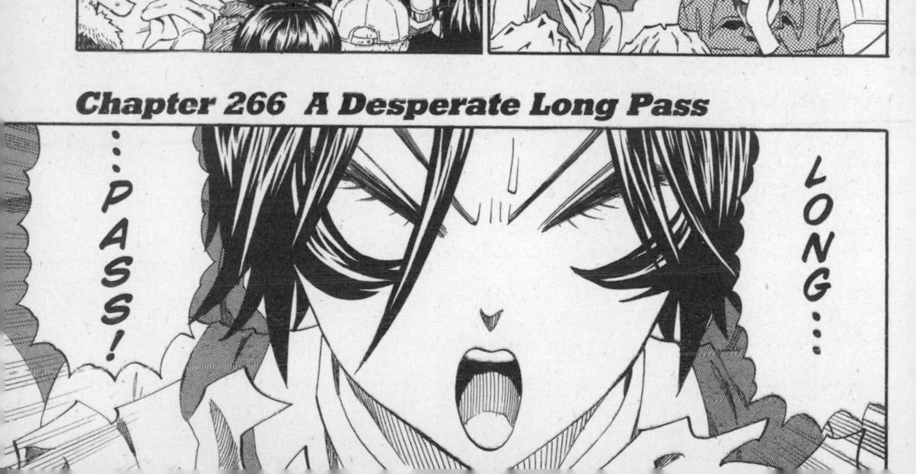
LONG...
...PASS!

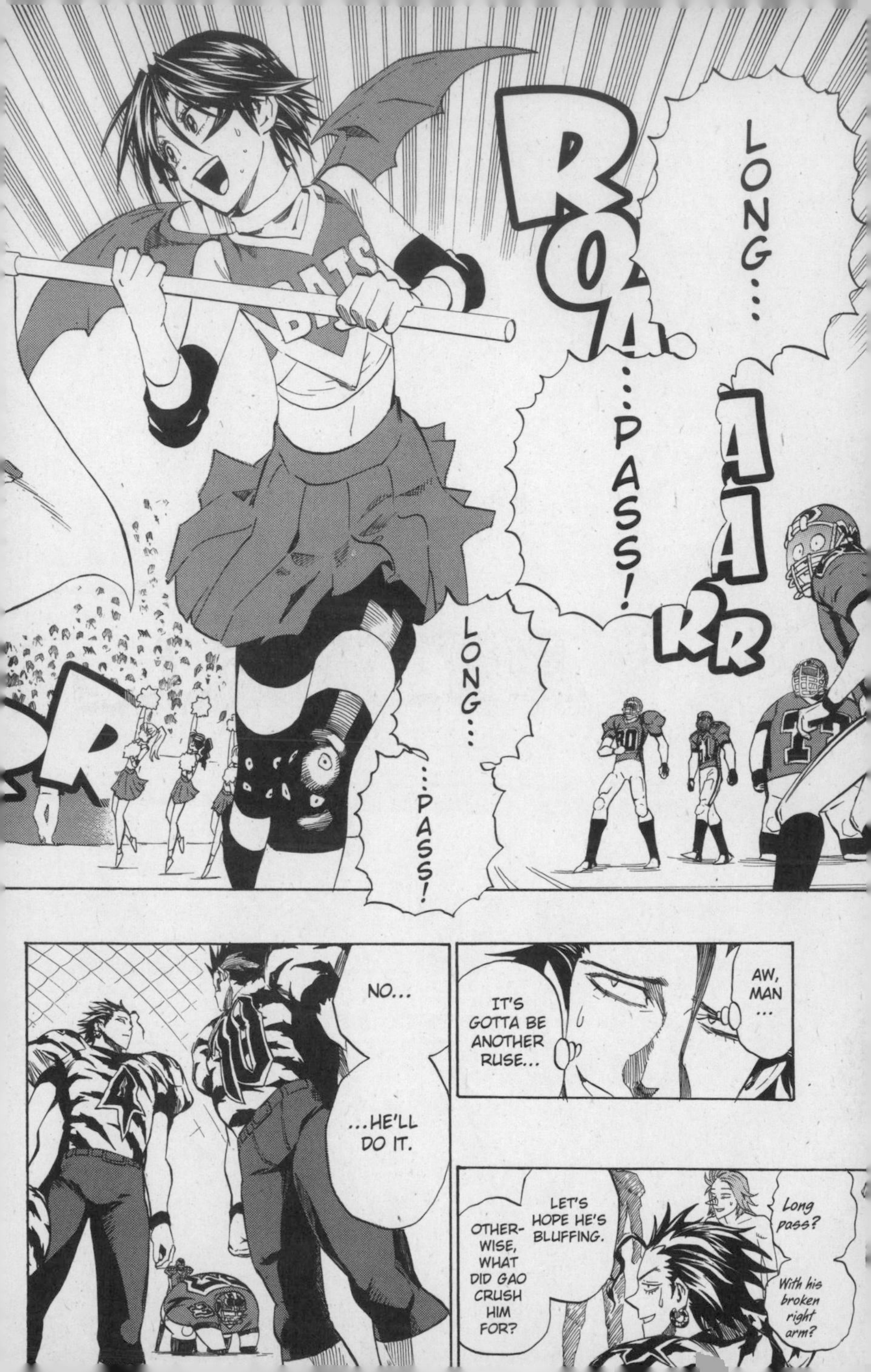
LONG... ...PASS!
ROAAARR
LONG... ...PASS!
AW, MAN...
IT'S GOTTA BE ANOTHER RUSE...
Long pass?
With his broken right arm?
LET'S HOPE HE'S BLUFFING.
OTHERWISE, WHAT DID GAO CRUSH HIM FOR?
NO...
...HE'LL DO IT.

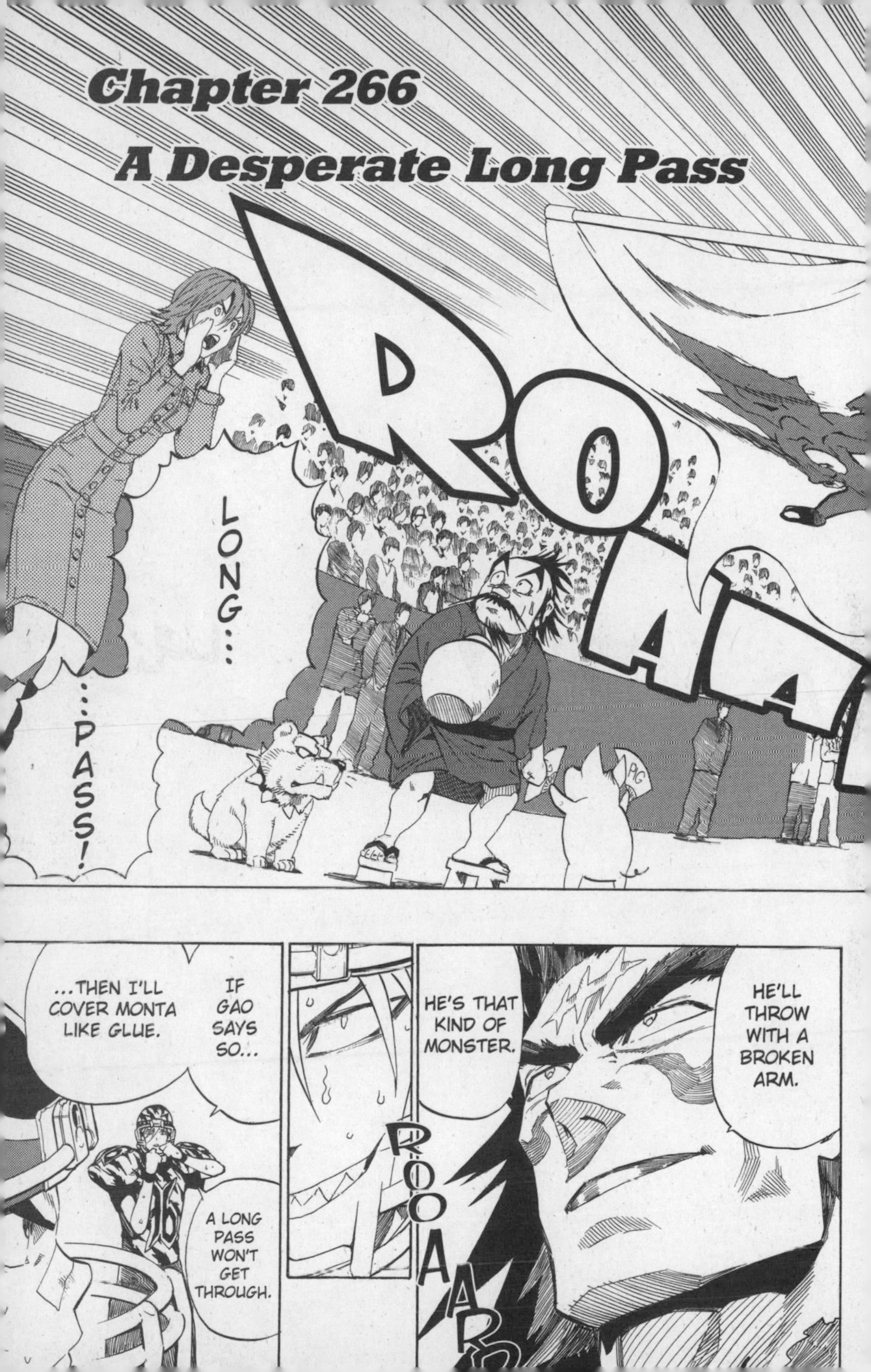
Chapter 266
A Desperate Long Pass
ROAA
LONG...
...PASS!
PIG
HE'LL THROW WITH A BROKEN ARM.
HE'S THAT KIND OF MONSTER.
ROOAA
IF GAO SAYS SO...
...THEN I'LL COVER MONTA LIKE GLUE.
A LONG PASS WON'T GET THROUGH.

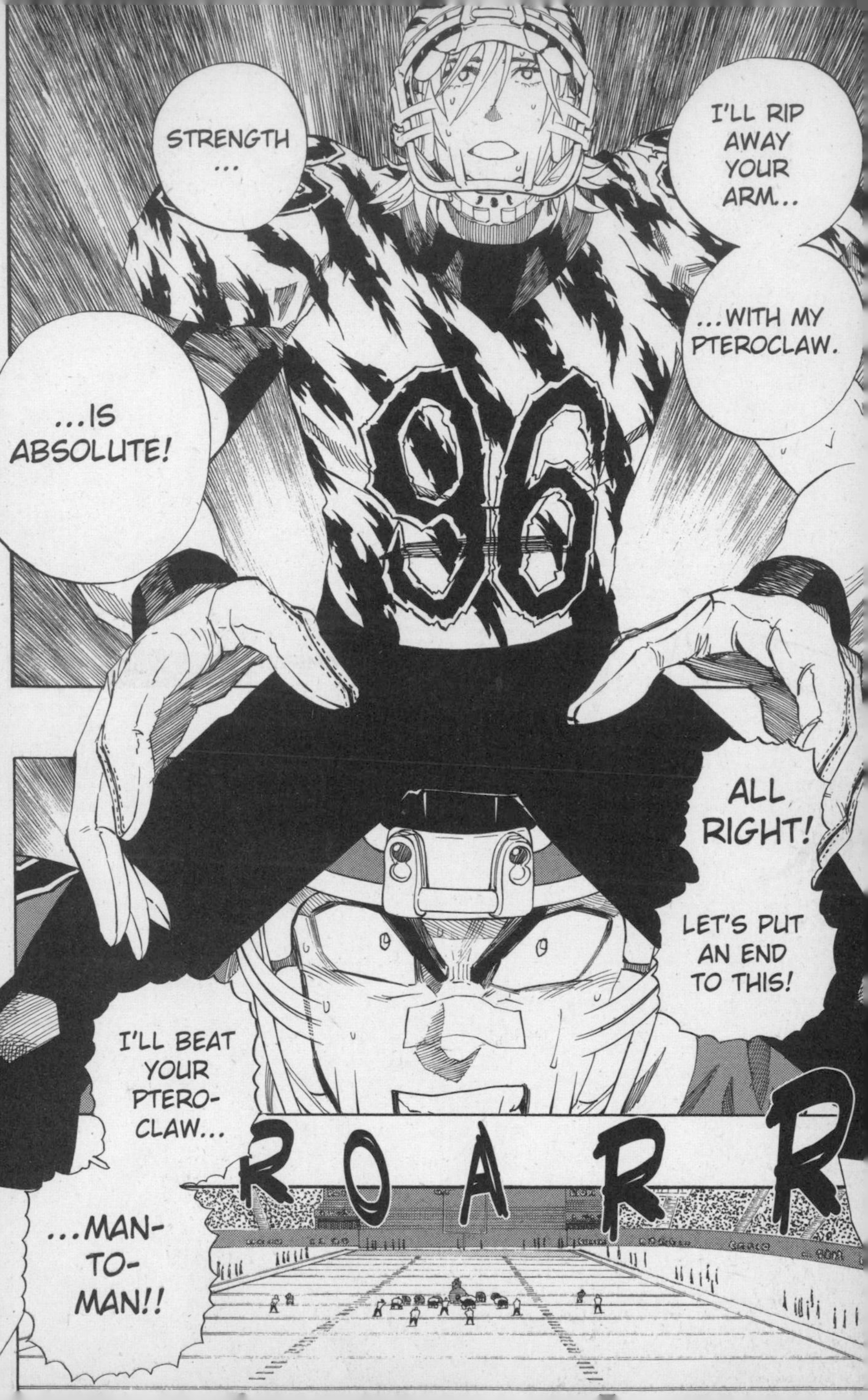
I'LL RIP AWAY YOUR ARM...
...WITH MY PTEROCLAW.
STRENGTH...
...IS ABSOLUTE!
ALL RIGHT!
LET'S PUT AN END TO THIS!
I'LL BEAT YOUR PTERO-CLAW...
...MAN-TO-MAN!!
ROARR

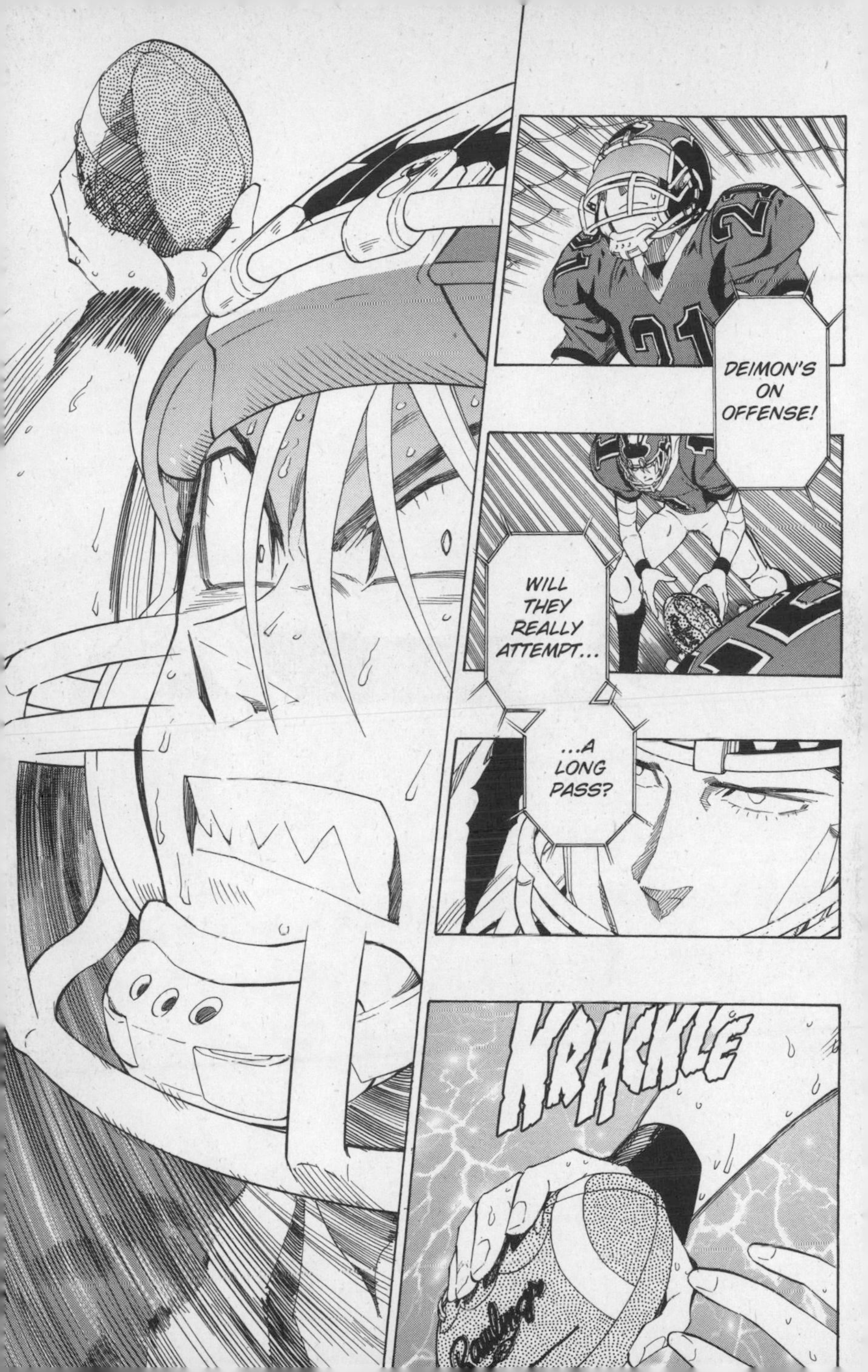
DEIMON'S ON OFFENSE!
WILL THEY REALLY ATTEMPT...
...A LONG PASS?
KRACKLE

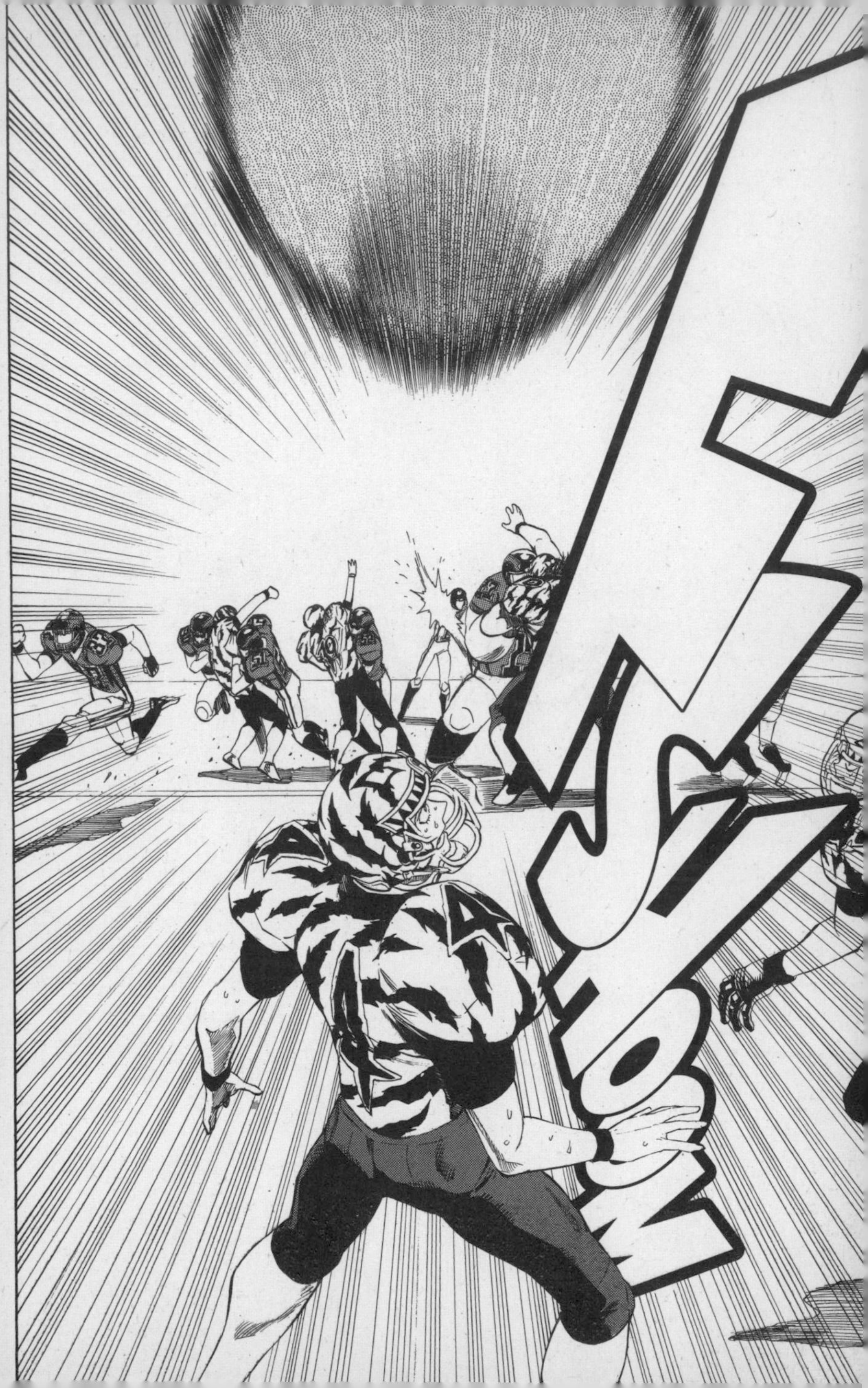
WHOOSH

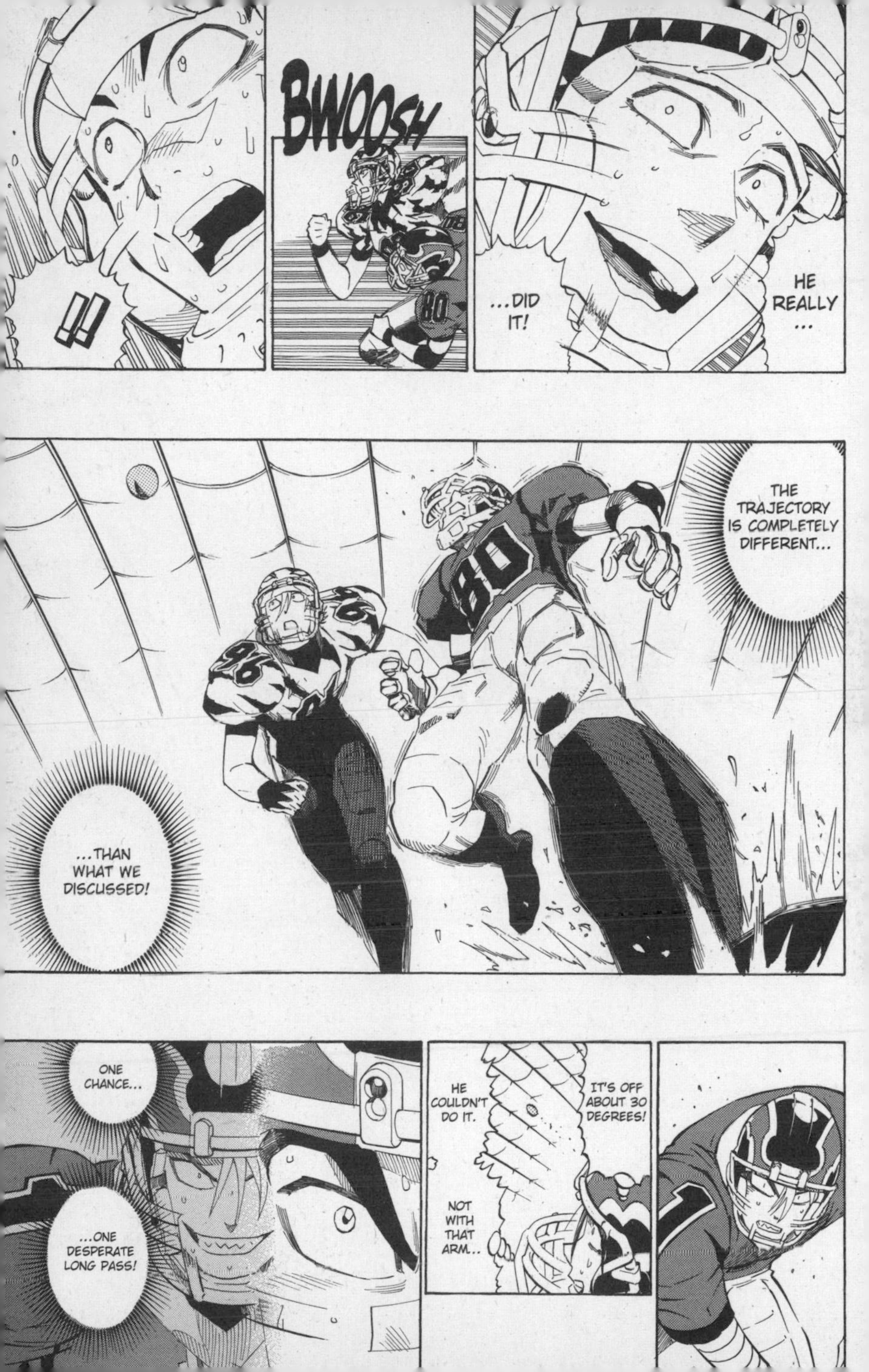
HE REALLY ...
...DID IT!
BWOOSH
!!
THE TRAJECTORY IS COMPLETELY DIFFERENT...
...THAN WHAT WE DISCUSSED!
IT'S OFF ABOUT 30 DEGREES!
HE COULDN'T DO IT.
NOT WITH THAT ARM...
ONE CHANCE...
...ONE DESPERATE LONG PASS!

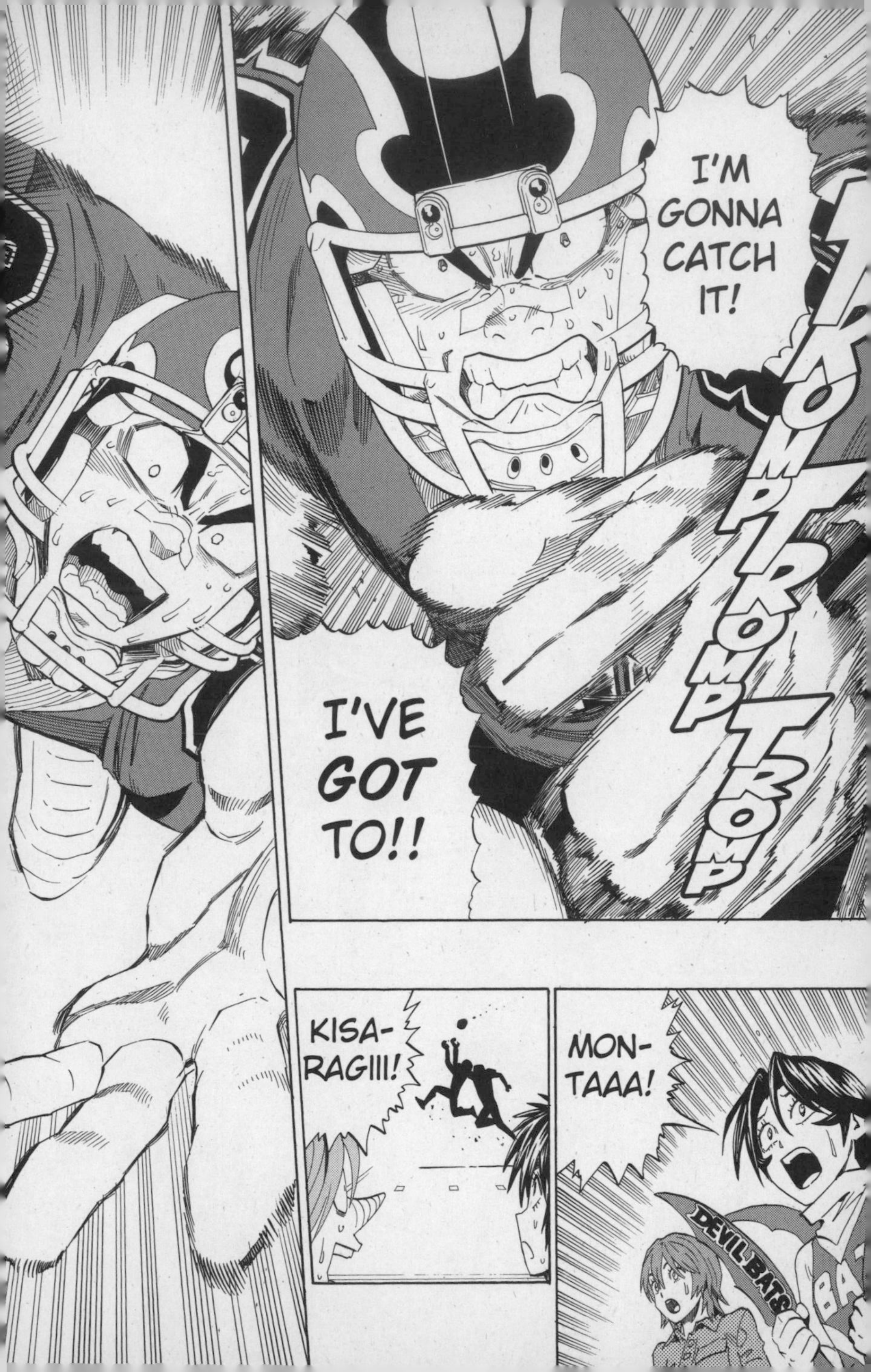
I'M GONNA CATCH IT!
KOMP TROMP TROMP
I'VE GOT TO!!
MON-TAAA!
DEVIL BATS
KISA-RAGIII!

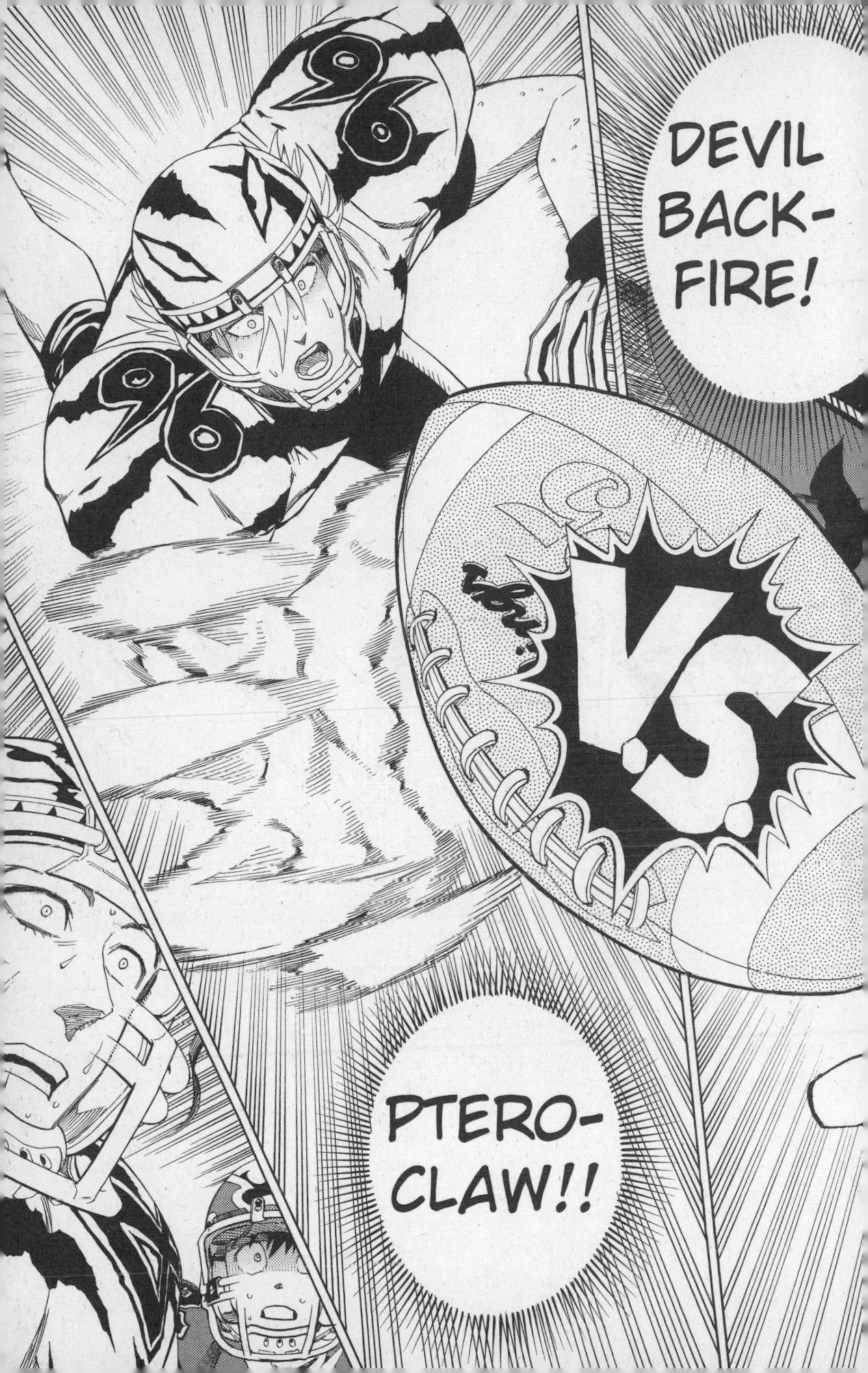
DEVIL BACK-FIRE!
V.S.
PTERO-CLAW!!

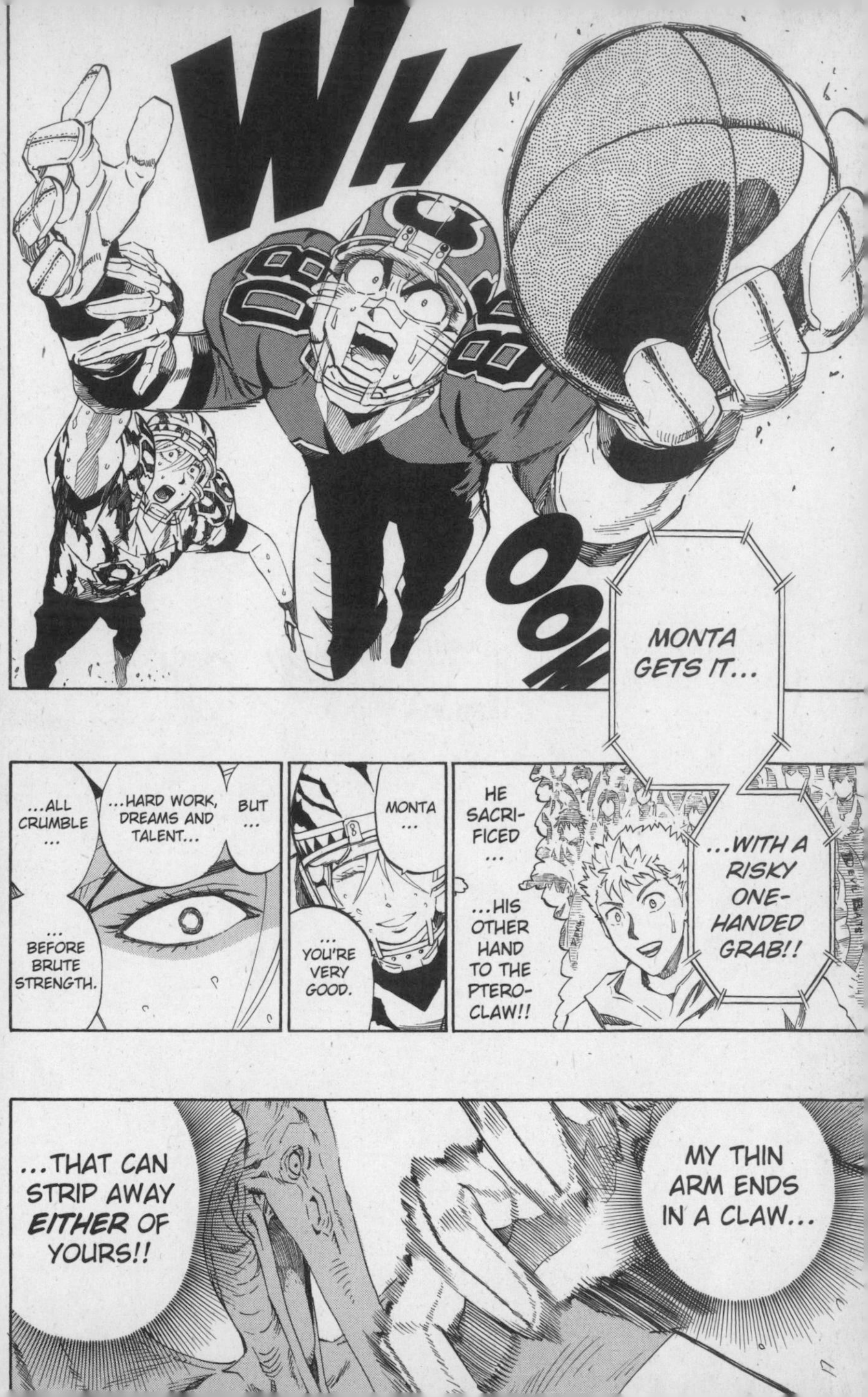
WHOOOM
MONTA GETS IT...
...WITH A RISKY ONE-HANDED GRAB!!
HE SACRIFICED ...
...HIS OTHER HAND TO THE PTERO-CLAW!!
MONTA ...
... YOU'RE VERY GOOD.
BUT ...
...HARD WORK, DREAMS AND TALENT...
...ALL CRUMBLE ...
... BEFORE BRUTE STRENGTH.
MY THIN ARM ENDS IN A CLAW...
...THAT CAN STRIP AWAY *EITHER* OF YOURS!!

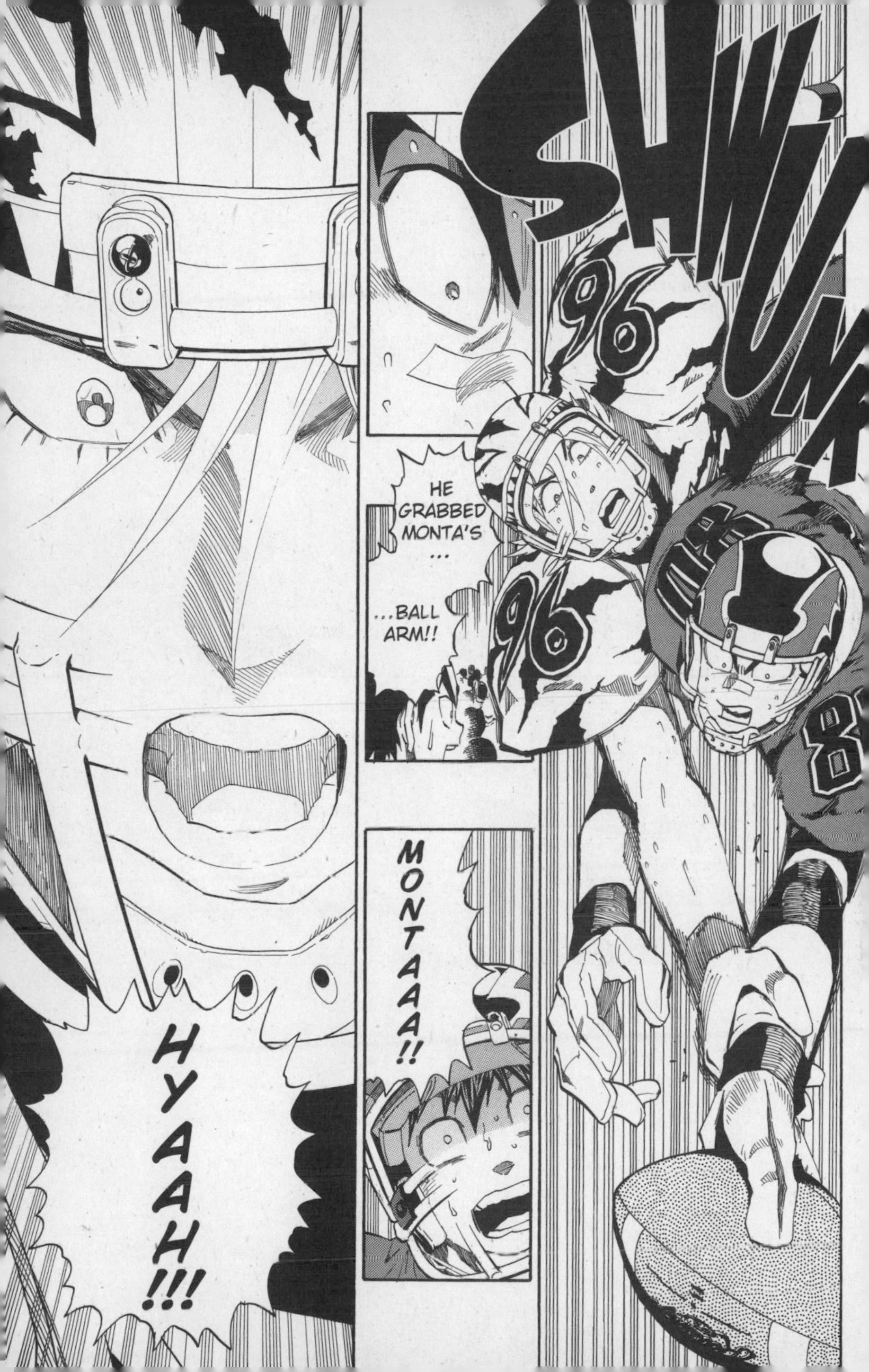
SHWUM
HE GRABBED MONTA'S ...
...BALL ARM!!
MONTAAAA!!
HYAAAH!!!

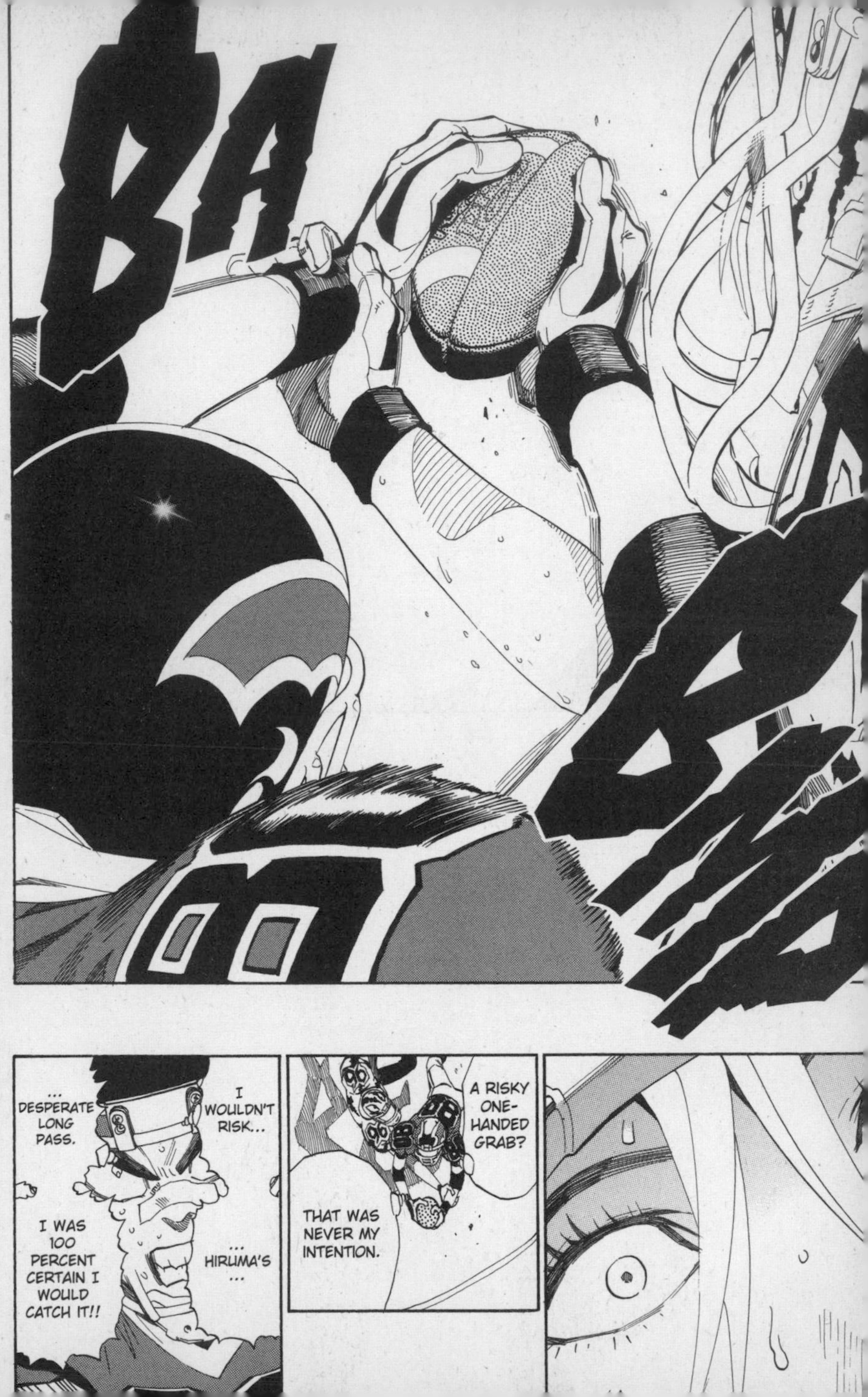
BA
A RISKY ONE-HANDED GRAB?
THAT WAS NEVER MY INTENTION.
I WOULDN'T RISK...
... DESPERATE LONG PASS.
... HIRUMA'S ...
I WAS 100 PERCENT CERTAIN I WOULD CATCH IT!!

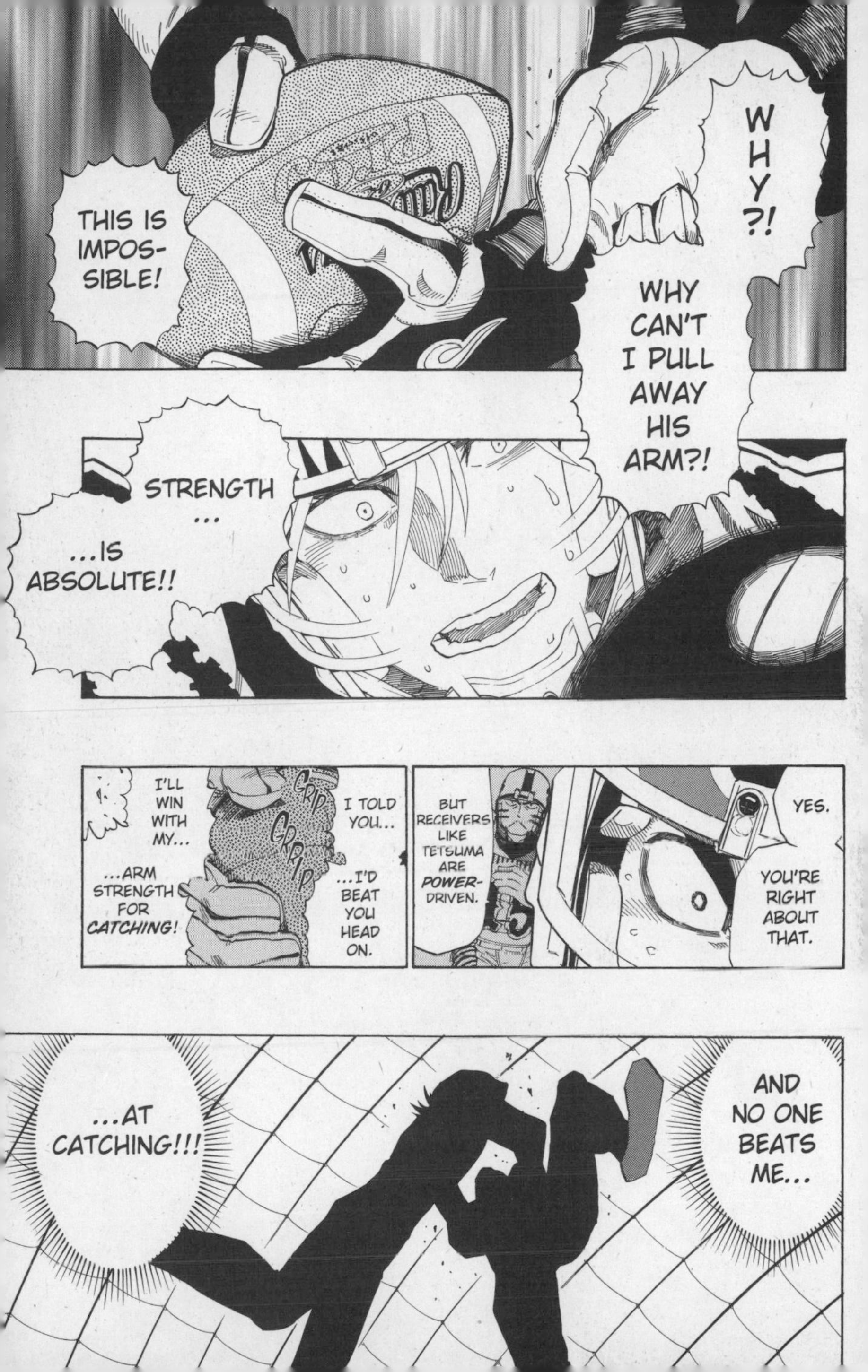
WHY?!
THIS IS IMPOSSIBLE!
WHY CAN'T I PULL AWAY HIS ARM?!
STRENGTH...
...IS ABSOLUTE!!
YES.
YOU'RE RIGHT ABOUT THAT.
BUT RECEIVERS LIKE TETSUMA ARE *POWER*-DRIVEN.
I TOLD YOU...
...I'D BEAT YOU HEAD ON.
GRIP
GRRIP
I'LL WIN WITH MY...
...ARM STRENGTH FOR *CATCHING*!
AND NO ONE BEATS ME...
...AT CATCHING!!!

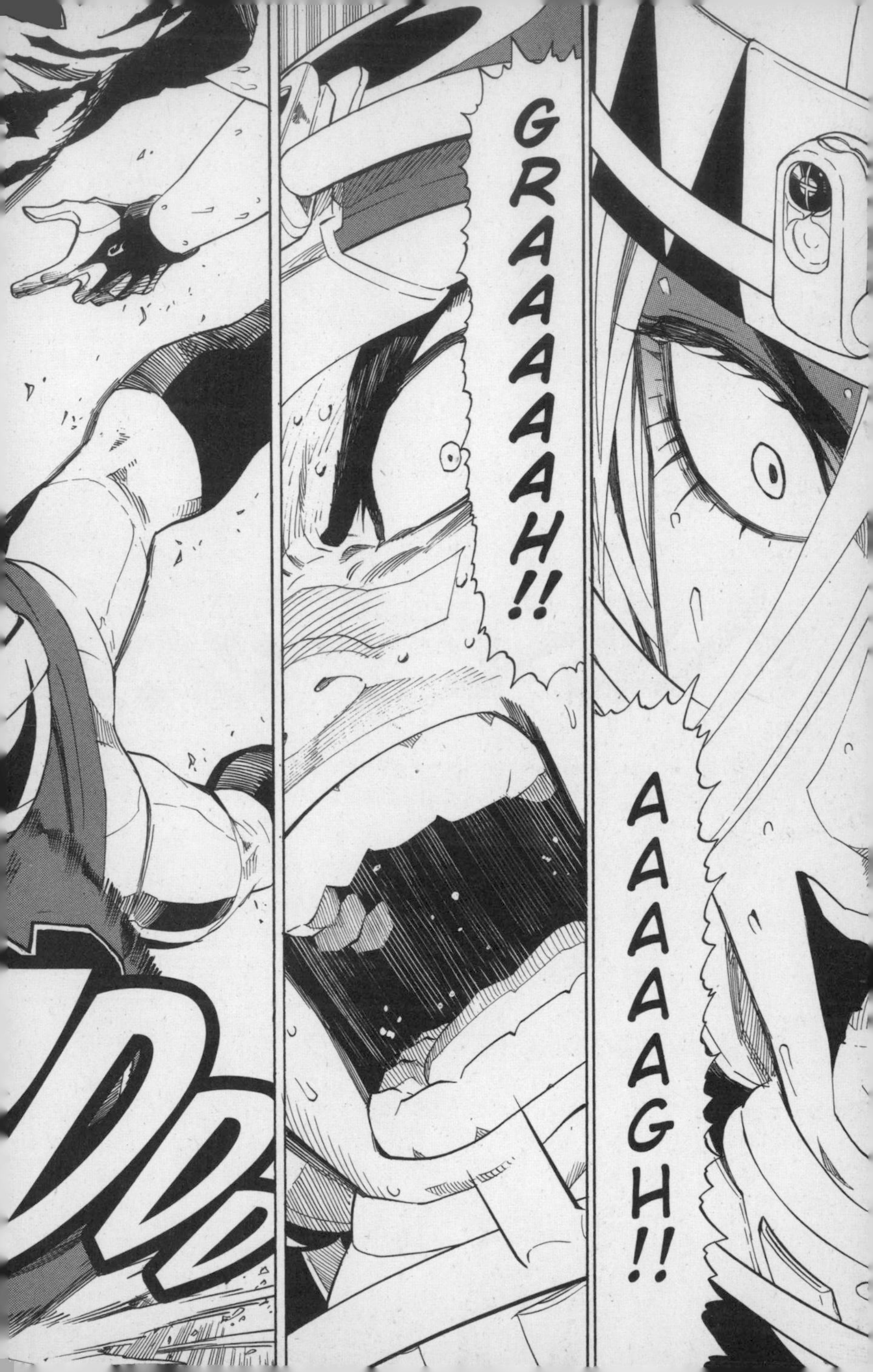
AAAAAGH!!
GRAAAAAH!!

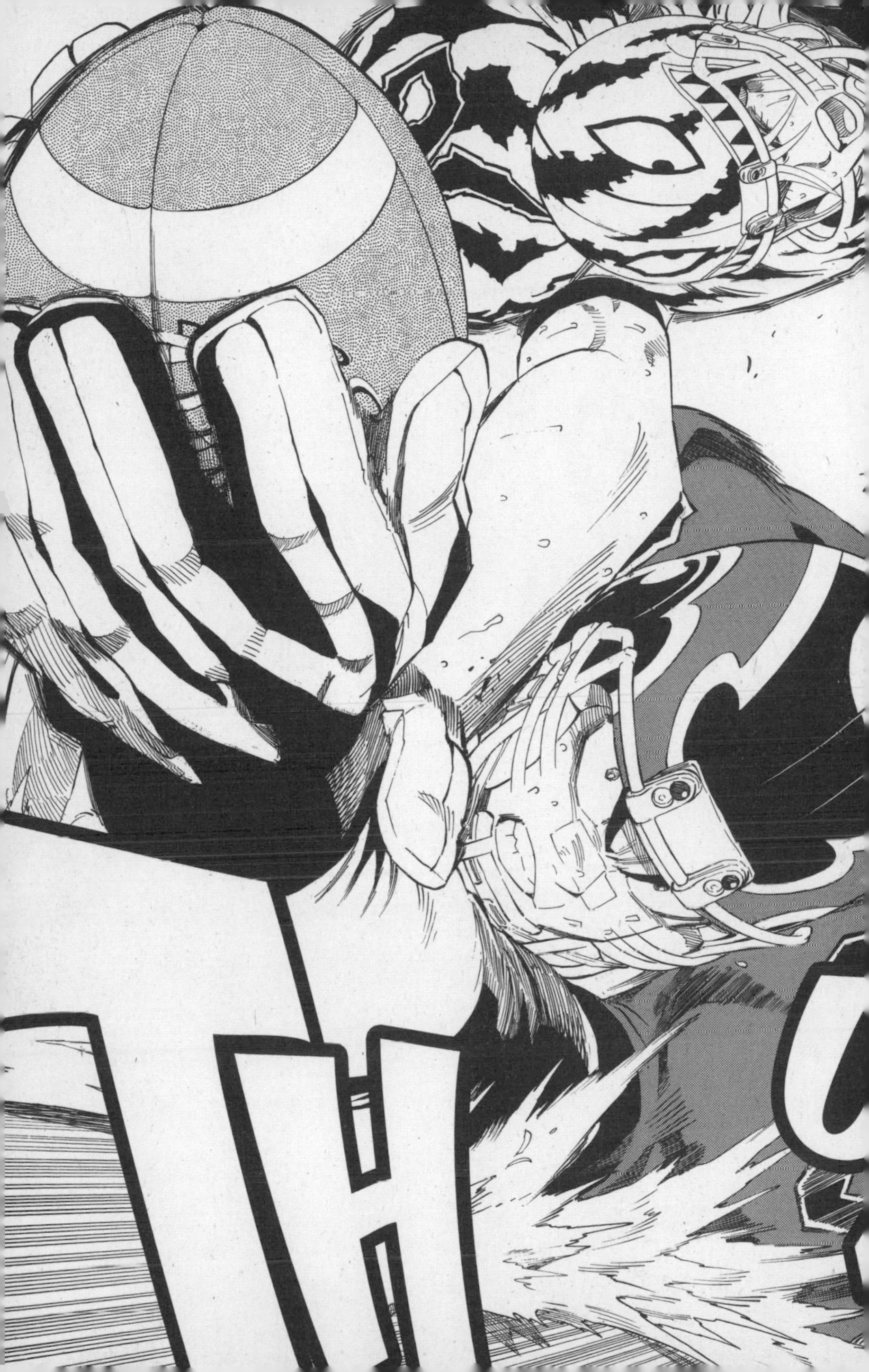

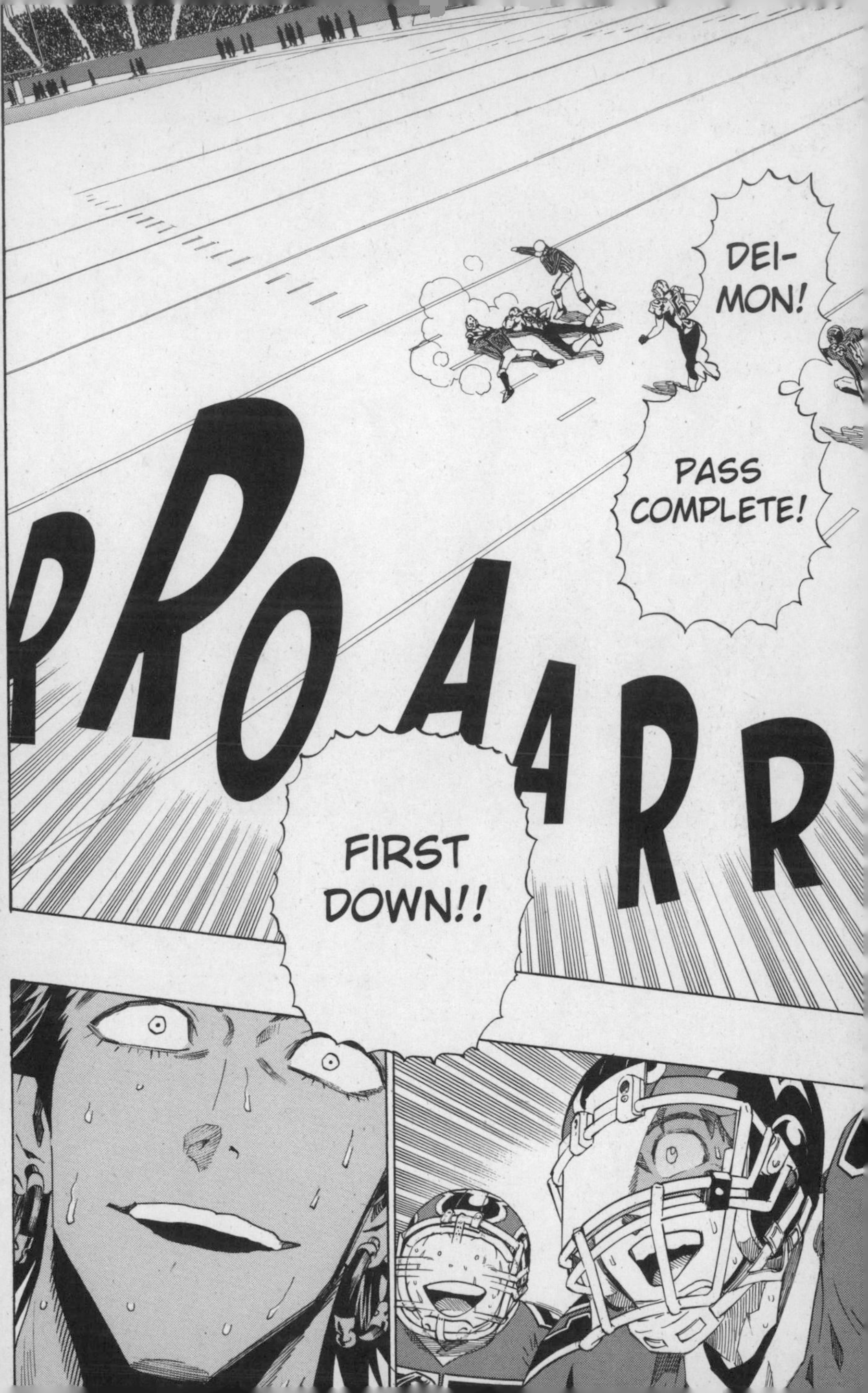
DEI-MON!
PASS COMPLETE!
ROAARR
FIRST DOWN!!

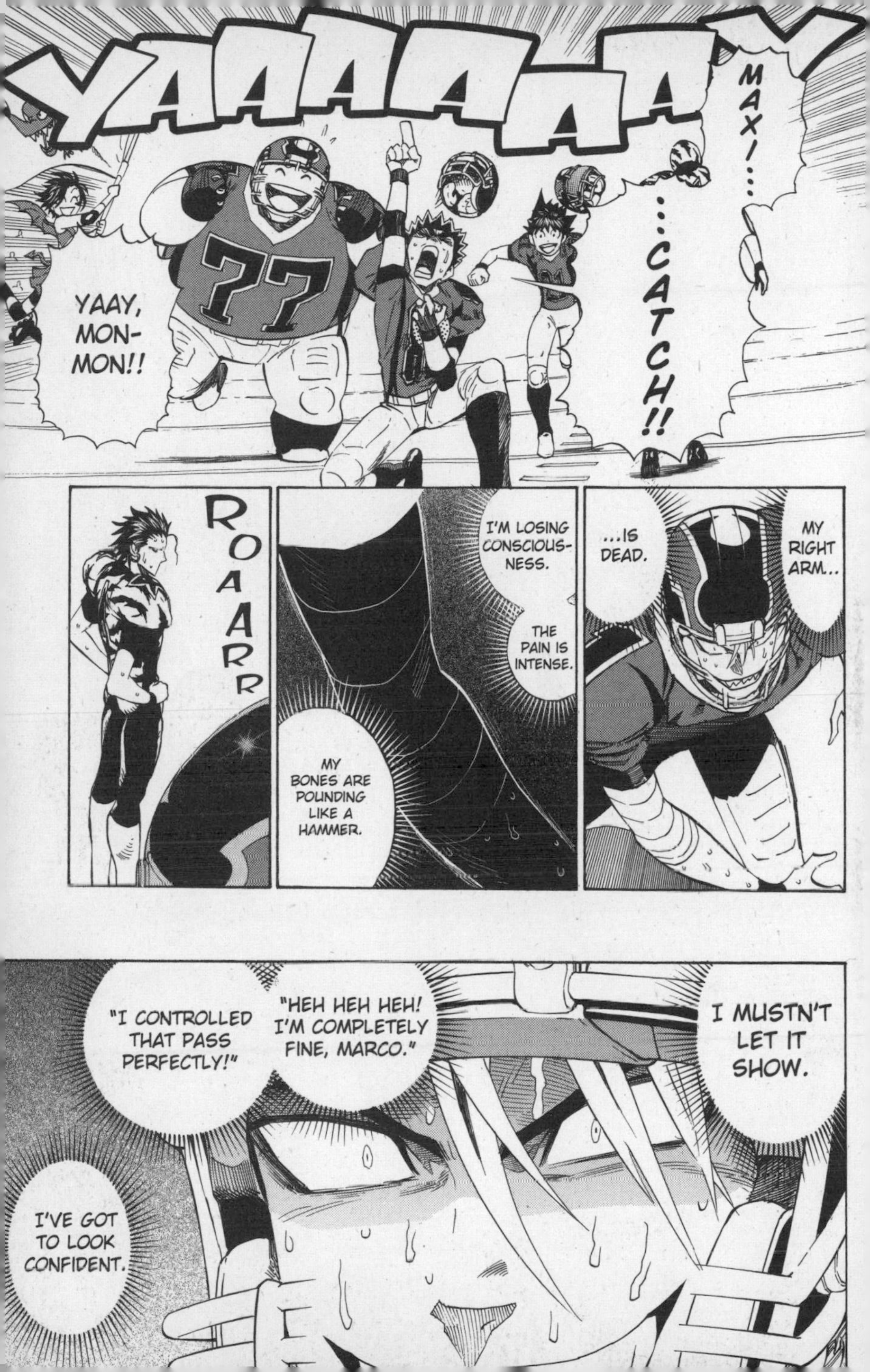
YAAAAAAY
MAXI... ...CATCH!!
YAAY, MON-MON!!
MY RIGHT ARM...
...IS DEAD.
I'M LOSING CONSCIOUSNESS.
THE PAIN IS INTENSE.
MY BONES ARE POUNDING LIKE A HAMMER.
ROAARR
I MUSTN'T LET IT SHOW.
"HEH HEH HEH! I'M COMPLETELY FINE, MARCO."
"I CONTROLLED THAT PASS PERFECTLY!"
I'VE GOT TO LOOK CONFIDENT.

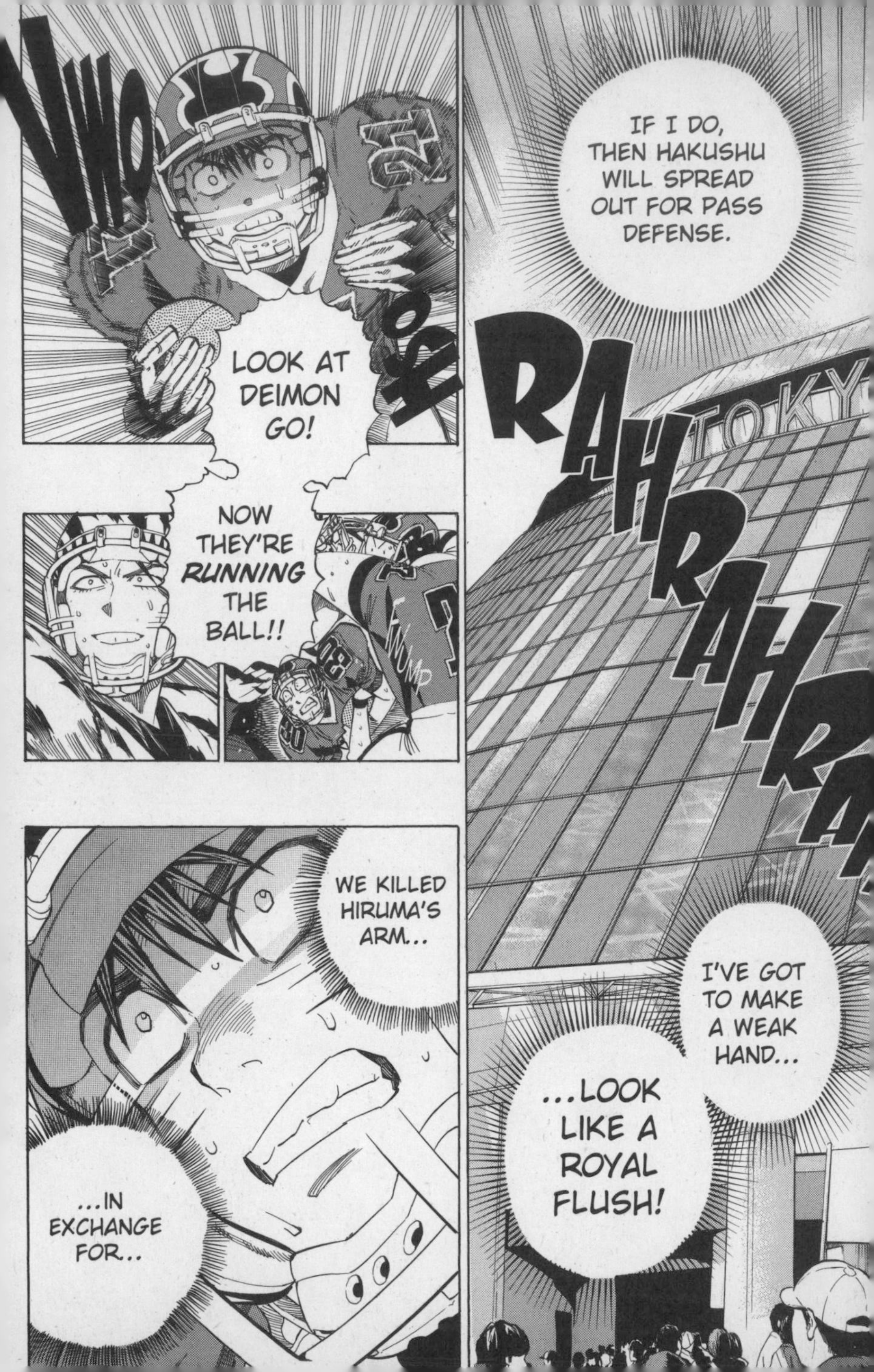
IF I DO, THEN HAKUSHU WILL SPREAD OUT FOR PASS DEFENSE.
RAHRAHRAHRA
TOKY
I'VE GOT TO MAKE A WEAK HAND...
...LOOK LIKE A ROYAL FLUSH!
WHOOSH
LOOK AT DEIMON GO!
NOW THEY'RE *RUNNING* THE BALL!!
WE KILLED HIRUMA'S ARM...
...IN EXCHANGE FOR...

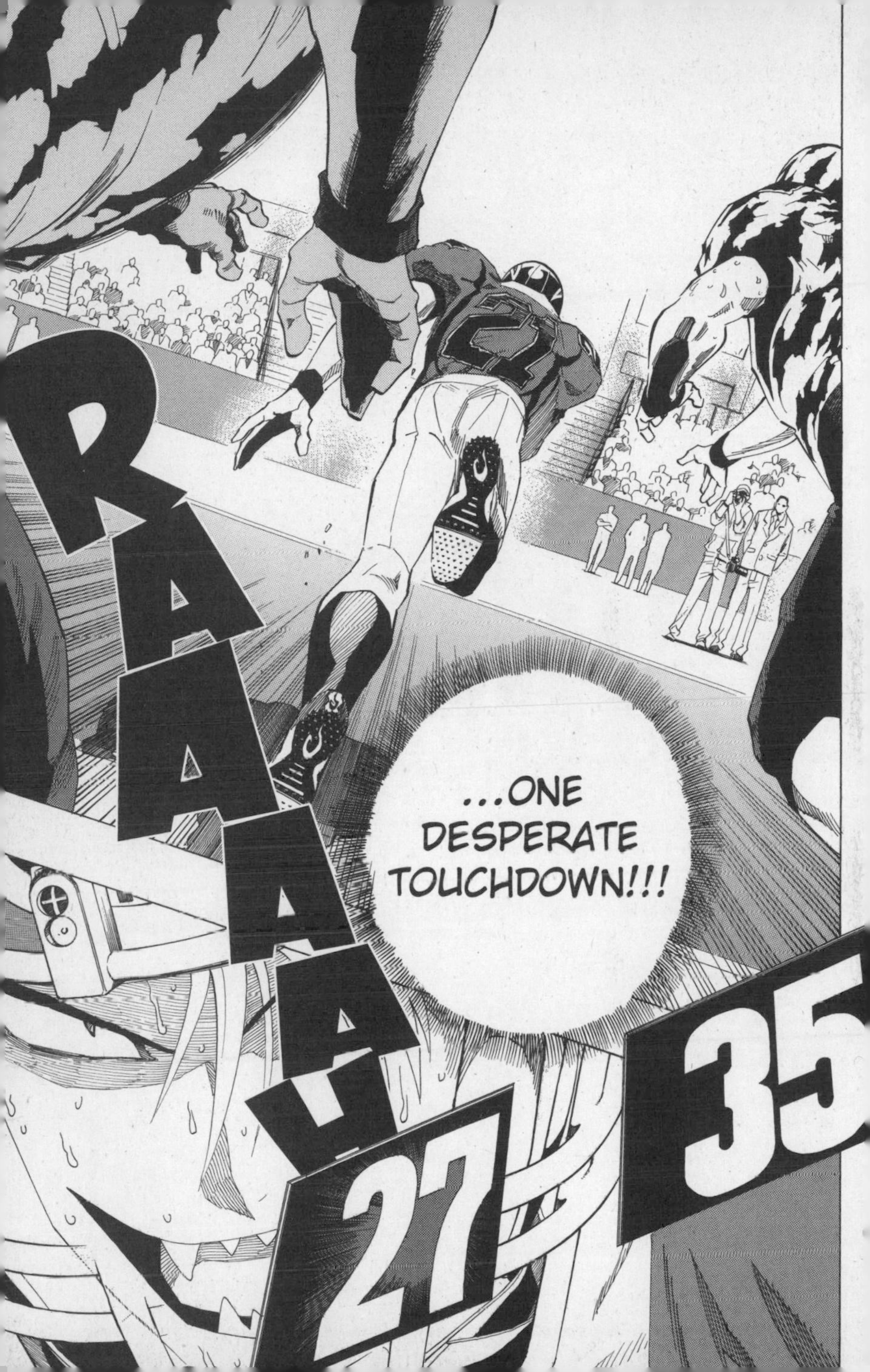
...ONE DESPERATE TOUCHDOWN!!!
RAAAAH
27
35

Eyeshield 21 Survey Corner **Devil Bat 021 SPECIAL!**

Investigation File #132

We saw the difference between Mamori's and Taki's luck at the casino. How lucky is everyone on the team?

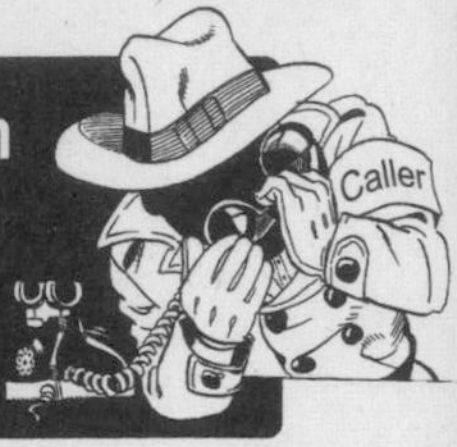
Caller

G.S. in Saitama Prefecture

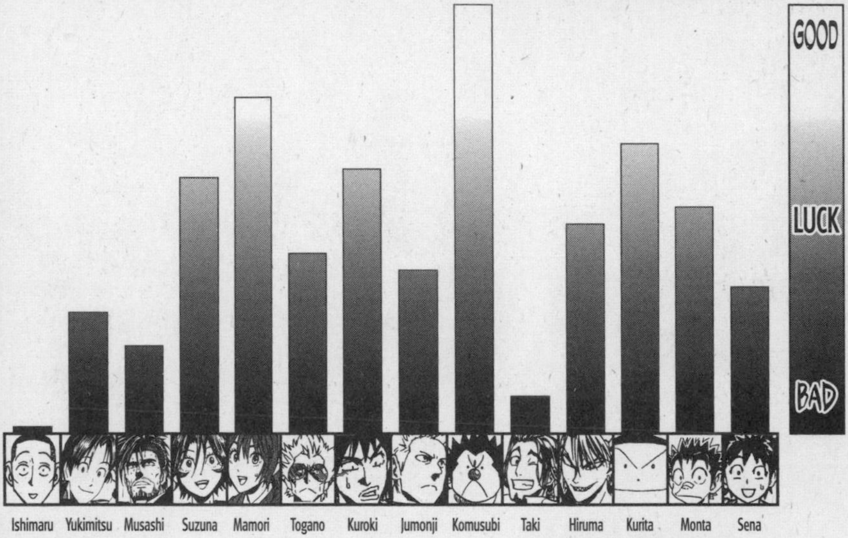
GOOD
LUCK
BAD
Ishimaru
Yukimitsu
Musashi
Suzuna
Mamori
Togano
Kuroki
Jumonji
Komusubi
Taki
Hiruma
Kurita
Monta
Sena

Send your queries for Devil Bat 021 here!!

Devil Bat 021
Shonen Jump Advanced/Eyeshield 21
c/o VIZ Media, LLC
P.O. Box 77010
San Francisco, CA 94107

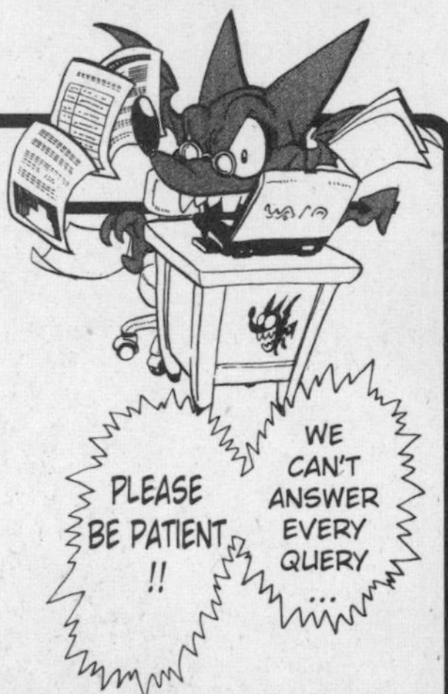
WE CAN'T ANSWER EVERY QUERY...
PLEASE BE PATIENT !!

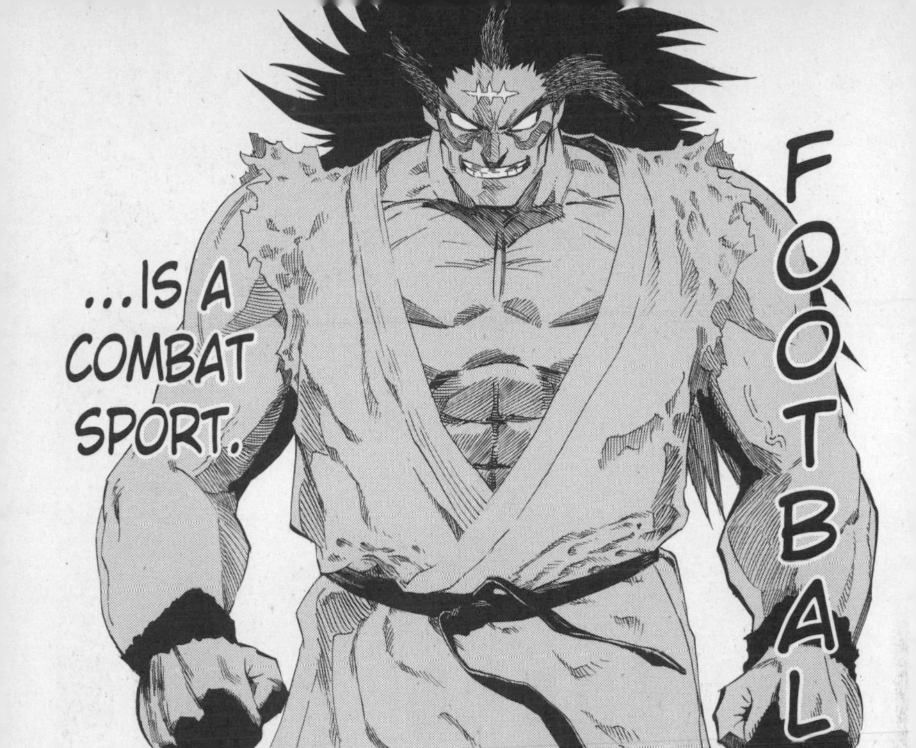
FOOTBALL...
...IS A COMBAT SPORT.

Chapter 267 A Crushing Blow

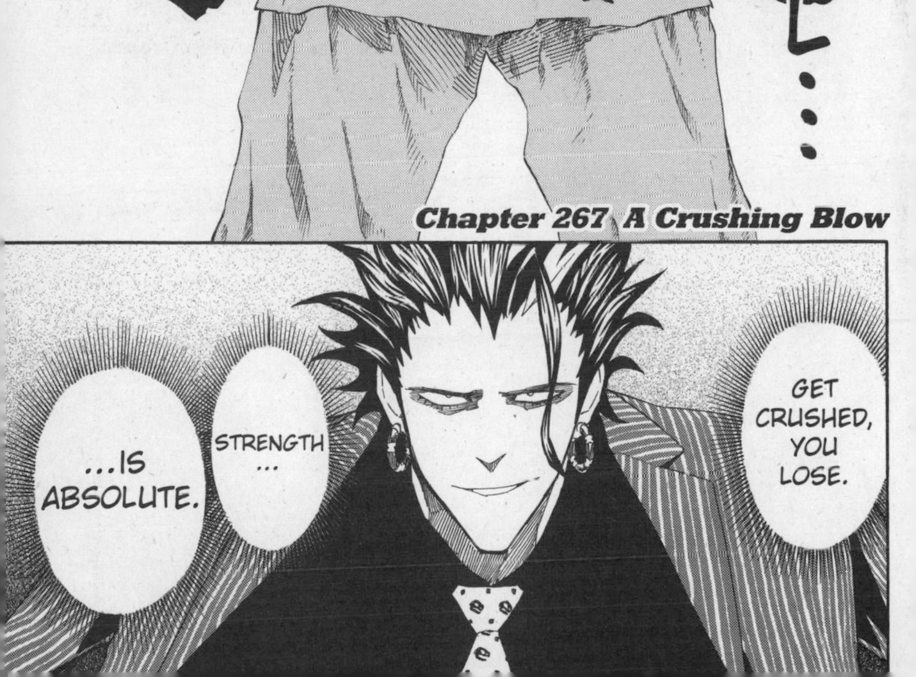
GET CRUSHED, YOU LOSE.
STRENGTH...
...IS ABSOLUTE.

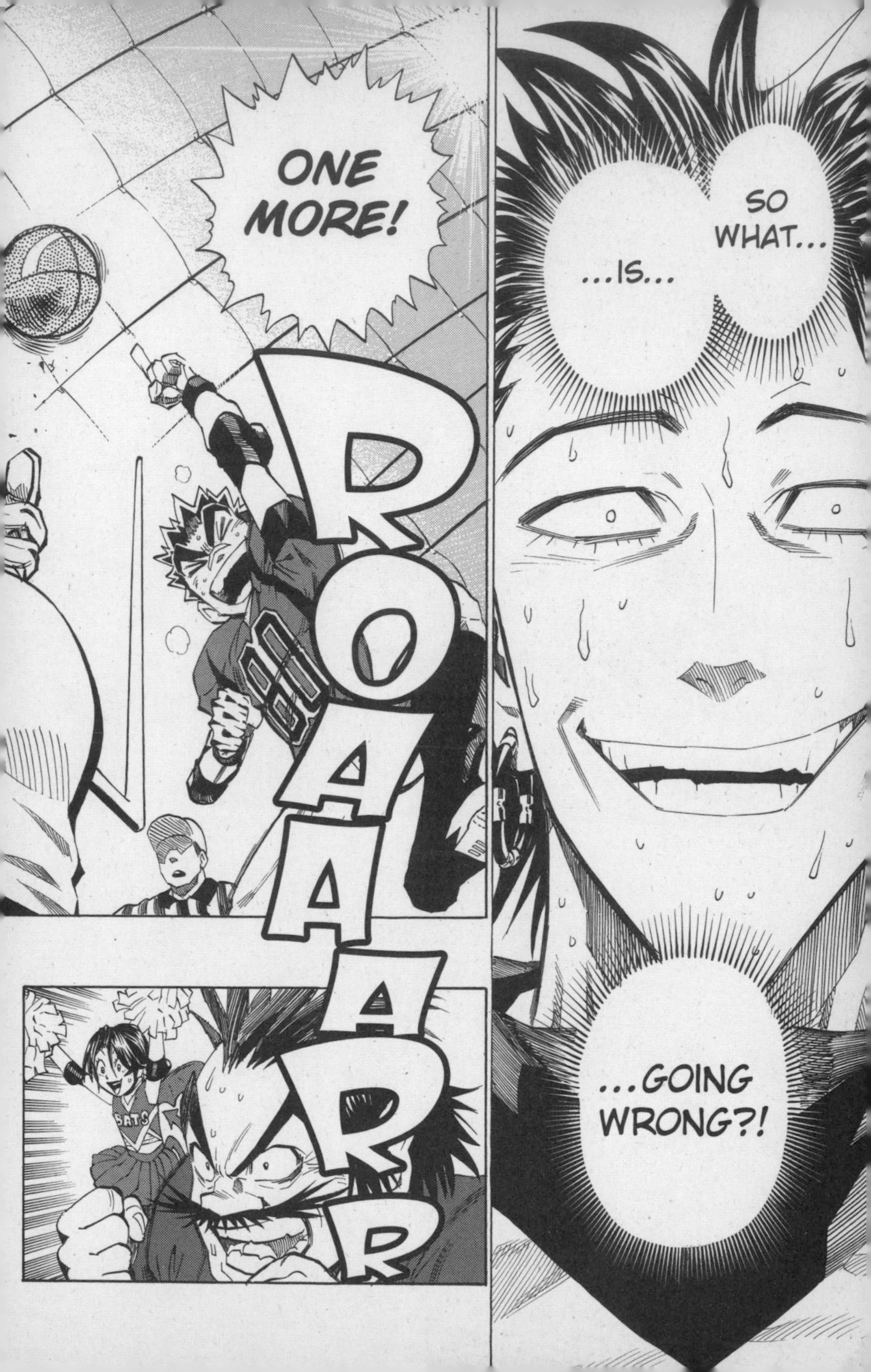
SO WHAT... ...IS...
...GOING WRONG?!
ONE MORE!
ROAAARR

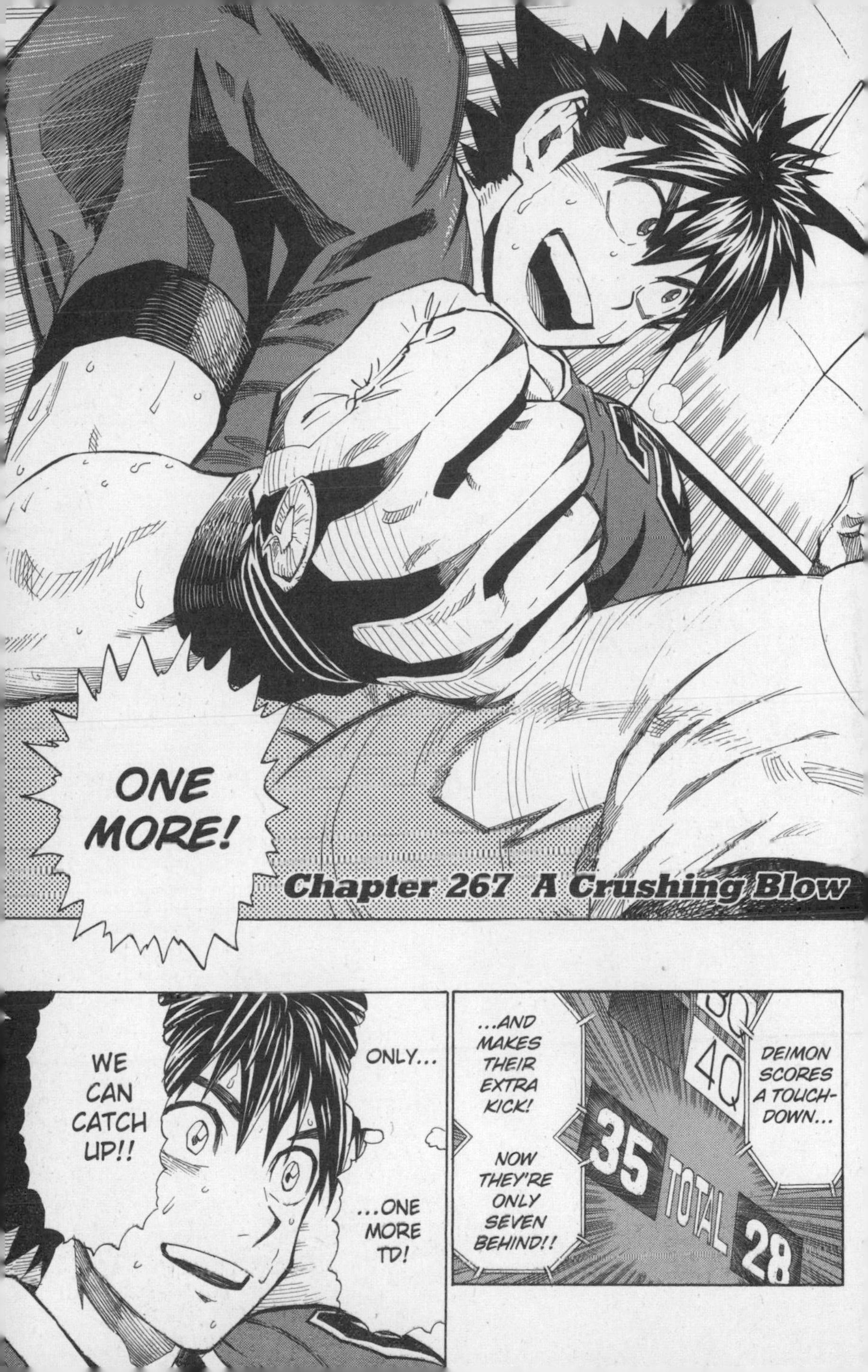
ONE MORE!
Chapter 267 A Crushing Blow
DEIMON SCORES A TOUCH-DOWN...
...AND MAKES THEIR EXTRA KICK!
NOW THEY'RE ONLY SEVEN BEHIND!!
4Q
35 TOTAL 28
ONLY...
...ONE MORE TD!
WE CAN CATCH UP!!

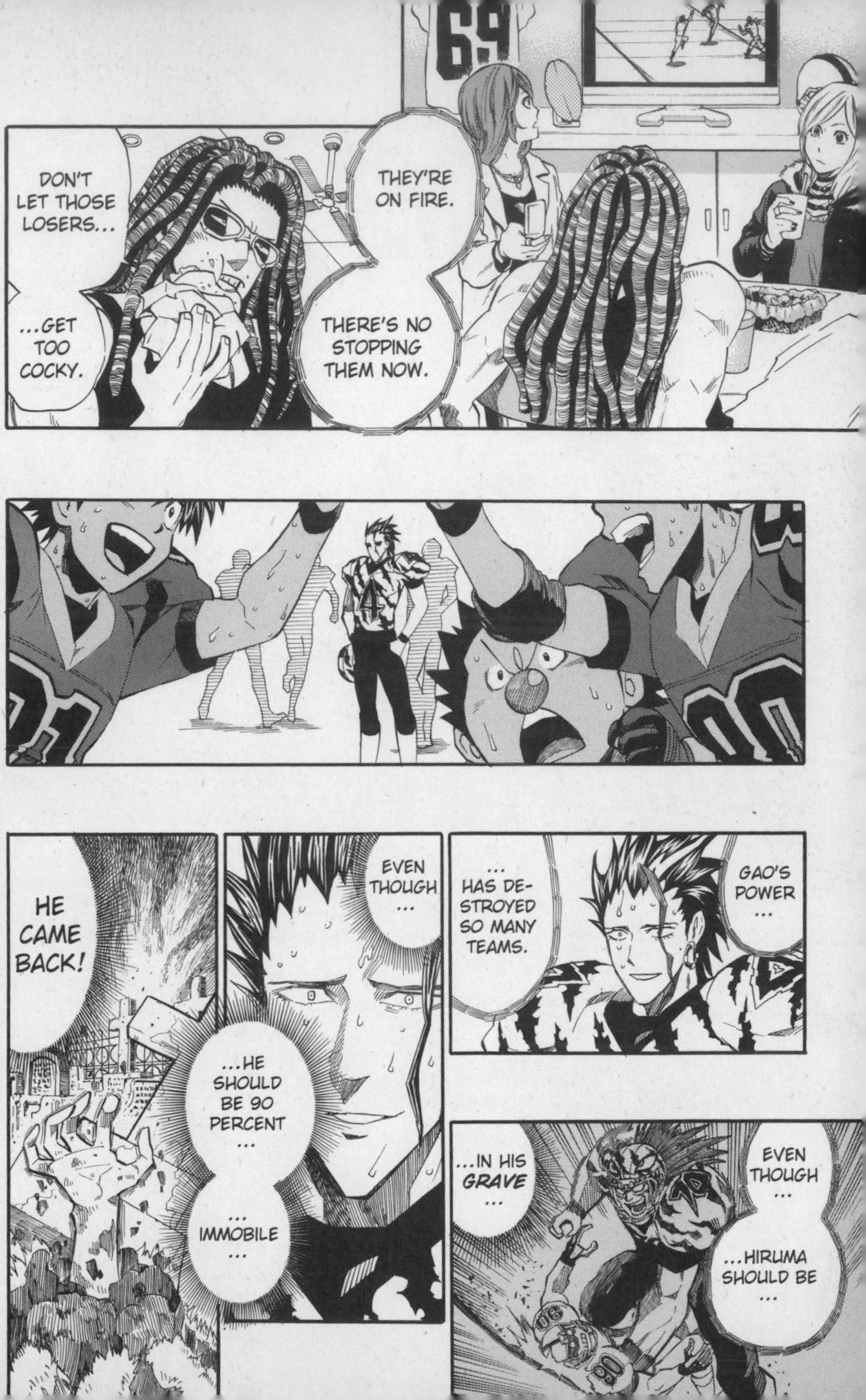
THEY'RE ON FIRE.
THERE'S NO STOPPING THEM NOW.
DON'T LET THOSE LOSERS...
...GET TOO COCKY.
GAO'S POWER ...
... HAS DE-STROYED SO MANY TEAMS.
EVEN THOUGH ...
...HIRUMA SHOULD BE ...
...IN HIS *GRAVE* ...
EVEN THOUGH ...
...HE SHOULD BE 90 PERCENT ...
... IMMOBILE ...
HE CAME BACK!

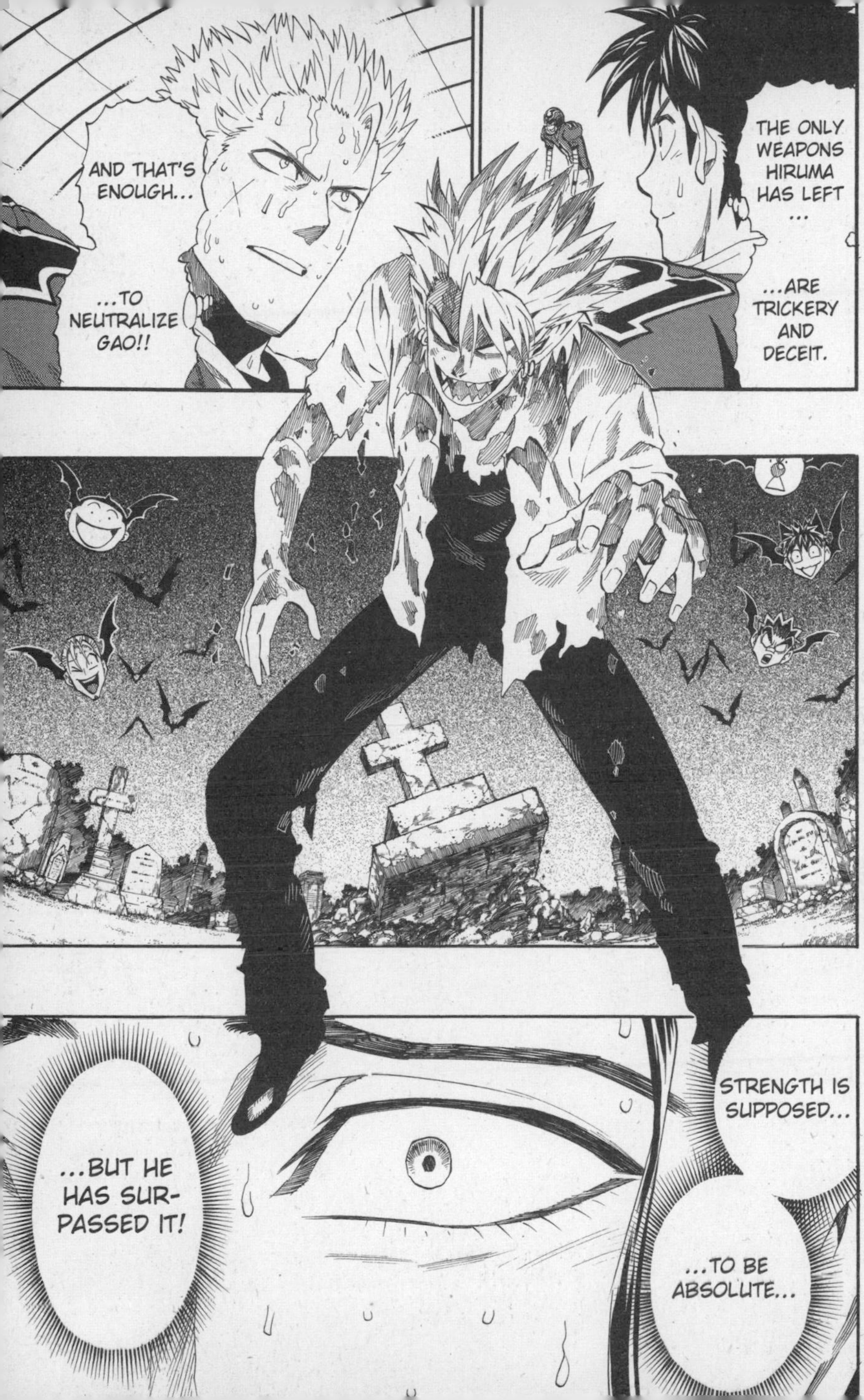
THE ONLY WEAPONS HIRUMA HAS LEFT ...
...ARE TRICKERY AND DECEIT.
AND THAT'S ENOUGH...
...TO NEUTRALIZE GAO!!
STRENGTH IS SUPPOSED...
...TO BE ABSOLUTE...
...BUT HE HAS SUR-PASSED IT!

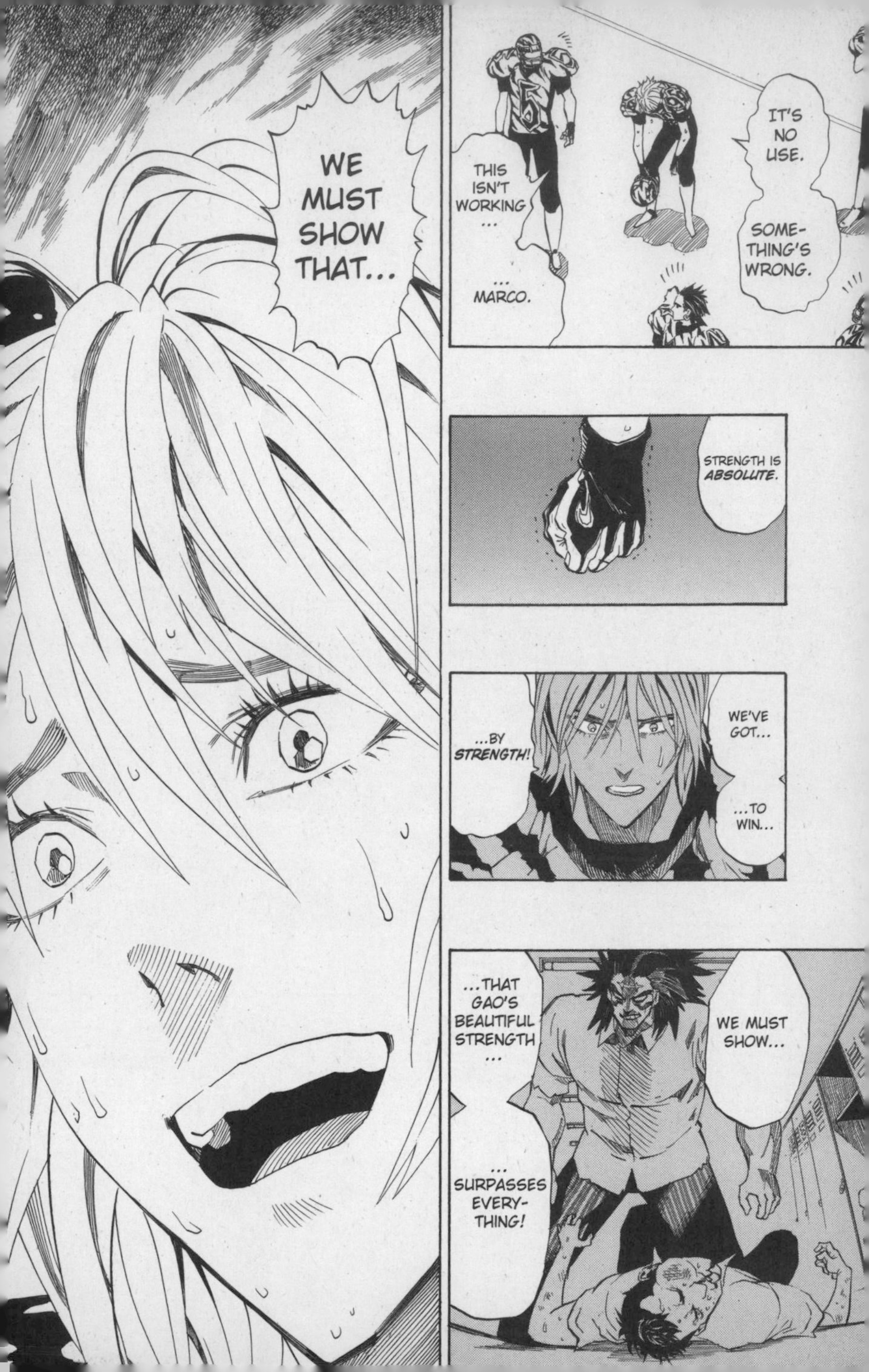
IT'S NO USE.
SOME-THING'S WRONG.
THIS ISN'T WORKING...
...MARCO.
STRENGTH IS ABSOLUTE.
WE'VE GOT...
...TO WIN...
...BY STRENGTH!
WE MUST SHOW...
...THAT GAO'S BEAUTIFUL STRENGTH...
...SURPASSES EVERY-THING!
WE MUST SHOW THAT...

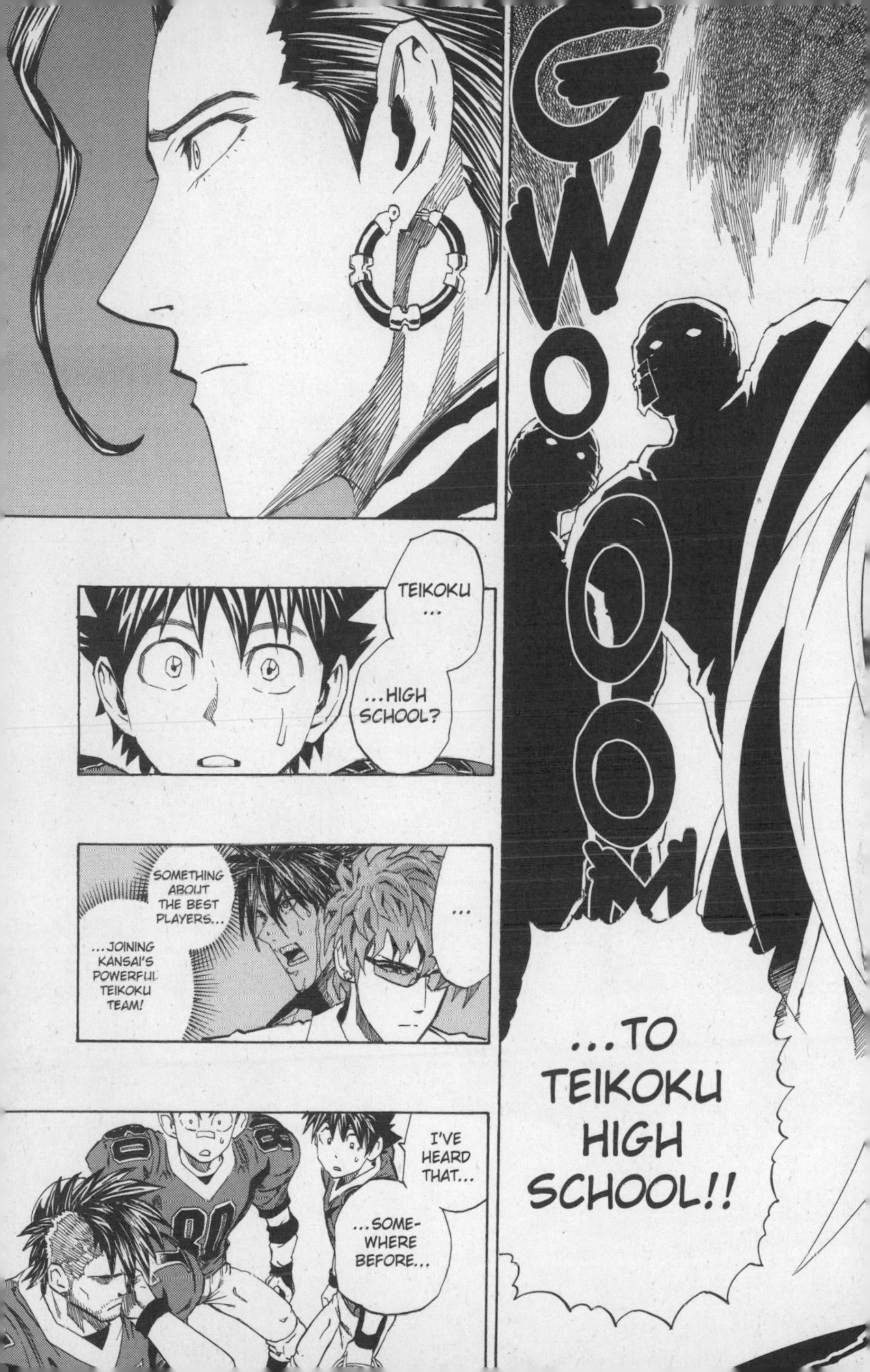
GWOOOOM
...TO TEIKOKU HIGH SCHOOL!!
TEIKOKU ...
...HIGH SCHOOL?
...
SOMETHING ABOUT THE BEST PLAYERS...
...JOINING KANSAI'S POWERFUL TEIKOKU TEAM!
I'VE HEARD THAT...
...SOME-WHERE BEFORE...

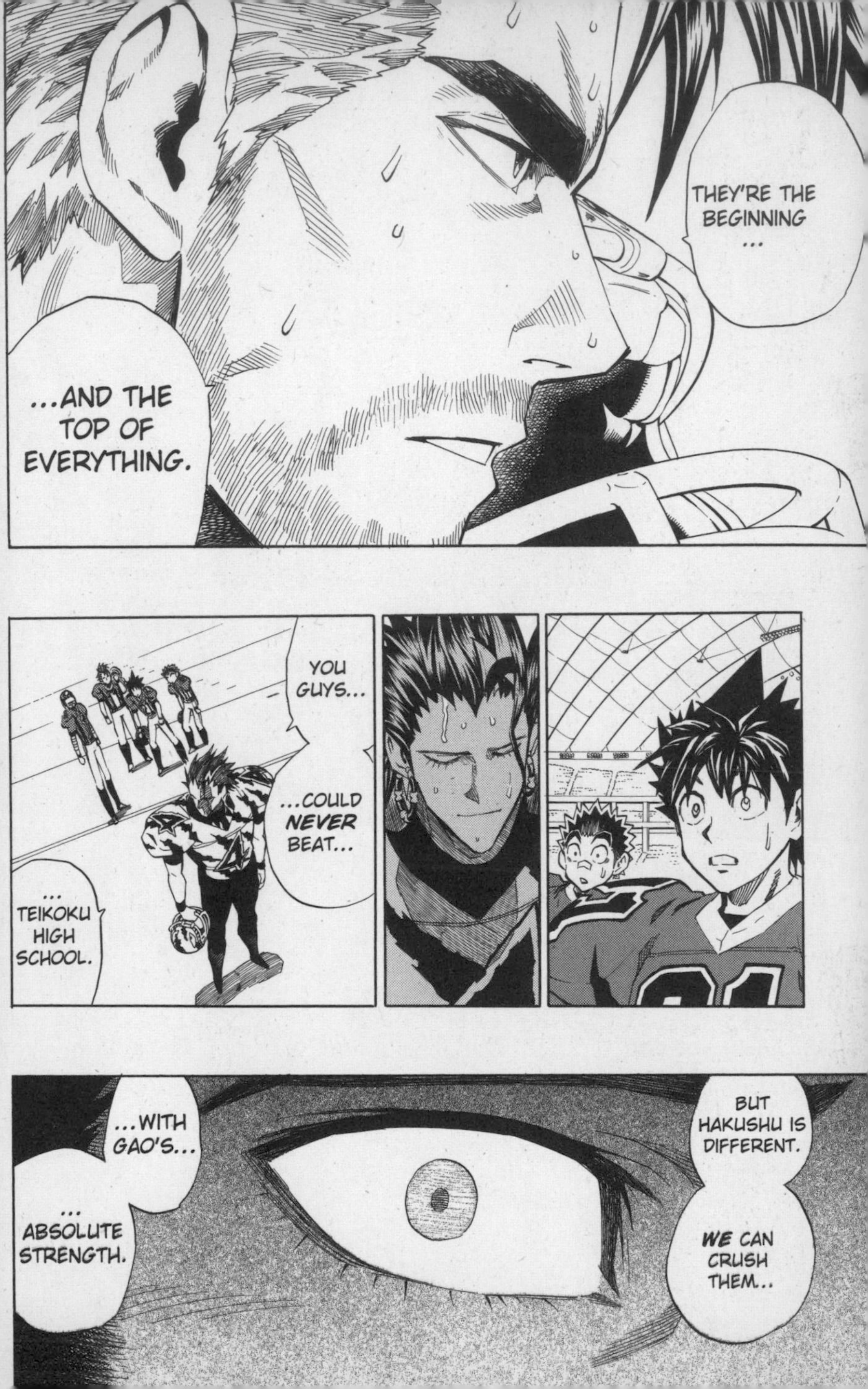
THEY'RE THE BEGINNING ...
...AND THE TOP OF EVERYTHING.
YOU GUYS...
...COULD *NEVER* BEAT...
... TEIKOKU HIGH SCHOOL.
BUT HAKUSHU IS DIFFERENT.
WE CAN CRUSH THEM..
...WITH GAO'S...
... ABSOLUTE STRENGTH.

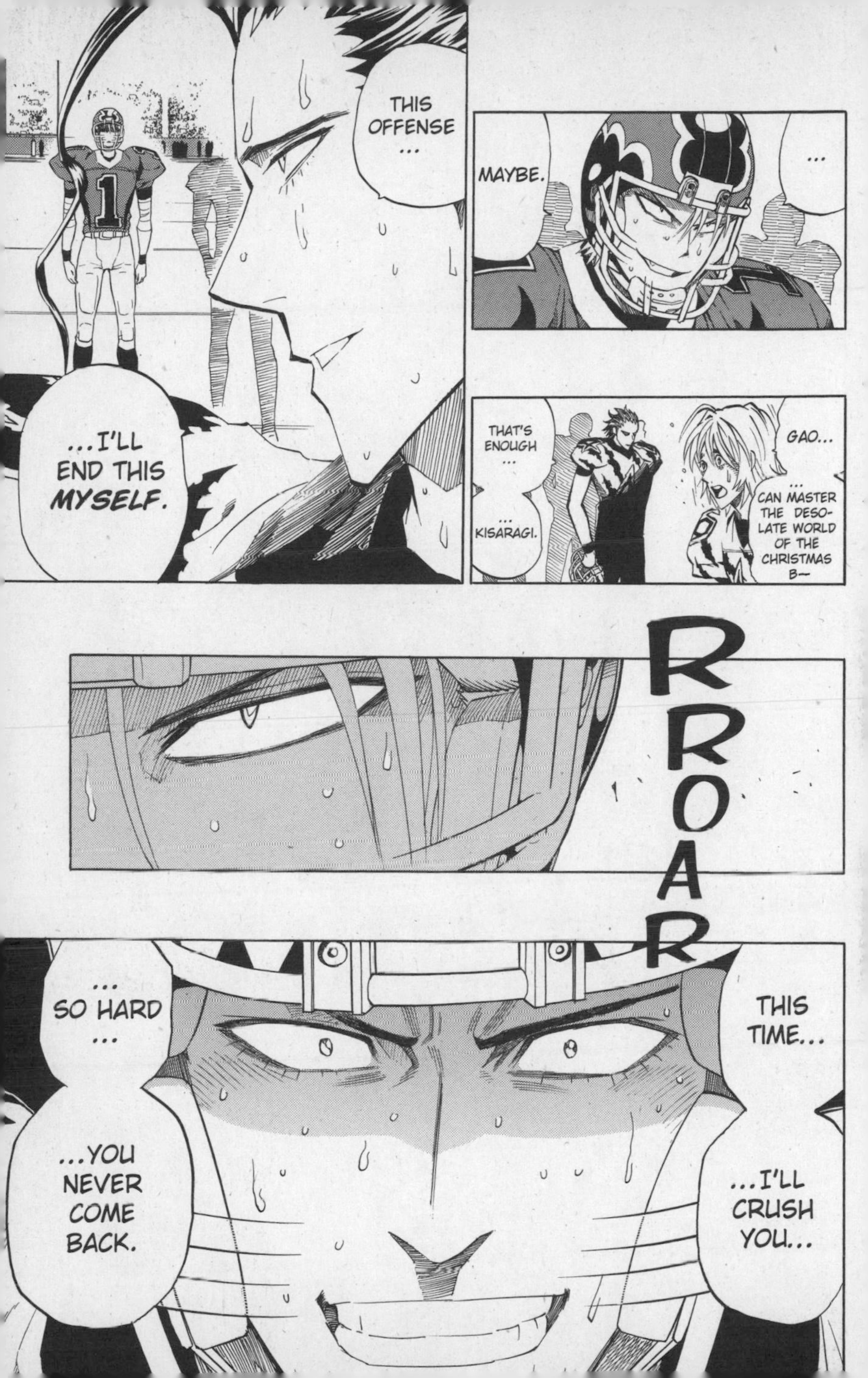
...
MAYBE.
GAO... ...CAN MASTER THE DESOLATE WORLD OF THE CHRISTMAS B—
THAT'S ENOUGH... ...KISARAGI.
THIS OFFENSE...
...I'LL END THIS MYSELF.
RROAR
THIS TIME... ...I'LL CRUSH YOU...
...SO HARD... ...YOU NEVER COME BACK.

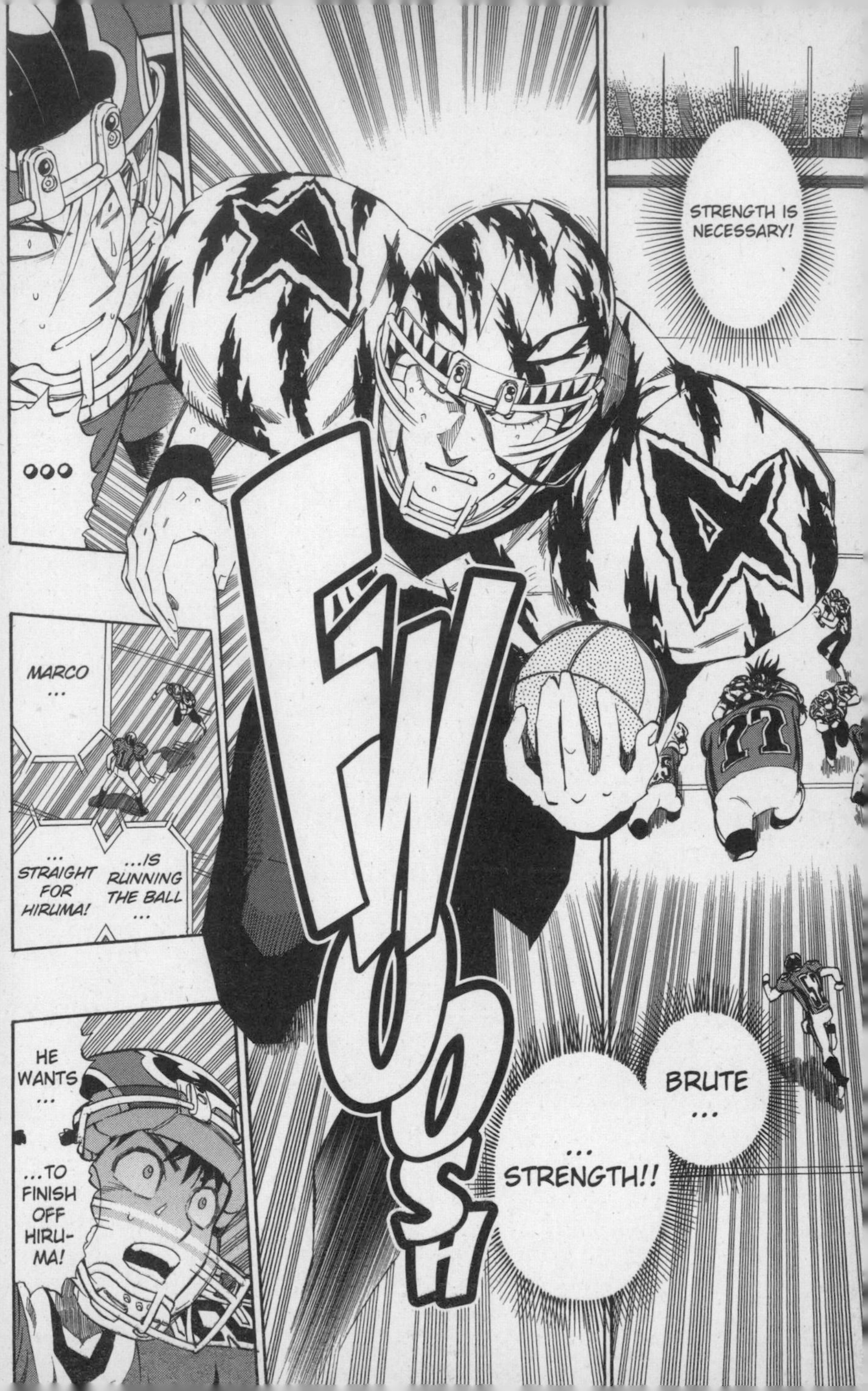
STRENGTH IS NECESSARY!
FWOOSH
BRUTE ...
... STRENGTH!!
...
MARCO ...
...IS RUNNING THE BALL ...
... STRAIGHT FOR HIRUMA!
HE WANTS ...
...TO FINISH OFF HIRU-MA!

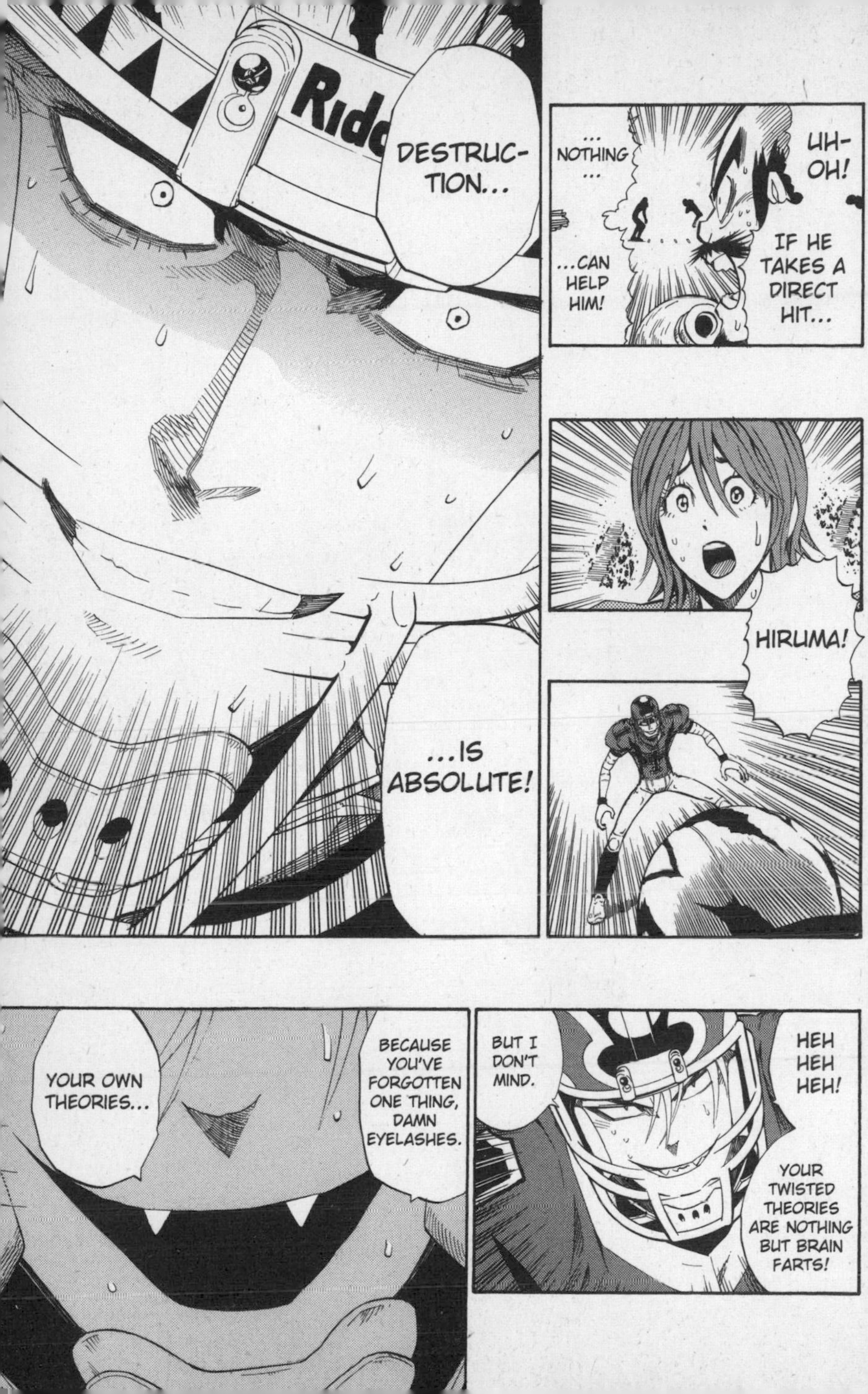
UH-OH!
IF HE TAKES A DIRECT HIT...
... NOTHING ...
...CAN HELP HIM!
HIRUMA!
DESTRUC-TION...
...IS ABSOLUTE!
HEH HEH HEH!
YOUR TWISTED THEORIES ARE NOTHING BUT BRAIN FARTS!
BUT I DON'T MIND.
BECAUSE YOU'VE FORGOTTEN ONE THING, DAMN EYELASHES.
YOUR OWN THEORIES...

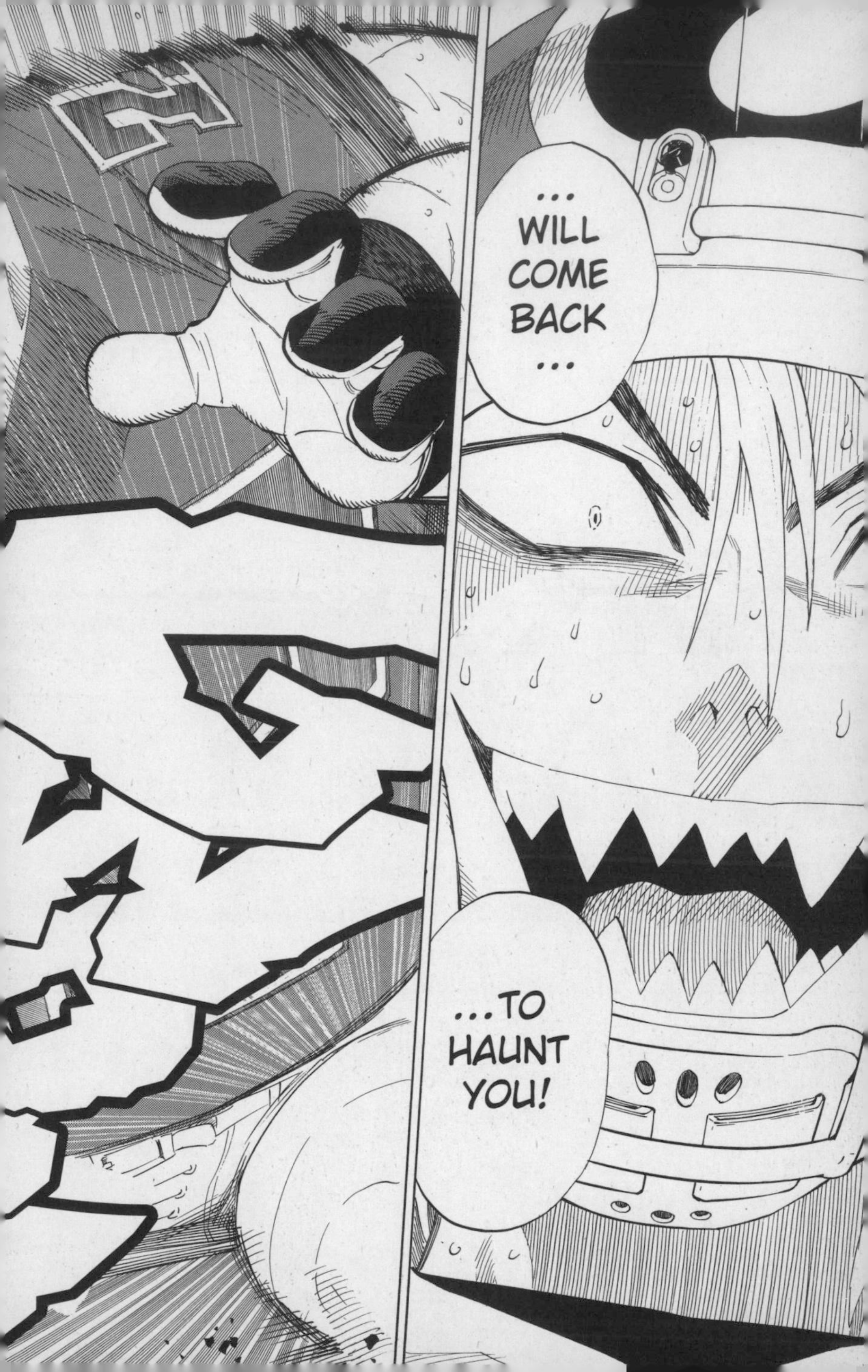
...WILL COME BACK...
...TO HAUNT YOU!

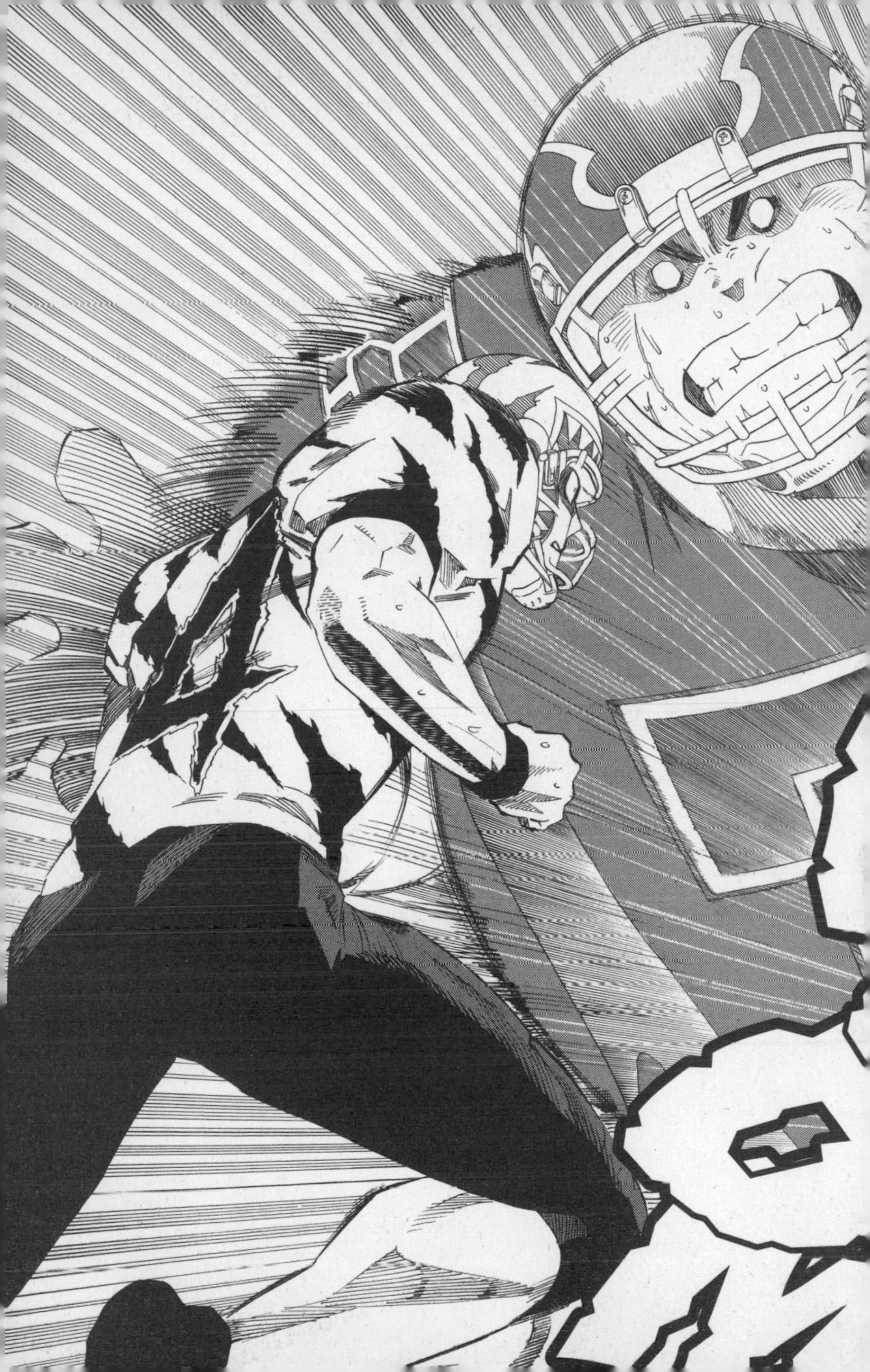

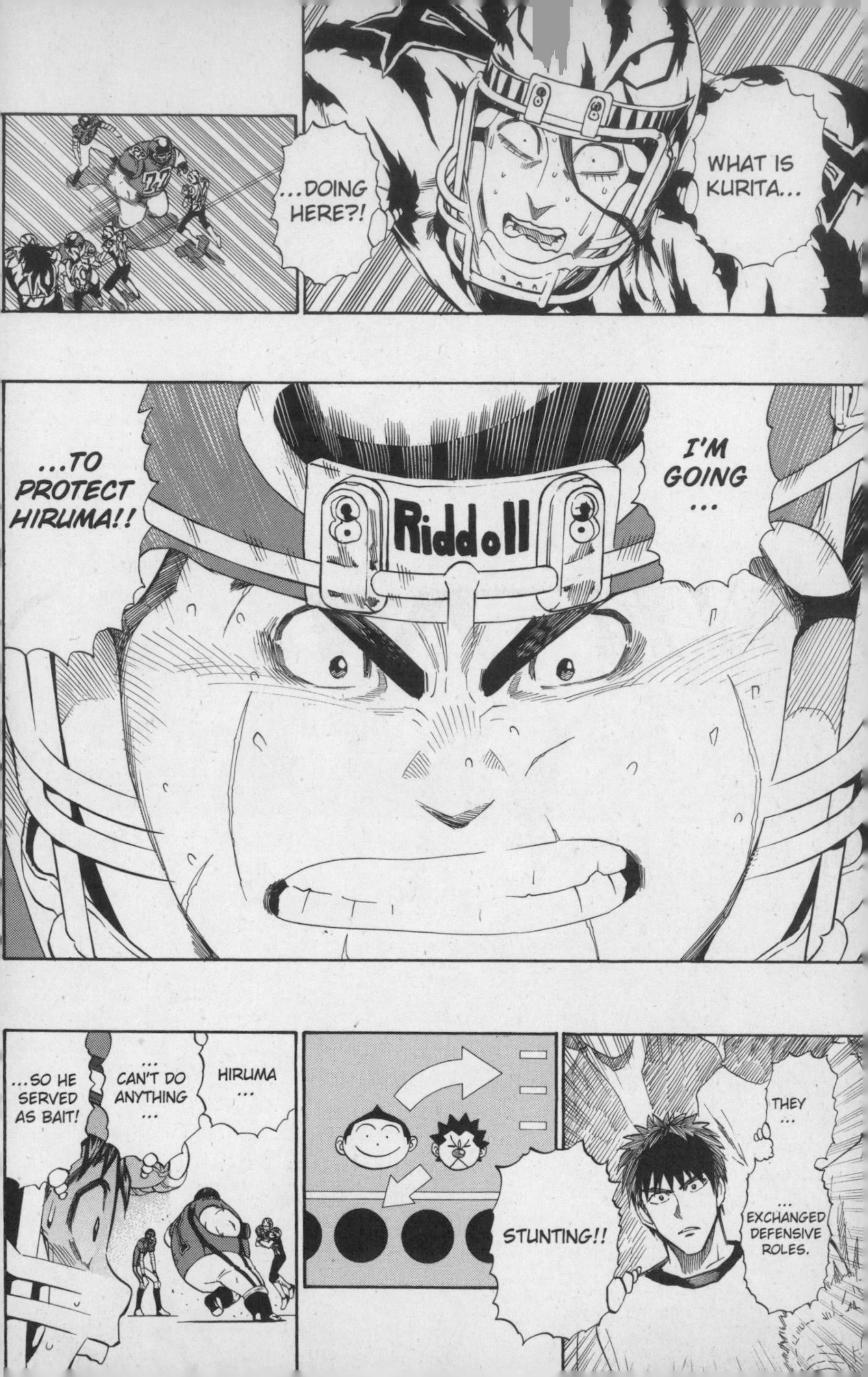
WHAT IS KURITA...
...DOING HERE?!
I'M GOING ...
...TO PROTECT HIRUMA!!
Riddoll
THEY ...
... EXCHANGED DEFENSIVE ROLES.
STUNTING!!
HIRUMA ...
... CAN'T DO ANYTHING ...
...SO HE SERVED AS BAIT!

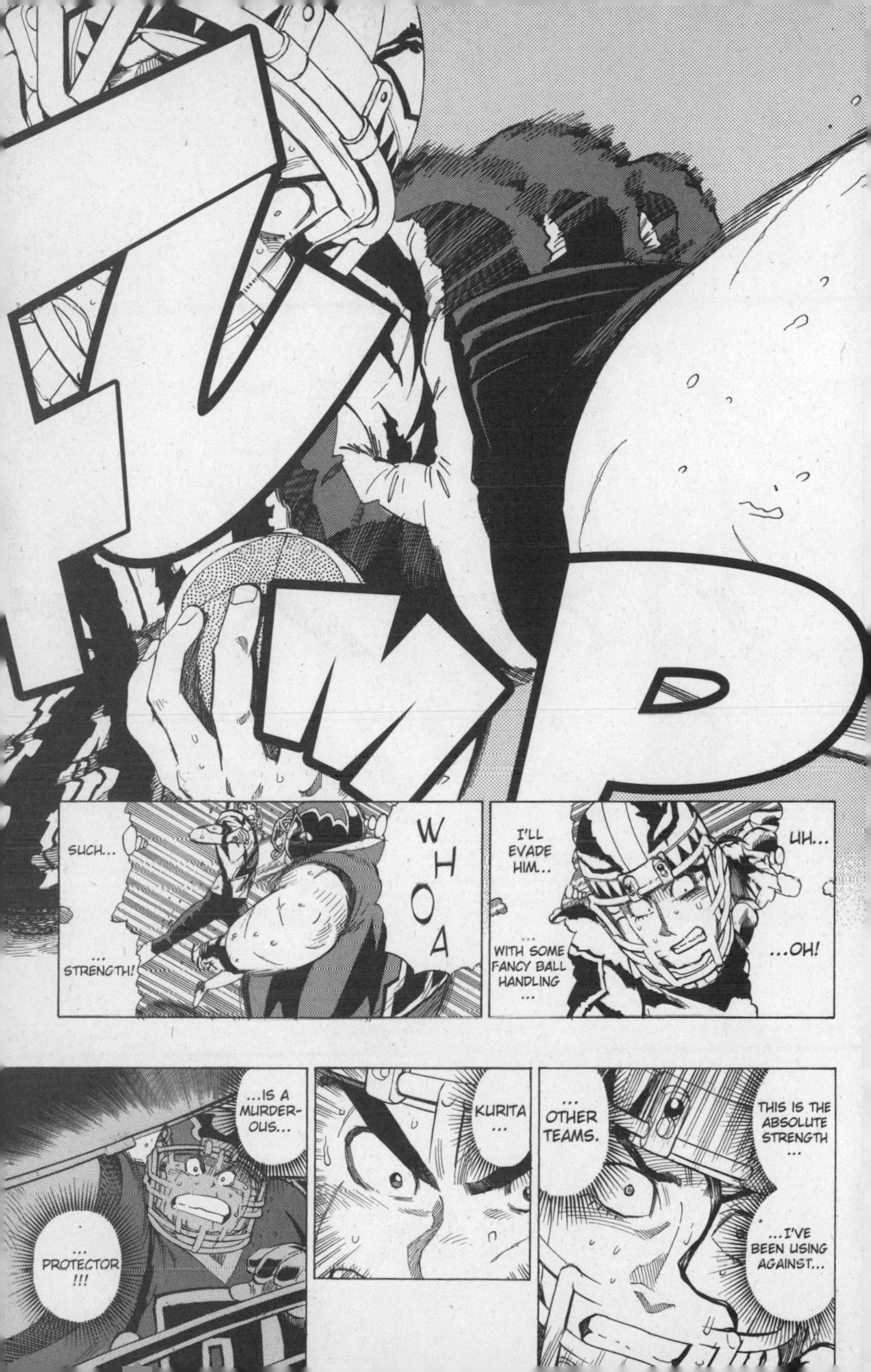
UH...
I'LL EVADE HIM...
...OH!
... WITH SOME FANCY BALL HANDLING ...
WHOA
SUCH...
... STRENGTH!
THIS IS THE ABSOLUTE STRENGTH ...
...I'VE BEEN USING AGAINST...
... OTHER TEAMS.
KURITA ...
...IS A MURDER-OUS...
... PROTECTOR !!!

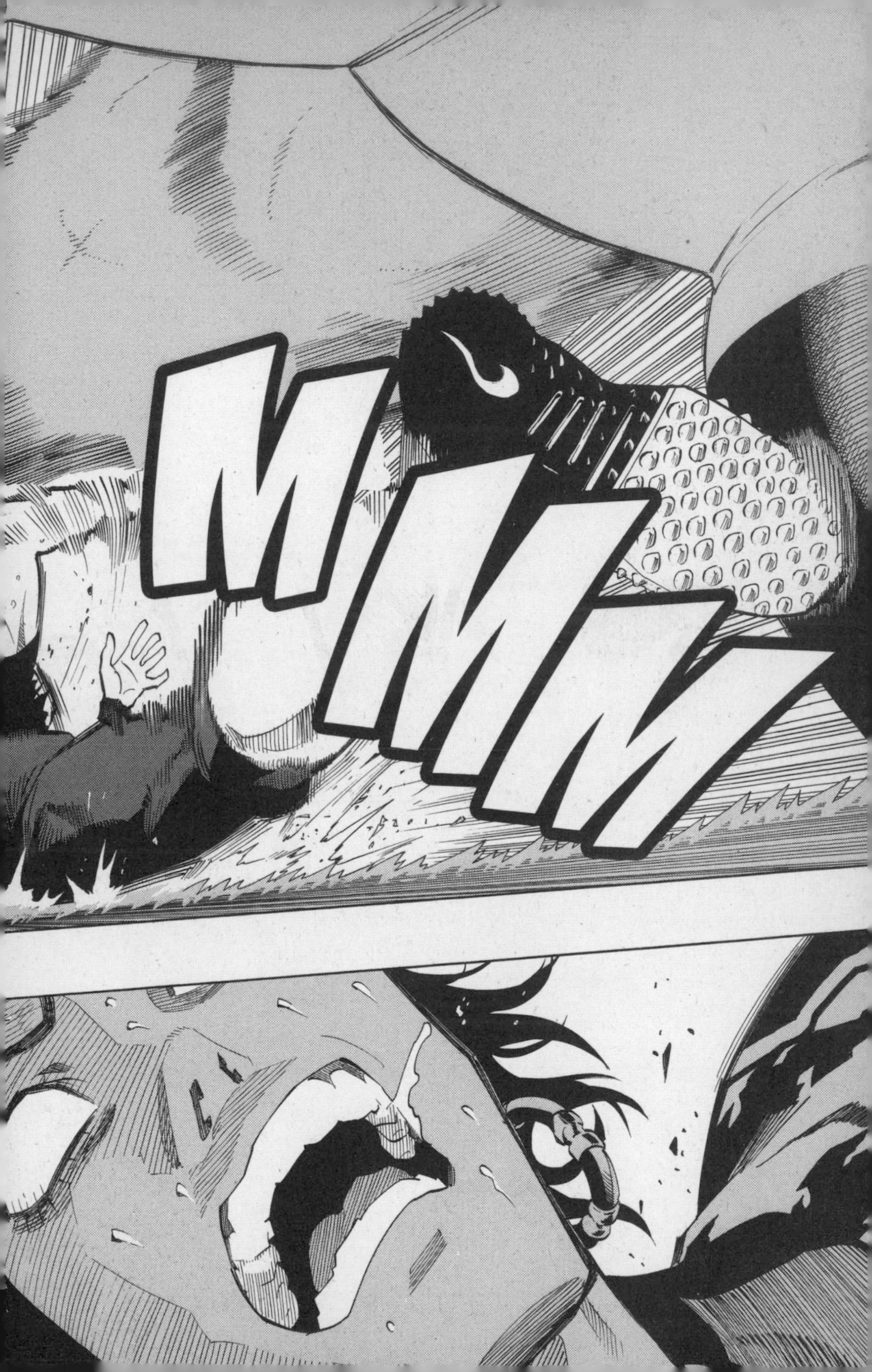
MMMM

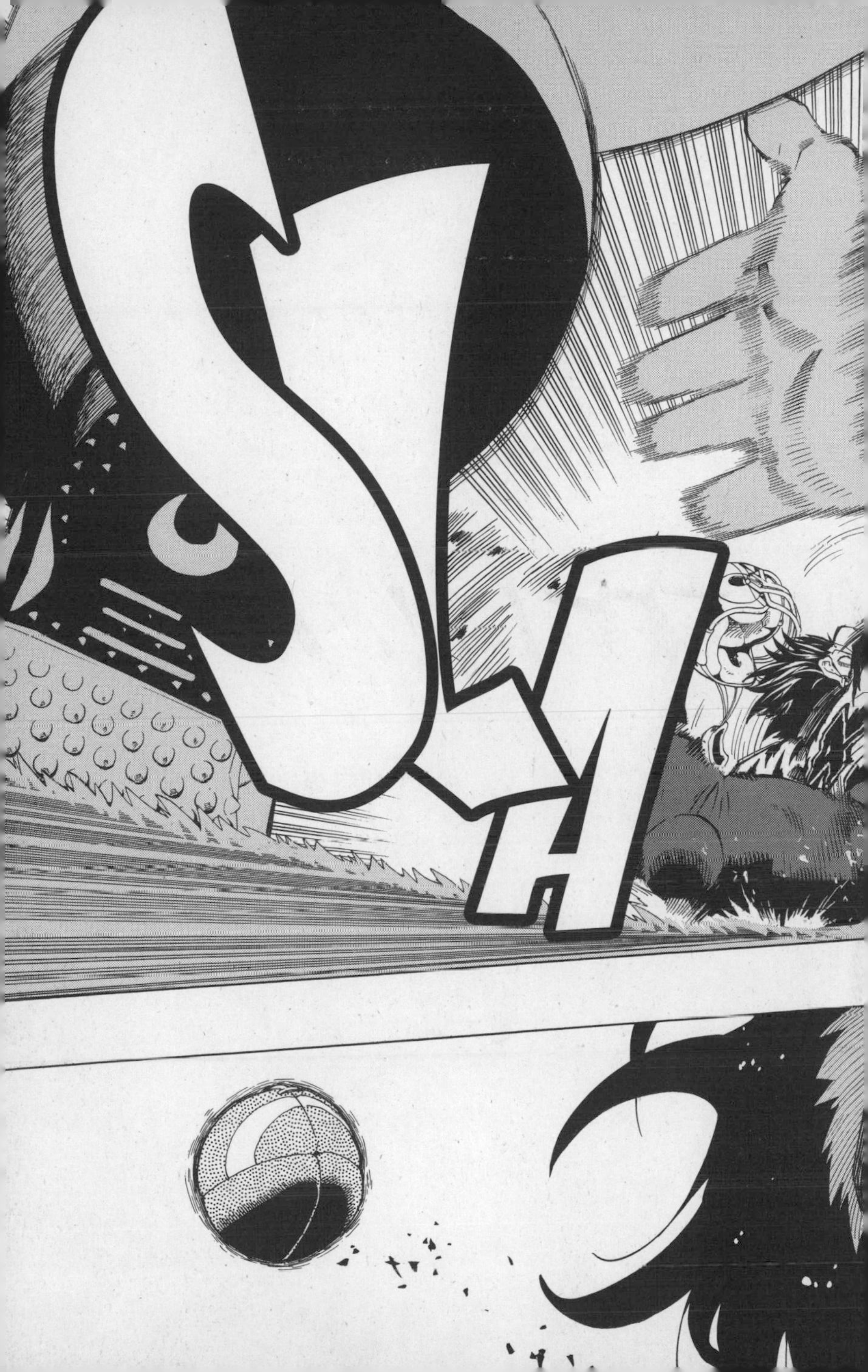
SH

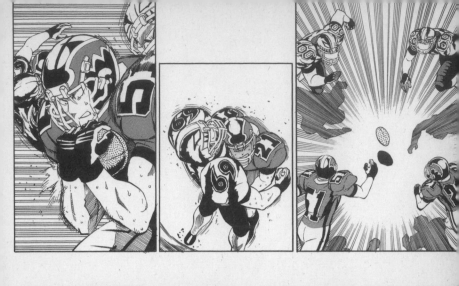

WITH ONLY FIVE MINUTES TO GO...

...THE SCORE...

...IS TIED!!

TOUCH... ...DOWN!!

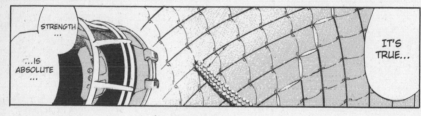

STRENGTH... ...IS ABSOLUTE...

IT'S TRUE...

...WHAT...

...YOU SOW...

YOU REAP...

Deluxe Biographies
of the Supporting Cast

Hakushu's Kicker: Saburo Mitsui

His driving motto in life is "I'll never be first! I always try to be third!!" He's *somewhat* ambitious.

But all the girls he likes put him *third* on their list, so his motto doesn't work at all when it comes to romance…

Funurghbah Dog & Funurghbah Pig

They appear on page 75. Kurita's fighting spirit even infects animals!

Cerberus's body changes so it can *deflect bullets*! Piggyberus's body loses fat so he tastes better!

Hakushu Junior High School

Fossils can be unearthed in the school yard, so at least when it comes to paleontology, it's an *abnormally great* school.

Marco's first-year summer project was to bring *dinosaurs back to life*. Good thing he failed.

ALLOSAURUS

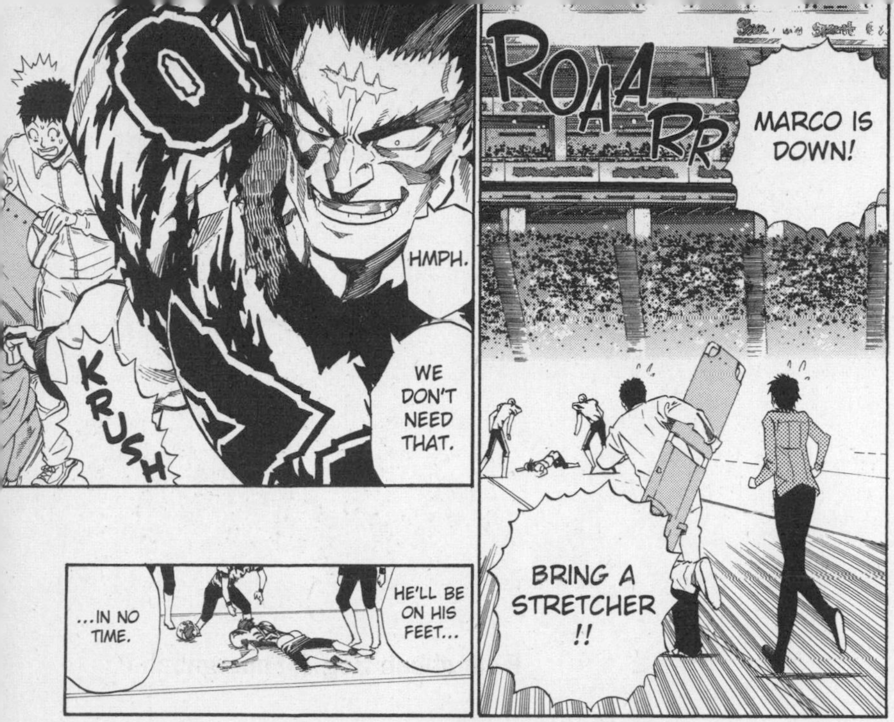
ROAARR
MARCO IS DOWN!
BRING A STRETCHER!!
HMPH.
WE DON'T NEED THAT.
KRUSH
HE'LL BE ON HIS FEET...
...IN NO TIME.

Chapter 268 He Only Sees the Top

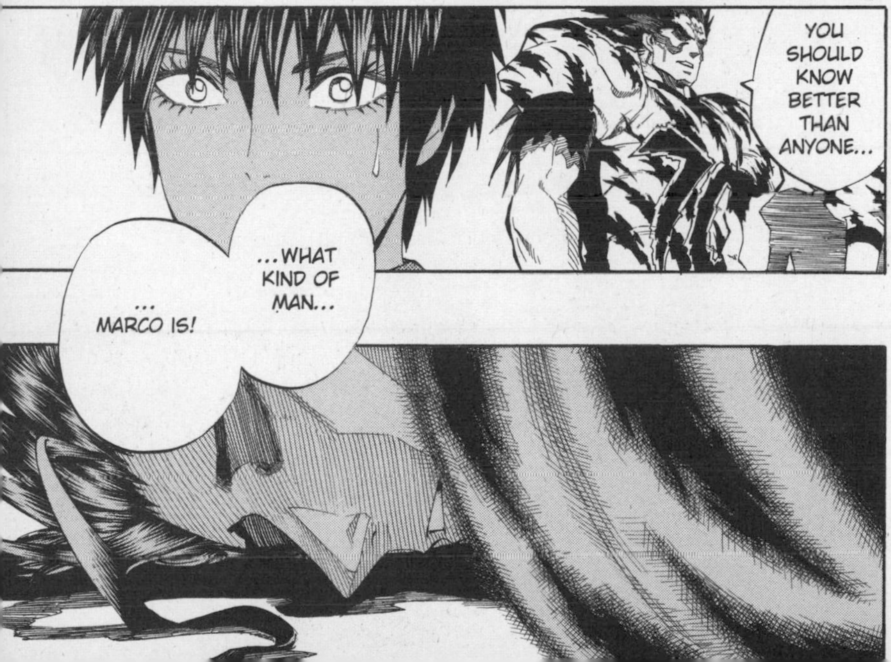
YOU SHOULD KNOW BETTER THAN ANYONE...
...WHAT KIND OF MAN...
... MARCO IS!

Chapter 268
He Only Sees the Top

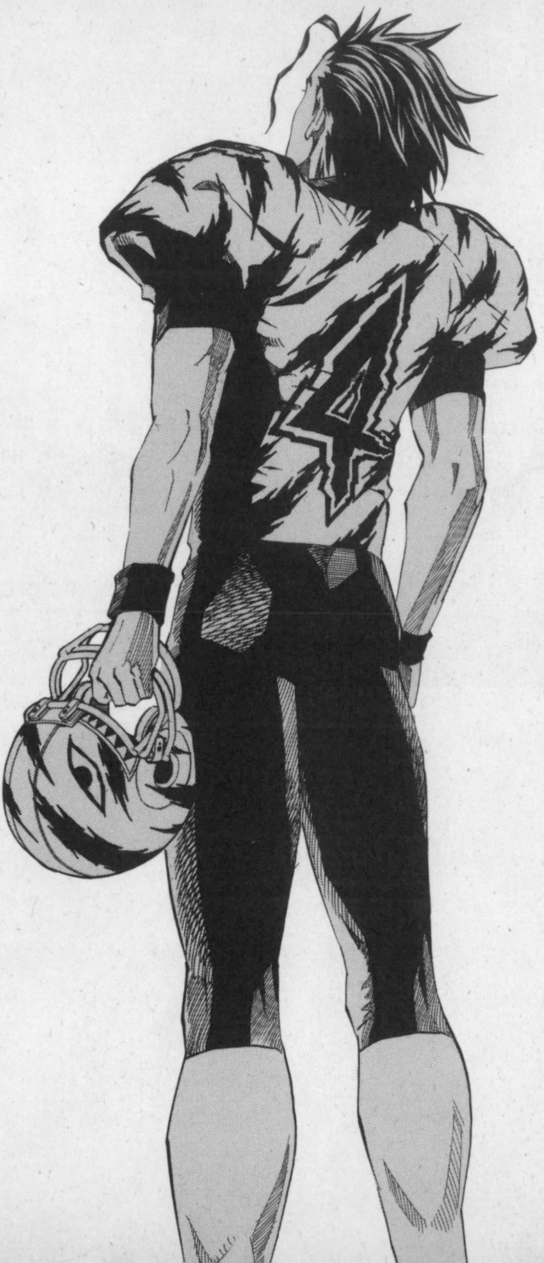

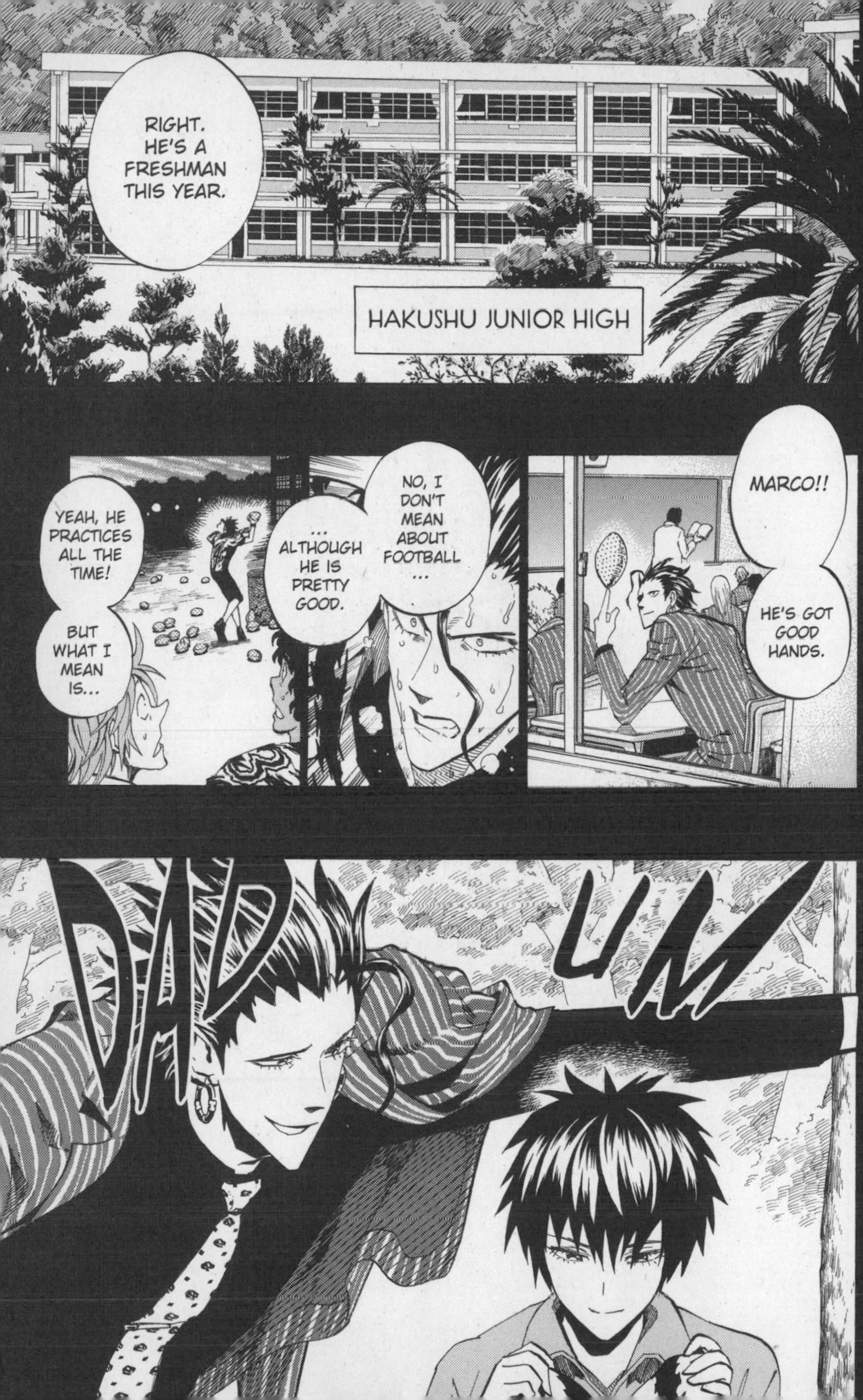
RIGHT. HE'S A FRESHMAN THIS YEAR.
HAKUSHU JUNIOR HIGH
MARCO!!
HE'S GOT GOOD HANDS.
NO, I DON'T MEAN ABOUT FOOTBALL...
... ALTHOUGH HE IS PRETTY GOOD.
YEAH, HE PRACTICES ALL THE TIME!
BUT WHAT I MEAN IS...
DADUM

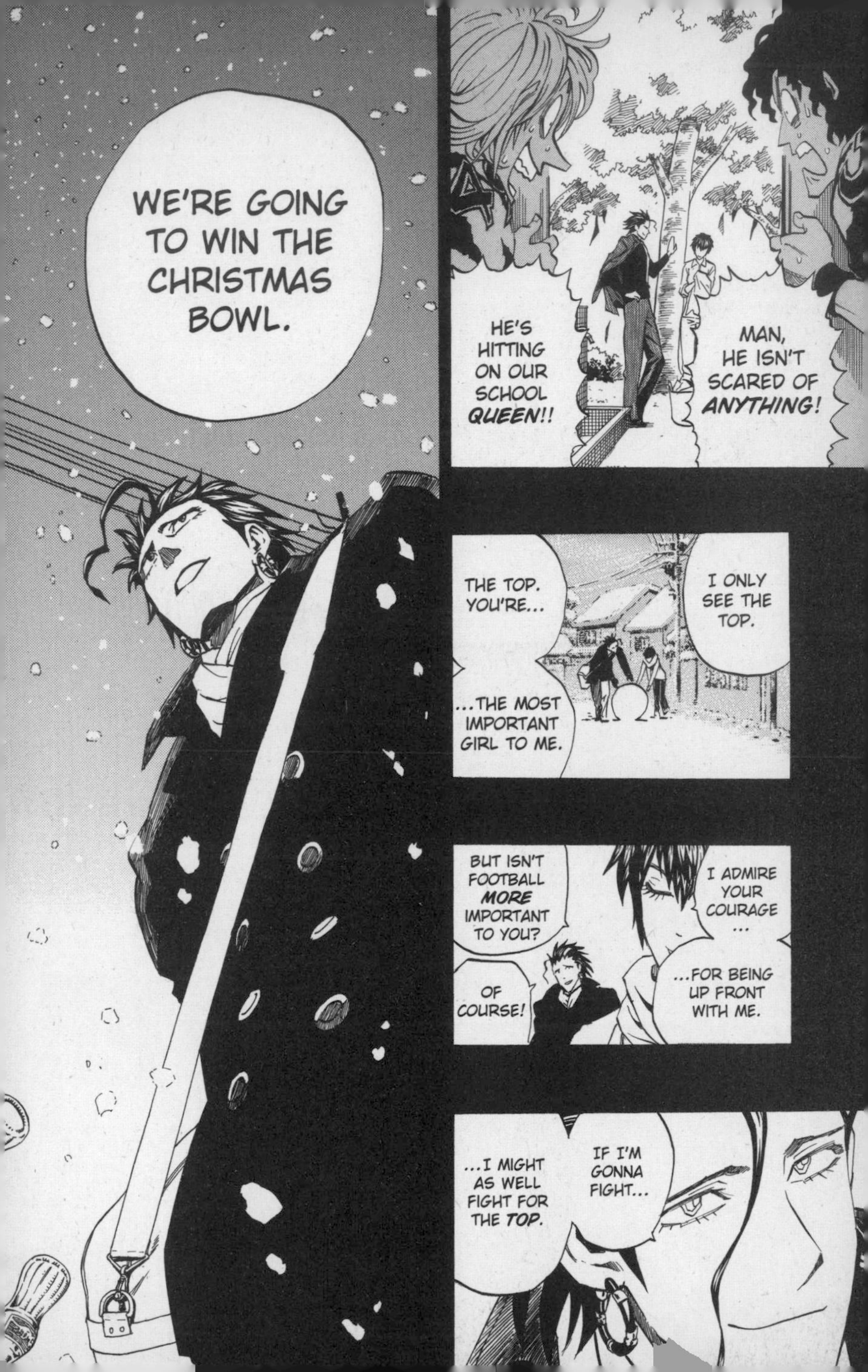
MAN, HE ISN'T SCARED OF ANYTHING!
HE'S HITTING ON OUR SCHOOL QUEEN!!
I ONLY SEE THE TOP.
THE TOP. YOU'RE...
...THE MOST IMPORTANT GIRL TO ME.
I ADMIRE YOUR COURAGE ...
...FOR BEING UP FRONT WITH ME.
BUT ISN'T FOOTBALL MORE IMPORTANT TO YOU?
OF COURSE!
IF I'M GONNA FIGHT...
...I MIGHT AS WELL FIGHT FOR THE TOP.
WE'RE GOING TO WIN THE CHRISTMAS BOWL.

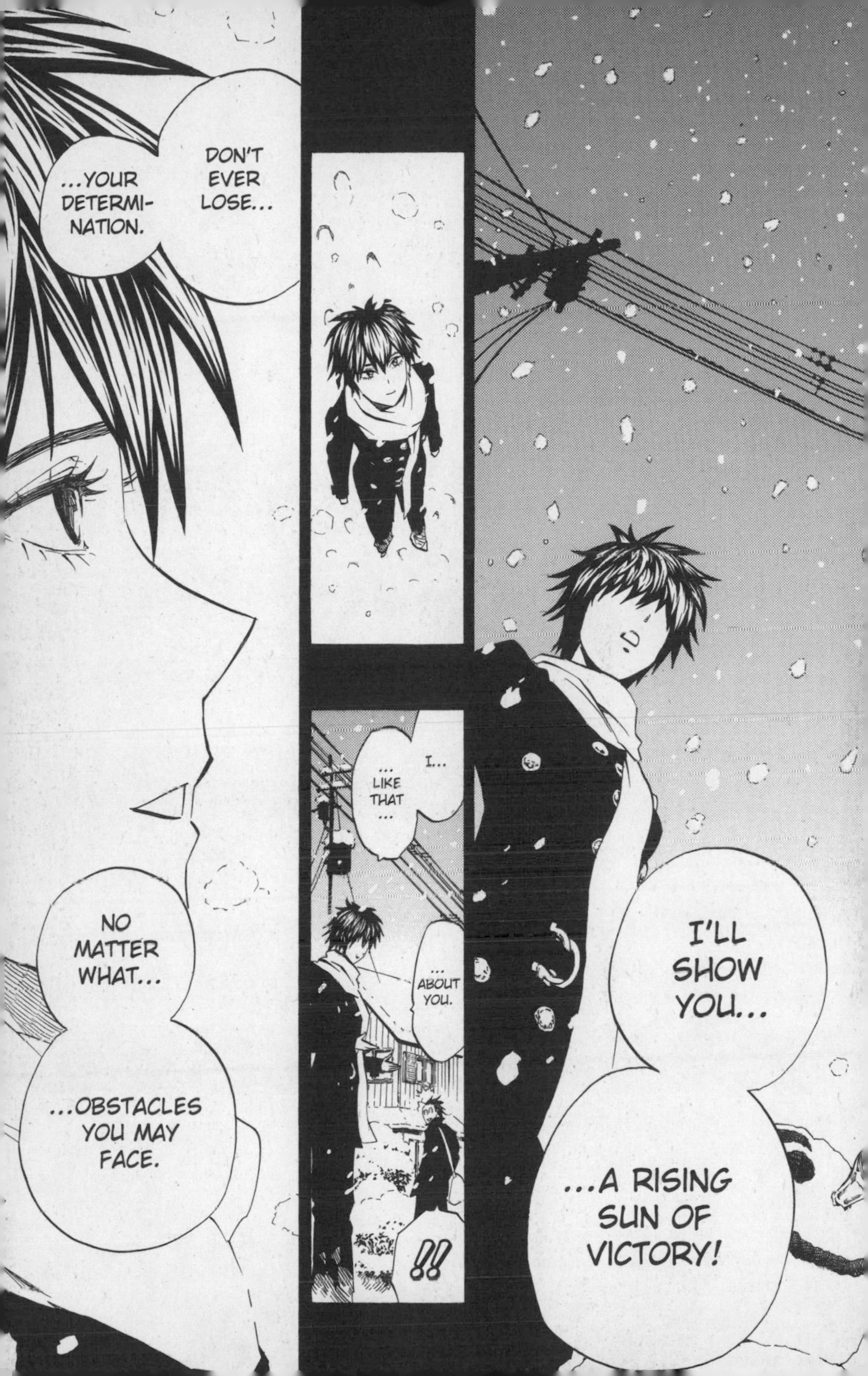
I'LL SHOW YOU...
...A RISING SUN OF VICTORY!
I... ...LIKE THAT...
...ABOUT YOU.
!!
DON'T EVER LOSE...
...YOUR DETERMINATION.
NO MATTER WHAT...
...OBSTACLES YOU MAY FACE.

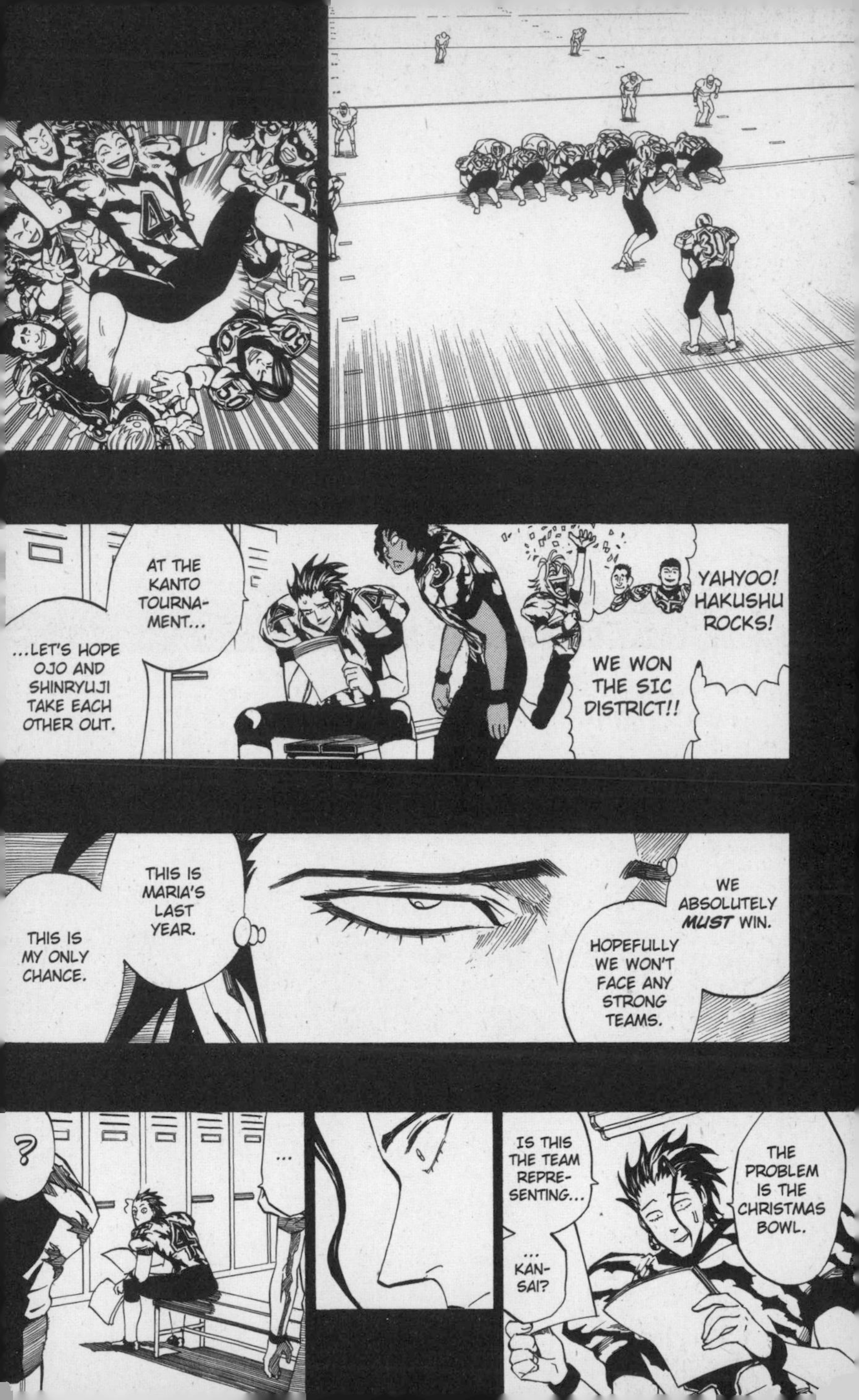
YAHYOO! HAKUSHU ROCKS!
WE WON THE SIC DISTRICT!!
AT THE KANTO TOURNA-MENT...
...LET'S HOPE OJO AND SHINRYUJI TAKE EACH OTHER OUT.
WE ABSOLUTELY *MUST* WIN.
HOPEFULLY WE WON'T FACE ANY STRONG TEAMS.
THIS IS MARIA'S LAST YEAR.
THIS IS MY ONLY CHANCE.
THE PROBLEM IS THE CHRISTMAS BOWL.
IS THIS THE TEAM REPRE-SENTING...
...KAN-SAI?
...
?

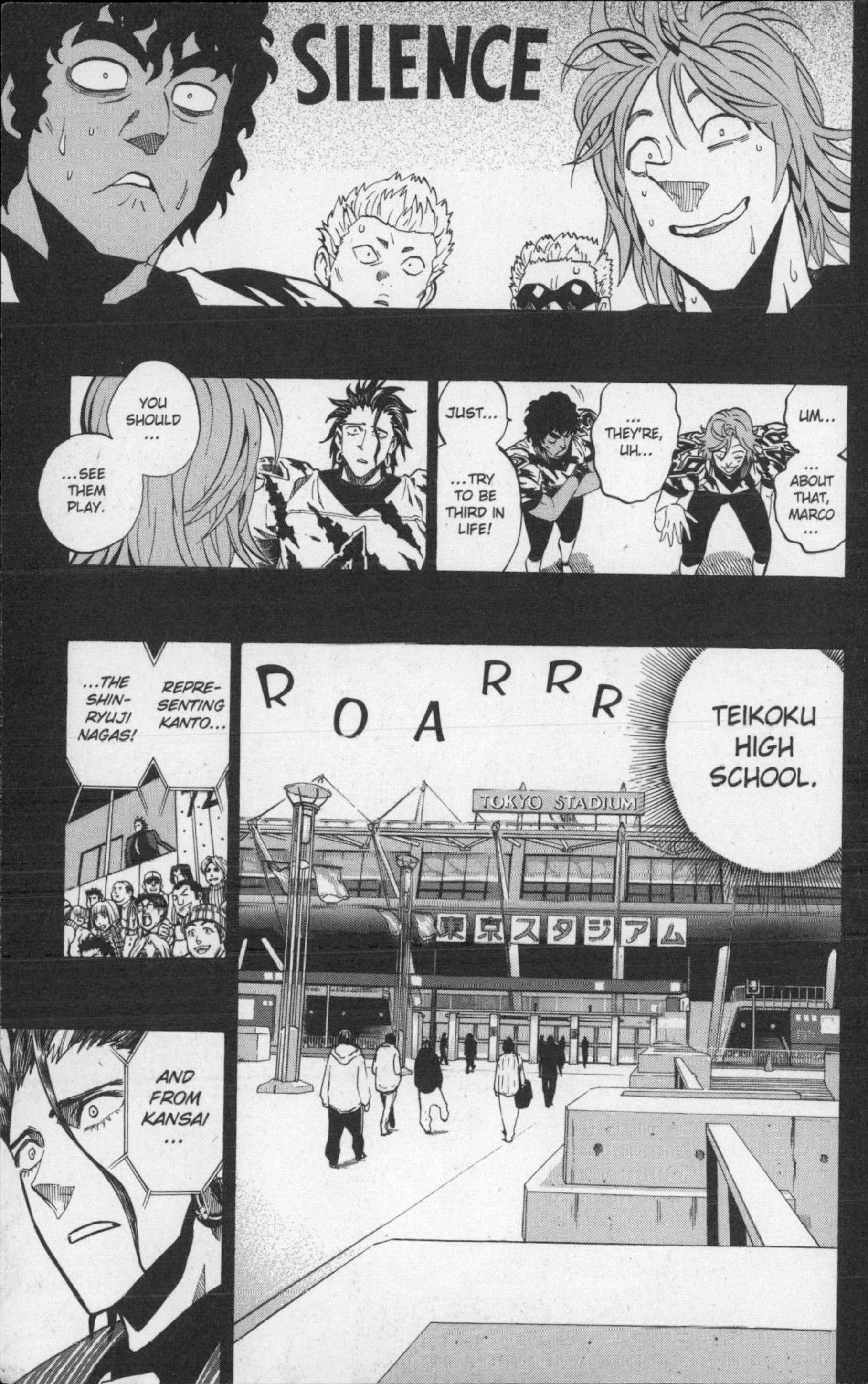
SILENCE
UM...
...ABOUT THAT, MARCO...
...THEY'RE, UH...
JUST...
...TRY TO BE THIRD IN LIFE!
YOU SHOULD...
...SEE THEM PLAY.
REPRESENTING KANTO...
...THE SHINRYUJI NAGAS!
AND FROM KANSAI...
ROARRRR
TOKYO STADIUM
東京スタジアム
TEIKOKU HIGH SCHOOL.

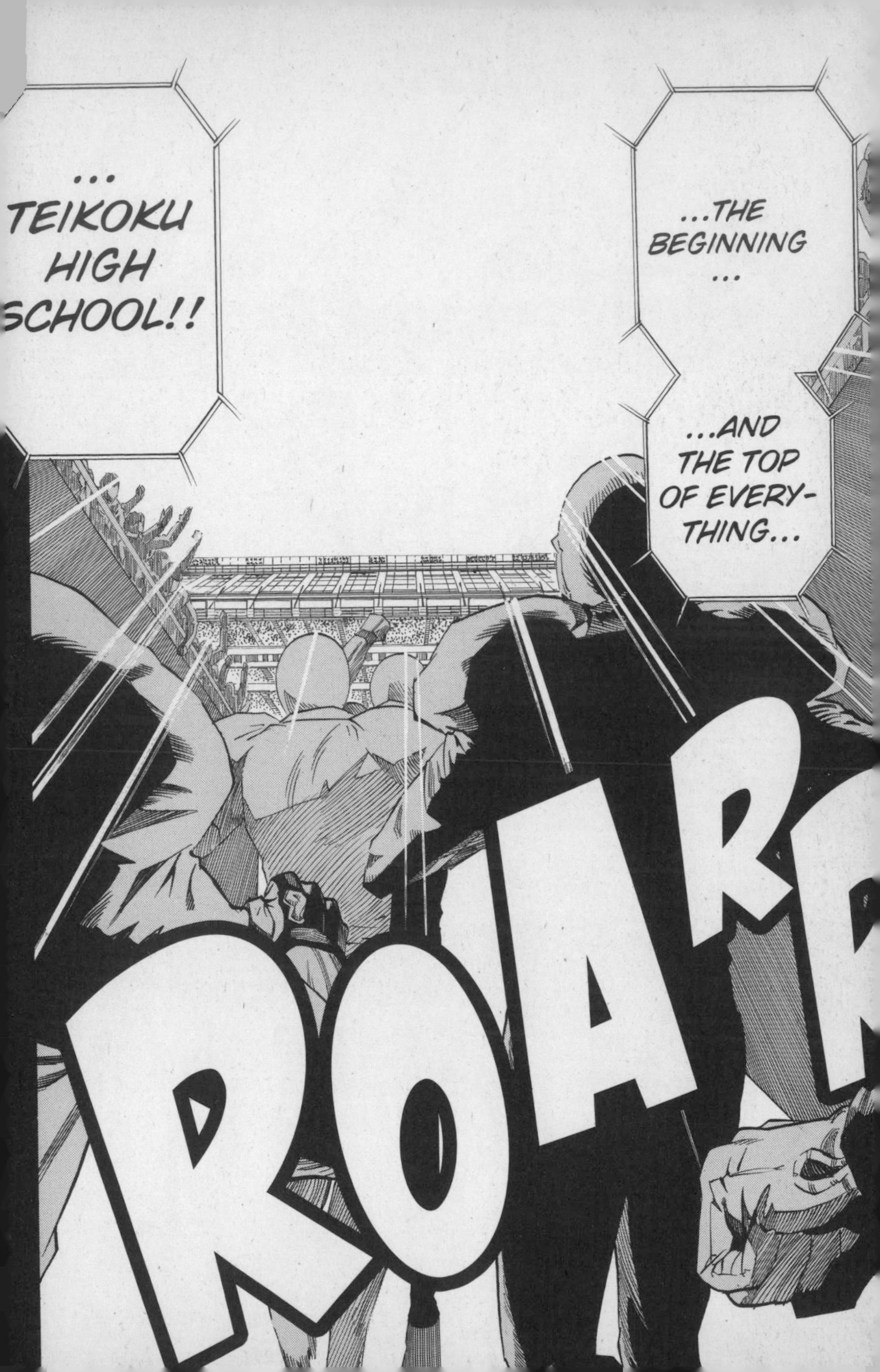
...THE BEGINNING ...
...AND THE TOP OF EVERY-THING...
... TEIKOKU HIGH SCHOOL!!
ROAR

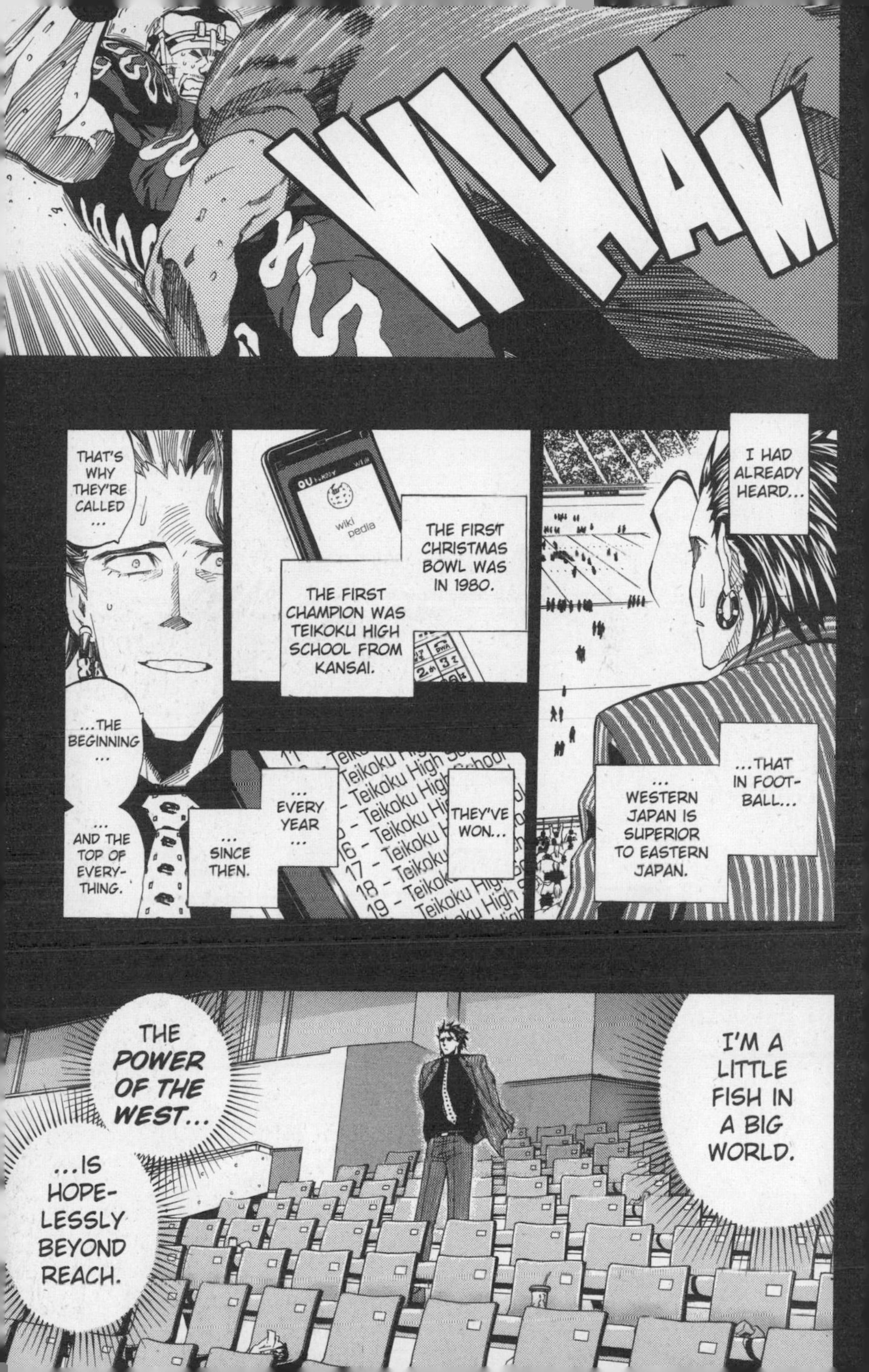
WHAM
I HAD ALREADY HEARD...
...THAT IN FOOT-BALL...
...WESTERN JAPAN IS SUPERIOR TO EASTERN JAPAN.
THE FIRST CHRISTMAS BOWL WAS IN 1980.
THE FIRST CHAMPION WAS TEIKOKU HIGH SCHOOL FROM KANSAI.
THEY'VE WON...
...EVERY YEAR...
...SINCE THEN.
THAT'S WHY THEY'RE CALLED...
...THE BEGINNING...
...AND THE TOP OF EVERY-THING.
I'M A LITTLE FISH IN A BIG WORLD.
THE *POWER OF THE WEST*...
...IS HOPE-LESSLY BEYOND REACH.

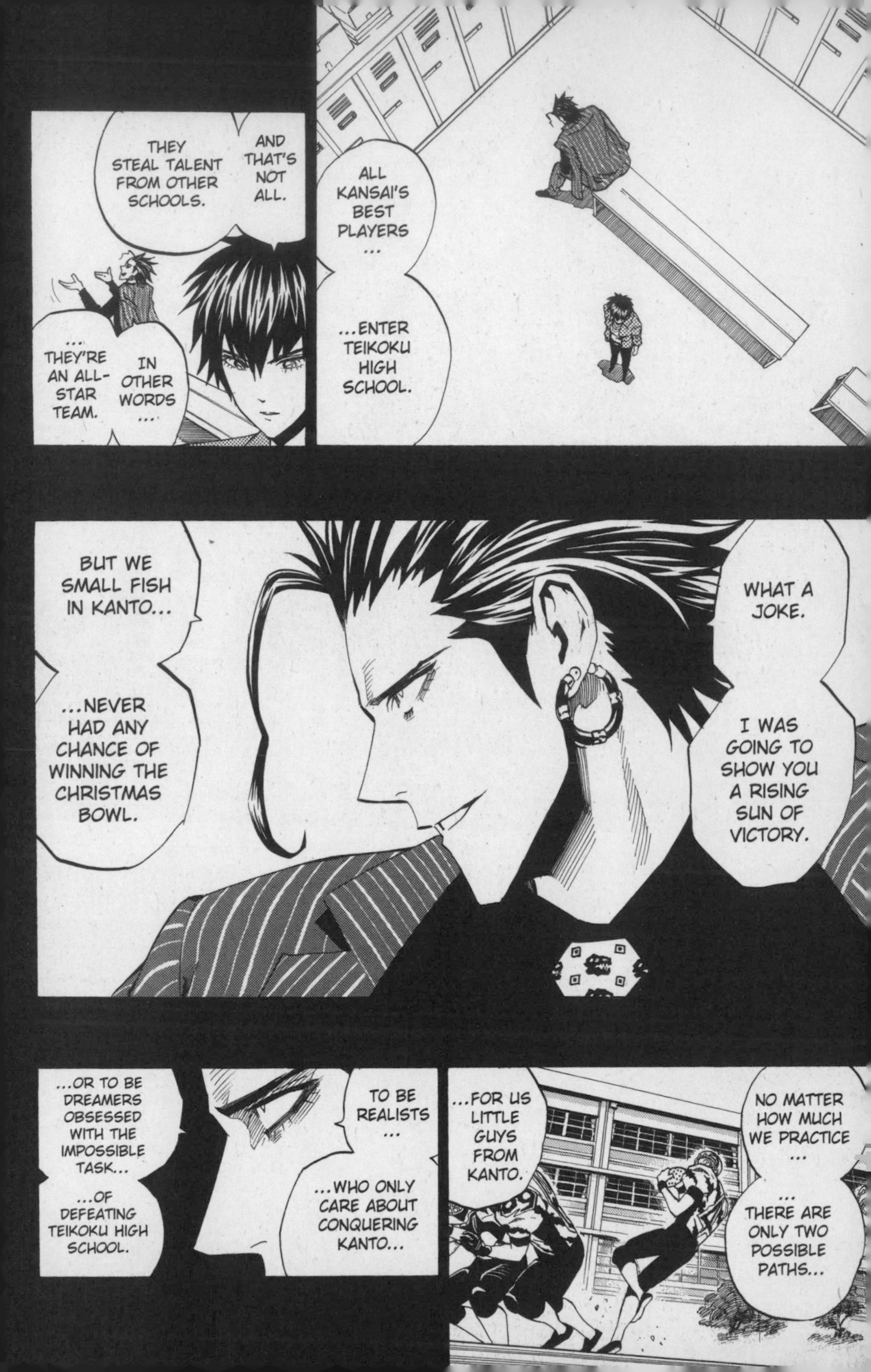
ALL KANSAI'S BEST PLAYERS ...
...ENTER TEIKOKU HIGH SCHOOL.
AND THAT'S NOT ALL.
THEY STEAL TALENT FROM OTHER SCHOOLS.
IN OTHER WORDS ...
... THEY'RE AN ALL-STAR TEAM.
WHAT A JOKE.
I WAS GOING TO SHOW YOU A RISING SUN OF VICTORY.
BUT WE SMALL FISH IN KANTO...
...NEVER HAD ANY CHANCE OF WINNING THE CHRISTMAS BOWL.
NO MATTER HOW MUCH WE PRACTICE ...
...FOR US LITTLE GUYS FROM KANTO.
... THERE ARE ONLY TWO POSSIBLE PATHS...
TO BE REALISTS ...
...WHO ONLY CARE ABOUT CONQUERING KANTO...
...OR TO BE DREAMERS OBSESSED WITH THE IMPOSSIBLE TASK...
...OF DEFEATING TEIKOKU HIGH SCHOOL.

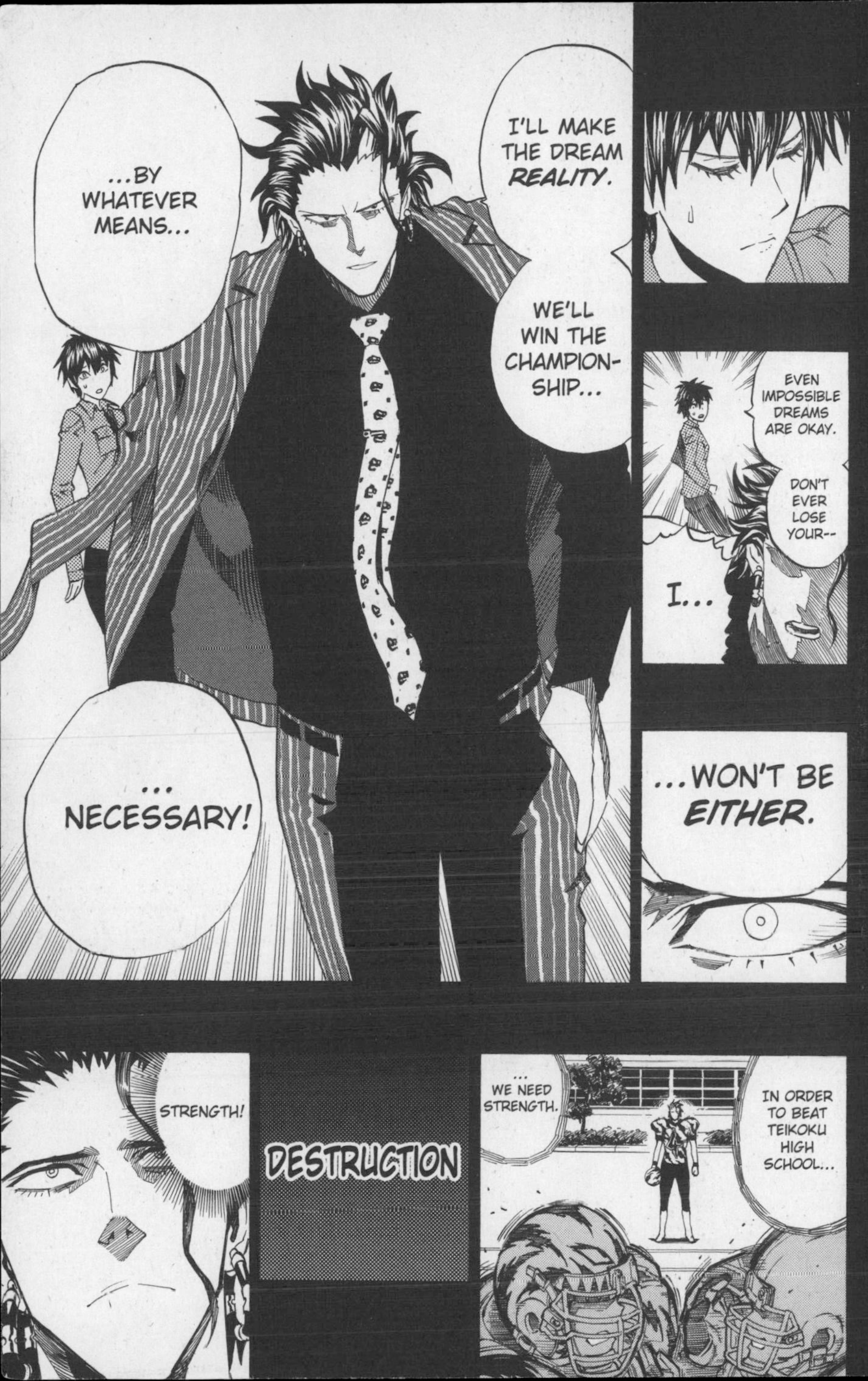
EVEN IMPOSSIBLE DREAMS ARE OKAY.
DON'T EVER LOSE YOUR--
I...
...WON'T BE *EITHER*.
I'LL MAKE THE DREAM *REALITY*.
WE'LL WIN THE CHAMPION-SHIP...
...BY WHATEVER MEANS...
... NECESSARY!
IN ORDER TO BEAT TEIKOKU HIGH SCHOOL...
... WE NEED STRENGTH.
DESTRUCTION
STRENGTH!

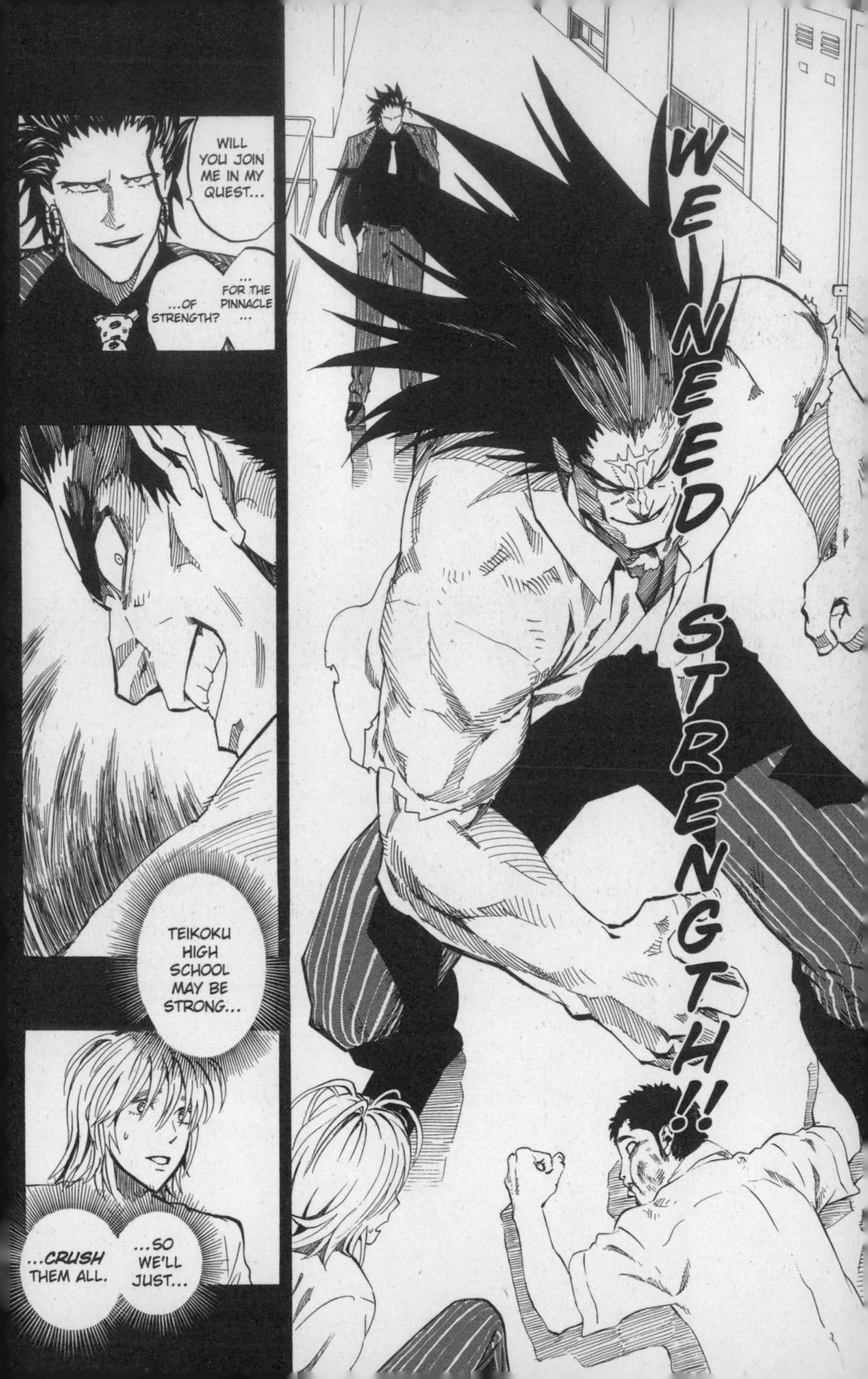
WE NEED STRENGTH!!
WILL YOU JOIN ME IN MY QUEST...
...FOR THE PINNACLE...
...OF STRENGTH?
TEIKOKU HIGH SCHOOL MAY BE STRONG...
...SO WE'LL JUST...
...CRUSH THEM ALL.

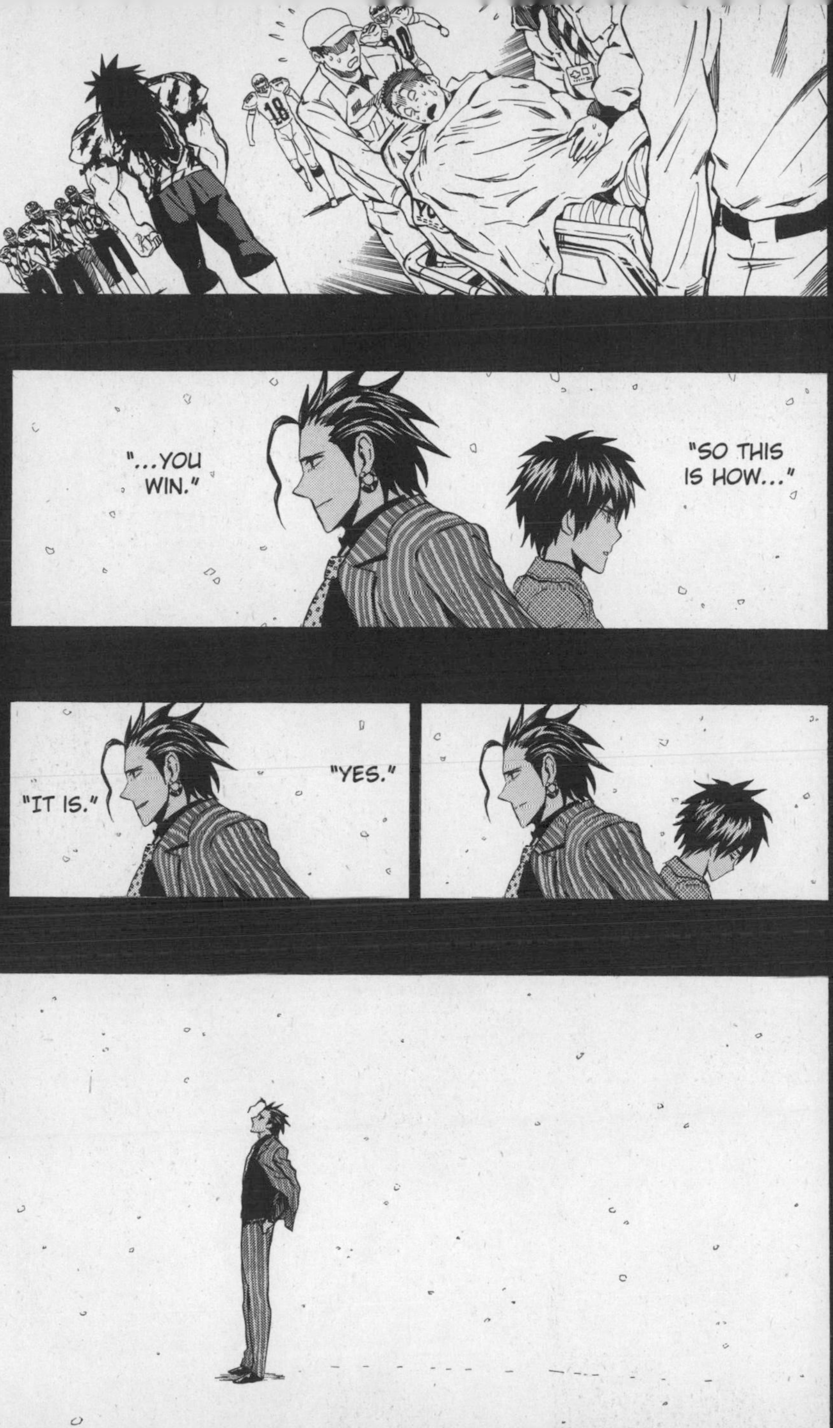
"SO THIS IS HOW..."
"...YOU WIN."
"YES."
"IT IS."

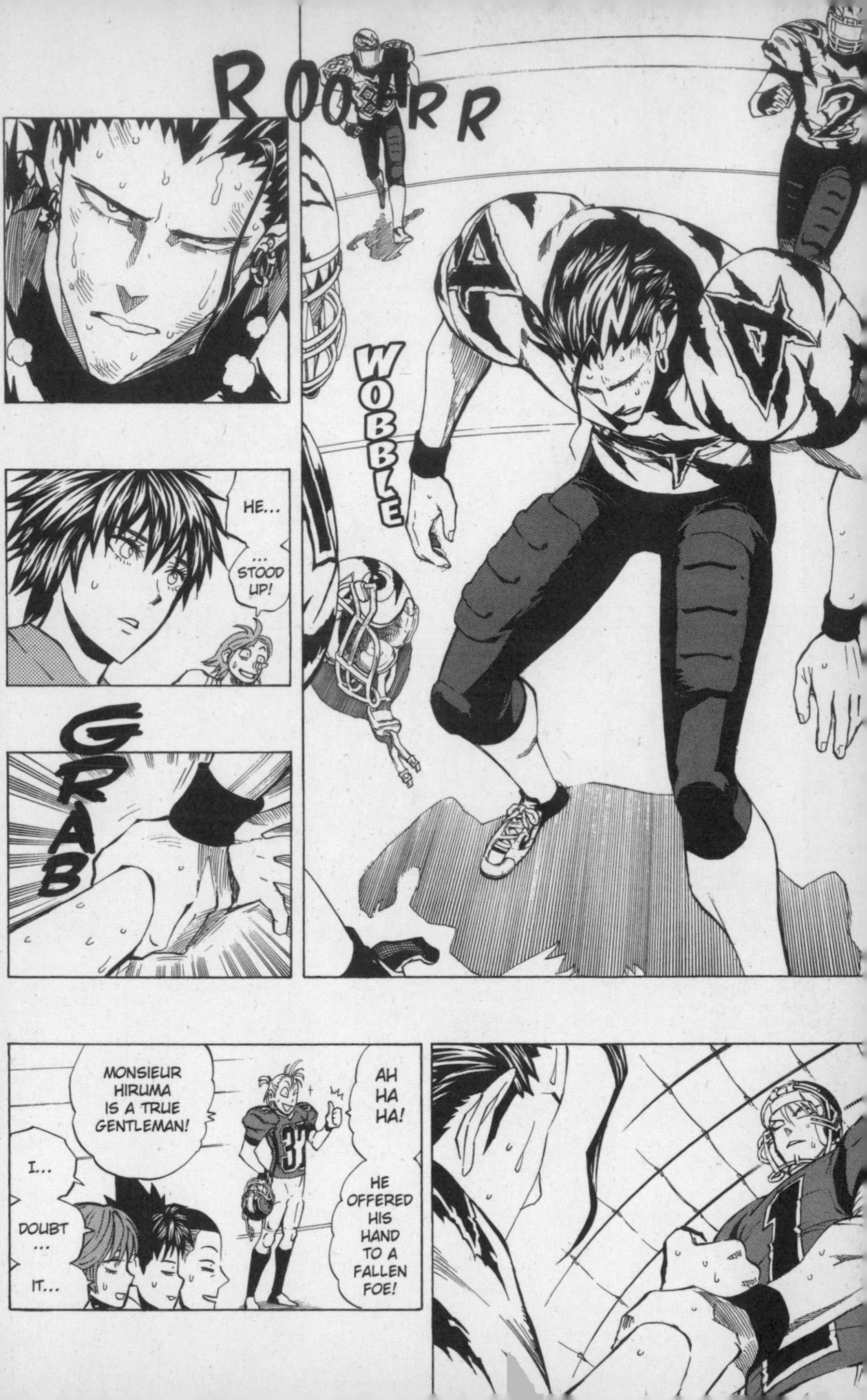
ROOARR
WOBBLE
HE...
...STOOD UP!
GRAB
AH HA HA!
HE OFFERED HIS HAND TO A FALLEN FOE!
MONSIEUR HIRUMA IS A TRUE GENTLEMAN!
I...
DOUBT...
IT...

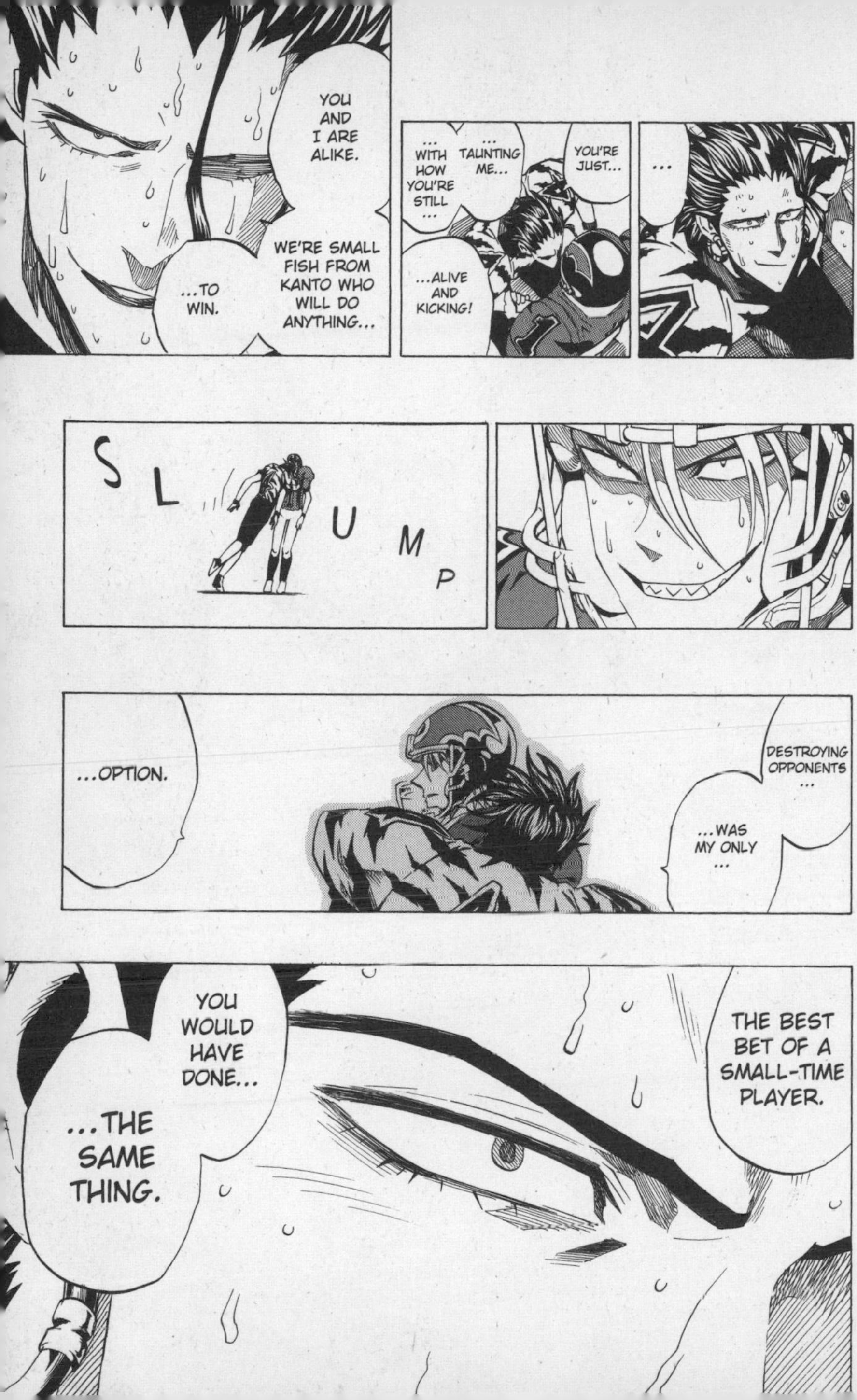
...
YOU'RE JUST...
... TAUNTING ME...
... WITH HOW YOU'RE STILL ...
...ALIVE AND KICKING!
YOU AND I ARE ALIKE.
WE'RE SMALL FISH FROM KANTO WHO WILL DO ANYTHING...
...TO WIN.
SLUMP
DESTROYING OPPONENTS ...
...WAS MY ONLY ...
...OPTION.
THE BEST BET OF A SMALL-TIME PLAYER.
YOU WOULD HAVE DONE...
...THE SAME THING.

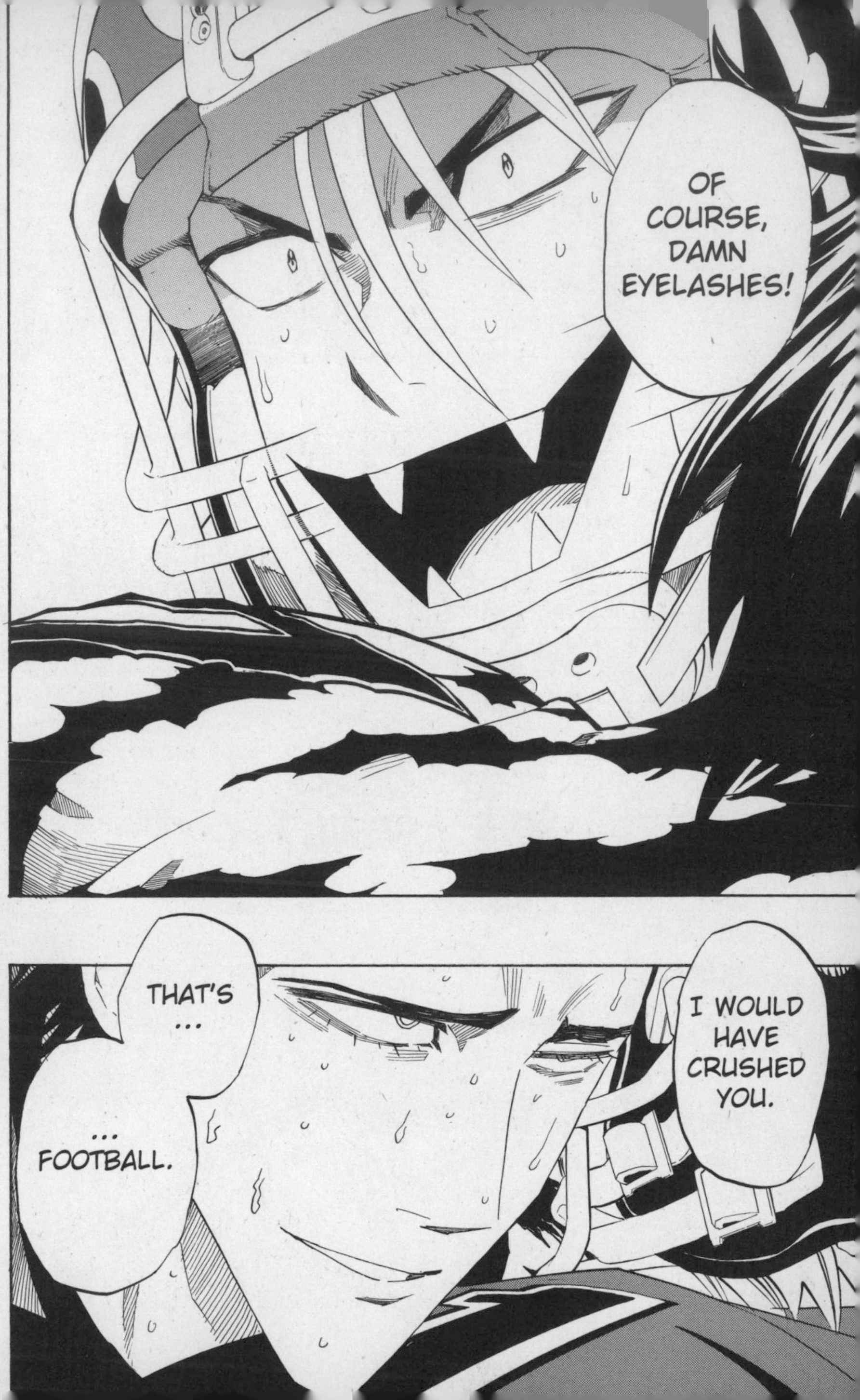
OF COURSE, DAMN EYELASHES!
I WOULD HAVE CRUSHED YOU.
THAT'S ...
... FOOTBALL.

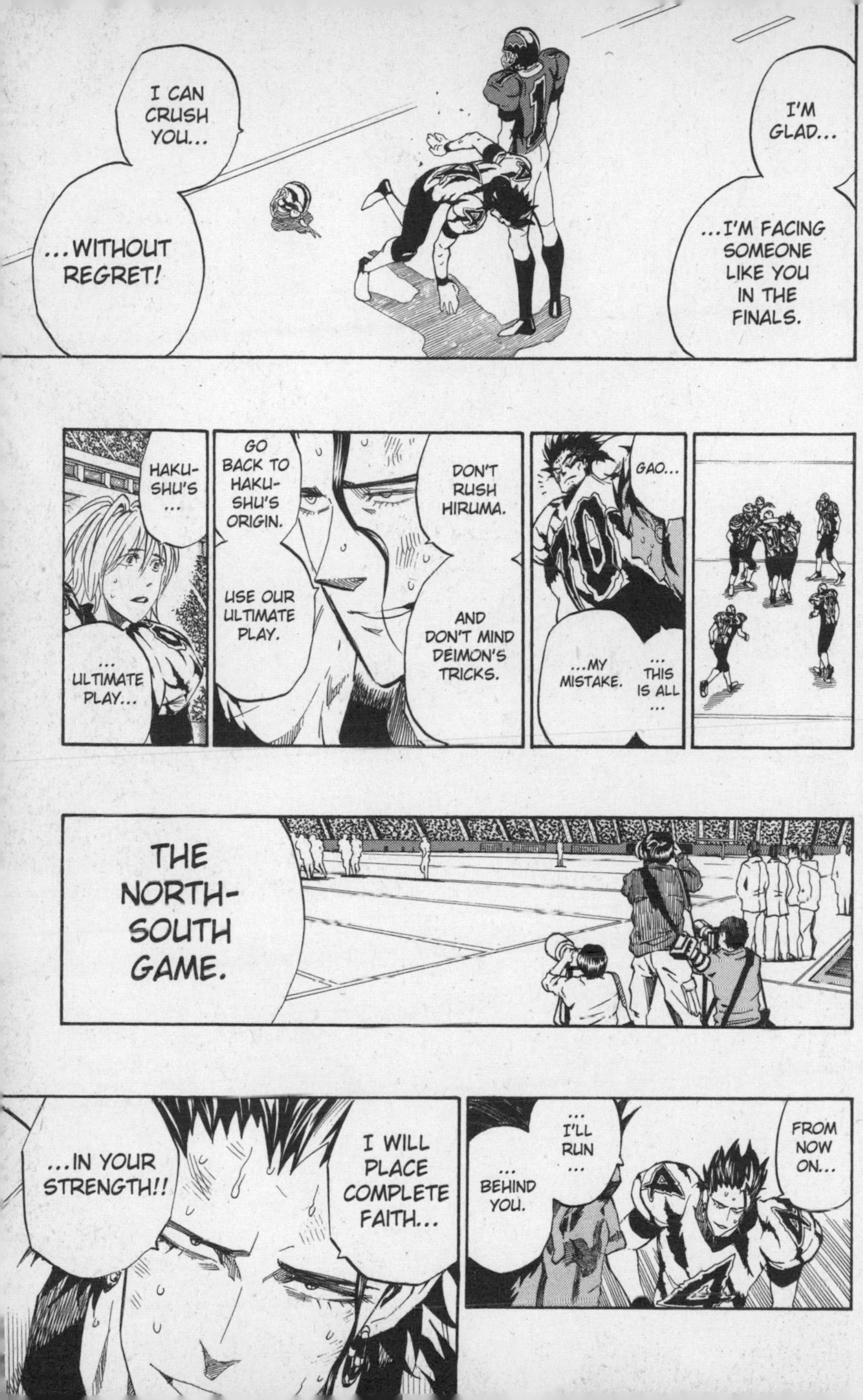
I'M GLAD...
...I'M FACING SOMEONE LIKE YOU IN THE FINALS.
I CAN CRUSH YOU...
...WITHOUT REGRET!
GAO...
... THIS IS ALL ...
...MY MISTAKE.
DON'T RUSH HIRUMA.
AND DON'T MIND DEIMON'S TRICKS.
GO BACK TO HAKU-SHU'S ORIGIN.
USE OUR ULTIMATE PLAY.
HAKU-SHU'S ...
... ULTIMATE PLAY...
THE NORTH-SOUTH GAME.
FROM NOW ON...
... I'LL RUN ...
... BEHIND YOU.
I WILL PLACE COMPLETE FAITH...
...IN YOUR STRENGTH!!

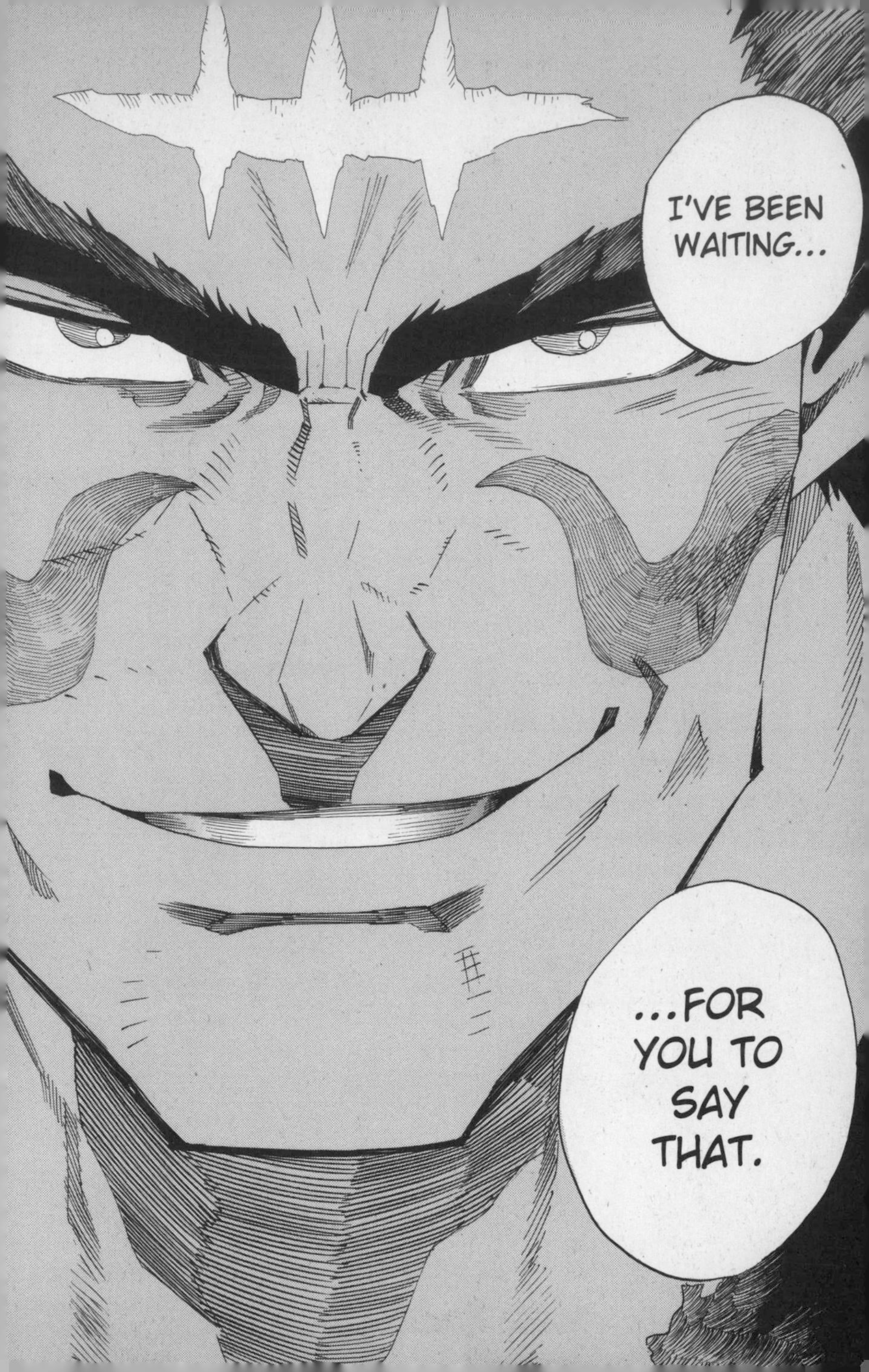
I'VE BEEN WAITING...
...FOR YOU TO SAY THAT.

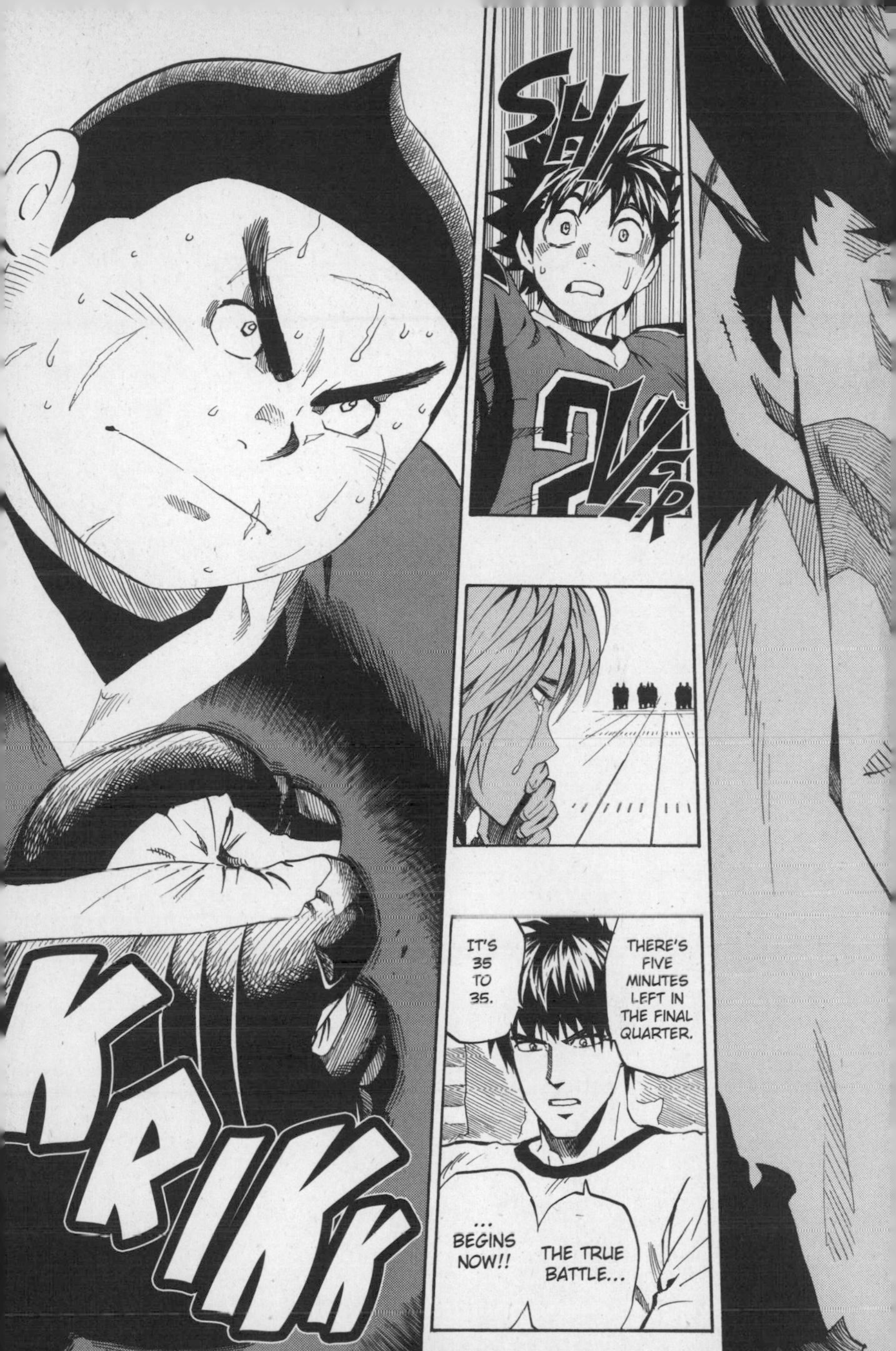

SHI
VER
THERE'S FIVE MINUTES LEFT IN THE FINAL QUARTER.
IT'S 35 TO 35.
THE TRUE BATTLE...
...BEGINS NOW!!
KRINK

End of Volume 30:
This Is Football

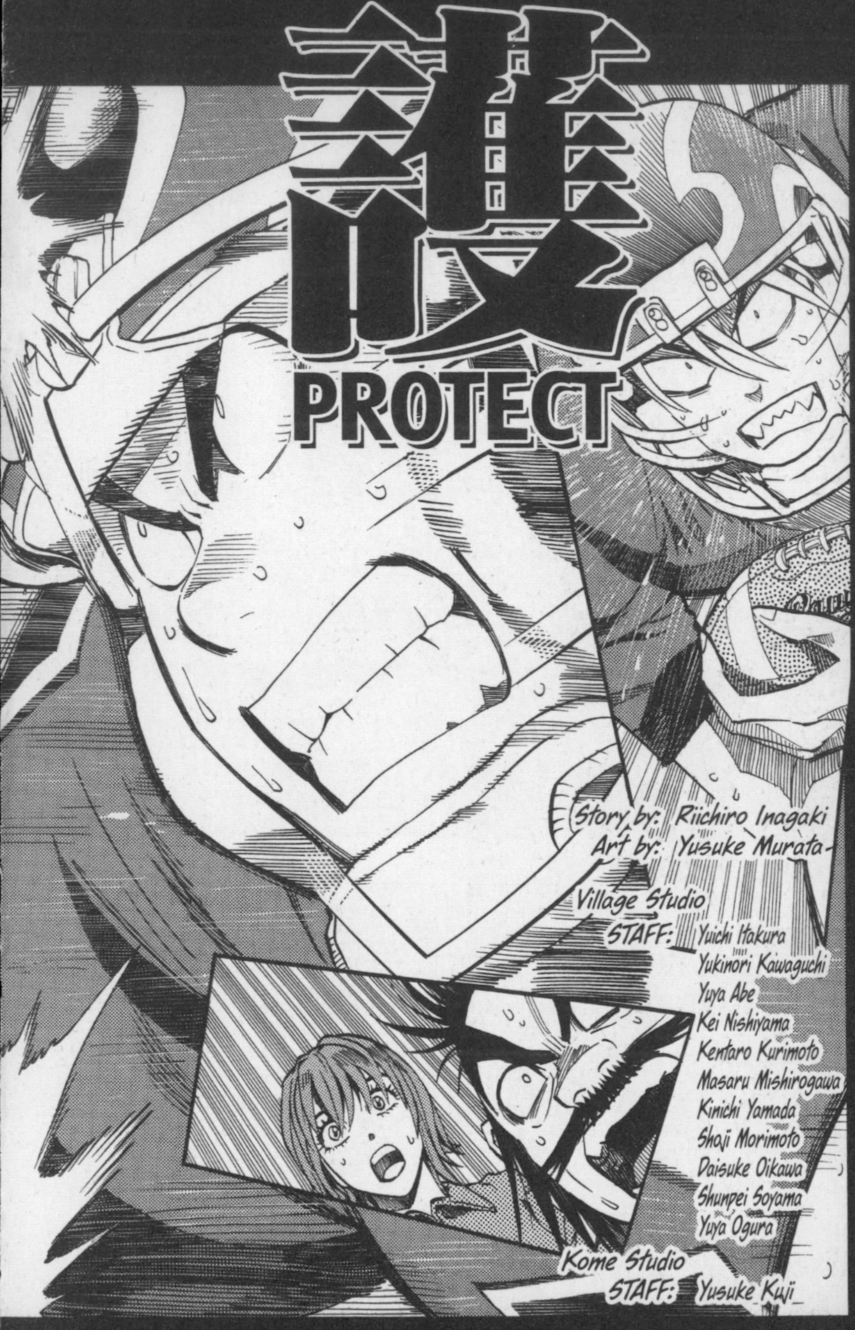
護
PROTECT
Story by: Riichiro Inagaki
Art by: Yusuke Murata
Village Studio
STAFF: Yuichi Itakura
Yukinori Kawaguchi
Yuya Abe
Kei Nishiyama
Kentaro Kurimoto
Masaru Mishirogawa
Kinichi Yamada
Shoji Morimoto
Daisuke Oikawa
Shunpei Soyama
Yuya Ogura
Kome Studio
STAFF: Yusuke Kuji

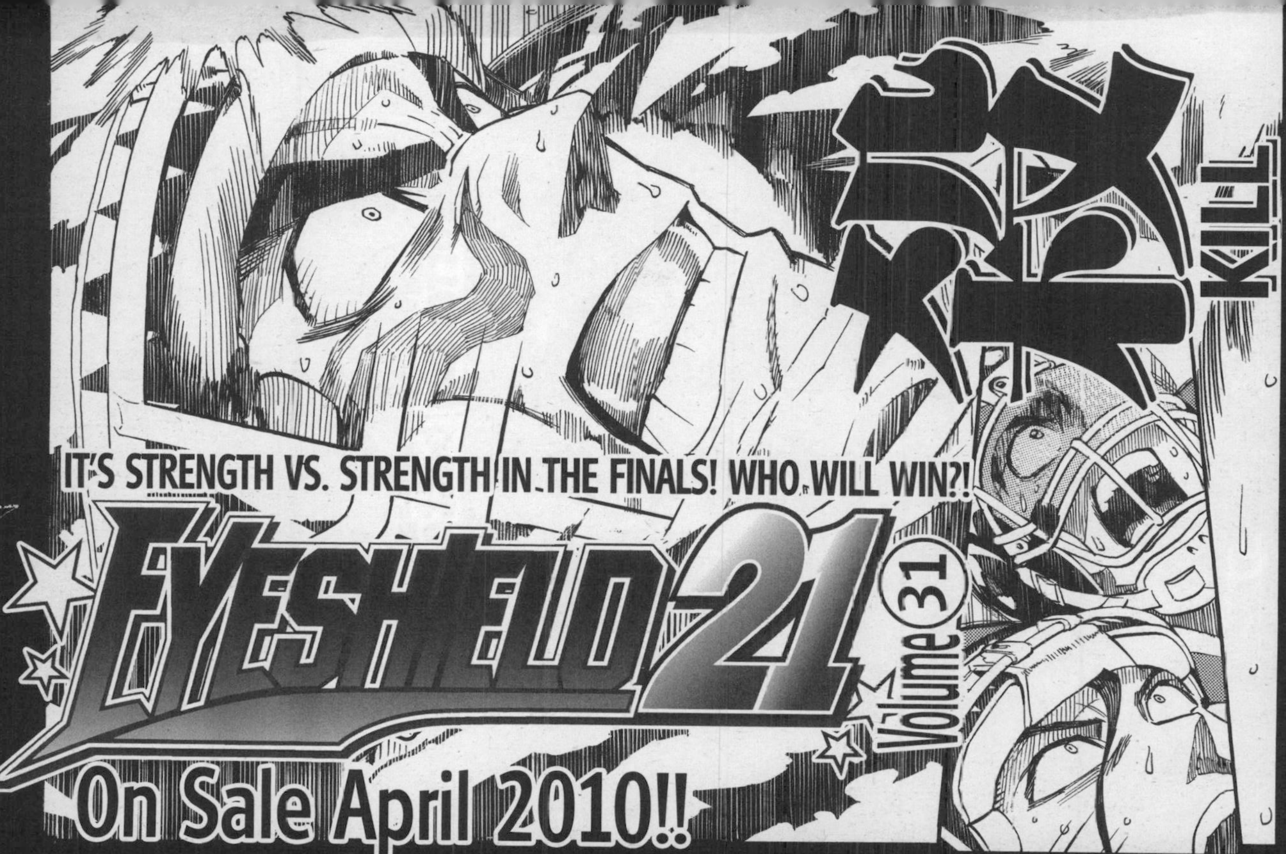
殺
KILL
IT'S STRENGTH VS. STRENGTH IN THE FINALS! WHO WILL WIN?!
EYESHIELD 21
Volume 31
On Sale April 2010!!